HOUGHTON MIFFLIN

Math

MATHEMATICS

Cover Activity: *Students investigate Patterns Made from Grids (Module 1, Investigations, pages 46–48). Students (shown here clockwise from upper left): Latoya Burton, Tim Wong, Cory Hodges, Betzaida Aguayo, William Wallace.*

HOUGHTON MIFFLIN

MATHEMATICS

Program Authors
Harry Bohan
Gerlena Clark
Heather J. Kelleher
Charles S. Thompson

Contributing Authors
Nadine S. Bezuk
Jean M. Shaw
Lucia Vega-Garcia

Houghton Mifflin Company · Boston

Atlanta · Dallas · Geneva, Illinois · Princeton, New Jersey · Palo Alto

Authors and Contributors

Nadine S. Bezuk
Associate Professor of Mathematics
  Education
San Diego State University
San Diego, CA

*Contributing Author,
Developer of Concept and
Materials for Math to Go*

Harry Bohan
Professor of Mathematics Education
Sam Houston State University
Huntsville, TX

*Program Author,
Developer of Philosophy
and Grades 3-6*

Gerlena Clark
Los Angeles County Mathematics
  Consultant
Los Angeles, CA

*Program Author,
Developer of Philosophy
and Teacher Training Materials*

Heather J. Kelleher
Former Classroom Teacher
  and Doctoral Student
University of British Columbia
Vancouver, BC, Canada

*Program Author,
Developer of Philosophy
and Grades 1–2*

Jean M. Shaw
Professor of Elementary Education
University of Mississippi
University, MS

*Contributing Author,
Developer of
Kindergarten Level*

Charles S. Thompson
Professor of Education
University of Louisville
Louisville, KY

*Program Author,
Developer of Philosophy
and Grades 3–6*

Lucia Vega-Garcia
Bilingual Education Director
Santa Clara County Office of Education
San Jose, CA

*Contributing Author,
Developer of Teacher
Support for Students
Acquiring English*

Acknowledgments
Grateful acknowledgment is made for the use of the following material: **30** "A Martian Named Harrison Harris" by Al Graham. —Continued on page 526

Printed in the U.S.A. ISBN: 0-395-67912-5

3456789-D-98 97 96 95

Developed and produced by Ligature

Specialists

Brenda Gentry-Norton
Research Associate
Program for Complex
  Instruction
Stanford University
Palo Alto, CA

*Consultant for Assessment
Philosophy and Materials*

Brenda Glen
Classroom Teacher
Balderas Elementary School
Fresno, CA

*Field Test Coordinator and
Developer of Teacher's Edition
Notes, Grades 5–6*

Joan L. Hopkins
Classroom Teacher
Escondido Elementary School
Palo Alto, CA

*Field Test Coordinator and
Developer of Teacher's Edition
Notes, Grades K–2*

Betty Iehl
Educational Consultant
San Gabriel, CA

*Developer of Teacher's Edition
Notes, Grades 4 and 6*

**National Center to Improve
the Tools of Educators**
Douglas Carnine, Director
Edward Kameenui, Associate
  Director
University of Oregon
Eugene, OR

*Developer of Alternate Strategies
Materials, Grades 2–6*

Mary Anne O'Neal
Educational Consultant
Carson, CA

*Developer of Teacher's Edition
Notes, Grades 3 and 5*

Annie Podesto
Staff Development Specialist
Stockton Unified School
  District
Stockton, CA

*Consultant for Assessment
Philosophy and Materials*

Sally Y. Wong
Title VII Adviser
Los Angeles Unified School
  District
Los Angeles, CA

*Developer of Teacher's Edition
Notes, Grades 3–6*

Field Test Teachers

Kindergarten Modules
Traci Assad, Fall River Summer School Program, Fall River, MA •
Susanne Burke, Holmes School, Dorchester, MA • **Leland Clarke,**
Holmes School, Dorchester, MA • **Beverly Letendre,** Fall River
Summer School Program, Fall River, MA • **Sarah Outten,** Slade
Regional Catholic School, Glen Burnie, MD • **Debbie L. Rea,**
Escondido School, Stanford, CA • **Pat Robinson,** Escondido School,
Stanford, CA

Grade 1 Modules
Robin Crawley, Holmes School, Dorchester, MA • **Suraya Driscoll,**
River Heights School, East Grand Forks, MN • **Nancy Matthews,**
Douglas School, Douglas, MA • **Mary Miller,** Holmes School,
Dorchester, MA • **Johanna Roses,** Baker School, Chestnut Hill, MA •
Elaine Kuritani Tsumura, Marrama School, Denver, CO

Grade 2 Modules
Najwa Abdul-Tawwab, Holmes School, Dorchester, MA • **Mary
Jane Brown,** Forwood School, Wilmington, DE • **Joan L. Hopkins,**
Escondido School, Stanford, CA • **Dorene Odom,** Holmes School,
Dorchester, MA • **Ida R. Wellington,** Washington School, Oakland, CA

Grade 3 Modules
Robin Burstein, Greenwood School, Des Moines, IA • **Joanne
Castelano,** Slade Regional Catholic School, Glen Burnie, MD • **Diane
Rezek Fator,** Emerson School, Berwyn, IL • **Linda Griffiths,** Kennedy
School, San Diego, CA • **Michele Hilbing,** Slade Regional Catholic
School, Glen Burnie, MD • **Sharnell Jackson** Decatur School,
Chicago, IL • **Janet M. Laws,** Lombardy School, Wilmington, DE •
Patricia Y. Lynch, Lombardy School, Wilmington, DE • **Efraín**

Meléndez, Dacotah Street School, Los Angeles, CA • **Doris Miles,**
Sandburg School, Wheaton, IL • **Ricki Raymond,** Piper School,
Berwyn, IL • **Deb Schantzen,** River Heights School, East Grand
Forks, MN • **Bonnie Schindler,** Kennedy School, San Diego, CA •
Theresa Sievers, Komensky School, Berwyn, IL • **Kimberly Bassett
Whitehead,** Lombardy School, Wilmington, DE

Grade 4 Modules
Lynda Alexander, St. Elizabeth School, Chicago, IL • **Betty
Coleman,** Parkman School, Chicago, IL • **Karen DeRon-Head,**
Armour School, Chicago, IL • **Keith Libert,** Escondido School,
Stanford, CA • **Joe Montoya,** Horace Mann School, Rapid City, SD •
Robert Poncé, Niños Heroes School, Chicago, IL

Grade 5 Modules
Lynnise H. Akinkunle-Gool, Niños Heroes School, Chicago, IL •
Doris Buffo, Balderas School, Fresno, CA • **Ronni K. Cohen,** Burnett
School, Wilmington, DE • **Valerie De George,** Greeley School,
Chicago, IL • **Brenda Glen,** Balderas School, Fresno, CA • **Brenda
Leigh,** River Heights School, East Grand Forks, MN • **Cynthia L. Lew,**
Madison School, Pomona, CA • **Lisa Palacios,** Pleasant Hill School,
Carol Stream, IL • **Kathryn Peecher,** Revere School, Chicago, IL •
Cindy Sardo, Burnett School, Wilmington, DE • **Henry A. Simmons,**
Balderas School, Fresno, CA • **Delorise Singley,** Oakwood Windsor
School, Aiken, SC • **Cecilia Maria Vasquez,** Balderas School, Fresno,
CA • **Michelle Wilson,** Jefferson School, Fresno, CA

Grade 6 Modules
Dorothy Cooper Jones, Banneker Achievement Center, Gary, IN •
Albert Martinez, Marianna Avenue School, Los Angeles, CA •

Reviewers

Kathryn A. Alexander, Macon Middle School, Brunswick, GA
(Grade 6 modules) • **Sherry Bailey,** Richland School District #2,
Columbia, SC (Grade 5 modules) • **Elsbeth G. Bellemere,**
Scarborough School District, Scarborough, ME (Grade 5 modules) •
Sharon L. Cannon, Myrtle Beach Middle School, Myrtle Beach, SC
(Grade 6 modules) • **Cleo Charging,** White Shield School,
Roseglen, ND (Grade K modules) • **Judy C. Curtis,** Colfax School,
Denver, CO (Grade 3 modules) • **Myra S. Dietz,** Carroll School #46,
Rochester, NY (Grade 6 modules) • **W. L. Duncker,** Midland School
District, Midland, TX (Grade 5 modules) • **Donna Marie Falat,**
Longfellow School, Bridgeport, CT (Grade 2 modules) • **Linda
Gojak,** Hawken School, Lyndhurst, OH (Grade 6 modules) •

Annette D. Ham, Waltersville School, Bridgeport, CT (Grade 5
modules • **Feliciano Mendoza,** Miles Avenue School, Huntington
Park, CA (Grades 5 and 6 modules) • **Kenneth Millett,** Department
of Mathematics, University of California, Santa Barbara, CA (Grade
6 modules) • **Rita Nappi,** Read School, Bridgeport, CT (Grade 4
modules) • **Mahesh Sharma,** Cambridge College, Cambridge, MA
(Grades K and 6 modules) • **Patricia E. Smith,** Crosswell School,
Easley, SC (Grades 3 and 4 modules) • **Bonnie Townzen,** Lubin
School, Sacramento, CA (Grade 1 modules) • **Angelia W. Whiting,**
Beardsley School, Bridgeport, CT (Grade 1 modules) • **Pamela
Yoka,** Covedale School, Cincinnati, OH (Grade K modules)

Contents

MODULE 3

Contents

tennis shoes

moosh ball

Teen-agers   Women Children Men

Moosh Ball
Popular toy
with broad
appeal.
Advertised:
Saturday
morning.

MODULE 4

One World, Many Parts

1 cup

$\frac{2}{3} \times \frac{2}{2} = \frac{4}{6}$ $\frac{2}{3} \times \frac{3}{3} = \frac{6}{9}$

Contents

MODULE 7

Fair Games

Math Power

The goal of this book is to help you build your **math power.** Math power means being able to understand and use math.

REASONING AND PROBLEM SOLVING

Learning to think mathematically and developing your skills as a problem solver are important parts of building math power.

CONNECT AND COMMUNICATE

By communicating about math, you can make your thinking clearer and find connections between new math ideas and the math you already know.

As your math power grows, you'll use math more and more in your daily life. Math power can help you in shopping, planning activities, or working on your favorite hobby.

Math power can also help people in their jobs. Whatever job you may have one day, you can be pretty sure that it will involve math. Discuss with your class some ways that store clerks, truck drivers, lawyers, and photographers use math in their work.

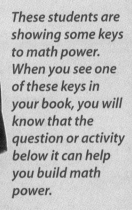

These students are showing some keys to math power. When you see one of these keys in your book, you will know that the question or activity below it can help you build math power.

TOOLS AND TECHNIQUES

Math power is knowing how and when to use tools such as calculators and computers and when it's faster to use mental math.

DRAWING TO LEARN

Building math power also involves drawing to help you understand and solve problems and to share your thinking with others.

Ongoing Investigation

Who We Are

First of all, what is an investigation? It's an open-ended problem. In other words, you won't reach a single right answer. In fact, your investigation can lead to many answers and even to other questions. You'll find lots of investigations in this book. The one described on these pages is called an ongoing investigation because you can work on it all year.

In 1990, the center of U.S. population was about ten miles from Steelville, Missouri. Where was the center of population 100 years ago? 50 years ago?

1 The Goal

This year investigate the U.S. population with your classmates. Find out "who we are" as compared with "who we were." Later, you'll use your data to predict "who we will be" in the future.

② Who We Are

The first U.S. census was taken in 1790. Since then, population records have been kept for a huge variety of categories. In the table are some data from the 1990 census.

1990 Census Data

- Total U.S. population: 249,924,000
- Average family size: 3.17 persons
- Median age: 32.9 years
- Most populated states:
  1. California (about 30 million)
  2. New York (about 18 million)
- Households with telephones: 93 out of 100, or 93%
- Number of births: 4,179,000

③ Who We Were

Which states had the highest population in 1900? How long were people expected to live in colonial times compared to today? You can answer such questions by tracing population statistics back through time. Look for these books to find statistics on your own: *Information Please Almanac* and *Statistical Abstract of the United States*.

④ Discover for Yourself

With your class, brainstorm for questions that you might investigate about the population. List each one. Then choose the question that interests you most and work with a group to gather data. Investigate the present population and trace the statistics as far back as you can.

1934

Irving Park School - Grades 5A-5B, 203.

1956

1978

LATIN SCHOOL

1978-79

Keep in Mind

Be sure to do the following things before you start:

☐ Clearly write your question. Be as specific as possible about what you want to know.

☐ Write a plan for how you will gather and organize your data.

5 **What to Do with Your Data**

Organize your data and write a short summary or conclusion. Then decide with your group how to display the data. Circle graphs, bar graphs, and charts are all excellent means of data display. See Data Collection in the Tool Kit, pages 468–469, for ideas on how to collect and present data.

6 **Looking Ahead**

As you begin your research, you'll discover a wealth of information about many aspects of the U.S. population. Jot down new questions that you want to research during future months. Eventually, you will compile a large amount of data that describes the United States in the present and past— enough data for you to make predictions about our future.

Who We Are

In 1880, 43 out of 100 Americans lived on farms. Today only about 2 in 100 do.

U.S. Rural and Urban Population 1890–1930

MODULE 1

Patterns and Design

With lines, shapes, and colors, artists and designers create patterns. More than a hundred years ago, quilters created this quilt using a pattern of squares. Architects use patterns when they design buildings. Mathematicians discover and use patterns of shapes and numbers. In this module you'll explore patterns of shapes and patterns of numbers. How would you describe to a friend what a pattern is?

SECTION A

Geometric Patterns

SECTION B

Using Shape and Number Patterns

SECTION C

Patterns on a Hundreds' Board

SECTION D

Multiplication Patterns

Pattern Hunt

Patterns are in everything. Check out the scene around you and record patterns from your everyday world. Look at the clothes you wear. Make rubbings of your sneaker treads or belt buckle. Track down the wildest patterns you can find.

This student is wearing patterns from around the world. The patterns in his hat are based on Ghanaian Ashanti weavings. His pants and vest were made in Guatemala, where making patterned cloth dates back many centuries. His sneakers were made in the United States.

Word Bank

- area
- common multiple
- composite number
- congruent
- expression
- perimeter
- prime number
- symmetry
- variable

1 Collecting

Make a visual record of patterns that you find. Draw them in your journal. On paper create rubbings of textured patterns with crayons or chalk. Paste these in your journal too. Use color! Use your imagination!

2 Sharing

For each pattern you collect, write a description in your journal. What are the basic shapes? Do they repeat? What makes it a pattern? Share what you found with your class.

Investigations Preview

As you learn about patterns of shapes and numbers, you can use this knowledge to explore how to design and plan familiar things.

Land Puzzles in the West (pages 11–13) How did early settlers in the West divide their land? You will be able to use what you learn about polyominoes to choose and plan a section of farmland.

Patterns Made from Grids (pages 46–48) How can you make a colorful quilt pattern using only squares? Symmetry and flips, slides, and turns, can help you analyze patterns in an Amish quilt. You can also design your own quilt. And you can watch a pattern grow!

LESSON 1

What's a Polyomino?

Do you recognize the quilt pattern below? If not, look back at the quilt on page 1. Discuss how the quilter arranged the pieces that make the design. The patterns made by these pieces look like shapes called **polyominoes**. This cross-shape of five squares is an example.

Patterns of squares and diamonds appear on many antique quilts, such as this one. Early quilters needed small, easily made shapes that could be cut from old clothing scraps.

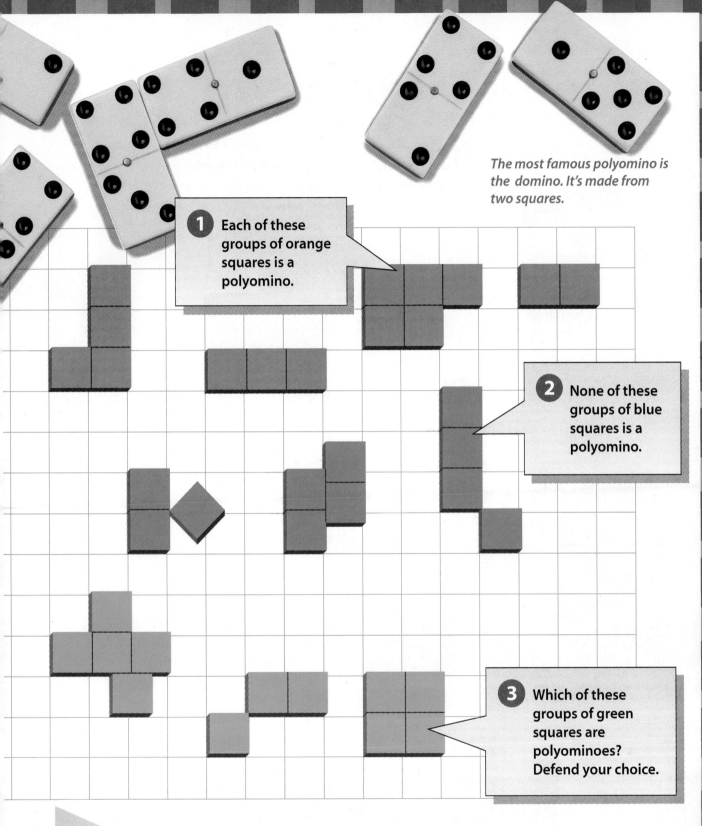

The most famous polyomino is the domino. It's made from two squares.

1 Each of these groups of orange squares is a polyomino.

2 None of these groups of blue squares is a polyomino.

3 Which of these groups of green squares are polyominoes? Defend your choice.

ACTIVITY 1 A Polyomino Is . . .

On Your Own Write a definition of a polyomino. Sketch some polyominoes as part of your definition.

What You'll Need

- *grid paper*
- *Tracing Tool*
- *scissors*

TOOLS AND TECHNIQUES

Cutting out your polyominoes so that you can slide, flip, and turn them will also help you find those that are congruent.

How Many?

With Your Group Polyominoes made of five squares are called **pentominoes.** How many different pentominoes are there? Try to find them all. Here are two.

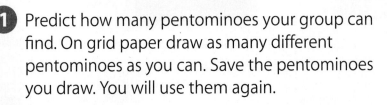

1 Predict how many pentominoes your group can find. On grid paper draw as many different pentominoes as you can. Save the pentominoes you draw. You will use them again.

2 Check the pentominoes you drew to see if they are **congruent.** Things that are the same size and shape are congruent.

Slide

Trace and cut out one of your pentominoes. If you can slide, flip, or turn your tracing to match another pentomino, they are congruent.

Flip

Turn

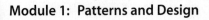

3 Use the pentominoes you drew and form groups that are congruent. How many different groups can you make?

4 Find other congruent figures. Use objects in your classroom. Name at least three groups you found.

5 How many different pentominoes did you find? Write your answer and your reasons. Explain why someone might disagree with your answer.

You can fold some pentominoes to make open boxes. Which pentominoes can you use? Write an explanation of how you know.

Do You Remember?

Try It!

Find the congruent figures. For each congruent pair, write whether the second figure is a slide, flip, or turn of the first.

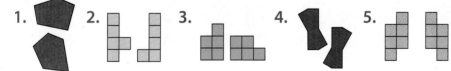

1. 2. 3. 4. 5.

Write the place value of each digit in the sum of 439 and 2,275.

6. 2   **7.** 7   **8.** 1   **9.** 4

10. Write the number of tens in the sum.

Think About It

11. How did you decide in Exercise 3 whether or not the figures are congruent?

Polyomino Puzzlers

◢ ACTIVITY 1 Area and Perimeter

With Your Class Use polyominoes to explore **area** and **perimeter**. Do these two polyominoes have the same area? Do they have the same perimeter? Defend your answer.

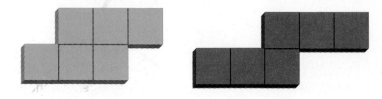

Perimeter is the distance around the edge of a shape.

Area is the space a shape covers.

On Your Own Answer any two questions. You may need the polyominoes you drew for Lesson 1.

1 The area of the tabletop is 18 square units. Each unit measures 10 in. on a side. What is the tabletop's perimeter?

2 What's the greatest perimeter you can have on a polyomino made with six squares? Defend your answer.

3 Draw or copy two polyominoes that have the same perimeters but different areas.

2 Symmetry Sketches

On Your Own Use polyominoes to explore **symmetry.** Answer the first question and two of the last three.

1 Which of these two polyominoes is symmetrical? Explain.

A shape has symmetry if you can fold it so that the two parts cover each other exactly. The two parts are congruent.

2 In a drawing, group the pentominoes you drew according to those that are symmetrical and those that are not.

CONNECT AND COMMUNICATE

3 Draw the pentomino that has the most lines of symmetry. Show its lines of symmetry. How many are there?

In Your Journal Explain how you decide whether two pentominoes are symmetrical.

4 Navajo women wove blankets using bold, colorful patterns. Does this pattern have any lines of symmetry? If so, make a sketch that shows them.

Navajo blanket, made before 1915

ACTIVITY OPTION

Find as many letters of the alphabet as you can that have two or more lines of symmetry. Draw their lines of symmetry.

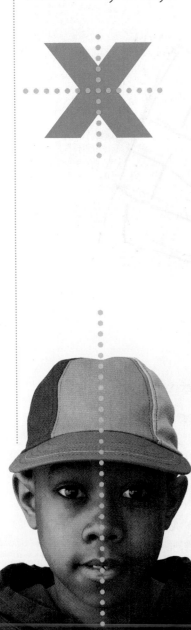

3 Choosing Sides

On Your Own Choose either 1 or 2.

1 You don't have a ruler! What unit can you use to estimate the area and perimeter of this page? Could you use an eraser? Choose any unit of measure and make an estimate. With the same unit, estimate area and perimeter of other surfaces.

2 Imagine that everything in your world is symmetrical. What would life be like? Write about what happens in a symmetrical world.

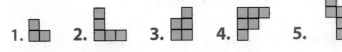

Do You Remember?

Try It!

Find the area and the perimeter. Sketch a figure with the same perimeter as the figure in Exercise 1.

1. **2.** **3.** **4.** **5.**

6. Which figures in Exercises 1–5 are symmetrical? Make a sketch to show how you decided.

Write *greater than*, *less than*, or *equal to* 3,085.

7. 3,058 **8.** 3,580 **9.** 308 tens
10. 3 thousand + 85 ones

Think About It

11. Write an explanation of how you found the perimeter and area of the figure in Exercise 4.

Investigation

Land Puzzles
in the West

After the Revolutionary War ended in 1783, the United States needed to raise money. The war alone had cost the new republic millions of dollars. The government decided to raise money by selling some of its land in the West. But how could all the land be divided into small pieces that people could afford?

Thomas Jefferson, with his knowledge of classical mathematics, had a plan. His plan divided the land into many equal units. How do you think Jefferson used mathematics in his plan?

Thomas Jefferson

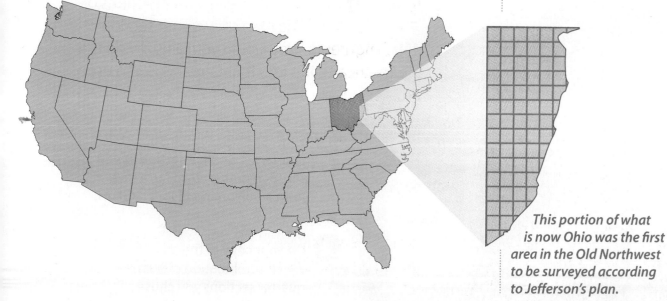

This portion of what is now Ohio was the first area in the Old Northwest to be surveyed according to Jefferson's plan.

Section B: Using Shape and Number Patterns 11

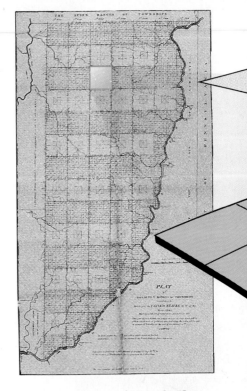

In 1785 government surveyors began drawing the first boundary lines in what is now Ohio. Surveyors used lines of latitude and longitude to create townships.

An early map shows the first townships surveyed under the Land Ordinance of 1785. During the next century this system of land division spread west across the nation.

A township, six miles (mi) long and six miles wide, is divided into 36 sections.

Stake Your Claim

Imagine you want to buy a section of land for yourself and three other farmers. Each of you will have four quarter-quarter sections of land. The map shows your section of land. How would you fairly divide the section into four farms? You can use your Tracing Tool to trace the map.

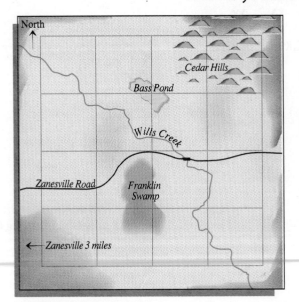

1. Show as many combinations of four farms within a section as you can. Remember, each farm must form a polyomino of four squares.

2. On your copy of the map, show which combination of quarter-quarter sections you chose.

Half Section (320 acres)

Quarter Section (160 acres)

Half - Quarter Section (80 acres)

Quarter - Quarter Section (40 acres)

Quarter - Quarter Section (40 acres)

Land purchasers arrange quarter-quarter sections so that one whole side of one square shares one whole side of another square. Each group of squares forms a polyomino.

A section was one mile long and one mile wide, or one square mile. A section could be divided several ways.

3 In a letter to the other three farmers, defend the combination of four quarter-quarters that you chose. Explain your reasoning. Also tell how you would decide fairly who got which four quarter-quarters.

Ask Yourself

☐ Where will you find examples of shapes like the quarter-quarter sections?

☐ What tools can you use to help you experiment with arrangements of quarter-quarters?

☐ What facts will help you decide on the best arrangement for the farms?

☐ What reasons will you give when you explain your arrangement to the three farmers?

☐ Think of an interesting way to present your arrangement of the section to your class.

LESSON 3

The Shape of Numbers

More than 2,000 years ago, math students in ancient Greece worked with patterns of shapes and numbers. They used sticks and pebbles to create their patterns.

What You'll Need
• *100 counters*

ACTIVITY 1 **Watch Them Grow!**

With Your Partner The pebbles on these pages show two patterns Greek students used. In this activity you'll extend these patterns and try to figure out how they grow.

1 Build Your Own L-numbers The patterns below are called L-numbers. Use counters to build the first six L-numbers. Record the number of counters at each step.

Step 1 **Step 2** **Step 3**

2 **Build Square Numbers** Now use counters to build the first six square numbers. Again, keep a record of the total number of counters as it grows.

Step 1   **Step 2**   **Step 3**

SQUARE NUMBERS

Step	Total
1	1
2	4
3	9
4	?

3 **Discover** Analyze your records of L-numbers and square numbers. In your journal, write an explanation of what you've learned.

With Your Class Discuss what you've learned about L-numbers and square numbers. Try talking about questions like these.

a. How would you describe the number patterns of L-numbers and square numbers?

b. Will all L-numbers be odd? How do you know?

c. What does the L-number pattern tell you about adding even and odd numbers?

d. How many counters are in the 20th L-number? in the 20th square number? Answer without drawing each step.

e. How are L-numbers and square numbers alike? How are they different?

TOOLS AND TECHNIQUES

Mathematicians often use charts like the one above as they work. Try a chart to follow the growth of L-numbers and square numbers. What would you include on your chart? Why?

Build Your Own!

On Your Own Look at some growth patterns that other students have built. Then try inventing your own patterns that grow according to a certain rule.

LIZARD STEPS

Step 1

Step 2

Step 3

Step 4

Button Squares

Color	Buttons
Yellow	1
Pink	8
Blue	16
Purple	?

1 Build your own growth pattern. You might draw your pattern, use counters, or make up your own way.

2 Record your pattern.

3 Write a paragraph describing your pattern. Give the pattern a name. Explain how your pattern grows.

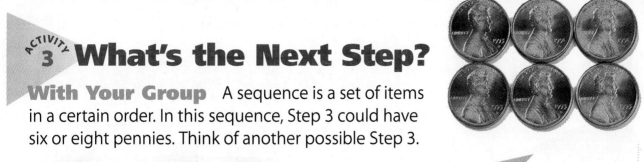

ACTIVITY 3 What's the Next Step?

With Your Group A sequence is a set of items in a certain order. In this sequence, Step 3 could have six or eight pennies. Think of another possible Step 3.

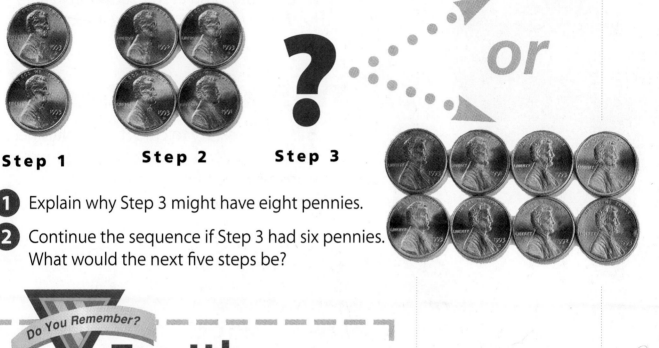

Step 1   **Step 2**   **Step 3**

1 Explain why Step 3 might have eight pennies.

2 Continue the sequence if Step 3 had six pennies. What would the next five steps be?

Do You Remember?

Try It!

Show two possibilities for Step 3 in each sequence. Defend your choices.

1. ● ●●   2. ■ ■▉   3. ▲ ▲▲

4. 3, 6   5. 5, 15   6. 4, 8

Estimate. Then add to find the exact answer.

7. 36 + 45   8. 77 + 44   9. 59 + 99

10. 181 + 399   11. 409 + 129 + 76 + 140

Think About It

12. Write an explanation of how you determined the relationships between the figures in Exercise 3.

REASONING AND PROBLEM SOLVING

To help figure out Step 3 of a sequence problem, try to decide what is happening as the steps go from 1 to 2. Are you adding? Are you multiplying? What other ways might the sequence be growing?

The 100th-Step Mysteries

You can probably predict the 10th step in a growth pattern. How about the 100th? If you know what clues to look for, it's not so hard.

ACTIVITY 1 Tri-Numbers Case

With Your Class Try to crack the Tri-Numbers Case. You need to predict the number of fingerprints for the 100th step in this pattern. Then you need to be able to predict any step.

Step 1   **Step 2**   **Step 3**

Investigate how two other student detectives searched for their clues.

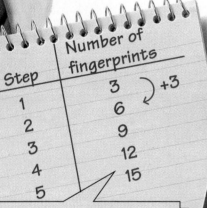

Step	Number of fingerprints
1	3 ⎫
2	6 ⎬ +3
3	9
4	12
5	15

Detective 1 made this chart to find the clues. What do you think of this method?

Step	Fingerprints	
1	→ 3	1 x 3 = 3
2	→ 6	2 x 3 = 6
3	→ 9	3 x 3 = 9

(n x 3) → This expression helps find any step.

100 x 3 = 300

Detective 2 made these notes and arrows. What do you think they mean?

Detective 2 finally wrote *n* x 3. Then she said, "The 100th step has 300 fingerprints." What do you think *n* x 3 means?

ACTIVITY 2 Solve This!

On Your Own Now solve the Pentagon Case. It's another 100th-step mystery. Think back to what a pentagon is. Remember, *penta* means "five." The clues in this folder will help you do your detective work. Use a calculator to help you find the 100th step. Here are the first two steps in the case.

Make up a new 100th-step mystery. Draw some clues. Write a paragraph explaining the case. Then see if a classmate can solve your mystery.

> The clue *n* x 5 is an **expression**— a way to represent a relationship. Some expressions use a letter to stand for an unknown number. The letter is called a **variable**.

1. What step in the pattern does the photograph show? Write a few sentences explaining how you know.

2. Try to predict the total for the 10th step and for the 15th step.

3. Explain how you made your predictions.

4. Now sort through the clues. On your paper, figure out the 100th step.

5. Write a short report telling how you cracked the Pentagon Case. Describe how you found the 100th step and how you can find any step.

The Game of n

What You'll Need
- *number cube*
- *game pieces*
- *gameboard*

TOOLS AND TECHNIQUES

To play the Game of n faster, try using a calculator to figure out your moves. Just use the number you get on the number cube in the expression.

³ ACTIVITY Using Expressions

With Your Group   In the 100th-step mysteries you used variables and expressions. Now play the Game of *n* to get more practice with variables and expressions.

1 **Set It Up!**   Collect 27 ones' cubes or other game pieces. Put one game piece on each space except the start.

2 **Get Started!**   Roll the number cube and move that many spaces. Take the game piece off the space and put it on your circle with the matching color. Now it's the next player's turn.

③ Keep Moving! On your next turn, look at the expression in the space you are on. Roll the cube. Your number will equal *n* in the expression. Find the value of the expression. Then move that many spaces.

Always work out the operation in parentheses ( ) first.

④ Collect All Four! Take the game piece off the space you land on next. Put it on your circle of the matching color. To win, you need to have a piece for each color. Don't take two pieces from the same color.

Which way? If the arrows point two ways, you decide.

Do You Remember?

Try It!

Find the 20th step in each sequence. Write the expression you used. Use your calculator.

1. 5, 10, 15, 20, 25, 30   **2.** 3, 4, 5, 6, 7, 8

3. 8, 16, 24, 32, 40, 48   **4.** 1, 4, 9, 16, 25, 36

Subtract the number from 7,000 only if the difference will be greater than 3,000.

5. 3,762   **6.** 1,728   **7.** 6,248

8. 1,002   **9.** 3,125   **10.** 4,109

Think About It

11. How do you know that your expression in Exercise 3 matches the sequence? Write an explanation.

Beads

For thousands of years people have made and traded beads. In most cultures beads have been used for decoration, for trade, or as symbols of power and control.

Precious bead necklaces, such as this one, were worn in the Imperial Chinese court between 1644 and 1912. Only the emperor and others of high rank could wear them. The arrangement of the beads was based on the number 3, which Chinese philosophers believed was sacred.

1 The large white beads separate the red beads into sections. How many red beads are in each section? How many red beads are in the necklace altogether? How are these numbers related to the number 3?

2 A jeweler has three necklaces. One has 108 beads, another 204, and the third 63. How many beads are in all three necklaces? Does the order in which you add matter? Explain.

3 After 1912, traders took necklaces like this to sell the beads separately. Imagine you had 5 necklaces but lost some beads when you took them apart to trade.
a. How many red beads did you lose if you have 489 left?
b. How many green beads did you lose if you have 124 left?

4 The green beads on the necklace were sometimes used for business calculations. Give an example of how the green beads could be used to add and subtract numbers greater than 30.

5 A necklace has 3 red, 9 black, 27 green, and an unknown number of white beads. Use this pattern to find the number of white beads, and find the total number of beads.

6 The ancient Chinese also made beads out of stone, shell, bone, teeth, and eggshell. Imagine that you found these beads: 30 stone, 12 shell, 18 bone, 16 teeth, and 14 eggshell. How many more beads do you need to make a necklace of 150 beads?

7 For how many centuries were beads like the ones shown worn by the Imperial Chinese court? How do you know?

Check Your Math Power

8 Plan a bead pattern. Write an expression that shows the pattern. Draw or describe your bead pattern.

9 Write two addition equations that use the same addends but in different ways. Why might one grouping be easier to add than another? What property of addition does this show?

10 Does the sum of any addition change if you add zero to it? Explain your answer in writing.

Mandarin chain, 1644–1912

LESSON 5
A Hundred Squares

Now try working with some new color and number patterns on a hundreds' board. You'll make predictions and wind your way through some mysterious math "pathways."

What You'll Need
- *3 colored markers*
- *hundreds' board*

ACTIVITY 1 Try Threes!

With Your Class Make a repeating three-color pattern on a hundreds' board. For instance, your class might choose red, yellow, and blue. If so, your pattern would be red, yellow, blue, red, yellow, blue, from 1 to 100 on the board.

1. Choose three colored markers. Decide on the order of the colors for your pattern.

2. Next take your markers or crayons and line up.

3. Take turns adding the next color of the pattern to each square.

4 Discuss questions like these.
  a. What does your finished pattern look like?
     What number pattern do you see?
  b. Do you see any stripes or diagonals? Why do
     you think they appeared?
  c. Will repeating four colors create different
     patterns? five colors? six? Explain.

Four and More

What You'll Need
- *set of markers or crayons*
- *hundreds' board*

With Your Group Now make repeating patterns with sets of four, five, six, seven, eight, and nine colors on the hundreds' board.

1 **Split Up the Task** The task might go faster if each member does one or more of the sets.

2 **Observe and Discuss** Describe each of your patterns.
   a. What diagonals or stripes do you see?
   b. Why do these diagonals or stripes appear?
   c. How are the patterns alike or different?

Do You Remember?

Try It!

On which of the patterns you made do these numbers share the same color? How do you know?

1. 6, 18, 34   **2.** 9, 63, 27   **3.** 3, 17, 10
4. 17, 35, 29   **5.** 10, 26, 42   **6.** 9, 27, 81

Write = or ≠. Explain how you know.

7. $(8 + 6) + 10 \bullet 8 + (6 + 10)$
8. $(15 + 26) + (14 + 9) \bullet 15 + (26 + 14) + 9$
9. $38 - (16 + 6) \bullet (38 - 16) + 6$
10. $25 + (15 + 12) \bullet (25 + 15) + 12$
11. $218 + 287 + 13 \bullet 218 + (287 + 13)$

Think About It

12. A classmate needs help on Exercises 1–6. Write a short explanation to help.

CONNECT AND COMMUNICATE

On page 25, you made some predictions about patterns of four, five, or six colors. Now look at the grids you've filled out. Were your predictions correct? Why or why not?

What Color Square?

Four plus four plus four plus one equals red? How can that be? To find out, look at the grid pattern below.

ACTIVITY 1 Imagine That!

With Your Group Suppose a group of students began painting a pattern of fours.

1 Think about the pattern they would make. Tell the order of the colors.

2 Which of the following squares will be red? Explain.
  a. 37   **b.** 47
  c. 61   **d.** 99

3 If the board went beyond 100, what color would these squares be? Tell how you know.

  a. 115   **b.** 151   **c.** 177   **d.** 642

ACTIVITY 2 Move On to Fives!

With Your Group Imagine the students painted another hundreds' board. This time they based their pattern on a set of five colors. The paint cans show the order. Answer the questions to make some generalizations for this pattern.

Red Yellow Blue Green Purple

1 What if the students want to paint all purple squares first? (They only have purple paint today.) How can multiplication help predict purple squares? Why?

2 The next day they have green paint. How will this chart help them find the squares to paint green?

3 Write an expression that shows how to find the green squares if you know the purple squares. Do the same for finding blue squares and yellow squares.

Hint: Try having *p* stand for purple.

Purple	Green
5	4
10	9
15	14
20	19

4 One student wants to know the colors of squares 55, 67, 72, 83, and 99.

   a. How can division help?
   b. What does a remainder tell the student?

5 Think of a pattern with six colors that has square 5 as green. Write the number of every square on the grid that will be green. How do you know? Do the same for patterns with seven colors, eight colors, and nine colors.

REASONING AND PROBLEM SOLVING

If square 5 is purple in a pattern of six colors, where will the second purple fall on the hundreds' board? How about the third? the tenth? Remember, the pattern ends at every sixth square.

On Your Own Here are two more color patterns the students might have painted.

6 Tell whether each of the numbered squares comes from pattern 1 or 2.

7 Choose pattern 1 or pattern 2. Will your pattern have stripes or diagonals? Explain how you know.

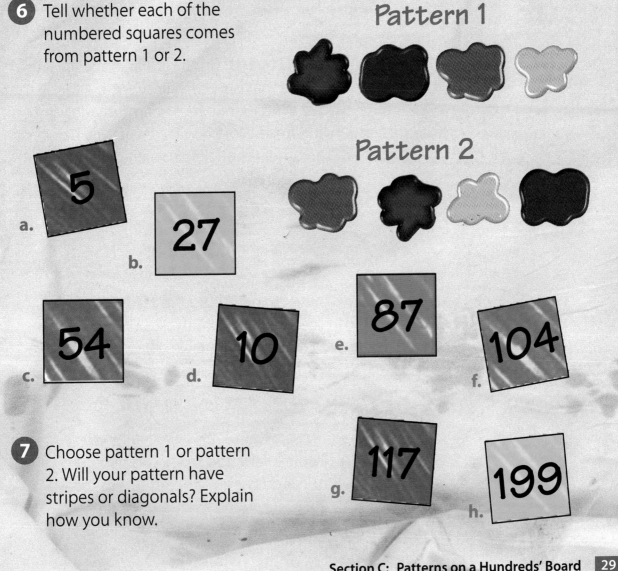

Pattern 1

Pattern 2

a. 5
b. 27
c. 54
d. 10
e. 87
f. 104
g. 117
h. 199

ACTIVITY 3 Limerick Patterns

LITERATURE

These poems called limericks have a pattern, too—a pattern of rhymes.

Interplanetary Limerick

A Martian named Harrison **Harris**
Decided he'd like to see **Paris**
    In space (so we **learn**)
    He took a wrong **turn**
And that's why he's now on **Polaris.**

by Al Grahm

The Fabulous Wizard of Oz

The fabulous wizard of **Oz**
Retired from business **becoz**
    What with up-to-date **science**
    To most of his **clients**
He wasn't the wiz that he **woz.**

Author unknown

With Your Group In "Interplanetary Limerick," look at the words that end each line. Write *A* for every "Harris" rhyme. Write *B* for every "learn" rhyme. What pattern do you find? Write it with *A*'s and *B*'s. Does the pattern fit the other limerick? Explain.

Do You Remember? Try It!

Use this pattern:  . Tell how division can help you predict the color of each square. Name the color of the square.

1. 11   **2.** 26   **3.** 42   **4.** 57   **5.** 64
6. 63   **7.** 17   **8.** 35   **9.** 31   **10.** 18

Think About It

11. Write an explanation telling how to predict colors in a pattern on the hundreds' board.

ACTIVITY OPTION

Find two or three other poems you like. Use A's and B's to show their rhyme patterns.

Pathways

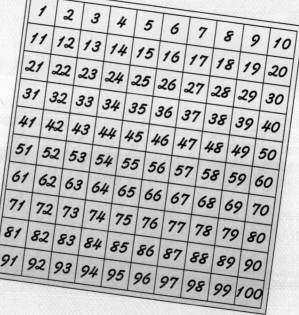

LESSON 7

The directions "Turn right and go two blocks" might help someone find your school. Think how you might direct someone on a hundreds' board.

ACTIVITY 1 Moving on the Board

On Your Own The compass rose on the map at the right shows directions. Try a new kind of compass rose that helps you move on a hundreds' board.

1 Draw! On a sheet of paper draw a simple compass rose.

2 Look! Choose any number on the grid. Call that number *y*. Notice that a move one space right adds one. That's $y + 1$. What expression describes a move one space left? up? down? Try the diagonals.

3 Label! Now label each point on your compass rose with an expression to describe a move one space in that direction.

4 Test It Out! Will your expressions work for all the numbers on the hundreds' board? Try it! Write an explanation of what happens.

What You'll Need
- *green marker*
- *red marker*
- *orange marker*

$y + 1$

The variable y stands for any number on the board. This expression describes a move one square to the right.

1	2	3	4	5	6	7	8	9	10
11	12	13	14	15	16	17	18	19	20
21	22	23	24	25	26	27	28	29	30
31	32	33	34	35	36	37	38	39	40
41	42	43	44	45	46	47	48	49	50
51	52	53	54	55	56	57	58	59	60
61	62	63	64	65	66	67	68	69	70
71	72	73	74	75	76	77	78	79	80
81	82	83	84	85	86	87	88	89	90
91	92	93	94	95	96	97	98	99	100

What You'll Need
- 2–4 hundreds' grids

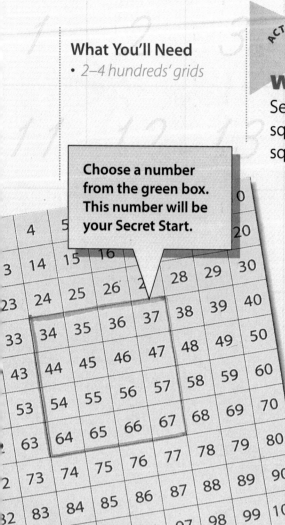

Choose a number from the green box. This number will be your Secret Start.

The Secret Start

With Your Partner Can your partner find the Secret Start? On your own board, start a path at any square from within the green box on the left. Call this square's number y.

1 **Begin** by drawing a line going two squares down from your secret start.

2 **Record** your move as $y + 20$.

3 **Continue** like this: three right, four up, six left, two down.

4 **Record** your path like this: $y + 20 + 3$, and so on, ending with "= (the last square)."

Your final record will be an **equation**—a number sentence with an equal sign.

5 **Use** the strategy of working backward to solve problems. Can your partner use your equation to work backward and find your secret start?

TOOLS AND TECHNIQUES

As you move around the hundreds' board, try using a calculator to help you write the equation.

Go Left at 7

On Your Own Write an equation to describe each path on the right.

Add to the equation to continue the pattern of each path.

The Maze Game

With a Partner Write an equation to describe an escape path from this maze. Start in square 1. You can only escape through square 100. You can't go over any orange squares.

Design a Maze Now design a maze of your own on a hundreds' board.

Color a starting square green.
Color an escape square red.
Color the obstacle squares orange.

Ask a classmate to write an equation to get through your maze.

1	2	3	4	5	6	7	8	9	10
11	12	13	14	15	16	17	18	19	20
21	22	23	24	25	26	27	28	29	30
31	32	33	34	35	36	37	38	39	40
41	42	43	44	45	46	47	48	49	50
51	52	53	54	55	56	57	58	59	60
61	62	63	64	65	66	67	68	69	70
71	72	73	74	75	76	77	78	79	80
81	82	83	84	85	86	87	88	89	90
91	92	93	94	95	96	97	98	99	100

Do You Remember?

Try It!

Which two expressions get you to 100 on the board? to 57? to 80? Tell why each pair gets you to the same place. Hint: Remember the commutative property of addition: $(5 + 7 = 7 + 5)$.

1. $1 + 9 + 90$ **2.** $23 + 4 + 30$ **3.** $23 + 7 + 50$
4. $23 + 30 + 4$ **5.** $1 + 90 + 9$ **6.** $23 + 50 + 7$

Find the value of z on the board.
7. $z + 40 = 90$ **8.** $44 + z = 64$
9. $17 + z = 20$ **10.** $42 - z = 12$

Think About It

11. How would you answer Exercises 7–10 without the hundreds' board?

DRAWING TO LEARN

Use these expressions to start designs on hundreds' boards. Then draw the designs on your own.

1. $1 + 1 + 10 - 1 + 10 + 3$

2. $91 - 10 + 1 - 20 + 1$

3. $11 - 9 + 11 + 9 + 11$

LESSON 8 Time Out

What You'll Need
- *colored markers*
- *multiplication tables*

CONNECT AND COMMUNICATE

Do you recall what a multiple is? Jot down a definition in your journal or share your definition with a classmate.

A multiplication table contains several hidden patterns. You'll learn how to find these patterns.

ACTIVITY 1 Number Pattern Hunt

With Your Group On copies of a 12-by-12 multiplication table, shade the multiples of every number from 1 to 12. Use one multiplication table for each number. You might find it helpful to begin by listing all the multiples of each number. That way you can check your work before you start shading the table. When you're finished, review your tables to be sure they're correct.

X	1	2	3	4	5	6	7	8	9	10	11	12
1	1	2		4	5	6	7	8	9	10	11	12
2	2	4	6	8	10		14	16	18	20	22	24
3	3	6	9	2	15		21	24	27	30	33	36
	4		12		20		28	32	36	40	44	48
				25		35	40	45	50	55	60
	5	10	15	2	25			60	66	72

With Your Class Display your shaded multiplication tables and compare the patterns of multiples. What do the patterns tell you? For example, on the table for the multiples of 6, every third number in the column below 2 is shaded. Why?

Use your calculator to find the multiples of any number. The constant function works on many calculators. Try pressing $3 + = = = =$ $= =$.

1 Why should each group have created the same pattern for the same multiple?

2 Why are some patterns simple and some complex?

3 Describe relationships you see between patterns.

Here's a pattern you might find on a tile floor or wall. Find at least three real patterns that remind you of patterns you found on your multiplication tables. Draw them.

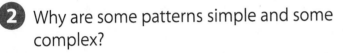

What You'll Need
- *2 colored markers*
- *multiplication tables*

ACTIVITY
2 Stripes and Plaids

With Your Partner You've seen the multiples patterns separately. Wait until you see what happens when you combine them! In these activities you'll discover what **common multiples** are and how you can find them.

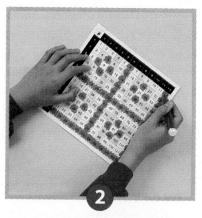

1

Choose a number 1 through 12 and color its multiples yellow.

2

Choose another number 1 through 12 and color its multiples red.

3

Outline the boxes that have numbers you shaded twice. Multiples shared by two numbers are called common multiples. List the common multiples of your numbers.

1	2	3	4	5	6	7	8	9	10	11	12
1	2	3	4	5	6	7	8	9	10	11	12
2	4	6	8	10	12	14	16	18	20	22	24
3	6	9	12	15	18	21	24	27	30	33	36
4	8	12	16	20			36	40	44	48	
5	10	15	20							60	
6	12	18	24	30						72	
7	14	21	28	35	42						
8	16	24	32	40	48	56					92
9	18	27	36	45	54	63	72				8
10	20	30	40	50	60	70	80	90			
11	22	33	44	55	66	77	88	99	1		

36

4 Look at your list of common multiples. Write a definition of what you think the **least common multiple (LCM)** is. Discuss your definition with another pair of students.

5 What is the greatest number in your list of common multiples? Do you think your two numbers have a *greatest* common multiple? Defend your answer.

Try It!

Estimate which of the following pairs of numbers will have the smallest common multiple. Then find the first two common multiples of each pair and check your estimate.

1. 11 and 7

2. 3 and 12

3. 6 and 9

4. 2 and 11

5. 1 and 5

6. 6 and 11

7. 4 and 9

8. 2 and 12

9. 7 and 8

Find the answers that will be even.

10. 7×10

11. $7 + 20$

12. 7×24

13. $5 + 30$

14. $5 + 33$

15. $(5 \times 6) + 2$

Think About It

16. Is the product of two numbers always a common multiple of those numbers? Is it always the least common multiple? Explain how you know.

New Combinations

Why is the Identity Property of Multiplication a good name for what happens when you multiply by 1? What do you think the Zero Property of Multiplication means?

ACTIVITY 1 Combinations of 12

With Your Group Your multiplication table is full of factors. Here are two of the factors of 12.

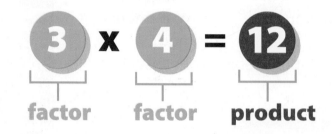

3 X **4** = **12**

factor   factor   **product**

1 You use factors each time you multiply. How could you use the multiplication tables you shaded to find other factors of 12? Make a list of all the factors of 12 that you find.

2 Now use your list of factors and write multiplication equations with 12 as the product. Did any of your equations use the same factors? Which ones?

On Your Own Find *Commutative Property of Multiplication* in the glossary. Use the property to group the equations you wrote into an organized list.

3 List the factors of each number in one of the following groups. Then write the multiplication equations for each product.
a. odd numbers 1 through 25
b. even numbers 2 through 24
c. multiples of 5 from 30 to 50

Write how knowing the Identity Property of Multiplication can help when you list factors.

ACTIVITY 2 Put It in Reverse

With a Partner How would you find factors that are not on the multiplication table?

1 How might writing the equation $5 \times n = 100$ as division help you find the answer? Write the division. What is the missing factor?

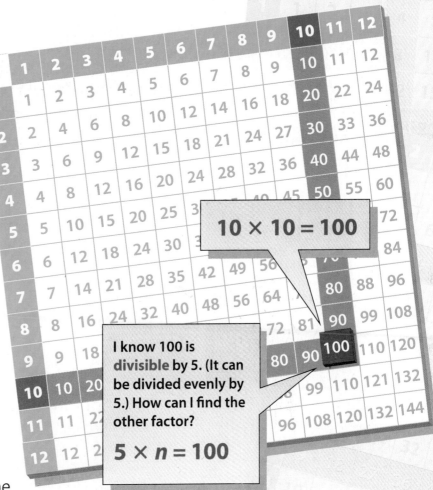

$10 \times 10 = 100$

I know 100 is **divisible** by 5. (It can be divided evenly by 5.) How can I find the other factor?

$5 \times n = 100$

2 Think about 100. How does knowing that it is an even number help you find more factors? Use your calculator to help you find more factors of 100.

On Your Own Look at the multiplication table. Make a list of all the numbers that have 3 as a factor.

1 Write a rule that will help you decide if a number is divisible by 3.

2 Try your rule on these numbers to see if it works. Check your thinking with a calculator.

    a. 39   **b.** 42   **c.** 48   **d.** 54   **e.** 60   **f.** 75

REASONING AND PROBLEM SOLVING

How can you decide if a number is divisible by 2, 5, or 10?

What You'll Need

- *multiplication tables*
- *tiles or small squares*

Remember that an array is a group of things arranged into equal rows and equal columns, like the tiles in the picture.

Equal columns

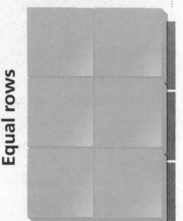

Equal rows

ACTIVITY 3 Prime Time

With Your Group Some of the numbers between 1 and 144 are missing from the multiplication table. Why?

1 Make a sketch or use tiles to show all the arrays of 15 squares. How could you find all the arrays without using the multiplication tables? How many different arrays did you find?

2 Now try making arrays of 17 squares. How many did you find? What did they look like?

3 Try making arrays of 39. Since 39 is not on the table, use your calculator to help you. How many did you find? Why do you think 39 is not on the table?

X	1	2	3	4	5	6	7	8	9	10	11	12
1	1	2	3	4	5	6	7	8	9	10	11	12
2	2	4		5	6	7	8	9	10	20	22	24
3	3		10	12	14	16	18		10	11	12	
				18	21	24	27	30	33	36		
5				28	32	36	40	44	48			
6	6			40	45	50	55	60				
7	7	14		48	54	60	66	72				
8	8	16	2		63	70	77	84				
9	9	18	27			80	88	92				
10	10	20	30									

Prime Suspects

On Your Own Here are two important ways for you to name numbers.

1 Find the factors of at least three numbers from the blue group. Then find the factors of at least three numbers from the red group. Explain how the factors of blue numbers and the red numbers are different.

35 8 28 21 48
17 2 11 31 43

2 The blue numbers are **composite numbers.** The red numbers are **prime numbers.** Use what you just discovered about these numbers to help you write a definition for each.

3 Make up a list of ten prime and ten composite numbers. Share it with a classmate. Can your classmate tell which numbers are prime and which are composite? If not, what hints can you give to help?

ACTIVITY OPTION

Choose three even numbers between 100 and 200. Use your calculator to make arrays with them.

• *Write your system for finding all the factors.*
• *Describe the patterns for prime numbers and for composite numbers.*

Exercises and Problems

The Art of the Grid

Artist Ellsworth Kelly used geometry to create the painting *Colors for a Large Wall.* Use the painting on the next page to answer the questions.

1 Name the arrays you could make with the same number of yellow squares Kelly used. Repeat for the number of white squares. Explain which number is prime and how you know.

2 One factor of the total number of small squares is 8. What are the other factors?

3 Find the number of small white squares and the total number of small squares. What is the greatest common factor of those two numbers?

4 How many squares are there that are four small squares long by four small squares wide? How do you know?

5 How many individual squares are painted red and how many are green? What is the least common multiple of those two numbers?

6 Is the number of white squares in the painting a prime or a composite number? the number of black squares?

7 Could all the squares in this painting be arranged in equal rows of two squares each? three squares? five squares? ten squares? Tell how you know.

8 List the colors Kelly used and note the number of times he used each color. Write all the factors of each number.

Oil on canvas, mounted on sixty-four wood panels; overall, 7ft 10 $\frac{1}{4}$ in. x 7ft 10 $\frac{1}{2}$ in. The Museum of Modern Art, New York. Gift of the artist.

Ellsworth Kelly, *Colors for a Large Wall*, 1951

9 How could you use multiplication to help you find how many small squares are in the painting? What factors would you use to find the product?

10 How could you use multiplication and division to find the total number of squares of any size in the painting?

43

Looking Back

Choose the best answer. Write *a, b, c,* or *d* for each question.

1. Which polyomino has the same perimeter as this one?

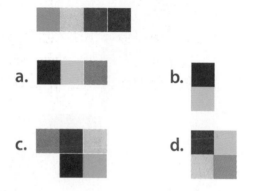

a.

b.

c.

d.

2. Which of these products does not match the others?

   a. $3 \times 6 = n$ b. $4 \times 6 = n$
   c. $2 \times 12 = n$ d. $3 \times 8 = n$

3. Which of these four letters has more than one line of symmetry?

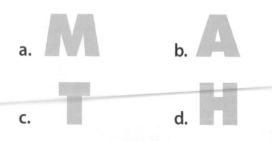

a. M

b. A

c. T

d. H

4. Which expression shows the pattern for square numbers?

   a. $n \times 3$ b. $n \times 2$
   c. $n \times n$ d. $4 \times n$

5. A border design uses five colors in a repeated pattern. The second color is yellow. Which of these sets of squares will be yellow?

   a. 5, 10, 15, 20   b. 7, 12, 17, 22
   c. 2, 5, 7, 12   d. 6, 11, 16, 21

6. The equation $p + 4 + 17 - 3 = 36$ shows a path on a grid. What is the value of p?

   a. 40   b. 9
   c. 6   d. 18

7. Write a number, letter, or expression for each of the following:
   a. a common multiple of 3 and 5 that is less than 50
   b. an example of the Commutative Property of Multiplication
   c. any composite whole number
   d. the next prime number that is greater than 20
   e. a variable

8. Write four equations that describe paths from a mystery starting box (*b*) to an ending box. Then show the value of *b*.

9. Write two equations using each of the following pairs of numbers.

   a. 3, 12   b. 11, 3
   c. 9, 10   d. 8, 7

10. Write an expression with a variable to predict any step in the following patterns.

    a. 3, 6, 9   b. 1, 4, 9, 16
    c. 15, 30, 45   d. 4, 8, 12, 16

    e.

11. A friend wants to start a paper route. She will be paid by the number of papers she delivers each day. She wants to figure out how many days it will take to make enough money to buy a bicycle. What does she need to know? Write an expression to describe the problem. Use variables for missing information.

12. Copy the grids below. Outline three figures on each that are congruent to the tetromino.

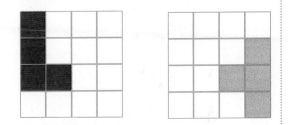

13. On grid paper make a chart of numbers from 1 to 42. Use six numbers per row. On the chart, shade multiples of any number you choose from 3 to 8. Describe the pattern. Try it again with a different number.

45

MODULE 1

Investigations

Patterns Made from Grids

This quilt, with a pattern called Jacob's ladder, is an example of a complex design made from a few simple parts. It was made in 1924 by an Amish quilt maker from Indiana. The Amish are a Christian group who follow a very simple way of life. They make quilts for practical use and for special occasions. The bright colors show that this quilt was probably made as a gift, perhaps for someone who was getting married or moving away. Quilts for everyday use are less colorful.

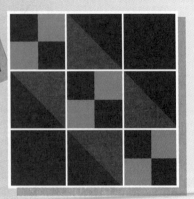

Take a look at the picture. Notice how a few basic squares are put together to make the whole pattern.

Choose one of the following investigations.

A Do-It-Yourself Jacob's Ladder

Your challenge is to write a set of directions for making a Jacob's ladder quilt.

1 **Use** the clues on these pages to analyze the overall pattern and figure out for yourself how it is put together.

2 **Write** directions for someone else to use in making the quilt. Your directions should include a sketch of each of the basic squares used and the number of each kind that will be needed.

3 **Create** diagrams and step-by-step directions to show how to put all the squares together.

Keep In Mind

Your directions will be judged on the following points:

☐ How did you use your knowledge of symmetry and slides, flips, and turns in solving the problem?

☐ Did you sketch all the basic squares? Did you accurately record the numbers of squares needed?

☐ How clearly did you present your thinking? How clearly do your words and diagrams communicate how to make the quilt pattern?

Types of squares

1.

2.

One Student's Process

Investigation B — Make Your Own Design

Try designing a pattern of your own. Your pattern should be a square made of one or more smaller basic squares. Feel free to use more than one basic square, as long as your design is symmetrical and has examples of slides, flips, or turns. Your report should include the following:

- your design mounted on paper or poster board
- a description that points out slides, flips, or turns as well as any lines of symmetry
- sketches of the combinations of squares you made in planning your design

Computer Option If you have a computer, you can use a drawing program for this investigation. Create your basic square and then make three copies. You can slide and turn the individual squares to make patterns. Then make three copies of the one you like best and arrange your final design.

Investigation C — Pattern Hunt Revisited

Take another look at the patterns you collected in the pattern hunt on pages 2–3. How would you use those patterns to make a poster that shows what you've learned in this module?

- Analyze your patterns for examples of symmetry and slides, flips, and turns.
- Use a grid to find the area and perimeter of shapes in your patterns.
- Make one of your patterns grow. Then write an expression that describes the growth pattern.

MODULE 2

Getting a Handle on Numbers

Learn about more numbers—and learn more about the numbers you know. That's the way to increase your number sense. In this module you will learn how to get a handle on greater numbers. You will also learn handy ways to multiply to reach even greater numbers.

SECTION A

Handling Millions

SECTION B

Estimation and Multiplication

SECTION C

Measurement and Multiplication

SECTION D

One-Digit Divisors

A Handful of Millions

You hear about a million a million times a day—or do you? About how many do you think a million is? Can you hold a million in your hand? Find out by collecting handfuls of items in your classroom.

① Hold a Thousand

Decide how many handfuls you would need to hold ten of each item.

- How many handfuls would it take to hold a hundred? a thousand?
- How did you decide? Make a chart of your items and predictions.

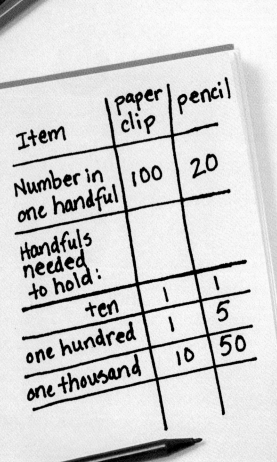

Item	paper clip	pencil
Number in one handful	100	20
Handfuls needed to hold:		
ten	1	1
one hundred	1	5
one thousand	10	50

Handle a Million

List at least three items that you might be able to collect one million of. List any difficulty you might have in trying to hold a million of the items.

③ Fill a Shoe Box

How big do you think a million is? Predict what size container you think you would need to hold a million of these items.

a. grains of sand
b. ones' cubes
c. leaves

Share your answers and how you got them.

Investigations Preview

Learn about numbers and get a sense of how large they are. Use your knowledge to move a million pennies or graph handfuls of popcorn.

You're a Winner (pages 76–77)

You've just won a million pennies. How will you collect your prize? You'll need your sense of a million to help you.

Grabfest (pages 110–112)

How many popcorn kernels can you hold in your hand? Can a relative with a larger hand hold more kernels? Use what you know about numbers to explore the relationship between hand area and the number of items in a handful.

LESSON ①

A Million's Place

Millions of stars dot the sky. **Millions** of people live in California. Millions of students go to school each day. In this lesson you will explore how big a million is.

What You'll Need

- *ones' cube*
- *tens' rod*
- *hundreds' flat*
- *thousands' cube*

ACTIVITY 1 **Grab a Million**

With Your Partner   You can use your base ten blocks to help you understand and even make a model of a million.

① Look at the chart below.

    a. How is the value of the digit in each place related to the value of the place on its right?

    b. How could you use your calculator to show the relationships among the places?

Millions	Hundred Thousands	Ten Thousands	Thousands	Hundreds	Tens	Ones
			1	1	1	1
			thousands' cube	hundreds' flat	tens' rod	ones' cube

**1 hundreds' flat
equals ■ tens' rods**

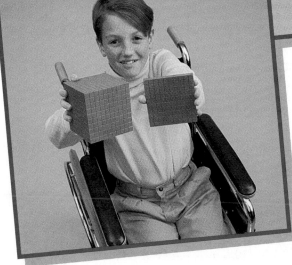

**1 thousands' cube
equals ■ hundreds' flats**

2 Look at the pattern of the place-value models. Tell how the models change as the place value increases.
  a. How can you show that the tens' rod is made of ten ones' cubes?
  b. Use what you know about the ten-to-one relationship among the places to explain how any model can be made with ten of the models to its right.

3 Use what you know about the relationship among the places in the place-value chart to describe and sketch a model for ten thousand.

4 Describe the models for the rest of the places in the chart. Explain how each would be made.

Use straws as tens' rods. Then use straws, tape, and string to make models for one thousand, ten thousand, one hundred thousand, and one million.

ACTIVITY 2 Too Big to Handle

With Your Partner Learn ways to handle numbers even greater than a million.

Period	Billions			Millions			Thousands			Ones		
Place	Hundreds	Tens	Ones	Hundreds	Tens	Ones	Hundreds	Tens	Ones	Hundreds	Tens	Ones
										3	4	9
							7	2	5	3	4	9

1 How are the place values for the thousands period the same as the place values for ones? How are they different?

2 Draw another place-value chart. Write a number greater than 999,999.

3 How could you use a millions' cube to model one **billion?** How tall and how wide would your model be?

In Your Journal Tell why you can read any number if you can read a three-digit number and if you know the names of the periods.

A billion ball-point pens laid end to end would wrap around Earth at the equator 4.1 times!

It is estimated that by 1996 there will be a total of fifty million, seven hundred fifty-nine thousand students enrolled in elementary and secondary schools in the United States. Of these students, thirty-one million eight hundred seventeen thousand will be between ten and thirteen years old.

from *Projections of Education Statistics to 2002* from the U.S. Dept. of Education, 1991

On Your Own Two of the different ways we express numbers are **word form** (like one billion) and **standard form** (like 1,000,000,000). Rewrite this report in standard form.

TOOLS AND TECHNIQUES

Remember that the word and is not used when you read or write whole numbers.
- *Standard form: 120,055*
- *Word form:
  one hundred twenty
  thousand, fifty-five*

₃ Handy Expressions

ACTIVITY 3

With Your Partner Greater numbers can be written in many different ways. The Incas, an ancient South American people, used knots tied in ropes to represent numbers. The ropes were called *quipus*. The Incas used periods and a base ten system.

1 What numbers do these ropes show?
  a. How is a quipu like our system?
  b. How is it different?

2 How do you make a greater number on a quipu?

The Incan Empire (above, in orange) lasted from 1438 to 1532. It extended more than 2,500 miles along the western coast of South America.

In the blue rope the knots at the far left are hundreds.

In the yellow rope the knots to the right are ones.

In the red rope the knots at the left are tens.

DRAWING TO LEARN

Making a mini–place-value chart can help you rename when you subtract greater numbers.

Number Sense

With Your Partner Numbers can be named in many ways for different purposes. Think about the ways you can name 24,032.

1 List all the names you can think of for 24,032.
   a. Why could you name the number 24 thousands, 32 ones?
   b. How would you name 24,032 in hundreds?

2 When you subtract, you need to know many names for a number. Explain how and why you rename 24,032 as you subtract.

$$24,0\overset{2}{\cancel{3}}\overset{12}{\cancel{2}} \longrightarrow \textbf{2 tens, 12 ones}$$
$$-15,564$$

3 Give an example of when you might use each of these number names for 642,000.

a. 642 thousands

b. 6 hundred-thousands,
   4 ten-thousands,
   2 thousands

c. 642,000 ones

Calculating Millions

On Your Own You can use your calculator to explore place value of large numbers. Be sure to look for a pattern as you do the activity.

1 **Enter 1** 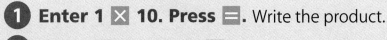 **10. Press** ▇. Write the product.

2 **Enter** ▇ **10. Press** ▇. Write the product.
Repeat until you reach 1,000,000. Use the constant
function if you wish. What pattern do you see?

3 Undo the multiplication.
Enter 1,000,000 ▇ **10.** Write the quotient.
Continue dividing by 10 until you reach 1.
Tell what pattern you see.

4 Once you reach 1, what will happen if you
continue to divide by 10?
a. What numbers will you get?
b. How could you add the numbers to the
place-value chart?
c. What names could you give the numbers?

Try It!

Write each number in at least two ways.

1. one thousand thirty 　　2. 18,492 　　3. 56,813

4. four million, four hundred thousand, forty-four

5. two hundred twelve thousand, two hundred eleven

6. seventy thousand, four hundred

Add or subtract to find only the even sums or differences.

7. 134 − 39 　　8. 467 + 139 　　9. 433 + 267

10. 941 − 755 　　11. 597 − 398 　　12. 6,411 + 4,913

Think About It

13. Write why you think trading and place value help you
think of other names for numbers.

LESSON 2 Compare and Order

People holding hands stood side by side and stretched across the country. "Hands Across America" made this dream come true. In 1986, about 4.9 million Americans joined hands to raise money for hunger and homelessness. They stretched from coast to coast.

ACTIVITY 1 Hand-Picked Data

With Your Group Decide on a way to divide fairly the data collection for all the states among the groups in your class. Use an encyclopedia or almanac.

1 Collect data about each state's population and its greatest distance east–west and north–south.

2 Organize your data into charts. Which data might be best organized from greatest to least? Why?

What You'll Need
- *encyclopedia or almanac*
- *index cards*

State	Population	Greatest Distance East to West	Greatest Distance North to South
Texas	16,986,510	774 mi	737 mi

3 Decide whether there are enough people in the states you researched to reach across the states east to west or north to south.

   a. You know a **mile (mi)** is a unit we can use to measure long distances. What do you need to know to answer the question?

   b. How can you get the information you need?

Present your conclusions to the class. Be prepared to explain how you made your decisions.

About 10 feet, or about 5 feet per person

With Your Partner Use the data and number facts your group collected to make up 20 questions. Write each question on an index card and provide an answer for each. Use your questions to play Twenty Questions with another group.

Databases are great tools for organizing lots of similar data. Try creating a database of your state information. What data will you include?

Information States

Maps, charts, and almanacs can provide a variety of information about people, places, and things. Use the information on the map and in the chart to answer the questions.

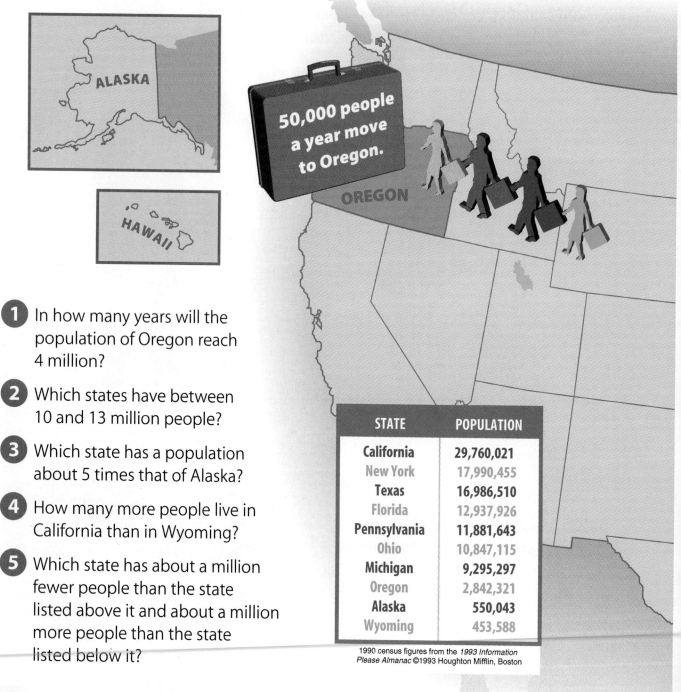

50,000 people a year move to Oregon.

ALASKA

HAWAII

OREGON

1 In how many years will the population of Oregon reach 4 million?

2 Which states have between 10 and 13 million people?

3 Which state has a population about 5 times that of Alaska?

4 How many more people live in California than in Wyoming?

5 Which state has about a million fewer people than the state listed above it and about a million more people than the state listed below it?

STATE	POPULATION
California	29,760,021
New York	17,990,455
Texas	16,986,510
Florida	12,937,926
Pennsylvania	11,881,643
Ohio	10,847,115
Michigan	9,295,297
Oregon	2,842,321
Alaska	550,043
Wyoming	453,588

1990 census figures from the *1993 Information Please Almanac* ©1993 Houghton Mifflin, Boston

6 What will be the population of Florida and New York after the people move?

7 What are ten possible populations for Illinois? Explain how you know.

8 Which states' combined population is about that of California's population?

9 Which of the states listed have more than four representatives in the House of Representatives?

10 Make a pictograph to show the populations of the states. Use 1 symbol = 2 million people.

Population ranks between Florida and Ohio

NEW YORK

ILLINOIS

100,000

1 representative for every 500,000 people

House of Representatives

FLORIDA

LESSON 3

About a Handful

Everyone uses estimates. Even when you think you are using exact numbers, you might be using an estimate. But don't worry, sometimes using an estimate is the right thing to do.

Roberto Clemente was a professional baseball player from 1954 to 1972. When he was a child he worked hard to earn the money to buy a bicycle. He kept all the money he earned in a glass jar.

Sometimes, when he was not in school or playing baseball, Roberto would earn a few extra coins working for his father. Don Melchor owned an old truck that he used to carry sand and gravel for construction work. Roberto and his brothers worked long hours loading and unloading the truck.

Finally, after three years of hard work, there was $27.00 in the big glass jar. Roberto took the money he had earned and bought a secondhand bicycle. He cleaned it and polished it until the metal sparkled in the sun. Don Melchor and Doña Luisa watched proudly as Roberto pedaled down the dirt road in Barrio San Antón.

From *Pride of Puerto Rico: The Life of Roberto Clemente*
by Paul Robert Walker

- When Roberto kept the coins he had earned in a big jar, do you think he figured out exactly how much money he had or do you think he used an estimate? Explain your choice.
- How might Roberto have estimated how much money he had in the jar?
- When do you think he needed to figure out exactly how much money he had?
- When do you use exact or estimated numbers?

ACTIVITY 1 Estimate or Exact?

On Your Own Look at the data on pages 58–59. Were the numbers you used exact or estimates? Explain.

1 Make a list of ten numbers from an almanac that you think are estimates and ten you think are exact. Explain how you made your decisions.

   a. Is the following an exact number? Roberto Clemente had 3,000 career hits. How did you decide?

   b. There are 58,729 seats at Three Rivers Stadium in Pittsburgh. If a game is sold out, do you know how many people will be in attendance or do you need to estimate? Explain.

What You'll Need
- *almanac*

2 Handy Estimation

With Your Class Below are listed four reasons you might want to estimate. Discuss with your class when these might occur. Give some examples for each and record them on a class chart.

You use an estimate in the following situations:
- when an estimate is as good as an exact answer
- when there is no way to get an exact answer
- when you could get an exact number but it would be too messy
- when you want to check whether an answer is reasonable

$$24.6$$
$$+ \; 26.7$$
$$?$$

The answer should be around 50.

For example, in 1985, 124,000,000,000 gallons of water were used per day in California. In which category would you put this estimate? In which category would you put an estimate of the number of snowflakes in a snowball the size of a baseball? Explain your answers.

Around and About

With Your Group A **line graph** is a good way to show change. Are the populations on the graph exact numbers or estimates? Why?

Why do you think students in the United States are taught that the halfway number, 5, always rounds up?

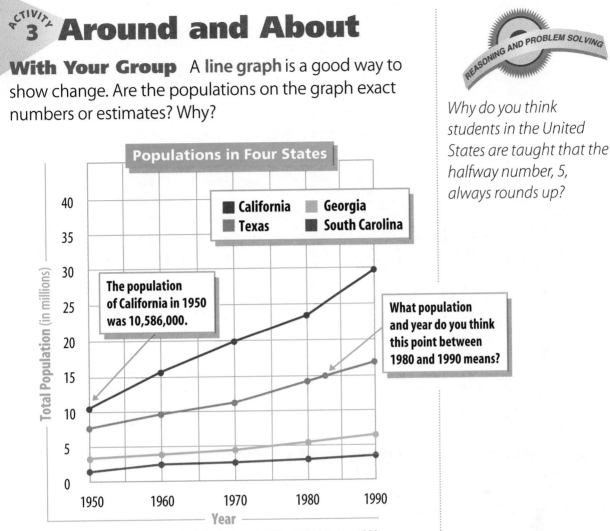

Populations in Four States

■ California ■ Georgia
■ Texas ■ South Carolina

Total Population (in millions)

The population of California in 1950 was 10,586,000.

What population and year do you think this point between 1980 and 1990 means?

Year

Source: *Statistical Abstract of the United States, 1992*
Historical Statistics of the United States, Part 1

1 Look at the estimate for California's population in 1950. This number has been rounded to the nearest thousand.
  a. What two millions is the number 10,586,000 between? How do you know?
  b. Why would you look at the number to the right of the millions' place to help you decide how to round?
  c. Why would it help to know that 500,000 is half of 1,000,000?

2 Write five questions and answers about the graph. Trade questions with another group and solve.

Look up populations for several years for cities or states in your part of the country. Use a line graph to show how population has changed over time.

4 Close Enough

With Your Group Think of problems that a classmate would probably use estimation to solve.

1 As a group write at least four problems. On a separate sheet of paper write the estimates you would expect to get and the method you used to get those estimates.

2 Trade questions with another group. Solve the problems and record how you solved them.

3 Share the problems with your class. Discuss the methods you used to solve them. Were the methods you used the same ones used by the group that wrote the problems? Do both methods work? Why?

Problem:
How many ½-pt cartons of milk will my classmates drink this week?

Answer:
Our class has 25 students. All of them drink milk each day at lunch. Five students a day drink milk at snack time.

30 × 5 =
150 cartons

ACTIVITY

5 A Lot and a Little

With Your Group What is the population of your class? Suppose there are 25 students in your class. That's a lot of students when you need to travel in a car but not a lot if you travel by bus. How do you know when a number means a lot or a little?

Make a list of 5 items and numbers to go with them, like 10 sneakers or 18 tires. Trade lists with another group. In 5 minutes write as many situations as you can in which each number of things is large, reasonable, or small.

A chart can help you organize your list. Use Large, Reasonable, and Small as your headings.

Do You Remember?

Try It!

Round to the underlined place.

1. 14**7**,392,610 **2.** 22,**5**40 **3.** 1**6**,498,499

4. 1**9**,800 **5.** 163,**8**21,421 **6.** **1**,501

7. Name a time when Exercise 1 would be an exact number and when it would be an estimate.

Choose the best method to find each product. Write *P* (paper and pencil), *M* (mental math), or *C* (calculator). Find the product.

8. 4×367 **9.** 9×14 **10.** 5×330 **11.** 6×400

Think About It

12. Write a rule for rounding to any place value.

Hands-on Multiplication

✓ **Self-Check** *Why would a ruler not be a good way to measure your hand?*

How big is your hand? You can answer this question in many ways. You might say that your hand is smaller than your foot or larger than your nose. How might you measure your hand?

- What is your hand's length and width? How did you decide?
- How could you find the area your hand covers? How would using grid paper help you?

ACTIVITY 1 **Sizing Up Your Hand**

What You'll Need
• *grid paper*

With Your Partner Place your hand on a sheet of grid paper and have your partner trace around your hand. Trade roles.

1 Estimate how many square units your hand covers. Explain how you made your estimate.

2 Draw the smallest possible rectangle that still includes the whole outline of your hand.

3 Draw the largest possible rectangle that totally fits inside the outline of your hand.

4 How can you use the rectangles to improve your estimate? How could using multiplication help you?

5 Describe at least two more ways to improve your estimate.

What You'll Need
- *grid paper*

Hand Me Ten

With Your Partner Now that you know the area of your own hand, try to find the area of ten of your hands.

1 Tell which of these expressions you would use to find out the area of ten of your hands. What does *n* stand for in these expressions?

$$n + 10 \qquad n \times 10 \qquad n - 10$$

2 Think of a simpler or related problem to find a way to solve this problem. Suppose your hand covered 2 square units. You know the following:

If *n* = 2   **If *n* = 3**   **If *n* = 4**

$2 \times 10 = 20 \qquad 3 \times 10 = 30 \qquad 4 \times 10 = 40$

3 Find the area when *n* equals 5, 6, 7, 8, 9, and 10 square units.

4 Think about what you know about the patterns of tens. How could you use mental math to find the area of ten of your hands? Find it.

5 Use grid paper. Find the area covered by ten of each: your foot, your mathematics book, a pencil. Explain how you got your answers.

CONNECT AND COMMUNICATE

In Your Journal Write a rule that you can use whenever you multiply by ten. Make a chart to help you and give some examples to support your rule.

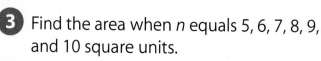

On Your Own Use mental math and the **Associative Property of Multiplication** to match each product with its factors. Explain your reasoning. Write at least two number sentences for each product.

b. 5×10

c. (6×2)×10

d. (2×5)×5

50

a. (2×2)×10

40

e. 32×10

f. (8×4)×10

320

120

g. (4×3)×10

h. 4×10

Do You Remember?

Try It!

Use mental math to find y.

1. $6 \times 10 = y$ **2.** $10 \times y = 100$ **3.** $15 \times y = 150$

4. $17 \times 10 = y$ **5.** $y \times 10 = 240$ **6.** $y \times 10 = 300$

Use the Associative Property to match the number sentences.

7. $(19 + 24) + 26$ **a.** $64 + (4 + 5) + 91$

8. $(64 + 4) + (5 + 91)$ **b.** $(3 + 5) + (32 + 10)$

9. $3 + (5 + 32) + 10$ **c.** $19 + (24 + 26)$

10. $(40 + 4) + 16$ **d.** $40 + (4 + 16)$

Think About It

11. What pattern do you see when you multiply by 10? How can you use it to help you multiply by 100?

Multiplying by Ten

Now that you know how many square units 10 of your hands would cover, you can find how many 20, 30, 40, 50, or even 100 hands would cover. You'll discover a method to help you multiply by even larger numbers.

ACTIVITY 1 Hand over Hand

With Your Partner Use what you know about place value, multiplying by 10, and multiplication properties to help you solve these problems.

1 Write the expression for finding 20 of your hand areas. (Hint: Think $20 = 2 \times 10$.) How could you use the Associative Property of Multiplication to make the expression easier to work with?

2 You can use the **Commutative Property of Multiplication** to change the order of the factors and the Associative Property to change the grouping. Write your expression so that it is easier to solve. Explain how you used the properties and then solve.

3 How will you decide whether your answer is reasonable?

4 Use the properties to find the area of 30, 40, 50, and 100 of your hands.

DRAWING TO LEARN

ACTIVITY 2 Laying It Out

With Your Partner What is the greatest number of gloves you can cut from this piece of leather? How many pairs is that? Use the area of your hand for a pattern. Each pattern needs a top and bottom stitched together. Draw a diagram to show how you would fit the patterns on the leather.

How many gloves? How many hands? Draw an array to help you find out. Every glove needs a front and a back. Every pair needs 2 gloves.

What You'll Need
• *grid paper*

1 meter

1 meter

Remember:
    1 year = 365 days
    1 day = 24 hours
    1 hour = 60 minutes
    1 minute = 60 seconds

ACTIVITY
3 The Hands of Time

On Your Own Look at these faces. Could any of these people be 1 million days old? 1 million hours old? 1 million minutes old? 1 million seconds old? You can use multiplication by multiples of 10 to find out.

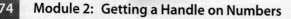

1 Decide whether anyone in the picture is a million days, hours, minutes, or seconds old. Explain how you made your decision.

2 Describe how you would find the number of days in 10 years, 20 years, and 50 years.

   a. What would multiplying 60 minutes × 24 hours tell you?

   b. What would multiplying the number of minutes in a day by 60 tell you?

Do You Remember?

Try It!

Rewrite the number sentences using the Associative or Commutative Property. Then find the product.

1. 10 × 20   **2.** 10 × 100   **3.** 10 × 14

4. 40 × 61   **5.** 30 × 19   **6.** 50 × 70

Label the pair *symmetrical, congruent,* or *neither.*

7.    **8.**

9.   **10.**

Think About It

11. How can patterns and properties help you find products when you multiply by 10 or by multiples of 10?

Investigation

You're a Winner

1,000,000 PENNIES!!!

GREAT NEWS!
* FIFTH GRADER *
YOU ARE A WINNER!!

CONGRATULATIONS!

Dear Fifth Grader:

You have JUST WON **1,000,000 PENNIES**!
Yes, Fifth Grader, you are the lucky winner of one million pennies.
That's **1,000,000 pennies**!
And all you have to do is collect your prize.

Sincerely,

Diana M. Suarez
Contest Coordinator

Rules (fine print!)

1. Your prize is located at a bank eight blocks from your home.
2. You have one week to move **ALL 1,000,000 PENNIES** from the bank to your home.
3. You must take the pennies. The bank will not exchange paper money for pennies.

> Imagine you've just received this letter. How would you go about collecting your prize?

1,000,000 PENNIES
1,000,000 PENNIES
1,000,000 PENNIES
1,000,000 PENNIES

Collect your prize today!

PAID

Fifth Grader
58A Anystreet
Anytown, USA

OPEN IMMEDIATELY!

1 **Decide** whether you want your prize. List reasons for and against collecting your prize. For instance, how much do the pennies weigh? How much space do they take up? How many dollars are they worth?

2 **List** several ways you can move the pennies. Pick three. Write the good and bad points of each. Choose the best plan for moving the pennies.

3 **Find** out how much space you'll need to store the pennies. You may need to use what you know about 1 penny and 100 pennies to make a model. Be sure to test your model.

Ask Yourself

☐ What do I know about pennies that can help me find out what my prize is worth and how big it is?

☐ How can drawings or a model help me plan the move?

☐ What can I do to see whether my plan will work?

☐ How can a model help me plan how to store my prize?

☐ How can I share my plan with the bank so that I can collect my prize?

Give Yourself a Hand

You can find large numbers in small places. Your hand, for example, is full of large numbers.

A normal handshake grip has about 100 pounds of force.

1 A politician can shake 180 hands in 1 hour. How many hands can she shake in 8 hours?

2 How much force will the politician have used in shaking hands for 1 hour?

3 About how many hand movements will you make in 10 days? 100 days?

4 Horses are measured in hands. One hand equals 4 in. If a horse is *n* hands tall, write an expression to show how to find the height of the horse in inches.

5 If a horse measures 16 hands, what is the height of the horse expressed in feet and inches?

There are three joints per finger, including the thumb.

6 About how many nerve endings are there in five fingertips? ten fingertips? Assume one square inch per fingertip.

7 Write an expression to show how many joints there are in 20 hands.

There are 1,300 nerve endings in one square inch of fingertip.

4 inches

Check Your Math Power

8 Do you think that 1,000 hand movements in 1 day is an estimate or an exact number? Explain.

9 Six people are standing in a line. The first person shakes hands with the second. Then the second person shakes hands with the third person, and so on. How many handshakes will there be?

10 There are two pairs of blue gloves and two pairs of red gloves in a box. The pairs are not attached. Without looking, you reach in and take out two gloves. Name four different possibilities of the two gloves you will pick.

A hand makes about 1,000 movements in a day.

LESSON

6

Helping Hands

Suppose your neighborhood wants to change vacant land into a park. You will want to know how much the park will cost to build and keep up.

What You'll Need
• *grid paper*

ACTIVITY

1 **Park Presentation**

With Your Group   Plan a presentation that will answer the questions below. Answer the questions in any order. Then prepare a presentation and explain how you found your answers.

Flower Border   Look at the cost of a flower border. Remember that a **foot (ft)** is a unit of length. It is 12 **inches (in.)**.

1 What else do you need to know?

2 Tell how this formula can help you find the cost of the border.

Perimeter = 2 × (length + width)
or $P = 2 \times (l + w)$

3 Why does the formula work?

4 How do people get into the park?

5 How does an entrance affect your perimeter?

Plants to Go

Flower border
is $8.00
per foot.

411 W. 87th
Leawood, Kansas
00483

Bob's Mulch and Grow
3300 N. Main St.
Chicago, Illinois 60606

Wood chips cost $4.00 per square foot.

Covering Chip Costs For safety, toddler areas need to be covered with wood chips.

1 How can you find out how much area needs to be covered by wood chips?

2 How can you find out the cost of covering the play area?

Maintenance Money

1 Draw a square. Label it *1 foot by 1 foot*. Why can you say the area is 1 square foot or 1 foot^2?

2 Draw a picture of the park you are planning. Show the park divided into square-foot parts.
   a. How many square feet is the park?
   b. How much money will you need to maintain the park?

BUDGET

Maintaining the Park costs $10 per square foot.

TOOLS AND TECHNIQUES

Architects and landscapers use models when designing houses, buildings, and open spaces. Would three-dimensional models be helpful for your planning? Why or why not?

Riverside Park 2 mi wide by 2 mi long

ACTIVITY 2 · Nearest Square Foot

What You'll Need
- *tape measure*
- *grid paper*

With Your Partner Measure three rectangular areas to the nearest foot. Choose places like a room, a playground, or a park.

1 Make a drawing of each place and label the measurements.

2 Find the perimeter and the area of each.

ACTIVITY 3 · Number Power

What You'll Need
- *2 cubes labeled 1–6*

On Your Own As you planned your park, you used feet^2 as a short way to write *square feet*. You can also use raised numbers, or **exponents,** as a short way to show the number of times a number is used as a factor.

1×1 can be written as 1^2

5×5 can be written as 5^2

10×10 can be written as 10^2

These are square numbers.

1 Look at the sentence below.

$$1 \times 1 \times 1 = 1^3$$

REASONING AND PROBLEM SOLVING

If a base number is used as a factor three times, the number is written with the exponent 3. These numbers are called cube numbers. Tell why you think they got their name. You may want to draw a picture to show your reasoning.

Compare the sentence to what you already know about square numbers. How do you think you would write the following numbers?

a. $10 \times 10 \times 10$ **b.** $5 \times 5 \times 5$ **c.** $30 \times 30 \times 30 \times 30$

With Your Partner Use what you know about exponents to play the following game.

 1 Toss two number cubes. Write the numbers from your toss in your notebook.

2 Use one number as the base number, the other as the exponent. Have your partner use the same numbers, but in reverse.

3 Predict which product will be greater. Use your calculator or your own way to check your prediction.

4 Now let your partner follow Steps 1–3.

5 Keep taking turns and follow the pattern of scoring. How many points will you get for your fourth and fifth correct predictions?

6 Try to be the first to reach 254 points!

✔ **Self-Check** To figure the scoring, write an equation for the number multiplied by itself. Decide how to find the value if the exponent is 3. Work forward or backward. Look for patterns. Check using a calculator.

How to Keep Score

1st correct prediction: 2^1 **points**

2nd correct prediction: 2^2 **points**

3rd correct prediction: 2^3 **points**

With Your Group You may want to add more activity areas to your park, maybe a ball field or a sprinkler fountain. You can use grid paper, letting 1 ☐ = 10 ft by 10 ft, to cut out shapes or shade the areas of the fields or courts.

1 Choose your own way to plan the area. Use estimates and rounding if you need to. Think about the amount of space between areas. Separate the activities that might disturb one another.

2 Label your park with the areas and uses of areas that will require fencing.

3 Be prepared to explain how you found the areas and perimeters.

PROPOSED PARK ITEMS

Item	Dimensions
Baseball Field	325 ft x 325 ft
Tennis Court	78 ft x 27 ft
Horseshoes Court	10 ft x 50 ft
Volleyball Court	60 ft x 30 ft
Bocce Ball Court	75 ft x 8 ft
Shuffleboard Court	52 ft x 6 ft
Basketball Court	94 ft x 50 ft
Kiddie Pool	8 ft x 8 ft
Field House	185 ft x 65 ft
Chess / Checkers Pavilion	16 ft x 16 ft
Fountain	55 ft x 55 ft

1,000 ft

2,000 ft

KEY

▨ AREA TO BE DEVELOPED

❀ BUSH

❁ TREE

RIVERVIEW PARK

W.O.#: 2305	
Prod. Mgr.: MJ	
Drawn: TKP	
Checked: ðбб	

84

Greater Park Areas

With Your Partner

1 Write one number from 0 to 9 on each of ten slips of paper. Put the papers in a box.

To find the combinations, draw the shapes you'll get with each set of numbers.

2 Take four slips from the box. Arrange them to make two-digit numbers for length and width. Find four possible combinations of two-digit numbers.

3 What combinations do you think will give the greatest area? the greatest perimeter?

4 Check your predictions. Use your own way or use a calculator. Repeat the activity.

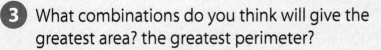

Do You Remember?

Try It!

Find the area and perimeter for rectangles with length of 3 ft and these widths.

1. 2 ft   2. 3 ft   3. 4 ft   4. 5 ft
5. 6 ft   6. 7 ft   7. 8 ft   8. 9 ft

Substitute these values in each expression: $w = 2$ ft; $l = 5$ ft; $s = 6$ ft.

9. area $= l \times w$ 10. perimeter $= 2\,(l + w)$ 11. area $= s^2$

Think About It

12. In Exercises 1–8 describe how the perimeters increase as the length of one side increases by 1 ft.

LESSON 7 *Distributing the Wealth*

Your class probably used many ways to find the areas in the parks you designed. You probably used some properties of multiplication without even knowing it!

What You'll Need
• *grid paper*

ACTIVITY 1 Court Size

With Your Partner Suppose you decide to set aside space in your park for a horseshoes court for senior citizens. The space will need to be 47 ft long by 21 ft wide.

1 Show the court on a grid with each square equal to 1 square foot. How would you find the total area of the court?

The drawing shows one way to find the total area by distributing or breaking up the area into parts.

$21 \times 47 = (20 \times 47) + (1 \times 47)$

2 The number sentence above shows the Distributive Property of Multiplication. Write an explanation of this property in your own words.
  a. What is the area of the field? How do you know?
  b. What other ways can you find to distribute the area?

21 × 47

47

20 + 1

3 Use grid paper. Mark out the dimensions of these playing courts. Show how you can use the Distributive Property to find the areas.

Trade the plan you made in step 3 with your classmates. Use the areas to tell which items are in the plan.

   a. basketball court 94 ft × 50 ft
   b. volleyball court   60 ft × 30 ft
   c. tennis court   78 ft × 27 ft

4 The picture shows how one student drew a rollerskating area 120 ft by 78 ft. What other ways can you find to divide the area?

2 Break It Up

On Your Own You may not always have a grid handy to draw a picture of multiplication. Think about how you can use the Distributive Property to find a more efficient way to write the multiplication.

- You know how to multiply by a one-digit number.

$$\begin{array}{r} 47 \\ \times\ 1 \\ \hline 47 \end{array}$$

- And you know how to multiply by a multiple of 10.

$$\begin{array}{r} 47 \\ \times\ 20 \\ \hline 940 \end{array}$$

- So how would you multiply any two-digit numbers?

$$\begin{array}{r} 47 \\ \times\ 21 \\ \hline \end{array}$$

CONNECT AND COMMUNICATE

When you multiply 47 × 21 the product of 7 × 21 and the product of 40 × 21 are called partial products. Why do you think this is so?

1 Show how you can use the Distributive Property of Multiplication to find these products.

a. 12 × 12   **b.** 14 × 23   **c.** 64 × 14

2 Write three more multiplication examples with two-digit factors. Trade examples with a classmate. Use the Distributive Property to help you find the products.

ACTIVITY 3 Drawing Fields

With Your Partner Design a new playing field for a school. Include areas for baseball, soccer, and volleyball. You might want to include a running track and an area for warm-up exercises.

What You'll Need
- *grid paper*

1. Draw your design on grid paper and mark the dimensions of the different areas.
2. Trade drawings with another set of partners. Find the total area of the playground designed and label the areas of all the different parts of the playground.

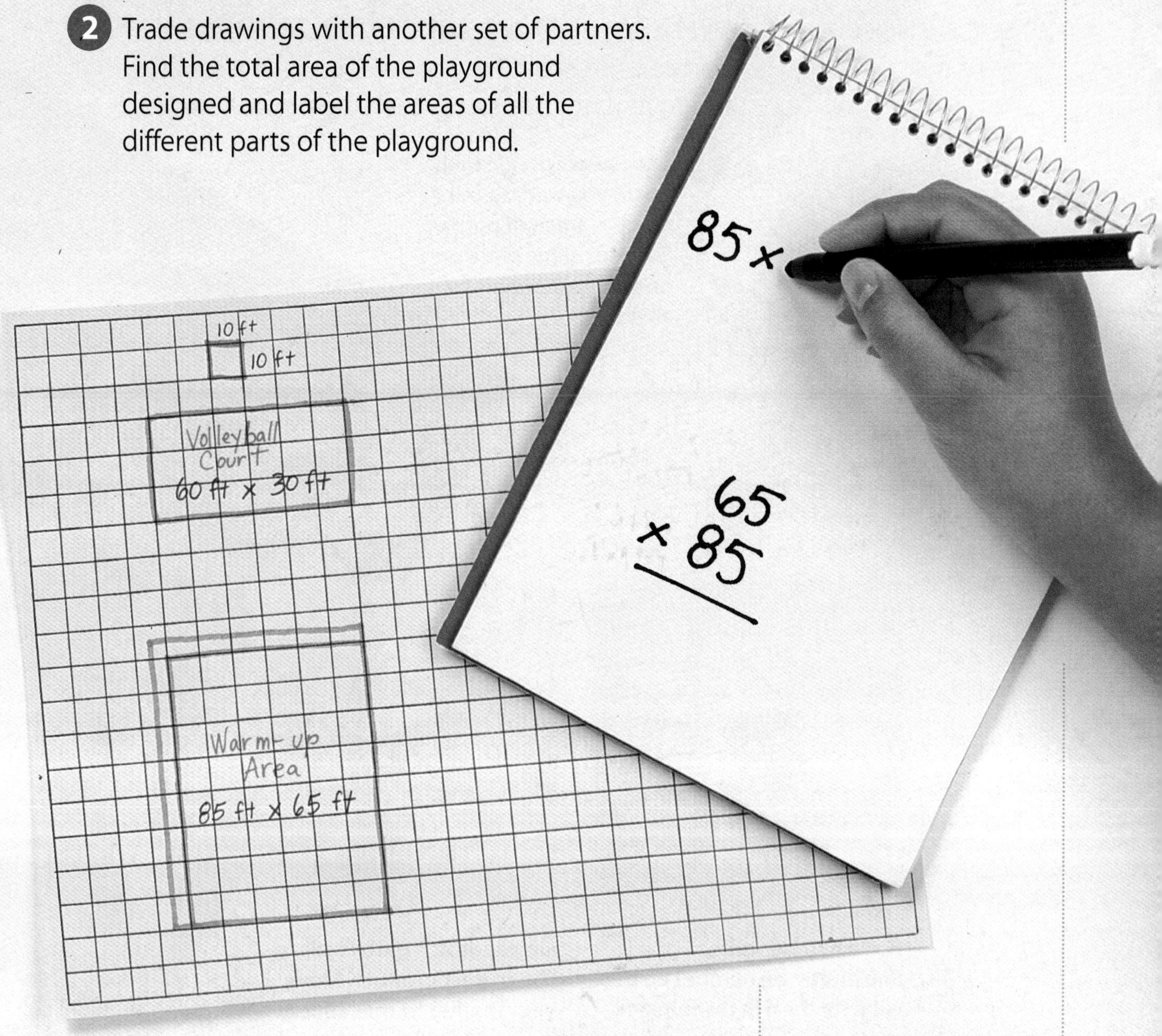

10 ft
10 ft
Volleyball Court
60 ft x 30 ft
Warm-up Area
85 ft x 65 ft
85 x
65
x 85

Distributive Dash

ACTIVITY 4 How to Play

What You'll Need
- *gameboard*
- *game pieces*
- *cube labeled 1–6*

With Your Partner Play this game with a partner. The goal of the game is to dash across the board and be the first to reach the opposite side.

1 Choose which side of the board you want to call home—green or purple. Put your game piece on one of the numbers by an arrow.

2 Roll a number cube. Substitute the number on the cube for the *n* in the number sentences along the paths.

3 Decide which path leads to the correct product. Move your marker to that space.

4 If you roll a number that does not correctly complete any of the expression paths, you have two choices.
  a. You may choose to roll again.
  b. You may tell what number will lead you to another space and move to that space.

5 Your opponent can challenge your move at any time during the game. If you are incorrect, you lose a turn.

6 Roll again to continue your dash to the other side.

Distributive Dash

Do You Remember?

Try It!

Rewrite the number sentences using the Distributive Property. Estimate. Only find products greater than 500.

1. $16 \times 17 = n$ 2. $23 \times 26 = n$ 3. $18 \times 28 = n$
4. $22 \times 23 = n$ 5. $19 \times 33 = n$ 6. $17 \times 22 = n$

Find the quotients. Describe any remainder.

7. $7\overline{)87}$ 8. $9\overline{)43}$ 9. $8\overline{)58}$

10. $6\overline{)47}$ 11. $9\overline{)73}$ 12. $7\overline{)47}$

Think About It

13. Explain in writing how you estimated products in Exercises 1–6.

Popcorn, by the Handful

LESSON 8

What is the average number of popped popcorn pieces that a fifth grader can hold in one hand? Use a bowl of popcorn to find out!

What You'll Need
- bag of popped popcorn

ACTIVITY 1 Handy Averages

With Your Group Do you think everyone in your group can hold the same number of popcorn pieces? Try it. Each person in the group should grab three handfuls of popcorn and count the number of pieces each time. Record the number. Did everyone get the same number of pieces every time? Why do you think that is?

CONNECT AND COMMUNICATE

	Number of Popcorn Pieces
Handful 1	25
Handful 2	
Handful 3	
Total	

In Your Journal Write an explanation of what *average* means to you. Tell how you use or hear about averages in your daily life.

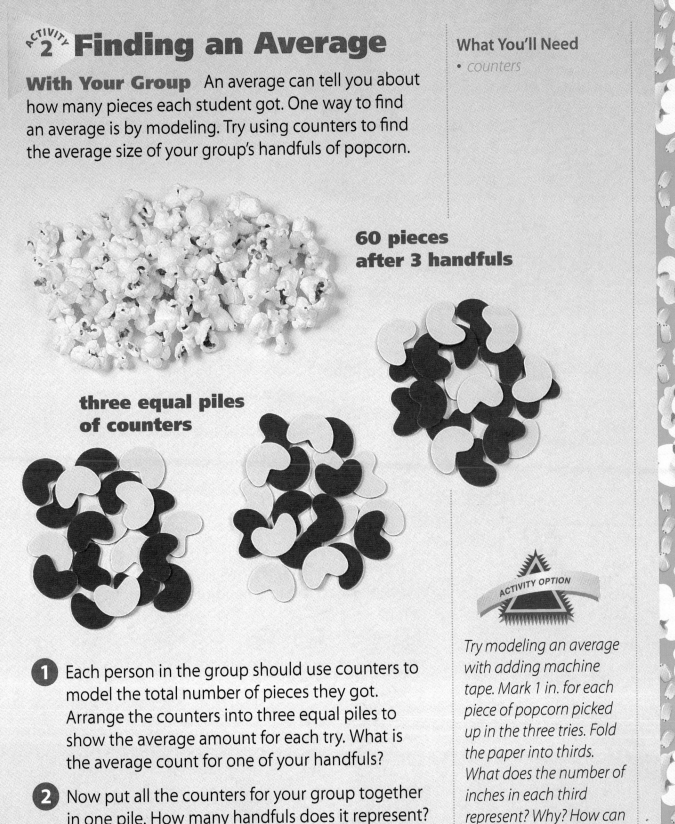

ACTIVITY 2 — Finding an Average

With Your Group An average can tell you about how many pieces each student got. One way to find an average is by modeling. Try using counters to find the average size of your group's handfuls of popcorn.

60 pieces after 3 handfuls

three equal piles of counters

ACTIVITY OPTION

1 Each person in the group should use counters to model the total number of pieces they got. Arrange the counters into three equal piles to show the average amount for each try. What is the average count for one of your handfuls?

2 Now put all the counters for your group together in one pile. How many handfuls does it represent? How many equal piles should you make? What is your group's average?

Try modeling an average with adding machine tape. Mark 1 in. for each piece of popcorn picked up in the three tries. Fold the paper into thirds. What does the number of inches in each third represent? Why? How can you find the average for your whole group?

3 Looking for Averages

On Your Own Try using a scattergram to find an average. Look at the example below. Around what numbers can you see many of the items clustered? What would you visually estimate the average of this group to be? Create your own scattergram. What does it tell you about your group's average?

Results from 3 Handfuls

Number of Pieces

40
30
20
10
0

John Ashira Theresa Ling

4 Cluster Averages

With Your Partner One way to help you estimate when you have a list of numbers is **clustering.** Look at this list of the total number of pieces grabbed in three handfuls by eight people.

75, 80, 80, 80, 85, 80, 82, 78

- Around what number do most of the numbers cluster?
- What would you estimate the average to be?
- Will clustering work with all sets of numbers?

Write a list of ten numbers for which clustering will help you find the average and a list of ten for which clustering probably won't help. Explain how you decided which numbers went into each group.

Operation Average

On Your Own Think about the process you just went through. Usually you will not want to go to the trouble of modeling the average. Find a way to use numbers to represent the situation. Think about the operations: addition, subtraction, multiplication, and division.

1 When you put all the pieces together to find the total number you grabbed, which operation did you use?

2 When you made equal-sized groups, which operation did you use? Write a rule for finding an average. Test your method by using it to check the average you found for your group. Share your method with the class.

✓ **Self-Check** *You may want to model a few averages as you begin to make sure you are correctly performing the operations.*

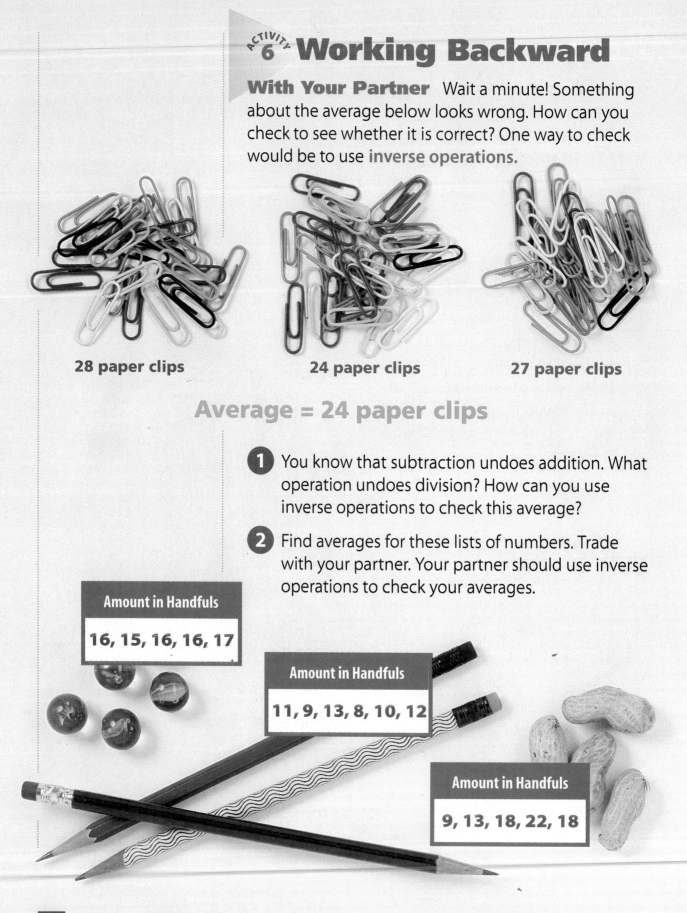

Working Backward

With Your Partner Wait a minute! Something about the average below looks wrong. How can you check to see whether it is correct? One way to check would be to use **inverse operations.**

28 paper clips   **24 paper clips**   **27 paper clips**

Average = 24 paper clips

1 You know that subtraction undoes addition. What operation undoes division? How can you use inverse operations to check this average?

2 Find averages for these lists of numbers. Trade with your partner. Your partner should use inverse operations to check your averages.

Amount in Handfuls

16, 15, 16, 16, 17

Amount in Handfuls

11, 9, 13, 8, 10, 12

Amount in Handfuls

9, 13, 18, 22, 18

ACTIVITY 7 Handful of Zero

With Your Partner Have you ever tried to divide zero by any number? Have you ever tried dividing any number by zero on your calculator? What happens? Understanding inverse operations can help you.

1 Think about this equation: $n = 0 \div 5$. Writing the inverse $n \times 5 = 0$ works. Why? What value works for n?

2 If $n = 5 \div 0$ then the inverse would be $5 = n \times 0$. Are there any values that work for n? Why?

3 Think about why you cannot divide by zero. Write an explanation for the fourth graders to use when they get to division this year.

Do You Remember?

Try It!

Find the averages of the following lists of numbers. For which of the lists could you estimate averages using a scattergram?

1. 5, 9, 12, 14   2. 2, 12, 13, 13   3. 12, 87, 123

4. 34, 36, 52, 58   5. 8, 9, 9, 10   6. 138, 144, 146, 152

Calculate. Prove your answers by using inverse operations.

7. $54 + 23$ 8. $76 - 45$ 9. $190 - 24$

10. 67×5 11. $6 \times 5 \times 11$ 12. $5 + 2 \times (7 \times 4)$

Think About It

13. How might you use the Associative Property to help you find an average? Explain.

Handy Work

Think about getting a job done. Why will there be more work per person if two people do the job than if three or four people do the job?

ACTIVITY 1 **Classroom Hands**

With Your Group Make a list of daily jobs for the classroom, like keeping things picked up. Each group in your class will take a turn doing a job every day.

1 Decide how often your group will do each job. Most school years are around 180 days. About how many turns do you think your group would have? 100 turns? 10 turns?

a. How do you know if your answer is reasonable?

b. How can you use what you know about multiplying and dividing to solve this problem? Share your method and solution with the class.

2 Discuss each group's method. Did everyone solve the problem the same way? Which way do you think worked best? Why?

ACTIVITY 2 · Divide Fairly

With Your Group   There is another way to divide the tasks in your classroom. You could divide the classroom into equal parts. Each group could be responsible for doing all the jobs in one area.

1 Decide the number of groups that should be in your class and the number of people that should be in each group.

2 Use your own method to find the number of square feet each group should be responsible for.

3 Draw a sketch of the classroom and then show the number of square feet each group will be responsible for and the location.

4 Present your plan to the class and vote to see who has the best plan.

REASONING AND PROBLEM SOLVING

Can you think of any other way to organize classroom tasks? Why do you think division would or would not be the appropriate operation to use when organizing?

OCTOBER

S	M	T	W	TH	F	S
				1	2	
5	6	7	8	9		
	13	14	15	16		
	20	21	22	23		
	27	28	29	3		

99

DRAWING TO LEARN

How does a calendar help you divide? What other visual models are good to use for division?

ACTIVITY 3 Lending a Hand

With Your Partner Getting started is sometimes the hardest part of any project. In this activity, you will discover how an estimate can help you get started.

Question

Suppose your class decides to read to senior citizens each Friday throughout the school year, which has 180 days. How many times a year would your class be able to do this?

Start

Why would you need to divide 180 by 5 first? Use what you know about place value to think about the number of digits that must be in the quotient.

quotient

$$\begin{array}{c} ??? \\ 5\overline{)180} \end{array}$$

divisor   dividend

Estimate

Are there enough Fridays for the class to go 100 times? Are there enough Fridays for the class to go 10 times? How did knowing about place value help you estimate? Explain.

1. What digit will I try first?

2. Where should it go in the quotient?

3. what would be a good estimate for the quotient?

Answer

Now that you have an estimate, use your own method to find the exact number.

Dear

On Your Own Senior citizen centers also appreciate having volunteers who write letters for residents throughout the year. If your class visited a senior citizen center every Monday, Wednesday, and Friday for a school year, about how many visits would your class make? Would this be reasonable? If not, what plan could you make that would be reasonable?

ᴬᶜᵀᴵⱽᴵᵀʸ 4 Just Dropping By

With Your Partner When you divide, you often need to get an exact answer, not an estimate. Here is one method you might use. Act it out with base ten blocks if you wish.

During the year, 8 groups will take turns visiting a senior citizen center each day for 365 days. How many days will each group be able to visit?

1 How many digits?

a. Are there enough days for each group to go 100 days? How do you know?

b. How many places will be in the quotient?

c. If you change the hundreds to tens, how many tens will there be?

hundreds tens ones

8)365

2 Deciding the tens

a. Now that you have made the trade, are there enough days for each group to go 10 days?

b. Think about your basic facts. What number will you try in the quotient first?

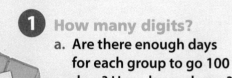

tens ones

8)365

3 **Any left over?**

   a. Once you have shared
      the tens, how many tens
      are left over?

   b. What would you need to
      do if the remainder here
      was eight or more?

   c. What trade do you need
      to make now?

4 **Deciding the ones**

   a. Share the 45 ones. What
      number will you try first?
      Why? Where will you write it?

   b. Finish the problem. Is there a
      remainder? Think about the
      problem you need to solve.
      What will you do with the
      remainder?

   c. How was this method like the
      methods you and your
      classmates used on pages
      98–101? How was this
      method different?

On Your Own Use the method you like best to
solve these. Describe any patterns you see.

  1. $5\overline{)85}$ **2.** $6\overline{)85}$ **3.** $7\overline{)85}$

  4. $8\overline{)260}$ **5.** $4\overline{)130}$ **6.** $2\overline{)65}$

Can you use inverse operations to check your work for these exercises? Which operations would you use with which exercises?

ACTIVITY
5 Hand-Me-Downs

With Your Partner Use what you know about division to complete Exercise 1. Then choose one of the remaining exercises to complete.

1 Collect data and find some handy averages. Choose one or more of these suggestions. Show your data and your work.

- the average temperature in your area for one week
- the average score in your last five times playing your favorite game
- the average number of minutes you spend doing homework in one week
- the average number of students in three classrooms at your school

2 Solve along the columns and diagonals to find the missing numbers. Then make up a puzzle of your own. Trade puzzles with a partner and solve.

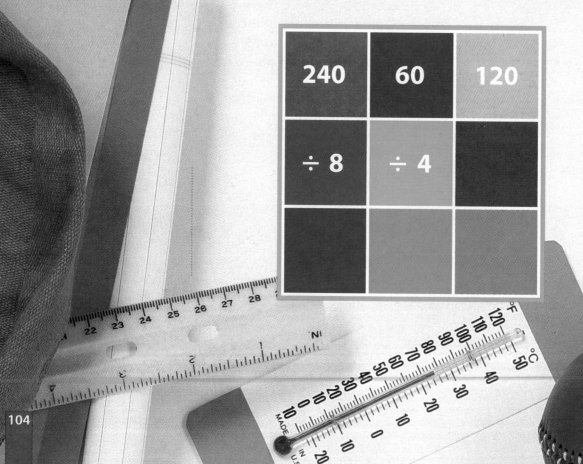

240	60	120
÷ 8	÷ 4	

3 Write down any number from 10 to 100. Add the number to itself. Multiply by 4. Then divide by 2. Divide by 2. Then divide by 2 again. What number did you end up with? Try it several more times with different numbers. What happens?

6 Find the Factors!

With Your Partner

What You'll Need
- *box or bag to hold slips of paper*

1 Write the numbers 2–9 on separate slips of paper and place in a box. Pull one of the numbers from the box and multiply any number from 10 to 100 by this secret number. Write the product on a piece of paper and give it to your partner.

2 Your partner gets one turn to find a divisor for which the quotient has no remainder. Players get one point for getting a quotient with no remainder and two points for getting the secret number.

3 Trade roles with your partner and try again. Try to get ten points each.

Hand Me a Hammer

In cities and towns across the country, people get together for a week or two at a time. They work very hard during this time, and when they are finished another family has a home. Use the information on these pages to answer the following questions.

1 How many people will have homes if there are an average of 3 people per family? 4 people per family?

2 How many weeks do you have for the project? How do you know?

3 How many workdays do you have for the project? Explain.

4 How many houses can a crew of nine build in 85 days?

400 families on waiting list

300 plots of land for 400 units

Budget $480,000

5 How many houses can 2 full crews build in 85 workdays?

6 Do you think 20 crews will be able to complete 400 houses in 85 days? Explain.

7 How much money do the crews need to raise each month to meet the budget?

8 How could you find the amount they need to raise each week to meet the budget?

4 months (120 days) to complete project

9 Are there enough plots of land so that one house could be built on each plot?

10 A crew member works 8-hour days. Would that person work more than 100 hours in 3 weeks? Explain.

A crew of 9 that works 5-day weeks can complete a house in 6 days.

Looking Back

Choose the right answer. Write *a, b, c,* or *d* for each question.

1. 1,356 can also be expressed as:

   a. 135 tens and 56 ones
   b. 1 thousand, 35 hundreds, and 6 ones
   c. 1 thousand, 3 hundreds, 56 ones
   d. 13 hundreds and 56 tens

2. Two hundred thirty thousand, eight hundred nine can also be expressed as:

   a. 230 hundreds, 80 tens; and 9 ones
   b. $230,000 + 800 + 9$
   c. $23 + 10,000 + 800 + 9$
   d. 230 thousands and 809 tens

3. 2 millions, 39 thousands, 46 tens, and 1 ones can also be expressed as:

   a. 2,390,047
   b. 2 millions, 394 hundreds, 6 tens, 1 one
   c. 2,039,047
   d. 2,030 thousands, 461 ones

4. Which number sentence below is true?

   a. $245 = 24 + 100 + 5 = 205 + 40$
   b. $51 + 27 + 350$
      $= 3 \times (9 + 18) + 350$
   c. $290 + 11 + 3 = 300 + 10 + 4$
   d. $4 \times 56 = (4 \times 50) + (4 \times 6)$

5. Which number sentence in Exercise 4 shows the Distributive Property of Multiplication?

   a. a   b. b
   c. c   d. d

6. If $n = 7$, which expression below gives the answer 89?

   a. $(40 \times n) + n$ b. $n \times (n + 40)$
   c. $n^2 + 40$ d. $(2 \times n) + 40$

7. Which equation below is true if $n = 3$?

   a. $n + n^2 = 6 + 6$
   b. $n \times (n + n) = (n \times n) + n$
   c. $0 \times (n + n) = 2 \times (n + 0)$
   d. $3 \times n \times 3 = n \times 2 \times 2 \times 2$

8. Which expression below shows how the Distributive Property of Multiplication can help you find the product of 48 × 64?

   a. 8 × (6 × 8)
   b. (60 × 48) × (4 × 48)
   c. (6 × 8) × (8 × 8)
   d. (40 × 64) + (8 × 64)

9. What is the product of 48 × 64?

   a. 348   b. 3,072   c. 288   d. 512

10. Which factors have a product less than 400?

    a. 14 × 27   b. 13 × 37
    c. 16 × 47   d. 17 × 27

11. Which factors in Exercise 10 have a product greater than 700?

Plan a community garden. Use the drawing below to help you answer Exercises 12–15.

12. What is the total area of your garden?

    a. 1,000 ft   b. 100 ft²
    c. 10,000 ft²   d. 200 ft²

13. Which expression shows how to find the width of the broccoli patch?

    a. 20 × n = 240
    b. 20 × (6 + 6) = 240
    c. 1,000 − 240
    d. 240 − 20

14. What is the width of the broccoli patch?

    a. 120 ft   b. 12 ft
    c. 260 ft   d. 220 ft

15. You would like to use the remaining 9,760 square feet for equal-sized plots of corn, tomatoes, spinach, and green beans. What size will you make each patch?

    a. 2,500 ft²   b. 2,440 ft²
    c. 1,900 ft²   d. none of these

Check Your Math Power

16. What do you know about multiplying by 10 and 100 that you can use to help you multiply 4,635 by 1,000?

17. Explain how you and two friends can share 3 dollar bills, a quarter, and 2 pennies equally.

18. What numbers can you use to estimate the product of 22 × 59? Explain your choices.

MODULE 2 Investigations

Grabfest

As you grab for marbles, popcorn, or pennies, would bigger hands help you grab more? Choose one of these three investigations to find out.

Investigation A Corn-y Grab

Popcorn is a food that is okay to eat with your hands. Explore the relationship between the area of your hand and the amount of popcorn you can hold.

1 Collect Data
Find the hand areas of at least five of your friends or family members. Count the number of popcorn kernels each person can grab. Have them make several tries.

2 Represent Your Data
Organize your data into a chart. Decide which data you will list from least to greatest. Use the data in your chart to make a graph to display your data.

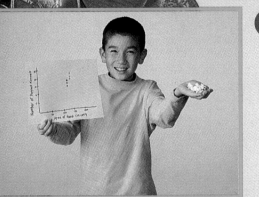

3 Analyze Your Results

Describe any patterns or relationships between the data you find in a report. Tell how you collected and organized your data. Explain how you came to your conclusions.

Number of Popped Kernels

25

20

15

10

5

0   50   100   150   200

Area of Hand (square units)

Keep in Mind

Your report will be judged by how well you do the following things.

☐ Show the relationship between hand area and number of kernels.
☐ Use division to represent the data.
☐ Organize your data.
☐ Use information to support your conclusions.

● = Vanessa
● = Marco
● = Anthony
● = Tanisha

Investigation

Grabbing for Dollars

Suppose you entered a charity coin-grabbing contest. How could you be sure you would grab the greatest number of coins in one minute? Should you scoop up the coins? Will you get more if you grab the coins with your palm down?

1 With your partner describe a method that will give the most coins, popcorn, or counters in one grab.

2 Then do an investigation and compare the results to your prediction.

Ongoing Investigation

"Who We Are" on Average

How can you use averages to describe the population you are investigating? You might, for example, find the amount of growth in the U.S. population for each decade. Then find the average amount of growth from decade to decade. During which decades did the population grow more than the average. less than the average?

Getting Your Money's Worth

We all want to get our money's worth, but sometimes doing so takes work. In this unit you'll learn how to use math to help you use money wisely.

What Will I Spend?

LA COCINA MARKET
784 N. PAULINA

CACTUS LEAVES   .27
.27LB @ .99/LB

JALAPEÑOS   .23
.12113 @ 1.89/LB

POPCORN   .70
2 @ .35

THE OAK STREET MARKET
1615 OAK AVENUE

GINGER
.19 LB @ 2.99/LB

BEAN THREAD   .57
NOODLES

PEA PODS   1.05

DRIED MUSHR   1.

How much do you know about the way your family spends money? For example, do you know the prices of food items such as the ones shown here? Do you know how much money it costs to feed your family a well-balanced meal?

1 Plan

Plan a meal to celebrate your family's ethnic heritage. Decide what foods you will serve and how many people you will feed. You may want to make up a menu that describes each item. Be sure to include all the food groups needed for a healthful meal.

Word Bank

- axis
- front-end estimation
- pictograph
- unit price

2 Estimate

What ingredients will you need to buy to make your meal? How much will they cost? Estimate the total cost as closely as you can.

3 Investigate

Find out what your meal will really cost. You can find real prices in a grocery store or in newspaper ads. You might also ask an adult who shops for food.

Investigate! Investigate! Investigate! Investigate! Investigate! Investigate! Investigate! Investigate! Investigate! Investigate! Investigate! Investigate! Investigate!

Investigations Preview

Learn about using money, units of measure, and dividing with two-digit divisors. With these skills you can do anything from designing a package label to planning a zoo's feeding budget.

Look at Labels (pages 140–141)
What information would you include on a label for a food product? Knowing units of measure will help you.

Please Feed the Animals (pages 174–176)
How would you prepare a feeding budget for several zoo animals? Using what you learn about money and budgeting will help you.

Investigate! Investigate! Investigate! Investigate! Investigate! Investigate! Investigate! Investigate! Investigate! Investigate! Investigate! Investigate! Investigate! Investigate! Investigate!

kite
$2.58

bike lock
$3.81

SPORTS CORNER

save $1.00 on any purchase

LESSON 1 Shopping Spree

You pay for things that you buy all the time. Do you always know how much to pay? Do you know which coins or bills to use and how much change you'll get?

What You'll Need
- *gameboard*
- *number cube*
- *game markers*
- *play money*

✔ **Self-Check**

Counting-on is one way to find out how much change you'll get. How would you explain counting-on to someone? What other ways of figuring out change can you think of?

ACTIVITY 1 Making Change

With Your Group Use play money to practice giving change in the game Pay $.

1 Pick one group member to be the cashier.
- The cashier accepts payment and gives change.
- The cashier will give each player the following money: two $10 bills, two $5 bills, five $1 bills, five quarters, ten dimes, eight nickels, ten pennies.

2 Starting in the center, take turns rolling one number cube to move around the board.
- You can move in either a clockwise or counterclockwise direction.
- You must buy any item you land on.
- Anyone who lands on more than one item in a store must total his or her prices and pay for all the items.

LAKESHORE SCHOOL MONEY
PLAY MONEY
ONE

PAY-$

pay with a five

pay with a ten

pay any way you like

pay with ones and dimes

pay any way you want to

pay with a ten and quarters

shop

cards $1.84

rice $1.23

salsa $2.37

sunblock $.92

crackers $2.08

peaches $3.54

LAKESHORE SCHOOL MONEY · PLAY MONEY

MONEY

GRAND ST

Grace

buy one, get one free!

3 After you buy at least one item, go to the cashier's line. The space you land on tells how to pay.
- Pay the cashier and make sure you receive the correct change.
- Move to the center of the board and start for the next store.
- You must buy at least one item from each of the four stores to finish.

4 The shopper with the most money left after all players have finished wins the game.

Exercises and Problems

Getting Change Back

See if you can tell whether you got the correct change. If you didn't, tell what the correct change should be.

1 You owe $2.53. You pay with **$5**.

Is **$1 $1 25¢ 1¢ 1¢ 10¢** the correct change?

2 You owe $.57. You pay with **$1**.

Is **25¢ 10¢ 5¢ 1¢ 1¢ 1¢** the correct change?

3 You owe $4.28. You pay with **$5**.

Is **25¢ 25¢ 10¢ 1¢ 1¢** the correct change?

4 You buy all three items and pay with **$10**.

How much change should you get?

5

Suppose you owe $.89. You pay with $1. What is the correct change?

6

You owe $2.06. You pay with $10. What is the correct change?

7

You owe $4.77. You pay with $5 1¢ 1¢. What is the correct change?

8

Develop a math rule that will help you know whether you get the right change. Explain your rule to a partner.

LESSON
② How Much?

$.55 Oat Bars — 100% NATURAL — Made with Honey

ACTIVITY OPTION

Bring in a few grocery store cash-register receipts. Black out or cut off the totals and exchange receipts with a partner. Estimate each other's totals.

I magine this. You've finished shopping and waited in a long cashier's line. Then you find that you don't have enough money for all of your items. You can avoid times like that by estimating totals in advance.

ACTIVITY 1 — Estimate Shopping

On Your Own   Use estimation to answer these questions as quickly as you can.

1. How much would all of the items on these pages cost? Estimate to the nearest dollar.

2. Suppose you had $10. Which items would you buy if you could buy only one of each item? List the items and their prices.

$.35 each

$.64 — Stone Ground Corn Tortillas — 12 Corn Tortillas — NO CHOLESTEROL

$.99 — Regular Firm — TOFU — Japanese Style Soybean Cake — NET WT 14 OZ (397 g)

$2.17 — Frank's Fruit Spread — Grape — NET WT. 32 OZ.

3 Now name one item and estimate how many of this item you could buy for $20.

4 Name three pairs of items you could buy for less than $2 per pair.

$.46 each

$.87

$3.55

PEANUT BUTTER
EXTRA CRUNCH
NET WT 28 OZ (1LB 12 OZ)

Sun in a box
FRUIT PUNCH

$2.27

BUBBLE BATH

15 fl. oz.

$.89

Rollo

TOWELS

$.97 each

$2.49

Ways of Estimating

On Your Own

1 Here are two ways to estimate totals. Do you use either of these methods? What other ways to estimate can you think of?

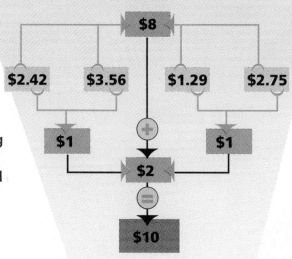

Round each amount to the nearest dollar.

$.75	$1.89	$1.29	$2.35
$1	$2	$1	$2

$6

$8

Use front-end estimation.
First add the front-end digits—the whole dollars.

Then combine the remaining amounts—the cents part of each price—into dollars, and add that to the front-end amount.

| $2.42 | $3.56 | $1.29 | $2.75 |

$1 ⊕ $1

$2

$10

CONNECT AND COMMUNICATE

In Your Journal Draw a diagram showing how you can use rounding and front-end estimation together in estimating a total of several prices.

2 Use each method to estimate the total price for the items in the picture on pages 120–121.
   a. Which method is easier? faster?
   b. What is the exact total? Use a calculator.
   c. Which method of estimating is more accurate in this case?

3 When would you want the faster estimate? When might you want the more accurate estimate?

ACTIVITY 3 Roll and Estimate

With Your Group Use three number cubes to roll three digits. Write them down as a price. For example, a 1, a 2, and a 3 would be written as $1.23. After you have written six prices, estimate a total. Someone in your group will check your estimate with a calculator. As group members take turns, challenge yourself by rolling four cubes or by estimating totals of seven or eight prices.

What You'll Need
• *number cubes*

Do You Remember?

Try It!

Use front-end estimation to find the total dollars for each group of prices.

1. $4.55 $1.22 $2.55
2. $1.88 $3.49 $2.69

3. $3.33 $4.17 $1.49
4. $2.09 $5.79 $3.05

Estimate the result for one-digit quotients. Find the solution for two-digit quotients.

5. $7\overline{)33}$
6. $5\overline{)47}$
7. $3\overline{)164}$

8. $8\overline{)432}$
9. $6\overline{)99}$
10. $9\overline{)346}$

Think About It

11. When might it be useful to use more than one method of estimating? Explain why.

LESSON 3 Dividing by Tens

REASONING AND PROBLEM SOLVING

Think What pattern do I see in the numbers on my chart? Explain to your partner how to divide by tens mentally. Use $10\overline{)360}$ as your example.

ACTIVITY 1 Multiply to Divide

With Your Partner Even if you've never held a hundred-dollar bill, there's no reason you can't know how to break one into smaller bills. To divide by 10 and multiples of 10, think multiplication and use guess and check.

1 How many $10's make $100? $200? $300? $800? Record the results in a table. Continue recording with the following amounts.

$20 $50 $150
$250 $350 $420

2 How many 10's make up 100? 1,000? 10,000? How many 10's make up 150? 1,500? 15,000? Add these numbers to your charts. What pattern do you see in your answers? What happens when you divide by 10 and the number of zeros in the dividend increases?

Amount	Divided by	How many?
100	10	10
200	10	20
300	10	
800		
20		
50		
150		

Amount	Divided by	How many?
100	20	5
1,000	20	50
10,000	20	

3 Now find a way to divide by a multiple of 10. You may want to think about multiplication.

$$30\overline{)210}$$

4 Record your answers to the following exercises. Try these items on your own and add them to your chart.

a. $20\overline{)100}$ $20\overline{)1,000}$ $20\overline{)10,000}$

b. $50\overline{)400}$ $50\overline{)4,000}$ $50\overline{)40,000}$

c. $80\overline{)240}$ $80\overline{)2,400}$ $80\overline{)24,000}$

5 Explain the patterns. How can this explanation help you divide by a multiple of 10?

TOOLS AND TECHNIQUES

You can use mental math to divide by 10 or a multiple of 10. To find 200 ÷ 40, for example, think of 20 ÷ 4. Why does that work? How did the dividend and the divisor both change?

Different Currencies

Practice dividing in your head by using currencies
from other countries. Remember to use multiplication
to check your estimates.

1 Canada
dollar (from German word *taler*, a coin
named after a town where coins were
made hundreds of years ago)
You need to divide 1,200 Canadian
dollars by 30. How many places will
there be in your answer?

2 Mexico
peso (Spanish for *weight*)
a. How many 50-peso coins
would you need to total
1,600 pesos?
b. How many 20-peso coins
make up 1,600 pesos?

3 Turkey
lira (Italian word for *pound*)
a. You have 1,550 liras in 10-
lira coins. How many coins
are there?
b. You must trade your 10-lira
coins for 50-lira coins.
How many will you get?

4 Zambia
kwacha (from a word that means
"dawn" in Zambia)
a. If 2,800 kwacha must be shared by
70 people, what will each one get?
b. How would your answer change if
the money was shared by only 7
people?

5 United Kingdom

pound (originally, the value of one pound weight of silver; abbreviated £)

a. There are 100 pennies in a pound. How many pounds equal 57,000 pennies?

b. You buy £1.55 worth of postcards and pay with a £5 note. What change should you get?

6 Poland

zloty (Polish word for *golden*)

In June 1993, 1 U.S. dollar was worth 18,200 zloty. How many zloty would you get for a quarter at that exchange rate?

7 India

rupee (from a Sanskrit word for *silver*)

a. You ask for 40,000 rupees in 20-rupee bills. How many bills will you get?

b. Complete the following sequence: 80 rupees, 120 rupees, 180 rupees, 260 rupees, n.

8 China

yuan (Chinese for *round coin*)

a. There are 10 jiao in 1 yuan. How many yuan equal 11,870 jiao?

b. If you divided your answer by 10, what remainder would be left?

LESSON 4 Capacity and Weight

ACTIVITY 1 Comparing Measures

With Your Class Collect labels from grocery products and try this activity with your class.

What You'll Need
- *product labels*
- *large paper*
- *tape or tacks*
- *crayon or colored markers*

1 Create a wall chart with the headings *Weight* and *Capacity*. Place each label under the correct heading.

2 Divide the labels into groups depending on the unit of measure used and place them under the correct heading.

 Discuss these questions.

From The Sun
RAISINS
18 oz (1 lb 2 oz)

a. **Why do you think this package shows the amount in two ways?**

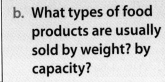

SUNFLOWER seeds

b. What types of food products are usually sold by weight? by capacity?

c. How many fluid ounces make up a quart? This label should help you answer.

Salsa

HOT

NET WT 12 OZ

APPLE JUICE

100% NATURAL

48 fl oz (1.5 QT)

d. How many of these packages would equal one pound?

e. What's the difference between an ounce and a fluid ounce?

4 oz

Sparkling Water

SUGAR FREE

16 fl oz (1PT)

f. Which measures are used for weight? Which are used for capacity?

Abbreviations	
cup	c
fluid ounce	fl oz
gallon	gal
ounce	oz
pint	pt
pound	lb
quart	qt
ton	t

2 What's the Measure?

With Your Group How well can you picture the size of each unit of measure?

1 One group member will name a product—anything from a bottle of perfume to a truckload of coal. The next person must tell which unit of measure—ounce, gallon, ton, and so on—would be the best one to use to measure its weight or capacity. The remaining group members will judge the answer.

POPS A LOT

ow Popcorn

NET WT. 1 LB

1-lb bag

1 oz each

2 Try another game. One person will name a unit of weight or capacity. The next person must name a unit of measure that is either greater or smaller.

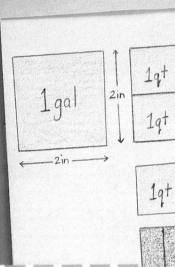

ACTIVITY 3 Units of Measure

On Your Own Show the relationship among the different units of capacity.

1 On a sheet of paper, draw a square about 2 in. wide and 2 in. deep. Write *1 gal* in the square.

2 How many quarts make up a gallon? Draw another square the same size as the first one. Divide it into the right number of equal parts. Label each part *1 qt*.

3 Draw a square the size of one quart. Divide this square into pints. Continue with cups and fluid ounces.

Do You Remember?

Try It!

Convert each amount to a larger unit of measure. Which ones can you convert to a smaller unit? Name the unit.

1. 1.5 c   **2.** 64 oz   **3.** 5 pt
4. 24,000 lb   **5.** 12 qt   **6.** 40 fl oz

Find the value of *n*.

7. $32 \times 16 = n$ **8.** $74 \times 21 = n$ **9.** $24 \times 20 = n$
10. $53 \times 45 = n$ **11.** $109 \times 33 = n$ **12.** $741 \times 86 = n$

Think About It

13. When you convert to a larger unit of measure, how does the number of units change? How does it change when you convert to a smaller unit?

LESSON 5

Big Bag Lunch

Over the next few days, you will plan a lunch menu for a class field trip. You'll have to decide what you'll serve and what you'll have to buy to feed a class of 23 students. Then you'll need to find out how much everyone will have to pitch in to pay for it.

ACTIVITY 1 What's to Drink?

With Your Group Your group will be the lunch-planning committee for your class field trip. To start, decide which drink you will provide for the class. Plan on a serving size of about 12 fl oz.

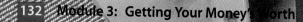

First find out how many servings each drink will provide. How many 12-fl-oz servings can you get from one package of the lemonade drink mix? How can the division below tell you the number of servings in 8 qt of the lemonade drink?

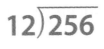

Where does the 256 come from? How many fluid ounces are there in 1 qt? in 8 qt?

 Work with your group to find the answer. If you use a calculator, pretend that the division key is broken. Be ready to share your answer and your method of finding it with the class.

3 Does the lemonade mix make enough lemonade for 23 students? If not, how much more mix would you need?

4 Use the method you discovered above to find the number of 12-fl-oz servings the punch and the orange juice will provide. How many containers of each drink would you need to serve 23 students?

5 Which drink would you suggest your class buy? Be ready to defend your choice.

In dividing, try the guess-and-check strategy. Guess the quotient and multiply to check it. If your result is too high or too low, make another guess and check it. Keep guessing and checking to narrow in on the correct quotient.

GROCERY GOODS
2314 West Avenue
Anywhere, USA

Natural Punch
$3.69

Sunbright O J
$2.27

Lemonade Drink Mix
$3.29

real orange juice from concentrate
makes 48 fluid ounces

Sun Bright

ACTIVITY 2 Dividing with Money

With Your Class Suppose your group decides to buy 2 gal of fruit punch for your class. What is the price per serving for the fruit punch?

Find the prices of other drinks you could serve. Use the method on this page to find the cost per 12-oz serving of each one.

1 What is the cost of 2 gal of fruit punch? Write the cost in cents.

   a. How does it help to think of the cost as 738¢ rather than $7.38?

   b. Why will the division below help you find the cost of each of the 23 servings?

2 Think about multiplication.

   a. Is the answer greater than 10? How do you know?

   b. Is the answer less than 100? How do you know?

   c. Use guess and check to find the answer.

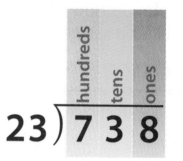

How can knowing that the answer has two places help you guess and check?

hundreds	tens	ones
7	**3**	**8**

23)

3 How many digits will there be in each quotient?

   a. 53)345   **b.** 53)1,387

   c. 23)345   **d.** 53)8,387

9

How Many Digits?

What You'll Need
• *paper bag or hat*

With Your Partner Practice using mental math to find the number of digits in a quotient. Take turns estimating in the following game.

1 Take ten small pieces of paper, and write the numbers 0 through 9 on them. Fold the numbered papers and place them into a bag or hat. Shake them to mix them up.

2 Pick six numbers, one at a time, from the bag and write them as an example of division. The first four numbers will be the dividend, and the last two will be the divisor.

3 Your partner will estimate the number of digits in the quotient for your example. Use multiplication on a calculator, and guess and check to decide if your partner is right. Then trade parts. Your partner picks, you estimate, and your partner checks.

How many different kinds of sandwiches with one filling can you make from the fillings listed below? Try to work out a diagram that shows the number.

ACTIVITY
4 What's for Lunch?

With Your Group Now plan the rest of your lunch menu for 23 students. You'll need to decide what to offer. Each student should get one sandwich, a piece of fruit, and a drink. Decide what filling or fillings each sandwich should contain. You'll also need to find out how much money to collect from each student.

1 Find the price per serving for each kind of bread. (Remember, it takes two slices of bread to make one sandwich.) Which bread is the most expensive per serving? the least expensive? What other factors should you consider when you make your choice?

The Sandwich Shop

Breads			Fillings		
Whole Wheat	24 slices	$2.29	American Cheese	24 slices	$3.07
Rye	20 slices	$2.19	Fruit Jelly	15 servings	$1.74
Cinnamon Raisin	19 slices	$2.25	Peanut Butter	12 servings	$2.68
Pita Pockets	12 pockets	$2.79	Smoked Turkey	14 slices	$4.87
			Chicken Salad	8 servings	$2.59
Fruit			Leaf Lettuce	16 servings	$1.44
Apples	1 apple	$.25	Roast Beef	10 servings	$4.09
Bananas	1 banana	$.15	Egg Salad	12 servings	$2.76

2 Now find the total cost for your class lunch. List all the items you will need, and then total their prices.

3 Divide your total price by 23 to find out how much each person will have to pay. Will it be more than $10 each? more than $1 each? How do you know?

4 Present your plan to the class. Compare lunches with other groups. Find out which lunch your class would like best.

Do You Remember?

Try It!

Estimate quotients that have two places. Use guess and check to solve the ones with only one place.

1. $32\overline{)276}$

2. $18\overline{)787}$

3. $43\overline{)249}$

4. $32\overline{)488}$

5. $24\overline{)911}$

6. $81\overline{)723}$

7. $48\overline{)432}$

8. $93\overline{)592}$

9. $35\overline{)849}$

10. $17\overline{)924}$

Think About It

11. When using guess and check, how could you refine your estimated quotients to make a better guess each time?

✓ **Self-Check** *Use guess and check to estimate the cost per serving of each filling shown in the price list on page 136. Compare your results with those of other students in your class.*

LESSON 6

The Best Buy

REASONING AND PROBLEM SOLVING

How can I use rounding and guess and check to find unit prices?

Of course you want the best buy. To get it, you often need to compare prices. The best way is to compare **unit prices.** A unit price is the price per unit of measure (per ounce, pint and so on).

ACTIVITY 1 Comparing Unit Prices

With Your Group

1. Analyze the ads on these pages to find the best buy for dog food. Estimate the unit price at each store.

2. Make a chart to compare the unit prices at the three different stores.

BUY IT AT BARKER'S

CANINE TREATS

ONLY
$6.98
for 10 lb

Get a FREE
dog bowl
with purchase

10 lb

OPEN 9–4 M–F, 1–5 SAT.

PUPPY PALACE

40 lb for $15.95

FIDO'S FEAST

FREE bone
with every
40-lb bag!

12 Locations — Open 10 a.m. to 10 p.m.

What unit should you use to compare the three dog-food prices?

Make sure you divide the total price by the total number of units.

Make Tracks to PAW'S

Buy two 10-lb bags of

PUP'S DELIGHT

at $7.95 each & get a third bag

FREE!

...day

3 Now try comparing unit prices for some actual supermarket products. Which is the best buy in each group?

Do You Remember?

Try It!

Write as an addition or subtraction equation.

1. Yoshi has 3 more dollars than the $10 I have.
2. Only 8 of the 12 game pieces are here.
3. If 2 more people arrive, there will be 6 of us.
4. Of 11 balls, 1 was red, 3 were blue, and the rest were black.
5. After Mr. and Mrs. Sanchez left, 9 people remained.

Estimate the unit prices in each pair to find the better buy.

6. **a.** 12 oz for $.79   **b.** 2 lb for $1.89
7. **a.** 1 qt for $2.25   **b.** two 12-oz bottles for $1.58
8. **a.** 4 oz for $1.25   **b.** 9 oz for $2.89
9. **a.** 1 pt for $1.25   **b.** 1 gal for $7.95

Think About It

10. Is price the only factor you should think about in deciding what to buy? Explain the importance of at least two other factors.

Investigation

Look at Labels

The black bars below hold the product's universal product code, or bar code. The bars carry a computer code that names the product and the company that packaged it. A laser "reads" the bar code, and the store's computer sends the price to a cash register.

Are you eating the right stuff? Are you getting enough vitamins? too much fat? Just what's in the food you eat? To find out, pour yourself a glass of juice or a bowl of cereal. Compare the serving size you've taken with that shown on the package label. Now figure out how much of all those nutrients you're really getting.

Unused portion should be capped tightly and promptly refrigerated or transferred to a suitable container for freezing.

Use by date on lid.

NET WT. 14 OZ (397g)

PRI
SPAGHET

A label may include the term *Net Wt.* when showing the measure of its contents. What does *net* mean?

Nutritional information is given for single servings. How could you use the label to find out if your serving size was more or less than a single serving?

Almost all food products include a list of their ingredients, in order from most to least. Which three ingredients top the list for this spaghetti sauce? for your snack?

SERVING SIZE ....4 OZ. (113g)
SERVINGS PER CONTAINER 3.5
CALORIES 80
PROTEIN (GRAMS) 2
CARBOHYDRATE (GRAMS) 14
FAT (GRAMS) 2
SODIUM 420mg/SERVING

PERCENTAGE OF U.S. RECOMMENDED
DAILY ALLOWANCES (U.S. RDA)

PROTEIN	2	RIBOFLAVIN	4
VITAMIN A	2	NIACIN	6
VITAMIN C	40	CALCIUM	4
THIAMINE	6	IRON	6

INGREDIENTS: TOMATO PUREE, DICED TOMATOES, CORN SYRUP, GREEN PEPPERS, ZUCCHINI, CARROTS, MUSHROOMS, CELERY, VEGETABLE OIL (CONTAINS ONE OR MORE OF THE FOLLOWING: CORN, CANOLA, COTTONSEED), CONCENTRATED VEGETABLE JUICES, SALT, ONION POWDER, GARLIC* AND CITRIC ACID

Ask Yourself

☐ Why might you want to know how much fat, sodium, or vitamins are in the food you eat?

☐ What utensils will you need to measure your serving?

☐ What math will you use—multiplication, division, percentages, decimals?

☐ Was your serving larger or smaller than the serving size on the label?

☐ How could you explain the nutritional contents of your snack to a friend?

Section B: Packaging and Place Value 141

Animals

Are Consumers, Too

Good nutrition is as important for animals as it is for humans. The meals on this menu were planned by zookeepers to help animals stay in top shape. Each meal feeds one animal per day.

Jungle Cafe

Howler Monkey
Special

2 hard-boiled eggs	$0.10
2 bananas	$0.20
2 carrots	$0.16
$\frac{1}{4}$ lb celery	$0.22
$\frac{1}{4}$ lb green beans	$0.37
2 apples	$0.32
$\frac{1}{2}$ bunch spinach	$1.00

1 If you were to buy a meal for a panda, a howler monkey, and an anteater, how much would you spend in one day? in one year?

2 It costs $73.85 to feed a sea lion 112 lb of herring each week. What is the cost of feeding one sea lion each day? Explain how you would find the price of 1 lb of herring.

3 What is the average daily cost of feeding the mongoose? of feeding all the animals on the menu?

4 Describe the border of the menu in terms of the geometric shapes you see.

5 Where do you see symmetry in the border? congruence?

6 How much would it cost to feed a sea lion and a panda for a day? for a whole year?

Flamingo Feast

3 scoops
dog chow $0.45
2 scoops
trout chow $0.27
2½ lb krill $3.75
coloring $0.05

Anteater Feeder

4 16-oz cans
cat food $11.00
35 crickets $5.25
1 orange $0.20

Sea Lion Smorgasbord

112 lb of herring
per week.....$73.85

Mongoose Meal

Choice of one of
the following meals

Meal 1.....$0.50
1 tbsp feline chow
2¼ slices banana
1 grape
½ tsp ground
hard-boiled egg

Meal 2.....$1.80
12 crickets

Meal 3.....$0.16
12 wax worms

Panda Platter

40 lb bamboo $20.00
2 lb rice $0.75
2 lb carrots $1.00
2 lb apples $1.50
1 sweet potato....$0.30

7 If 1 scoop of the dog chow for flamingos weighs about 5 oz, what's the cost of a 20 lb bag of dog chow?

8 If the zoo spends $19.04 each week on carrots to feed its howler monkeys, how many howler monkeys live there?

9 What is the most expensive meal on the menu? How much more does it cost than the second most expensive meal? How did you find out?

Check Your Math Power

10 What does it cost to feed you for a day? Explain how you'd find out. Make up a menu for one day's meals for yourself. Include the price of each item. Use your knowledge of shapes to decorate your menu.

LESSON 7 Finding the Problem

LITERATURE

Did you ever get too much of something? Read this excerpt to find out just how much too much can be!

I dialed Rufus's number. "Rufus," I said. "I have a problem."

"Math?" Rufus said. I often call him when I'm having trouble with a math assignment.

"Well, sort of," I said. "Rufus—you know how much a gross is?"

"One hundred and forty-four," Rufus said. "A dozen dozen."

"That's right," I said. "I knew it had something to do with a dozen, Rufus. But I thought it was just one dozen."

"What was?" Rufus asked.

"Toothpaste tubes," I said. "Rufus, I just bought 50 gross by mistake. And the problem is that I don't think I can carry that many home on my bike."

"Oh," Rufus said.

There was a silence at the other end of the phone. It wasn't that Rufus was mad at me. He was just multiplying in his head.

"Seven thousand two hundred tubes?" Rufus asked after a minute. "Is that what you've got?"

"There are quite a few of them, Rufus," I said. "Five big boxes. I think I may need a truck."

There was another silence.

Then Rufus said, "Probably one tube weighs about an ounce. 7200 ounces is 450 pounds. Say about a quarter of a ton. Okay, Kate. I know what to do. Where are you?"

From *The Toothpaste Millionaire* by Jean Merrill

ACTIVITY 1 Looking at Equations

REASONING AND PROBLEM SOLVING

With Your Class Rufus Mayflower and his friend Kate MacKinstrey are in the toothpaste business. They are finding out that in business there is always a new problem to think about.

What information do you need to find out how many pounds are in a quarter of a ton? Why do you need to use the number 2,000?

1 How did Rufus know that 450 lb is about a quarter of a ton? Decide which of these equations he could use to represent the problem and explain your choice.

a. $2{,}000 \times 4 = n$ b. $2{,}000 \div 4 = n$

c. $2{,}000 \div n = 25$

2 Match each of these equations with the question it represents.

How many pounds are in 7,200 oz?

How many tubes are in 50 gross?

How much is a gross?

a. $12 \times 12 = n$ b. $50 \times 144 = n$

c. $7{,}200 \div 16 = n$

3 Discuss with a partner how you matched the questions and equations.

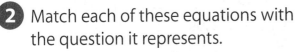

What's the Problem?

With Your Class Writing equations is one way to represent a problem so you can solve it.

1 Find the problem. What does Rufus know? What does he want to know?

Mr. MacKinstrey told Rufus there were more than 200,000,000 people in the United States. "I was thinking that everybody in the country probably uses about one tube of toothpaste per month," said Rufus. "And if they do, how many tubes of toothpaste are sold in a year?"

2 Thinking of a sentence that fits the problem can help you solve it. How does the sentence below fit Rufus's problem?

Two hundred million people times 12 tubes a year equals an unknown number of tubes sold per year.

3 Which equation matches the problem? Explain why it matches by showing how it fits the sentence.

a. $200{,}000{,}000 \div 12 = n$

b. $200{,}000{,}000 \times 1 = n$

c. $200{,}000{,}000 \times 12 = n$

✓ **Self-Check** *How will you decide which equation fits the problem? Will the total number of tubes sold per year be greater than or less than 200,000,000? How do you know?*

4 Asking yourself questions will help you write equations. Try asking questions for each problem. Then write an equation.

> What am I asked to find? How do I know what numbers to use?

a. Rufus thought he could sell 250,000,000 tubes of toothpaste in one year. If he made a profit of 1¢ a tube, what would his total profit be?

b. Rufus had 1,000 shares of stock. He gave 499 shares to his helpers and kept the rest for himself. How many shares of stock did Rufus own?

c. Postage costs from 5¢ to 9¢ a tube, depending on how far the toothpaste is mailed. What is the average cost of mailing one tube?

> How can I show how the numbers are related?

250,000,000
1¢ Profit each
1 year = 365 days

Do You Remember?

Try It!

If the quotient has an error, correct it. Write *C* if the quotient is correct.

41 R2	127	1,002 R3	72
1. 6)248	**2.** 5)585	**3.** 5)5,014	**4.** 3)219

Solve. Write problems to fit two of the equations.

5. $26 \times n = 130$ **6.** $927 \div 3 = n$ **7.** $365 - 180 = n$

8. $63 + n = 98$ **9.** $72 \times 16 = n$ **10.** $(6 \times 4) - n = 12$

Think About It

11. What can you do before dividing that will help you decide whether a quotient is reasonable?

Think About Division

ACTIVITY 1 Patterns

With Your Class Using patterns and making connections to what you already know about dividing will help you solve problems with larger numbers.

1 Look at these examples. What is the first digit in each quotient? What pattern do you see? Explain what happens to the quotient as the dividend becomes ten times greater.

$$4\overline{)24} \qquad 4\overline{)240} \qquad 4\overline{)2{,}400}$$

2 How do you know what the first digit in each quotient will be? Where will you write the first digit? Explain any pattern that you see.

$$5\overline{)45} \qquad 5\overline{)450}$$

$$50\overline{)450} \qquad 50\overline{)4{,}500}$$

3 Let's connect. You know how to divide this problem mentally.

You can also use mental math to solve this problem. Explain how.

$$50\overline{)450}$$

$$50\overline{)457}$$

4 Knowing how to divide by multiples of ten will help you estimate the quotient.

Why can't the quotient be 10? Where did the 450 come from?

Why is 450 subtracted from 487?

$$\begin{array}{r} 9\_ \\ 50\overline{)4{,}876} \\ -450 \end{array}$$

CONNECT AND COMMUNICATE

5 Estimate the first digit in each quotient. Check your estimate by multiplying.

a. $6\overline{)36}$ $6\overline{)360}$ $60\overline{)360}$ $6\overline{)368}$

b. $8\overline{)40}$ $8\overline{)400}$ $80\overline{)400}$ $80\overline{)410}$

In Your Journal Explain what is the same about dividing by a one-digit divisor (such as $5\overline{)487}$) and dividing by a multiple of ten (like $50\overline{)487}$). What is different?

Look at the following example: 54)786. How would drawing 786 as paper bills help you solve the problem? How could sketching help you explain the problem to your friend?

2 Sharing

With a Partner   Suppose you want to share $532 of your store's profits among 17 people who work for you. How much money will each person receive?

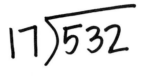

1 Think about sharing the money. Are there enough $100 bills for each person to get one? How can you share the 5 hundreds?

2 If you traded the 5 hundreds for tens, how many tens would you have to share?

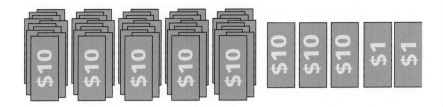

3 How can you decide the number of $10 bills for each person?

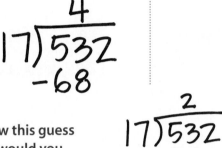

How do you know this guess is too high? How would you continue to divide if this were your first guess?

$$17\overline{)532} \\ -68$$ with quotient 4

How do you know this guess is too low? How would you continue to divide?

$$17\overline{)532} \\ -34 \\ \overline{19}$$ with quotient 2

4 Look at these examples. Find the first digit in each quotient. Explain your thinking.

a. $12\overline{)2,647}$ b. $55\overline{)1,892}$ c. $27\overline{)1,845}$

5 Share your method of finding the first digit with your class. Did anyone else use the same method you did? Is there a method you like better than yours? Why?

6 Use the method you like best to solve these.

a. $26\overline{)324}$ b. $23\overline{)92}$

c. $62\overline{)538}$ d. $45\overline{)1,280}$

3 Making Estimates

With Your Class When you divide by greater numbers, you usually have to estimate the first digit in the quotient. Discuss the ways of estimating shown here.

1 One way of making a problem simpler is to use friendly numbers. For example, you can think about money.

$$27\overline{)2{,}178}$$

$$\downarrow$$

$$25\overline{)2{,}178}$$

How many quarters (25¢) are in $2.17? How does thinking about money help you to find the first digit in the quotient? What is the first digit?

Write at least three other division examples that use friendly numbers. Explain how they make it easier to estimate.

2 You can think about the dividend in terms of 100. How many 27's are in 100? in 200? What will you use for the first digit of the quotient? Will this estimate be too high or too low? How do you know?

$$27\overline{)2{,}178}$$

Think:

$$27\overline{)200}$$

3 You can estimate by rounding the divisor. What is the first digit you try in the quotient? Would this estimate work? Why or why not? What is the correct number? How do you know? Would rounding the dividend help you estimate for this example? Think of an example where it would help.

If you would rather have your estimate be too low, will you round up or down? Explain why.

$$27\overline{)2{,}178}$$

Think:

$$30\overline{)2{,}178}$$

On Your Own Write an explanation of how you would use your own method or one of the methods shown here to estimate the first digit of the quotient. Then find the first digit and check your estimate.

1. $28\overline{)278}$ 2. $54\overline{)1{,}000}$ 3. $68\overline{)210}$ 4. $18\overline{)96}$

4 Here's what one student does when her guess is too low. What did this person do? Why does it work? What do you like about this method? How is your method the same or different from this method?

$$
\begin{array}{r}
7 \\
\cancel{8} \\
72\overline{)5680} \\
-432 \\
\hline
136 \\
-72 \\
\hline
64
\end{array}
$$

Do You Remember?

Try It!

Finish the division. Use any method you wish.

$$
\begin{array}{r}
7 \\
1.\ 35\overline{)285} \\
-245 \\
\hline
40
\end{array}
\qquad
\begin{array}{r}
9\_ \\
2.\ 46\overline{)4{,}444} \\
-414 \\
\hline
30
\end{array}
\qquad
\begin{array}{r}
6\_ \\
3.\ 16\overline{)1{,}207} \\
-96 \\
\hline
24
\end{array}
\qquad
\begin{array}{r}
7 \\
4.\ 65\overline{)520} \\
-455 \\
\hline
65
\end{array}
$$

Write or draw the next step in the pattern. Use a calculator if necessary.

5. ⣫ ⣺ ⣻

6. 5, 5, 6, 8, 11

7. 7, 49, 343

8.

9. ▲ ■ ⬠

10. 1, 100, 10, 1000, 100

Think About It

11. For Exercises 1–4 explain your method of division. Why might you use a different method for different problems?

Working It Out

ACTIVITY 1 ## Finding Your Way

With Your Partner Use pencil and paper to find this quotient.

1 Think about what you already know.

   a. How many digits will be in the quotient?

$$24{\overline{\smash{\big)}\,564}}$$

   b. What are some of the strategies you can use to help you find the first digit?

   c. What is a simpler or related example you can solve that will help you think through this division?

   d. How will you test if your first guess is correct?

   e. When you find the first digit, what will you do next?

2 You and your partner may have different ways of dividing. Explain your way to your partner.

155

2 Keep It Simple

With Your Group How would $564 in profit-sharing money be divided among 24 employees? How much would each person get? Look at this simple way of recording division with a two-digit divisor.

$$564 \div 24 = n$$

1 Set up the problem and think about it. Why will the first digit in the quotient be in the tens' place?

24)564

100's	10's	1's
5	6	4

2 Trade the hundreds in for tens. How many tens will you have?

3 56 tens, 24 people. How many tens for each? Find the first digit and multiply. Then subtract.

100's	10's	1's
	56	4

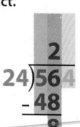

```
      2
24)564
  -48
    8
```

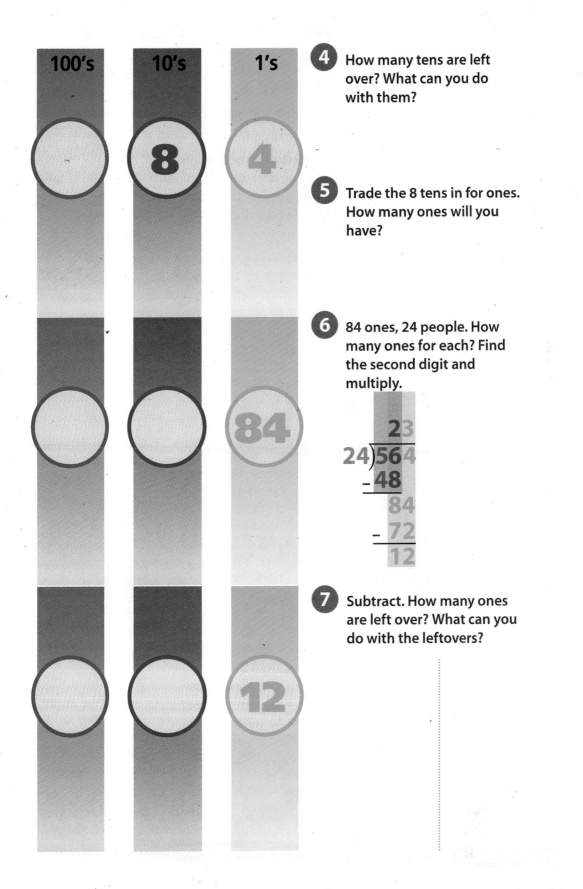

100's	10's	1's
	8	4

4 How many tens are left over? What can you do with them?

5 Trade the 8 tens in for ones. How many ones will you have?

6 84 ones, 24 people. How many ones for each? Find the second digit and multiply.

$$
\begin{array}{r}
23 \\
24\overline{)564} \\
-48 \\
\hline
84 \\
-72 \\
\hline
12
\end{array}
$$

7 Subtract. How many ones are left over? What can you do with the leftovers?

In Your Journal Describe how the same remainder is treated differently in the problems on this page. What does the remainder mean in each case?

ACTIVITY 3 What's the Answer?

With Your Class When you divide, you haven't solved the problem until you know what to do with the remainder. The answer depends on the situation.

1 If you share 3 dozen cookies equally with your class, how many cookies will each person get? Draw a picture to show what you will do with the cookies that are left.

$$16\overline{\smash{)}36} \\ \underline{-32} \\ 4$$

2 How can 36 pencils be shared among 16 people? What is the least number each person will get? What are two things you could do with the leftover pencils?

3 Thirty-six students and teachers are going on a field trip. One minivan holds 16 people. How many minivans will they need?

4 If each of your 16 classmates needs 3 crayons for a project, are 36 crayons enough? Explain.

On Your Own Write a problem situation that has the given answer and a two-digit divisor. Show the division for each problem.

5 The answer is "Thirty each with 17 left over."

6 The answer is "There aren't enough for each person to get 12."

7 The remainder is the answer.

Gather data about remainders in real-life situations. Your family, your friends, and your observations are sources. After a week, share your findings with the class.

Do You Remember?

Try It!

Arrange the numbers in order from least to greatest. Find the difference between the greatest and least numbers.

1. 100 million; 1,300,000; 130,000,000
2. 1,006; 1,600; sixteen hundred one
3. nine thousand; 900; 89,000
4. one million fifty-six; 1,560,000; 1,000,560
5. 8,378; 8,738; 8,700; 7,830; 8,003

Estimate the first digit. If the first digit is 1, use pencil and paper to find the answer.

6. $31\overline{)419}$
7. $84\overline{)5,544}$
8. $44\overline{)7,526}$
9. $53\overline{)287}$
10. $26\overline{)338}$
11. $17\overline{)7,344}$

Think About It

12. What is the greatest remainder you can have when you divide by 31? by 53? Write a sentence explaining the relationship between any divisor and the remainder.

LESSON 10 — TV Favorites

Television advertising is big business. Before spending millions of dollars on new commercials, advertisers must find out what people like to watch. To do this, they take surveys and collect data.

What You'll Need
• *sticky notes*

ACTIVITY 1 — Your Favorite Show

On Your Own Gather your own data about what fifth graders like.

The Simpsons

Beverly Hills 90210

Mystery Science Theater

1 What are your three favorite TV shows? List them on your paper. Then write the names of the shows on sticky notes. Put one show on each note.

2 Do you think most students in your class will have the same favorites as you? Why or why not? Write down your prediction for your class's three favorite shows.

ACTIVITY 2 Organizing Your Data

With Your Class Compile the class favorites and check your predictions.

1 Take turns sticking your three notes on the chalkboard. Tell the class the name of each show as you put it on the board. If you have the same favorite as someone else, place your note above or below the other note.

2 Describe the data. What could you say about the single notes? Are there clumps of notes in some places? What does this clumping mean?

3 Which three shows are your class's favorites? How many people predicted the three favorites correctly?
  a. Compare the actual favorites with your predictions.
  b. If you wanted to sell toys, during which show would you have a commercial? Why?

4 Explain what kind of graph your class has made.

ACTIVITY 3 Who Watches What?

With Your Group How do your class's favorite programs compare with what the graph shows?

How many viewers does each horizontal part of the graph represent? Why is the scale in millions?

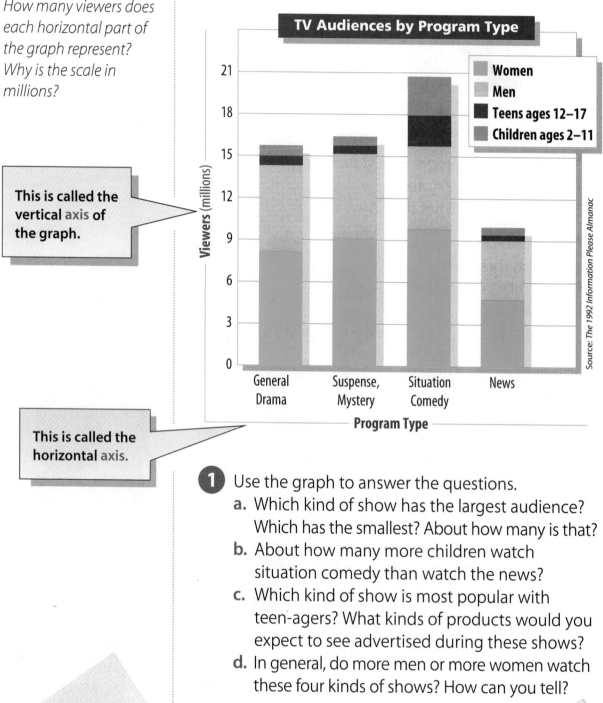

TV Audiences by Program Type

Legend:
- Women
- Men
- Teens ages 12–17
- Children ages 2–11

Vertical axis: **Viewers** (millions) — 0, 3, 6, 9, 12, 15, 18, 21

Horizontal axis: **Program Type** — General Drama, Suspense, Mystery, Situation Comedy, News

Source: The 1992 Information Please Almanac

> This is called the vertical **axis** of the graph.

> This is called the horizontal **axis**.

1 Use the graph to answer the questions.

a. Which kind of show has the largest audience? Which has the smallest? About how many is that?

b. About how many more children watch situation comedy than watch the news?

c. Which kind of show is most popular with teen-agers? What kinds of products would you expect to see advertised during these shows?

d. In general, do more men or more women watch these four kinds of shows? How can you tell?

Bugs Bunny

The Simpsons

Tom and Jerry

2 Sort your class's favorite shows into categories like the ones on the graph. Rearrange your sticky notes to make a new bar graph. Place the notes for each show in the bar for the correct category.

a. Which kind of show has the largest audience?

b. Which has the smallest?

3 How is your new graph like the graph on page 162? How is it different?

NBA Basketball

American Gladiators

Full House

Fresh Prince

In Living Color

Saturday Night Live

graph on page 162

Do You Remember?

Try It!

Use the information in the table to make a bar graph.

Viewers	Hours of TV Watched per Week
Children 6–11	21 hours, 19 minutes
Women 18–54	27 hours
Men 18–54	$24 \frac{3}{4}$ hours
People 55 and over	$39 \frac{3}{4}$ hours

1. What will each axis of your graph show?
2. Which bar will be the longest?

Solve the divisions with more than two places in the quotient.

3. $62 \overline{)548}$ 4. $32 \overline{)586}$ 5. $55 \overline{)3,653}$ 6. $16 \overline{)1,654}$

7. $22 \overline{)132}$ 8. $60 \overline{)7,200}$ 9. $78 \overline{)458}$ 10. $28 \overline{)1,568}$

Think About It

11. What does your graph show about television watching by various age groups? Write your answer.

LESSON 11 It Pays to Advertise

Write a paragraph or two explaining in words the information shown on the graph.

Television networks make money by selling time for commercials. This advertising time isn't cheap.

ACTIVITY 1 Advertising Costs

With Your Group This double-bar graph shows how much was spent to buy advertising time.

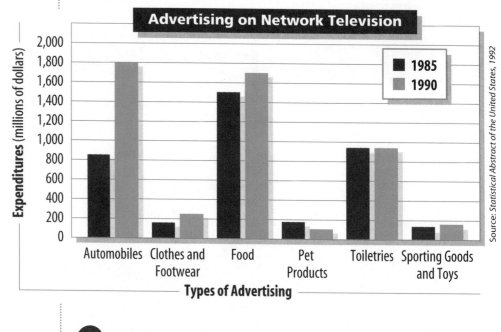

Advertising on Network Television

Expenditures (millions of dollars)

■ 1985
■ 1990

Automobiles Clothes and Footwear Food Pet Products Toiletries Sporting Goods and Toys

Types of Advertising

Source: Statistical Abstract of the United States, 1992

1 Use the graph to answer these questions.
  a. Which product had the highest total expenses in 1985? in 1990?
  b. Look at the changes in spending between 1985 and 1990. For which products did spending increase? decrease? stay the same? double?
  c. About how much more advertising money was spent on automobiles in 1990 than on food?
  d. About how much was spent all together in 1990?

2 What does the information in the graph tell you about the kinds of commercials that are shown on television?

Graph It!

With Your Group   Make a graph of your own. Use the data sheets you filled out as you watched one hour of television. What will this graph show?

1 Sort out your information. What kinds of products were advertised during each time period? Did anyone track commercials at any other time?

2 Work with your group to design one of the kinds of graphs described here. Decide which kind to make. Be prepared to explain why you chose the one you did.

If you have a computer graphing program, you could use it to graph your data.

Date   Nov 15
Time   4:00

Total Commercials
15

① Cars 卌

Date Sat/17th
Time   9:00

① Food 卌 I
② Toys 卌 III
③ Cars I
④ Shoes IIII

Double-Bar Graph   Design a double-bar graph that compares the number of commercials for certain kinds of products during two of the time periods your group watched. You might compare numbers of commercials for food, footwear, and pet products during after-school time and on Saturday morning.

165

Can you find more recent data on the amount of money spent on TV commercials? If so, make a graph like the one on page 164 and add a bar for the latest year.

Pictograph Make a **pictograph** that compares the number of commercials per hour during each of the time periods your group watched. Design a symbol to represent the number of commercials. Ask yourselves these questions as you plan your graph.

How many commercials should a symbol stand for?

Do any of the numbers of commercials require you to use a fraction of a symbol? If so, how should you show that?

3 Use a checklist like this as you make your graph. Think about where the labels for each time period will be.

Commercials Per Hour

Saturday AM	📺 📺
Prime Time	📺 📺 📺 📺
...ter Sch...	📺 📺
...enin...	
= 5 comm...	

Cars

Shoes

Cereal

Checklist for a Good Graph
☑ Choose a scale that clearly shows the range of your data
☑ Clearly label the axes
☑ Provide a key if necessary
☑ Give your graph an informative title

4 When designing your graph, show something you find interesting in the data you have collected. For example, you might show
- the numbers of commercials for the most frequently advertised products.
- the numbers of commercials for specific brands of a product.

5 Explain to the class how you made your graph and what it shows. Display all the graphs your class made. Use them during the next lesson.

Do You Remember?

Try It!

Write the appropriate unit of capacity or weight.

1. I poured myself a 12– _____ glass of juice.
2. Apples were on sale for 49¢ a _____ .
3. The truck weighed about 1.5 _____ .
4. The quart bottle was three fourths empty. Only one _____ was left.
5. The fish tank held about 10 _____ of water.

Use the graph on page 164 to identify the products.

6. Spent the most on TV ads in 1985
7. Spent nearly the same amount in 1985 and 1990
8. Increased its spending from 1985 to 1990 by $200 million
9. Showed the largest dollar increase between 1985 and 1990
10. Showed the largest dollar decrease between 1985 and 1990

Think About It
11. Write two more questions based on one of the graphs in this section. Share with your group.

LESSON 12 Buying Time

CONNECT AND COMMUNICATE

In Your Journal *Keep a record of all the advertisements you see in one day. Include radio, TV, billboards, magazines, newspapers, posters, and any others you see.*

Now it's your turn! You and your group have to decide how to spend an advertising budget on television commercials for three products. Before you begin, decide on a way to keep track of your decisions so that you can present your report to the class.

ACTIVITY 1 Choose Your Products

With Your Group You have a budget of $800,000 to spend on advertising three of the products described here. Your goal is to reach the largest number of likely buyers for your products at the lowest cost.

1 Tape Player
$75.00 This tape player has lightweight headphones and automatic tape reverse. Whom do you think it would appeal to?

2 Toastie Os
$4.95 for a 20-oz box This low-fat cereal has no sugar. Who would be interested in buying it?

Whole grain toasted oat cereal

Toastie Os

WHOLE GRAIN OATS

3 **Doggie Delights**
$3.79 for a 4-lb bag
This dog food is healthful and tasty. What is one thing you know about people who might buy this product?

4 **Super Sneakers**
$30.00 per pair
These are great all-purpose gym shoes. Who might be interested in buying them?

5 **Moosh Ball**
$1.59
A very popular item at toy stores everywhere! Why would this appeal to several groups of buyers?

With Your Group Discuss the questions. Then write down the answers you agree on.
a. What is a good mix of products to advertise? Why?
b. Should all three products appeal to the same buyers, or will you advertise to different groups?
c. Which three products did you choose? What groups of buyers do you hope to reach?

TOOLS AND TECHNIQUES

You don't have to use a calculator to find the cost per viewer. Try using smaller numbers and dividing by multiples of ten to estimate the cost.

ACTIVITY 2 **Look at the Data**

With Your Group You can advertise your products on any of the eight shows listed below.

1 How can the information in the table help you decide where to advertise your products?

Television Data		
Show	**Cost (30 seconds)**	**Number of Viewers**
The Cartoon Club	$15,000	2,100,000
Super Bowl XL	$800,000	79,000,000
Afternoon Drama	$10,400	5,460,000
After-School Movie	$10,400	3,200,000
Super Quiz Show	$47,400	17,500,000
Evening News	$47,400	31,670,000
Family Comedy	$106,400	20,640,000
The Mystery Hour	$106,400	17,100,000

a. Which show costs the most per ad? the least?

b. Which three shows reach the greatest number of people? How many watch each show?

c. Which show reaches the most people per dollar spent?

d. Who would be the audience for each show? Which audience do you want to reach?

2 How can information from the other charts and graphs in this section help you decide how to spend your money?

Market

Tape player
Tennis shoes
moosh ball

1. Teen-agers
2. College students
3. Business people?
4. Teachers

170

ACTIVITY 3 Present the Proposal

With Your Class Share your report with the rest of the class.

1

Describe your products and your market. Tell why you are aiming for those markets.

2

Explain how your budget will be spent and why you made the choices you did.

Do You Remember?

Try It!

How many viewers are there per dollar spent?
1. Program A: $15,000 for 4,400,000 viewers
2. Program B: $120,000 for 20,000,000 viewers
3. Half the viewers of each program A and B bought 3 of each product on pages 168-169. How much did each product earn?

What is the greatest common factor?

4. 12 and 15   5. 8 and 32   6. 18 and 42
7. 25 and 30   8. 21 and 49   9. 40 and 48

Think About It
10. What other facts would you need to decide which program above is the better buy? Explain why.

✔ **Self-Check** *Did you consider information from all the charts and graphs in this section to help you prepare your report?*

Looking Back

Choose the right answer. Write *a*, *b*, *c*, or *d* for each question.

You need to buy items with these prices:

$1.87 $2.23 $9.06

$3.76 $.90

1. Estimate the total cost.
   a. $5–$10   b. $11–$15
   c. $16–$20   d. $21–$25

2. Between what two amounts is the exact total?
   a. $15–$16   b. $17–$18
   c. $25–$26   d. $21–$22

3. If you pay with a $50 bill, you will get back how much change?
   a. $34–$35   b. $24–$25
   c. $28–$29   d. $32–$33

4. If you share the change with nine friends, about how much will each of you receive?
   a. between $3 and $4
   b. between $2 and $3
   c. between $4 and $5
   d. less than $3

You are in charge of making raisin bread for the school bake sale. Ingredients for 20 loaves cost $28.

5. What do you need to know to find out if you will break even?

6. How many loaves can remain unsold, if you charge $3 per loaf, to make a $24 profit?

Complete the tables to 20 loaves.

7. Profit/loss at $2 per loaf

Loaves sold	Profit/loss
0	−$28
1	−$26
2	−$24
3	−$22

8. Profit/loss at $4 per loaf

Loaves sold	Profit/loss
0	−$28
1	−$24
2	−$20
3	−$16

The San Diego Zoo orders 715,000 crickets per year. Each cricket costs 15¢. Each anole, a small chameleonlike lizard, eats 7 crickets a week.

9. What is the best way to find how much the San Diego Zoo spends on crickets each year?
   a. divide
   b. add
   c. multiply
   d. subtract

10. How much must a school raise to sponsor one anole for one year?
   a. more than $50
   b. more than $10
   c. more than $4,000
   d. more than $75

11. If the San Diego Zoo feeds all its crickets each year to anoles, about how many anoles live at the Zoo?
   a. 17,023
   b. 13,750
   c. 119,166
   d. 1,964

You are in charge of ticket sales for the school fair. Your goal is 3,750.

12. If you give 15 tickets to each student to sell, how many students are in your school?
   a. 200–300
   b. 100–200
   c. 300–400
   d. 400–500

13. Choose the correct number of students with needed ticket sales.
   a. 75 students, 50 tickets
   b. 150 students, 20 tickets
   c. 200 students, 15 tickets
   d. 250 students, 12 tickets

Check Your Math Power

An advertising agency has to make a proposal for a $2 million advertising account. The products that will be sold are clothing for 8–18-year-olds, recreational sports equipment, breakfast cereal, and various snack foods. Use this information to answer Exercises 14–15.

14. Make a proposal for spending the advertising dollars. Base it on your experiences watching television, listening to radio, and reading newspapers and magazines. Decide how much of the $2 million should be used in advertising on television, radio, and print advertising. Explain how you made your decisions.

15. You have decided the total amount to spend on each type of advertising—television, radio, and print. Now make a proposal in which you tell how much will be spent for each product in each medium. For example, how much do you propose to spend on advertising recreational sports equipment on television? Make a bar graph to show how the $2 million will be spent. Defend your choices.

MODULE 3 Investigations

Please Feed the Animals

Elephant
75 lb elephant chow $16.50
75 lb hay $20.00

The San Diego Zoo is home to more than 3,200 animals. The cost of feeding all of the animals is more than $520,000 a year. These cards include a few examples of the kinds and amounts of food needed in just one day at the San Diego Zoo.

Investigation A Feeding Time

Your zoo is about to buy some new animals. You can spend $30,000 per year to feed these animals. Make a spending plan to help you decide which ones to buy.

Penguin
5 lb herring $3.36
2 lb smelt $ .96
2 lb octopus $2.80
1 lb squid $1.40

Gecko
3 crickets $.45

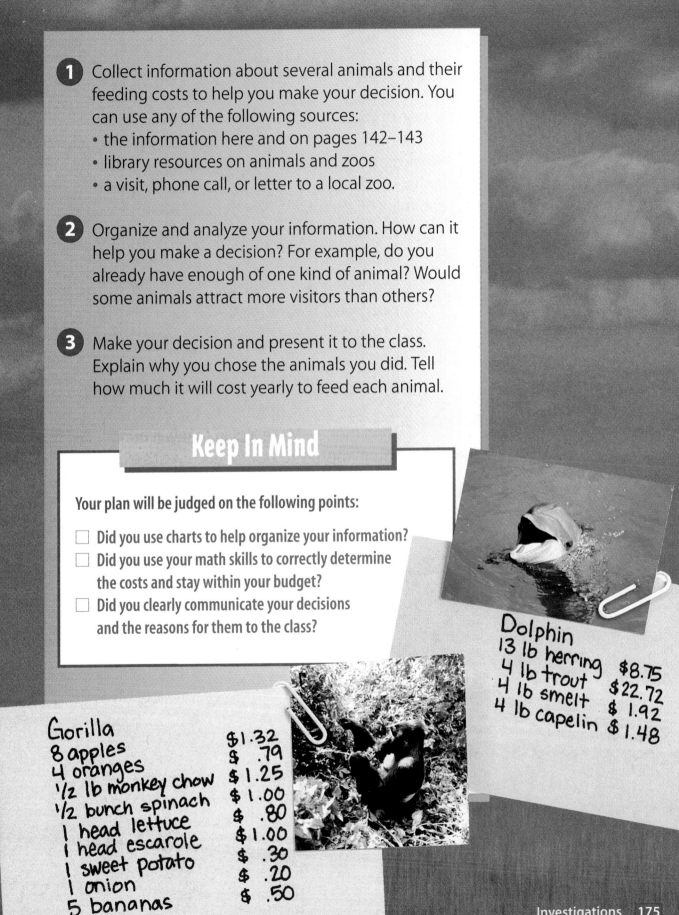

1 Collect information about several animals and their feeding costs to help you make your decision. You can use any of the following sources:
- the information here and on pages 142–143
- library resources on animals and zoos
- a visit, phone call, or letter to a local zoo.

2 Organize and analyze your information. How can it help you make a decision? For example, do you already have enough of one kind of animal? Would some animals attract more visitors than others?

3 Make your decision and present it to the class. Explain why you chose the animals you did. Tell how much it will cost yearly to feed each animal.

Keep In Mind

Your plan will be judged on the following points:

☐ Did you use charts to help organize your information?
☐ Did you use your math skills to correctly determine the costs and stay within your budget?
☐ Did you clearly communicate your decisions and the reasons for them to the class?

Dolphin
13 lb herring $8.75
4 lb trout $22.72
4 lb smelt $ 1.92
4 lb capelin $ 1.48

Gorilla
8 apples $1.32
4 oranges $ .79
½ lb monkey chow $ 1.25
½ bunch spinach $ 1.00
1 head lettuce $ .80
1 head escarole $ 1.00
1 sweet potato $ .30
1 onion $ .20
5 bananas $ .50

Investigation B — Funding a Zoo

Suppose your small zoo included only two each of the animals named on pages 142–143 and 174–175. What costs would you have besides feeding the animals? Gather information about every cost you can think of, and plan a yearly budget for the zoo.

1 List all the expenses and their prices. Remember to include services (such as workers) as well as goods (such as food). If you can't find the exact cost, make a realistic estimate.

2 Total all the costs, then figure out how your zoo can meet those costs. Admission fees, yearly zoo memberships, and gifts of money from people or businesses are among the possible ways of raising money. Make a plan that will bring in enough money to pay for each year's expenses. Explain your plan to the class.

Computer Option Try using a computer spreadsheet program to help you organize, calculate, and present your zoo's yearly budget. What data should you include? How can you organize the data so you can easily analyze it? Can you use formulas to help you calculate your costs?

Investigation C — A Zoo at Home

Do you have a pet at home? If not, what kind of pet would you like to have? Investigate the costs of keeping your real or hoped-for pet for a year. Don't forget to include any expenses other than food in your total. Share your findings with the class.

MODULE 4

One World, Many Parts

From a space shuttle our planet shows no division into countries, only land lapped by blue sea. Closer to home our planet divides into many parts. In this module you will learn how fractions separate wholes into parts and how the different parts relate to one another.

SECTION A

Fractions and Geometry

SECTION B

Multiplying Fractions

SECTION C

Discovering Differences

SECTION D

Adding and Subtracting Fractions

Parts of Your World

Fractions show the division of a whole, such as the world, into parts. Water and land cover the Earth's surface. The land breaks into continents. Some continents contain many countries.

Some of the divisions on this map show equal areas or fractions. For example, the equator splits the world into two equal parts.

Word Bank

- denominator
- equivalent fractions
- numerator
- percent

Shirin represents $\frac{1}{4}$ of the new students in her class.

1 Finding and Collecting Fractions

Your own world divides into parts. You spend about $\frac{1}{4}$ of your day in school. You are a fraction of the students in your class. Think of fractions that show parts in your world and record them in your journal.

Other divisions on this map show sets of unequal parts. How many continents can you count?

Fractions in my life

$\frac{1}{2}$ *of my books are blue.*

$\frac{1}{3}$ *of the coins in my pocket are pennies.*

$\frac{2}{3}$ *of my friends have long hair.*

2 Using Fractions

You will make a diorama at the end of the module. To complete this project, you will need to add and subtract fractions.

Investigate! Investigate! Investigate! Investigate! Investigate! Investigate! Investigate! Investigate! Investigate! Investigate! Investigate! Investigate! Investigate! Investigate!

Investigations Preview

Learn about fractions as parts of wholes and as parts of a set. Fractions can help you understand more about the whole world and your own world.

A Fraction of Time (pages 224–225)
What fraction of your day do you spend sleeping? Use fractions to see how you spend your day.

Sizing Up the World (pages 238–240)
What do statistics about countries really mean? Use fractions to compare different nations. Include this information on your diorama so that you can share it with your class.

LESSON 1 Parts of a Whole

What You'll Need
• *Tracing Tool or tracing paper*

Use the Tracing Tool to check your estimates. First, trace the fractional part of the flag. Then find the number of times that part fits on the whole flag.

You can find fractions everywhere you look. Examine these flags from around the world to find the parts or fractions of each one.

 ACTIVITY 1 Find the Fractions

With Your Class What methods can you use to find the fractions in the flags below?

Look at the flags of Thailand and France. Describe the fraction of each flag that is white. Now estimate the fraction for the other colors on the flags. Explain how you made your estimates.

Remember how to write the terms of the fraction:

$$\frac{1}{3}$$

1 numerator: *number of special parts*

3 denominator: *total number of parts*

France

Thailand

With Your Class It is not always easy to estimate the fractions for flags. Look at the flags below and answer the questions.

1 Which flag has a greater fraction of white, Bahrain or Central African Republic? Explain.

2 About what fraction of Papua New Guinea's flag is red? black? orange?

3 Not all of Gambia's flag is red, blue, or green. About what fraction is white?

Could knowing how to find the area of a flag help you determine the fractions in it? Explain.

 ACTIVITY 2 # Make It Whole

With Your Group Design a flag that is about $\frac{1}{3}$ white, $\frac{1}{6}$ red, $\frac{1}{6}$ blue, $\frac{1}{3}$ yellow. The parts you draw do not have to be rectangles. Share your flag with the class. Explain how your flag shows these fractions.

What You'll Need
• *grid paper*
• *crayons or markers*

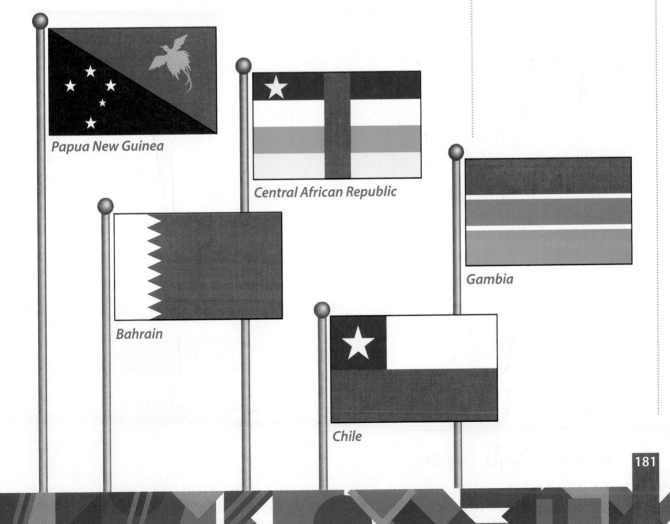

Papua New Guinea

Central African Republic

Gambia

Bahrain

Chile

What You'll Need

- *Tracing Tool or inch and centimeter rulers*
- *Geometry Tool G or right isosceles triangle shape*
- *dot paper*
- *crayons or markers*
- *scissors*

ACTIVITY 3 **Visualizing Fractions**

With Your Partner Work through the activities on these two pages in any order you wish.

1 What fraction of Tanzania's flag is green? black? blue? Record your estimates.

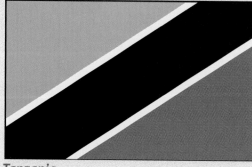

Tanzania

Use the grid on the Tracing Tool to check your estimates. Then draw a flag that has the same fractional parts as Tanzania's flag. Explain how you know the two flags show the same fractions.

2 Draw three right isosceles triangles like the ones below. How many squares can you make if you put them together edge to edge?

- Write your answer as a mixed number and as a fraction greater than one.
- Discuss your answers with a partner. Put your triangles together to make a flag.

REASONING AND PROBLEM SOLVING

How could you demonstrate that all the fractions in any shape will add up to a whole?

3 Choose two shapes from the chart to draw.
Draw them as big as you want. Find fractional
areas and shade them different colors like a flag.
Record the different fractional areas you shaded.

ACTIVITY OPTION

Draw several different-sized parallelograms without right angles. Compare each parallelogram with a rectangle that has the same area. Which shape has a greater perimeter?

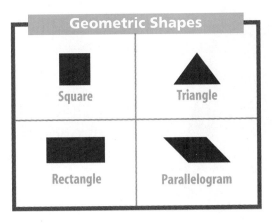

Geometric Shapes

Square

Triangle

Rectangle

Parallelogram

4 Draw a rectangular flag 1 square by 3 squares.
How could you divide it into triangles so that
you could shade $\frac{3}{4}$ of the area? How many
squares did you shade?
Compare answers.

What You'll Need
- *Fraction Tool or inch and centimeter rulers*
- *dot paper*
- *crayons or markers*
- *scissors*
- *tape, paste, or glue*

ACTIVITY 4 # Make Your Own Flag

On Your Own Design your own flag.

- Color it at least two different colors and use at least two different fractions to divide the area.
- Glue your completed flag into your journal.
- Write a description of your flag and include a count of its fractional parts. What number should all these fractions equal if you add them together? How do you know?

Do You Remember?

Try It!

Draw the whole if the triangle here equals the part given: Identify any lines of symmetry you find.

1. $\frac{1}{2}$ of a larger triangle   2. $\frac{1}{2}$ of a square   3. $\frac{1}{4}$ of a square

Draw a different shape and shade it to show these fractions.

4. $\frac{3}{4}$ 5. $\frac{2}{3}$ 6. $\frac{7}{8}$ 7. $\frac{4}{5}$ 8. $\frac{1}{5}$

Find the sum or difference.

9. 1 fifth + 3 fifths   10. 9 tenths − 0   11. 3 fourths + 1 fourth
12. 5 fifths − 2 fifths   13. 9 sixteenths − 9 sixteenths

Think About It

14. How did you use congruent figures to find answers for Exercises 1–3?

Equivalent Families

ᴬᶜᵀᴵⱽᴵᵀʸ 1 Half and Half

With Your Class Equivalent fractions have the same value. Look at Poland's flag in the picture and complete a chart like the one below.

How does the sketch show that $\frac{1}{2} = \frac{2}{4}$? What other equivalent fractions for $\frac{1}{2}$ can you find? Sketch them on dot paper. Show all the equivalent fractions you found. Find as many other equivalent fractions as you can. Discuss how the fractions are equivalent.

What You'll Need
- *dot paper*
- *crayons or markers*

DRAWING TO LEARN

Use your Fraction Tool to draw a shape like the flag in the picture. Then use the picture to show how rectangles, parallelograms, and triangles are related.

Poland

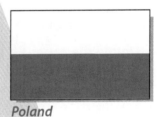

Total number	4		
Fraction white			
Fraction red			
How do I know?			

ACTIVITY 2 Folding Fractions

On Your Own How many equivalent fractions can you make for one fraction? Try this paper-folding experiment to find out!

1

2

3

Make a chart like the one shown above.

Divide a sheet of paper into thirds. Shade in one third.

Fold the paper in half perpendicular to the shaded part.

4

5

Unfold the paper. Record the total parts, the total shaded parts, and the new fraction shaded. How can you prove it is equivalent to $\frac{1}{3}$?

Refold the paper and make a new fold parallel to the first one. Record the parts and fractions in your chart.

6 Continue folding the paper as many times as you can. Which equivalent fractions did you find? Describe any patterns you see.

7 Why can't you keep folding paper to find more equivalent fractions? How do you know there are more fractions equivalent to $\frac{1}{3}$?

With Your Group Repeat the activity to find other equivalent fractions. Each person should choose at least one of the following fractions.

$$\frac{2}{3} \quad \frac{3}{3} \quad \frac{1}{5} \quad \frac{2}{5} \quad \frac{3}{5} \quad \frac{4}{5} \quad \frac{5}{5}$$

Shade a portion of paper to represent the fraction. Then fold the paper and record the equivalent fractions each time. Share the fractions you found with your group and explain any patterns you see.

✓ **Self Check** *What do all the equivalent fractions for a whole have in common? Write a few sentences to explain what you found.*

ACTIVITY 3 Changing Models

With Your Partner You used dot paper and folding paper to make equivalent fractions. You could also model equivalent fractions with the Fraction Tool or fraction circles. Use the fractions $\frac{2}{8}, \frac{4}{8}, \frac{6}{8}, \frac{8}{8}$.

1 Each partner should model five fractions equivalent to these fractions. You should model each of the fractions a different way.

2 Explain in writing how you know that your fraction models are equivalent to your partner's.

What You'll Need
• *Fraction Tool or other fraction models*

TOOLS AND TECHNIQUES

How could you use what you learned with the dot paper activity and this paper-folding activity to help you show more equivalent fractions? How could using patterns help you?

ACTIVITY OPTION

Draw a rectangle on a sheet of dot paper. Then divide it to show as many equivalent fractions for $\frac{1}{2}$ as you can. Draw four more rectangles and find equivalents for four different fractions.

ACTIVITY 4 Fair Shares

With Your Partner Think about the many ways you can represent fractions. Then try either of the activities on these two pages.

1 How can you find out if this shape has been divided into two equal parts?

2 On a sheet of dot paper, draw at least four more flags the same size as these. Divide each shape into two equal parts. Each shape should be divided in a different way.

ACTIVITY 5 Shapes in a Shape

On Your Own Use your Geometry Tool to find some other equivalent fractions. Start by tracing.

1 Which shape can be drawn twice to make the hexagon?

2 Which shape can be repeated 3 times to make the hexagon? 4 times? 5 times? 6 times?

3 Write the equivalent fractions you see for $\frac{1}{2}$ in your hexagons. Do you see any patterns in the fractions you drew? Explain. Write any other equivalent fractions you see with the hexagon.

4 Use the Geometry Tool to draw other equivalent fractions. Label your drawing and share it with a partner.

What You'll Need
- *hexagon shape on Geometry Tool or hexagon shape*

CONNECT AND COMMUNICATE

In Your Journal Write a rule that describes what happens to the numerator and denominator of a fraction as you make a list of equivalent fractions.

hexagon

Houghton Mifflin Mathematics
Drawing to Learn Geometry Tool

Do You Remember?

Try It!

Use paper folding or fraction models to find two fractions equivalent to each one below.

1. $\frac{5}{6}$ 2. $\frac{7}{10}$ 3. $\frac{3}{4}$ 4. $\frac{3}{8}$ 5. $\frac{1}{6}$

Write one equivalent fraction with a greater denominator and one with a smaller denominator for each fraction below.

6. $\frac{2}{10}$ 7. $\frac{7}{14}$ 8. $\frac{4}{12}$ 9. $\frac{10}{15}$ 10. $\frac{5}{40}$

Think About It
11. How could you use paper folding, fraction models, or a drawing to show that $\frac{5}{6}$ does not equal $\frac{3}{8}$?

LESSON 3 — Parts of a Set

Does each part of a set need to be of equal size? Why or why not?

You already know that fractions can represent parts of a whole. Fractions can also describe parts of a set. Look at the collection of state and territory flags on these pages.

Arkansas

New Mexico

Illinois

Puerto Rico

Maryland

What You'll Need
- *crayons or markers*

ACTIVITY 1 — Parts of Your Group

With Your Partner Make your own set of flags and discuss the questions on these pages.

1 Choose five to ten flags that you think go together in some way as a set. Make a sketch of the flags you chose. Then write a title that describes the set your flags make. You can include flags from other pages or books if you choose.

2 Answer these questions about your set of flags. Write your answers as fractions.

a. What part of your set has an animal as part of the design?

b. Look at flags in your set that have only red, white, and blue as the colors. What fraction have a triangle as part of the design?

c. What part of your set has red, white, and blue for colors and stars and stripes for the design?

d. Suppose you add your city, state, or territory flag to your set. How would this change the numerators and denominators of your answers to questions a, b, and c?

In Your Journal Make a sketch that shows several sets of fractions in your classroom, house, or life.

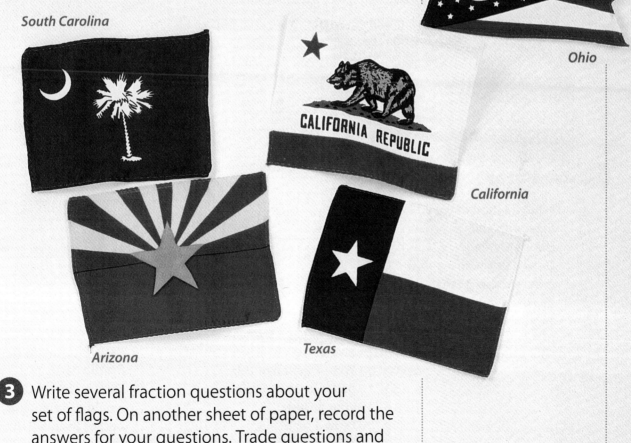

South Carolina

Ohio

California

Arizona

Texas

3 Write several fraction questions about your set of flags. On another sheet of paper, record the answers for your questions. Trade questions and sketches with another set of partners. Record and then discuss the answers you each wrote.

World of Fractions

Use what you know about fractions to answer the following questions. Use your Tracing Tool to help you.

1 United States

a. Look at the flags on these two pages. What fraction of them are red, white, and blue?

b. Identify at least five fractions on this flag. Explain what each fraction represents.

2 Honduras

a. What fraction of the flags with stars is Honduras' flag?

b. Draw a flag with a different design that has the same part blue as Honduras' flag.

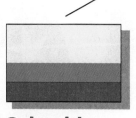

3 Colombia

a. What fraction of this flag is yellow? Explain your answer.

b. Draw a set of five different flags that have the same part red as the Colombian flag.

4 Brazil

a. What fraction of the flags with circles is Brazil's flag?

b. Explain how you would estimate the part of Brazil's flag that is white.

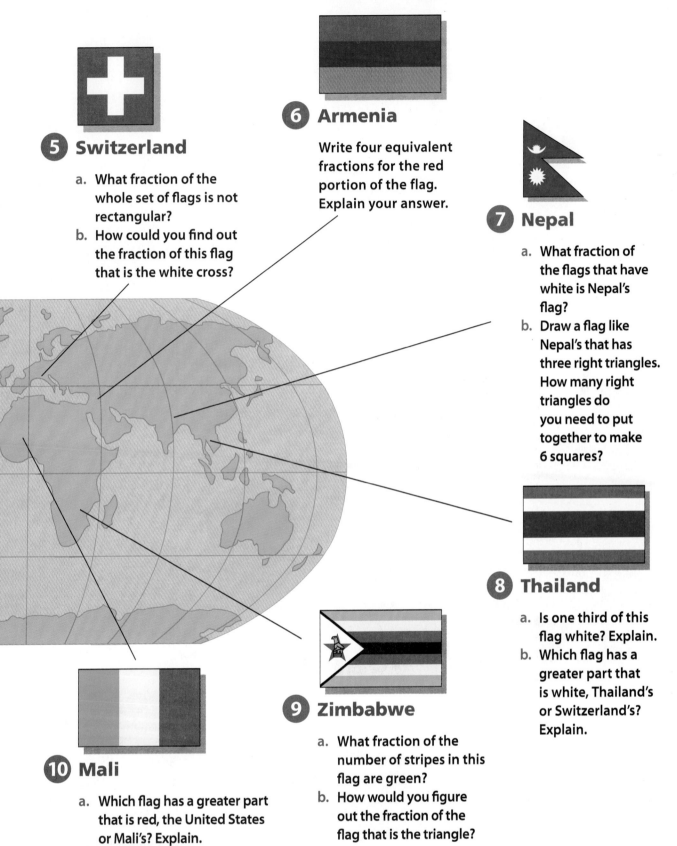

5 Switzerland

a. What fraction of the whole set of flags is not rectangular?

b. How could you find out the fraction of this flag that is the white cross?

6 Armenia

Write four equivalent fractions for the red portion of the flag. Explain your answer.

7 Nepal

a. What fraction of the flags that have white is Nepal's flag?

b. Draw a flag like Nepal's that has three right triangles. How many right triangles do you need to put together to make 6 squares?

8 Thailand

a. Is one third of this flag white? Explain.

b. Which flag has a greater part that is white, Thailand's or Switzerland's? Explain.

9 Zimbabwe

a. What fraction of the number of stripes in this flag are green?

b. How would you figure out the fraction of the flag that is the triangle?

10 Mali

a. Which flag has a greater part that is red, the United States or Mali's? Explain.

b. Write four equivalent fractions for the portion of the flag that is green and yellow.

LESSON
(4)

Many *Mouths* to Feed

People around the world share, trade, adapt, and adjust their favorite recipes. How can you find a way to make half a recipe of cookies for yourself or double a recipe to make cookies for your entire class?

Oatmeal Raisin Cookies

$2 \times \frac{2}{3}$ c white sugar

$2 \times \frac{1}{3}$ c brown sugar

$2 \times \frac{1}{2}$ c butter or margarine

2×1 egg

2×1 tsp vanilla

2×2 c flour

$2 \times \frac{1}{2}$ tsp baking soda

$2 \times \frac{1}{2}$ tsp salt

$2 \times \frac{1}{4}$ tsp cinnamon

2×1 c rolled oats

$2 \times \frac{3}{4}$ c raisins

Oatmeal Raisin Cookies

$\frac{1}{2} \times \frac{2}{3}$ c white sugar

$\frac{1}{2} \times \frac{1}{3}$ c brown sugar

$\frac{1}{2} \times \frac{1}{2}$ c butter or margarine

$\frac{1}{2} \times 1$ egg

$\frac{1}{2} \times 1$ tsp vanilla

$\frac{1}{2} \times 2$ c flour

$\frac{1}{2} \times \frac{1}{2}$ tsp baking soda

$\frac{1}{2} \times \frac{1}{2}$ tsp salt

$\frac{1}{2} \times \frac{1}{4}$ tsp cinnamon

$\frac{1}{2} \times 1$ c rolled oats

$\frac{1}{2} \times \frac{3}{4}$ c raisins

ACTIVITY 1 Predicting Products

With Your Partner How much of each ingredient will you need to make half the recipe of oatmeal raisin cookies? Write a recipe card showing the new amounts. Tell your class how you used estimation to find these amounts.

ACTIVITY 2 Finding Patterns

With Your Partner Multiply these pairs of factors using your calculator.

a. $\frac{1}{5} \times \frac{1}{4}$ **b.** $\frac{1}{5} \times \frac{2}{4}$ **c.** $\frac{1}{5} \times \frac{3}{4}$ **d.** $\frac{1}{5} \times \frac{4}{4}$

e. $\frac{2}{5} \times \frac{1}{4}$ **f.** $\frac{2}{5} \times \frac{2}{4}$ **g.** $\frac{2}{5} \times \frac{3}{4}$ **h.** $\frac{2}{5} \times \frac{4}{4}$

Take turns predicting the product and recording the result. Then come up with ten multiplication exercises of your own.

 Enter the first factor, numerator first, using **/** as the fraction bar.

 Press **x** to multiply.

❸ Enter the second factor and press **=** to find your product.

What patterns did you and your partner discover?

• Did you get better at predicting products?
• What helped you get better at estimating?

TOOLS AND TECHNIQUES

You may want to check your multiplication for half the recipe of cookies with a calculator. You can show fractions on the calculator by using the / sign.

ACTIVITY 3 Modeling Recipes

With Your Class Choose a recipe from this page or bring in a favorite recipe from home. Discuss how to change the amounts of ingredients to serve groups of 2, 3, and 24. To change the recipes you will need to know how to multiply with fractions.

From Sweden

Rice Pudding
serves 6

3 tbsp butter   1 c rice
$\frac{3}{4}$ c water   4 c milk
1 tsp cinnamon
$\frac{1}{4}$ c sugar
$\frac{1}{4}$ tsp salt
1 tsp vanilla

From Lebanon

Hummos Bi Tahini
serves 6

1 15-oz can chick peas or garbanzo beans
$\frac{1}{4}$ c sesame seed paste (tahini)
1 clove garlic, minced $\frac{1}{2}$ tsp salt
$\frac{1}{4}$ c lemon juice   2 tbsp olive oil
several sprigs parsley
6 pieces pita bread

From Ghana

Peanut Crunch
makes 16 balls

$\frac{1}{4}$ lb peanuts $\frac{1}{4}$ tsp salt
$\frac{1}{3}$ c water $\frac{3}{4}$ tsp vanilla
$\frac{1}{3}$ c sugar
$\frac{1}{2}$ tsp cinnamon

From Indonesia

Banana Delight

serves 4

4 bananas
2 c plain yogurt
2 c orange juice
½ c honey
1 tsp vanilla
ice

Slice the bananas or mash with a fork. In a blender or jar, blend the banana pieces with the rest of the ingredients. Pour over ice into two large glasses.

With Your Partner Suppose you choose to make the rice pudding for 3 people. To find the amount of any of the ingredients needed you can multiply by ½.

- Write an equation to find the amount of water you would need.
- How could you use models or estimation to help you?

Now it's time to cook! Choose one of these activities for changing recipes. Find a way to change the recipes without using a calculator.

1 Change one of the recipes to serve 2, 3, and 24 people.

2 Change all four recipes, but serve only 2, 3, or 24 people.

TOOLS AND TECHNIQUES

If you are having trouble, you may want to try the paper-folding activities on pages 198 and 199 before trying this activity.

4 Paper Models

With Your Partner Bread is one food that is common to most cultures in the world. How could you make half a loaf of bread, if the recipe for a whole loaf uses $\frac{2}{3}$ c of flour? How could a model help you change the recipe? Use a 1-×-1 array to model $\frac{1}{2} \times \frac{2}{3}$.

What You'll Need
- *inch ruler*
- *crayons or markers*
- *scissors*

CONNECT AND COMMUNICATE

Explain to your partner how you would use paper folding or another method to solve a different fraction multiplication.

1 Cut an $8\frac{1}{2}$-in.-×-$8\frac{1}{2}$-in. square to represent the array.

2 Fold the paper in one direction to show thirds. Unfold and describe where $\frac{2}{3}$ would be. Fold the paper perpendicular to the first folds to show halves.

3 Use the fold lines to think about where you would find $\frac{1}{2} \times \frac{2}{3}$. Shade your paper to show the array. How much is $\frac{1}{2} \times \frac{2}{3}$? How do you know? Do other students' arrays look the same? Why or why not?

On Your Own Use paper folding to find $\frac{1}{3} \times \frac{1}{4}$ and $\frac{2}{3} \times \frac{1}{4}$. How can you check your answers? Write an explanation of how you would find one of these pairs of products: $\frac{1}{3} \times \frac{2}{4}$ and $\frac{1}{3} \times \frac{3}{4}$ or $\frac{2}{3} \times \frac{2}{4}$ and $\frac{2}{3} \times \frac{3}{4}$.

Use the recipe on page 196. Suppose you want to make rice pudding for two people. Explain how you could use paper folding and shading to find the amount of water and salt needed.

Do You Remember?

Try It!

Estimate the products. Then use paper folding or your own way to find the answers.

1. $\frac{1}{4} \times \frac{1}{4}$ 2. $\frac{3}{5} \times \frac{2}{3}$ 3. $\frac{1}{4} \times \frac{1}{2}$ 4. $\frac{5}{8} \times \frac{3}{4}$

5. $\frac{1}{6} \times \frac{1}{3}$ 6. $\frac{2}{5} \times \frac{1}{2}$ 7. $\frac{3}{8} \times \frac{2}{3}$ 8. $\frac{4}{5} \times \frac{3}{4}$

Draw and label the dimensions of two different rectangles for each area listed.

9. 6 square centimeters

10. 24 square feet

11. 30 square centimeters

12. 48 square centimeters

13. 100 square inches

14. 1 square meter

Think About It

15. Did you find a pattern in your answers to the fraction multiplication exercises? Explain.

The equation for page...

LESSON 5 One *Little* Square

ACTIVITY 1 Arrays Large and Small

With Your Class How could you show fraction multiplication without folding paper? Make an array! Draw one that shows the part of $\frac{1}{3}$ c of water you need to make 8 balls of Peanut Crunch.

First think about what you already know.

1 Draw an array to show 3×5. How could you show 3×3? 2×2? 1×1?

2 You know that $0 \times 0 = 0$ and $1 \times 1 = 1$. So why should the product of $\frac{1}{2} \times \frac{1}{2}$ be between 0 and 1? Estimate what you think the product is.

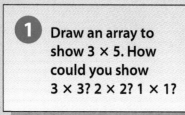

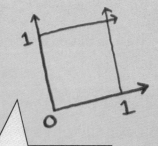

3 Draw a 1-×-1 array, or square. Use it like the paper you folded.

CONNECT AND COMMUNICATE

The equation
$$3 \times 2 = 2 \times 3$$
shows the Commutative Property of Multiplication. Does this property work for fractions as well? Give three examples to support your answer.

From Ghana

Peanut Crunch
makes 16 balls

$\frac{1}{4}$ lb peanuts $\frac{1}{2}$ tsp cinnamon

$\frac{1}{3}$ c water $\frac{1}{4}$ tsp salt

$\frac{1}{3}$ c sugar $\frac{3}{4}$ tsp vanilla

Here's a completed array showing $\frac{4}{5} \times \frac{2}{3}$. What part of the array shows $\frac{4}{5}$? What part of the array shows $\frac{2}{3}$? What fraction of the square shows the product?

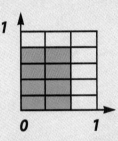

4 On your square, label the factors for $\frac{1}{2} \times \frac{1}{3}$. Draw a line across the square to show the fold for $\frac{1}{2}$.

5 How could you draw lines going up and down for thirds instead of folding the paper?

6 With your finger on the square go up $\frac{1}{2}$ and over $\frac{1}{3}$. Shade that array. What is the product? Why does this strategy work?

ᴬᶜᵀᴵⱽᴵᵀʸ **2 Drawing Arrays**

With Your Partner Make arrays for the pairs of factors below. Write the completed equations and then compare your arrays with your partner's. How could you find the answer without drawing the array?

a. $\frac{1}{2} \times \frac{1}{8}$ b. $\frac{2}{3} \times \frac{3}{5}$ c. $\frac{1}{6} \times \frac{2}{5}$ d. $\frac{2}{8} \times \frac{1}{2}$ e. $\frac{3}{8} \times \frac{4}{5}$

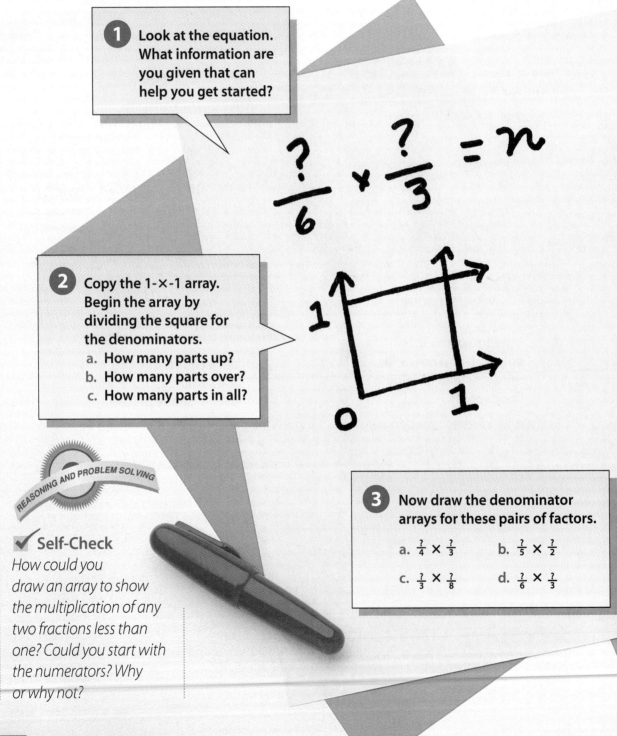

ACTIVITY 3 Drawing Conclusions

With Your Class A recipe serves 6 and calls for $\frac{1}{3}$ c of tomatoes and $\frac{2}{3}$ c of beans. How much of each ingredient is needed per person? Use what you know about fractions and arrays to find out.

1 Look at the equation. What information are you given that can help you get started?

$$\frac{?}{6} \times \frac{?}{3} = n$$

2 Copy the 1-×-1 array. Begin the array by dividing the square for the denominators.
  a. How many parts up?
  b. How many parts over?
  c. How many parts in all?

REASONING AND PROBLEM SOLVING

✔ **Self-Check**
How could you draw an array to show the multiplication of any two fractions less than one? Could you start with the numerators? Why or why not?

3 Now draw the denominator arrays for these pairs of factors.
  a. $\frac{?}{4} \times \frac{?}{3}$ b. $\frac{?}{5} \times \frac{?}{2}$
  c. $\frac{?}{3} \times \frac{?}{8}$ d. $\frac{?}{6} \times \frac{?}{3}$

4 Look at the factor pairs and think about your arrays. How could you find the denominator of any product without drawing an array?

5 What information do you need to shade the arrays? How many parts would you shade if you only had the numerators?

6 Shade each array and label it with the completed equation. How could you find the solution without drawing an array?

a. $\frac{1}{4} \times \frac{2}{3}$

b. $\frac{4}{5} \times \frac{1}{2}$

c. $\frac{2}{3} \times \frac{7}{8}$

Do You Remember?

Try It!

Find the product. Describe the methods you used.

1. $\frac{5}{6} \times \frac{5}{6}$
2. $\frac{2}{5} \times \frac{7}{8}$
3. $\frac{8}{10} \times \frac{5}{6}$

4. $\frac{3}{8} \times \frac{5}{6}$
5. $\frac{1}{3} \times \frac{5}{8}$
6. $\frac{3}{4} \times \frac{7}{10}$

Divide only exercises with quotients greater than 100.

7. $23\overline{)460}$
8. $40\overline{)16,000}$
9. $15\overline{)3,020}$

10. $6\overline{)361}$
11. $8\overline{)8,889}$
12. $32\overline{)7,759}$

Think About It

13. Write a rule that explains how to multiply fractions.

LESSON 6
Fractions and Wholes

Alice's adventures included growing and shrinking. How do you think you could shrink a whole number by multiplying?

What a curious feeling!" said Alice. "I must be shutting up like a telescope!"

And so it was indeed: she was now only ten inches high, and her face brightened up at the thought that she was now the right size for going through the little door into that lovely garden. First, however, she waited for a few minutes to see if she was going to shrink any further: she felt a little nervous about this, "for it might end, you know," said Alice to herself, "in my going out all together, like a candle. I wonder what I should be like then?"

From 'Alice's Adventures in Wonderland by Lewis Carroll

Shrinking can be tricky, as Alice found out! If Alice drinks more and shrinks to half her size, how tall will she be? Why does it make sense that multiplying $\frac{1}{2} \times 10$ will give a product less than 10?

Changing recipes, like changing size, sometimes means multiplying fractions and wholes. How would multiplying a whole and a fraction help shrink a recipe?

Is the product always greater than both factors when you multiply? Explain your answer.

Parts Times Wholes

With Your Class How could you triple this recipe? You already know everything you need to know to multiply a fraction times a whole number. Use paper folding if you want.

- Write an equation that describes how to triple the butter or margarine in the recipe.
- What is the numerator of the product? the denominator?
- How could you rearrange the parts to show the product as a mixed number?
- Could you draw an array? How?

Oatmeal Raisin Cookies

$\frac{2}{3}$ c white sugar

$\frac{1}{3}$ c brown sugar

$\frac{1}{2}$ c butter or margarine

1 egg

1 tsp vanilla

2 c flour

$\frac{1}{2}$ tsp baking soda

$\frac{1}{2}$ tsp salt

$\frac{1}{4}$ tsp cinnamon

1 c rolled oats

$\frac{3}{4}$ c raisins

What if you didn't want to draw an array or fold paper?
- Why could you write 3 as the fraction $\frac{3}{1}$?
- How could you show this as the multiplication of two fractions?
- Now find the product.

On Your Own Now rewrite the recipe with all the ingredients multiplied by 3. Then choose another recipe from pages 196–197. Explain how you would multiply fractions and whole numbers to make $\frac{1}{3}$ as many servings.

The equation 1 × n = n shows the Identity Property of Multiplication. How is the Identity Property being used to make an equivalent fraction here?

$$\frac{1}{2} \times \frac{3}{3} = \frac{3}{6}$$

ACTIVITY 2 Parts Times One

With Your Group You folded paper to find equivalent fractions on page 186. Multiplying fractions by different names for one can help you find equivalent fractions for your recipes much faster. Choose a fraction less than one to test your understanding of equivalence.

Look at these examples. What is the same about each of these arrays? What is different? Why is the shaded area in each array the same?

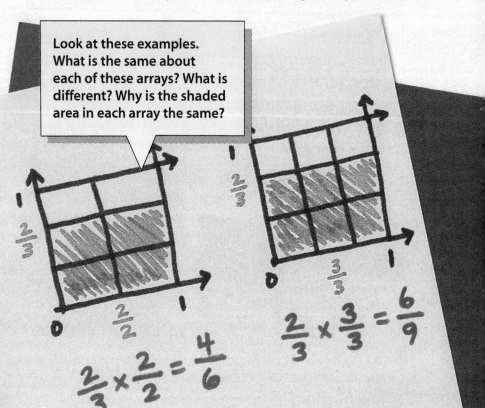

$$\frac{2}{3} \times \frac{1}{1} = \frac{2}{3}$$

$$\frac{2}{3} \times \frac{2}{2} = \frac{4}{6}$$

$$\frac{2}{3} \times \frac{3}{3} = \frac{6}{9}$$

1 Have each person draw and label an array. Then use the Identity Property of Multiplication to multiply your group's fraction.

2 Now answer these questions:
   a. How do your arrays and products compare?
   b. How would you order the fractions?
   c. Are all the fractions you made equivalent? Explain.

3 Based on your group's work, write a rule for making lists of equivalent fractions. Explain your rule to another group.

On Your Own Use the Identity Property of Multiplication to write five equivalent fractions for each fraction below. Use your calculator if you wish.

a. $\frac{2}{5}$ b. $\frac{3}{8}$ c. $\frac{5}{6}$ d. $\frac{1}{4}$ e. $\frac{2}{10}$

Try It!

Use the Identity Property of Multiplication. Write three equivalent fractions.

1. $\frac{4}{5}$ 2. $\frac{1}{8}$ 3. $\frac{2}{6}$ 4. $\frac{1}{3}$ 5. $\frac{1}{5}$

6. $\frac{2}{3}$ 7. $\frac{3}{5}$ 8. $\frac{1}{10}$ 9. $\frac{3}{10}$ 10. $\frac{5}{8}$

Round these numbers to the nearest 100.

11. 439 12. 5,435,678 13. 51 14. 106 15. 1,357,399

Think About It

16. Explain how you used multiplication of fractions and the Identity Property to find the equivalent fractions.

A Simpler Way?

CONNECT AND COMMUNICATE

Find a way to write $\frac{18}{24}$ in simplest terms and write the steps in your notebook.

Why do you suppose $\frac{1}{2}$ is not called $\frac{3}{6}$ or $\frac{30}{60}$? **Simplifying** the fractions you sometimes get when you multiply will make measuring and cooking a lot easier!

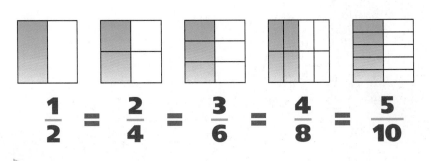

$$\frac{1}{2} = \frac{2}{4} = \frac{3}{6} = \frac{4}{8} = \frac{5}{10}$$

24/36

- Key in 24 **/** 36 on your calculator.
- Press **simp** and then **=**. What happened? Record the result.
- Press **simp** and **=** again. Record your results.
- Continue pressing **simp** and **=**. Record your results. What operation does the calculator do each time?

ACTIVITY 1 Simplifying Terms

With Your Class   Look at the equivalent fractions above. Why is $\frac{2}{4}$ in simpler terms than $\frac{8}{16}$? Which fraction do you think is in **simplest terms**? Explain your choice.

With Your Partner

1 Think about how you could simplify $\frac{24}{36}$. Try using a calculator. Read the instructions on this calculator to simplify.

2 Use your calculator to simplify the fractions on the top of the next page. What happens to the numerator and denominator at each step? How can you tell that the fraction is in simplest terms?

a. $\frac{6}{15}$ b. $\frac{30}{40}$ c. $\frac{48}{60}$ d. $\frac{24}{100}$ e. $\frac{42}{70}$ f. $\frac{25}{100}$

On Your Own You can find the simplest terms for a fraction such as $\frac{6}{24}$ in just one step—use common factors.

- Key in 6 $\boxed{/}$ 24 on your calculator.
- Press $\boxed{simp}$ then $\boxed{6}$ and then $\boxed{=}$. Why does this work?

Now simplify the fractions above to simplest terms in one step. Name the common factor you use.

✔ **Self-Check** *How does knowing common factors help you find the simplest terms for a fraction in one step?*

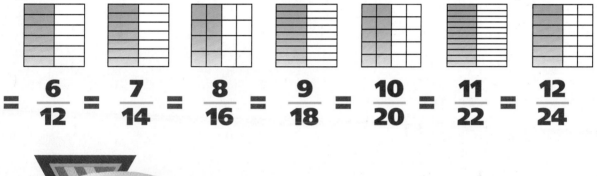

$= \dfrac{6}{12} = \dfrac{7}{14} = \dfrac{8}{16} = \dfrac{9}{18} = \dfrac{10}{20} = \dfrac{11}{22} = \dfrac{12}{24}$

Do You Remember?

Try It!

Find a pattern in the common factors you use to change these fractions into simplest terms.

1. $\frac{10}{14}$ 2. $\frac{6}{9}$ 3. $\frac{12}{20}$ 4. $\frac{20}{25}$ 5. $\frac{30}{36}$

Find the first two common multiples of each pair of numbers.

6. 2 and 3   7. 4 and 6   8. 3 and 5
9. 5 and 10   10. 3 and 4

Think About It

11. Write two more exercises that follow the pattern you found in Exercises 1–5.

A World of Spices

Let your nose be the guide at your neighborhood spice shop. There you'll find sweet cinnamon, hot curry, and saffron. Saffron is the most costly spice of all, because it takes about 50,000 crocus flower parts to make a pound.

1 A clove tree produces about 40,000 buds each year. Use a place value chart to show the total number of buds produced by a clove tree in ten years.

Cloves
Madagascar
75¢ per ounce

Curry Powder
India
29¢ per ounce

Coriander
Mexico
$4.80 per pound

Cloves.

Saffron
Spain
$183.00 per ounce

2 Choose any four spices. Find the average price for $\frac{1}{2}$ oz.

3 Curry powder is on sale for 10¢ off per ounce today. How much does it cost per pound?

4 If you had the weight of your textbook in saffron, estimate how much it would cost.

5 Europeans traded gold for peppercorns for hundreds of years. At today's prices estimate how many pounds of peppercorns you would need to buy something that costs $100.

 6 The United States imports 50,000,000 lb of pepper a year. What is the market value of this pepper?

7 Which spice is the least expensive? How do you know?

8 A recipe calls for equal parts of cinnamon and coriander. Can you buy $\frac{1}{2}$ oz of each and get change for 50¢? Explain.

 9 Your shopping list includes $\frac{1}{2}$ oz cinnamon, 1 oz nutmeg, and $\frac{1}{3}$ oz cloves. How much change should you get from a $5 bill?

Check Your Math Power

10 Choose a favorite food that includes some of these spices. Describe how you would estimate the weight of one spice and its cost.

Black Peppercorn
Brazil

$4.64 per pound

Cinnamon
China

38¢ per ounce

Nutmeg
Indonesia

$12.64 per pound

Sweet Basil
Italy

45¢ per ounce

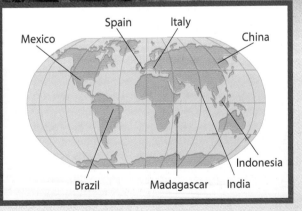

LESSON 8

Hello, World

How could you talk with a friend if you each spoke a different language? Having a common language or a translator helps people communicate. Giving fractions that have different denominators something in common makes them easier to compare.

What You'll Need
• *Fraction Tool or ruler*

Hello

ACTIVITY 1 ▶ Talking in Your Class

With Your Class People in the United States speak many languages besides English.

1. Survey your class. What fraction of it speaks a language other than English at home? What fraction does not? Record both fractions on the chalkboard. How could you sketch a model to show which fraction is greater?

你好

2 Compare your class's fraction with Colorado's. How could you compare these fractions by using mental math? Which is closer to 0? to 1? How could you use the Fraction Tool to show which is greater? Record and explain your answers.

☑ **Self-Check** *Why is it easy to compare fractions that have the same denominator?*

With Your Partner Which state listed on this page has the greatest fraction of people who speak a language other than English at home? List fractions from the chart in order from greatest to least. Share your answer with the class and explain how you decided the order.

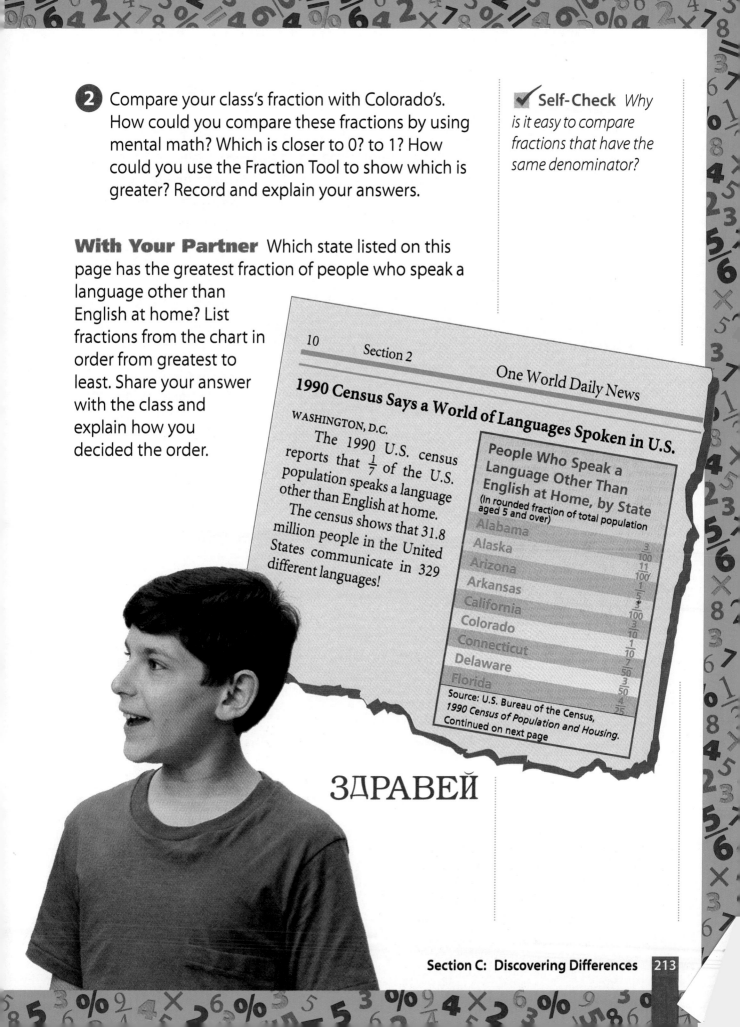

10   Section 2

One World Daily News

1990 Census Says a World of Languages Spoken in U.S.

WASHINGTON, D.C.
The 1990 U.S. census reports that $\frac{1}{7}$ of the U.S. population speaks a language other than English at home. The census shows that 31.8 million people in the United States communicate in 329 different languages!

People Who Speak a Language Other Than English at Home, by State
(In rounded fraction of total population aged 5 and over)

Alabama	
Alaska	$\frac{3}{100}$
Arizona	$\frac{11}{100}$
Arkansas	$\frac{1}{5}$
California	$\frac{5}{100}$
Colorado	$\frac{3}{10}$
Connecticut	$\frac{1}{10}$
Delaware	$\frac{7}{50}$
Florida	$\frac{3}{50}$
	$\frac{4}{25}$

Source: U.S. Bureau of the Census, 1990 Census of Population and Housing. Continued on next page

ЗДРАВЕЙ

In Your Journal
Synonyms are different words that have the same or nearly the same meaning. How are equivalent fractions like synonyms? How could equivalent fractions help you compare fractions that have different denominators?

ACTIVITY 2 Compare a Pair

On Your Own Writing equivalent fractions can help you compare fractions that have different denominators. Use what you know to figure out in which of the following states a greater fraction of the population speaks a language other than English at home.

1 Use mental math or sketching to compare the fractions for Minnesota and New Jersey. Which is greater? Record your estimate.

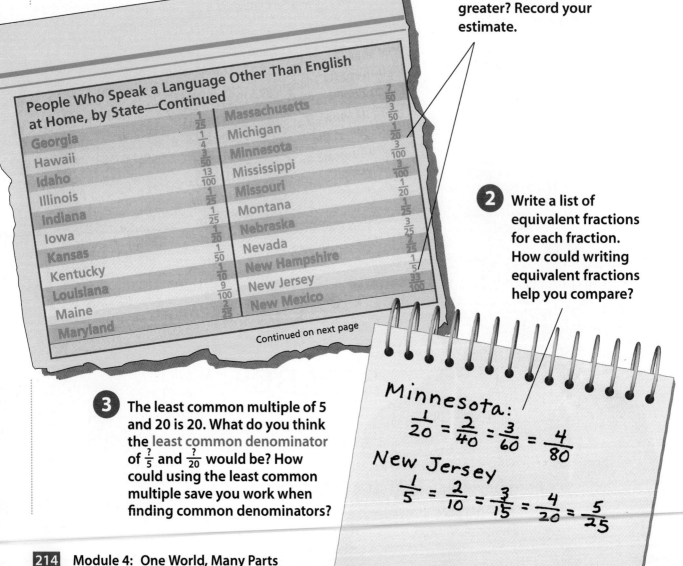

People Who Speak a Language Other Than English at Home, by State—Continued			
Georgia	$\frac{1}{25}$	Massachusetts	$\frac{7}{50}$
Hawaii	$\frac{1}{4}$	Michigan	$\frac{3}{50}$
Idaho	$\frac{3}{50}$	Minnesota	$\frac{1}{20}$
Illinois	$\frac{13}{100}$	Mississippi	$\frac{3}{100}$
Indiana	$\frac{1}{25}$	Missouri	$\frac{3}{100}$
Iowa	$\frac{1}{25}$	Montana	$\frac{1}{20}$
Kansas	$\frac{1}{20}$	Nebraska	$\frac{1}{25}$
Kentucky	$\frac{1}{50}$	Nevada	$\frac{3}{25}$
Louisiana	$\frac{1}{10}$	New Hampshire	$\frac{2}{25}$
Maine	$\frac{9}{100}$	New Jersey	$\frac{1}{5}$
Maryland	$\frac{2}{25}$	New Mexico	$\frac{33}{100}$

Continued on next page

2 Write a list of equivalent fractions for each fraction. How could writing equivalent fractions help you compare?

3 The least common multiple of 5 and 20 is 20. What do you think the least common denominator of $\frac{?}{5}$ and $\frac{?}{20}$ would be? How could using the least common multiple save you work when finding common denominators?

Minnesota:
$$\frac{1}{20} = \frac{2}{40} = \frac{3}{60} = \frac{4}{80}$$
New Jersey
$$\frac{1}{5} = \frac{2}{10} = \frac{3}{15} = \frac{4}{20} = \frac{5}{25}$$

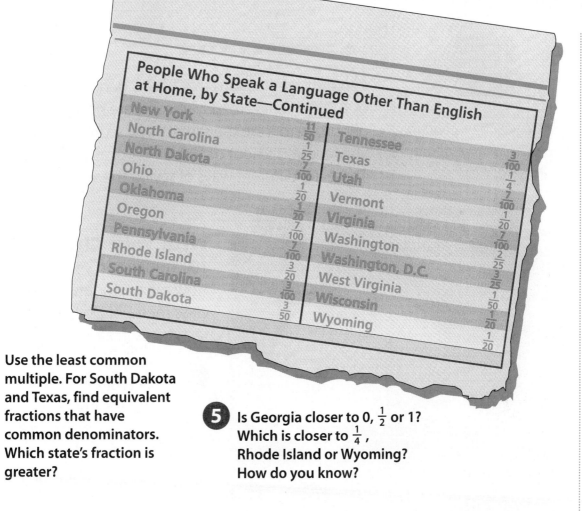

People Who Speak a Language Other Than English at Home, by State—Continued

New York			Tennessee	
North Carolina	$\frac{11}{50}$		Texas	$\frac{3}{100}$
North Dakota	$\frac{1}{25}$		Utah	$\frac{1}{4}$
Ohio	$\frac{7}{100}$		Vermont	$\frac{7}{100}$
Oklahoma	$\frac{1}{20}$		Virginia	$\frac{1}{20}$
Oregon	$\frac{1}{20}$		Washington	$\frac{7}{100}$
Pennsylvania	$\frac{7}{100}$		Washington, D.C.	$\frac{2}{25}$
Rhode Island	$\frac{7}{100}$		West Virginia	$\frac{3}{25}$
South Carolina	$\frac{3}{20}$		Wisconsin	$\frac{1}{50}$
South Dakota	$\frac{3}{100}$		Wyoming	$\frac{1}{20}$
	$\frac{3}{50}$			$\frac{1}{20}$

4 Use the least common multiple. For South Dakota and Texas, find equivalent fractions that have common denominators. Which state's fraction is greater?

5 Is Georgia closer to 0, $\frac{1}{2}$ or 1? Which is closer to $\frac{1}{4}$, Rhode Island or Wyoming? How do you know?

With Your Partner Refer to the charts in Activities 1 and 2 and present the data from all 50 states in a report. Order the fractions from greatest to least and identify your state on the list.

ACTIVITY 3 More or Less

With Your Partner Have each partner write fractions on ten strips of paper. Put them face down. Choose two strips and compare. Use estimation, modeling, or equivalent fractions to explain to your partner how you decided which one was greater.

TOOLS AND TECHNIQUES

Using a common multiple as a common denominator makes comparing fractions easy.

$\frac{2}{3}$ ■ $\frac{5}{8}$

The common multiple of 3 and 8 is 24.

$\frac{2}{3} = \frac{16}{24}$

$\frac{5}{8} = \frac{15}{24}$

Design your own chart to show the findings about your school.

ACTIVITY 4 **Percents**

Percents are fractions that have a denominator of 100. Percents are easy to compare because the denominators are the same. If you scored 95% on a test, you received 95 out of 100, or $\frac{95}{100}$ of all possible points. These are different ways of saying the same thing.

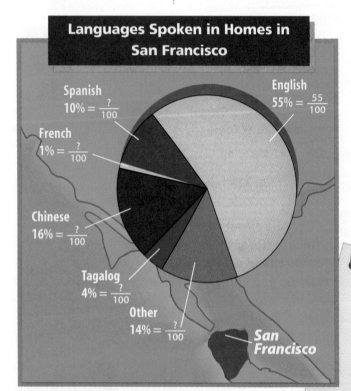

Languages Spoken in Homes in San Francisco

Spanish
$10\% = \frac{?}{100}$

French
$1\% = \frac{?}{100}$

Chinese
$16\% = \frac{?}{100}$

Tagalog
$4\% = \frac{?}{100}$

Other
$14\% = \frac{?}{100}$

English
$55\% = \frac{55}{100}$

San Francisco

Source: U.S. Bureau of the Census, *1990 Census of Population and Housing.*

With Your Class Survey 100 students in your school. How many students must each class member poll to get 100 responses in all?

1 During lunch or recess ask these questions:

• Have you been surveyed yet? If the answer is yes, you will have to find another student.

• Have you heard languages other than English?

• What languages do you speak?

Look at the charts for San Francisco and New York City. In which city does a greater fraction speak Chinese? French? Spanish?

2 Record your findings on the board in your classroom. Decide how to organize the data.

3 What fraction of students surveyed have heard languages other than English?

4 Record the fraction of students who speak each language.

5 Change these fractions into percents. Order the percents from least to greatest.

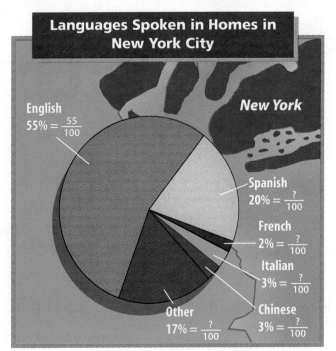

Languages Spoken in Homes in New York City

New York

English 55% = $\frac{55}{100}$

Spanish 20% = $\frac{?}{100}$

French 2% = $\frac{?}{100}$

Italian 3% = $\frac{?}{100}$

Chinese 3% = $\frac{?}{100}$

Other 17% = $\frac{?}{100}$

Source: U.S. Bureau of the Census, *1990 Census of Population and Housing.*

Do You Remember?

Try It!

Write the percents as fractions and fractions as percents.

1. $\frac{78}{100}$ **2.** $\frac{16}{100}$ **3.** $\frac{1}{100}$

4. 40%   **5.** 93%   **6.** 100%

Write number sentences for each situation using variables.

7. The number of boys is greater than 28.

8. The percent of buyers is less than 20%.

9. The number of boys is 9 more than the number of girls.

Solve.

10. $\frac{1}{4} \times \frac{2}{5} = n$ **11.** $\frac{7}{8} \times \frac{1}{2} = n$ **12.** $\frac{3}{4} \times 8 = n$

13. $\frac{4}{5} \times \frac{5}{4} = n$ **14.** $\frac{7}{12} \times n = \frac{7}{12}$ **15.** $\frac{4}{5} \times n = 0$

Think About It

16. Write why you think percents are easy to compare.

Measure Up

How far away are you from Montego Bay? How many miles? How many feet? Measurement can help you plan explorations in any part of the world.

What You'll Need
- *Fraction Tool or inch ruler*

ACTIVITY 1 Give 'em an Inch

With Your Partner Plan a trip to visit ten places around California in any order you choose.

1 Select and list your ten sites.

2 Use your ruler or Fraction Tool to measure the distance between places on the map to the nearest $\frac{1}{8}$ in. Record.

3 Use the scale to determine the number of miles between sites. Record.

4 Describe your entire trip in order and the distance between each site. Include the math you used.

Equivalents:
 1 mi = 5,280 ft
 1 yd = 3 ft
 1 ft = 12 in.

How can you determine the number of yards in a mile if you know the number of feet in a mile?

Notice that each inch is divided into 16 parts, or sixteenths.

How many sixteenths do you find in 1 in.? $1\frac{1}{8}$ in.? 2 in.? How do you know?

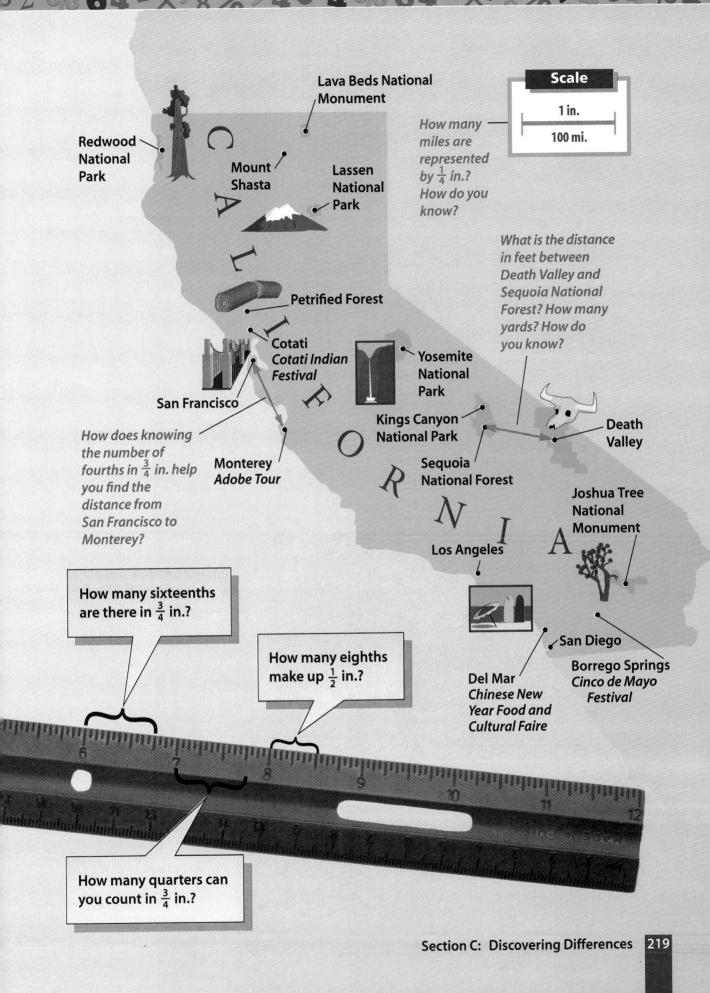

Scale

1 in.

100 mi.

How many miles are represented by $\frac{1}{4}$ in.? How do you know?

Lava Beds National Monument

Redwood National Park

C A L I F O R N I A

Mount Shasta

Lassen National Park

What is the distance in feet between Death Valley and Sequoia National Forest? How many yards? How do you know?

Petrified Forest

Cotati
Cotati Indian Festival

Yosemite National Park

San Francisco

How does knowing the number of fourths in $\frac{3}{4}$ in. help you find the distance from San Francisco to Monterey?

Monterey
Adobe Tour

Kings Canyon National Park

Death Valley

Sequoia National Forest

Joshua Tree National Monument

Los Angeles

How many sixteenths are there in $\frac{3}{4}$ in.?

How many eighths make up $\frac{1}{2}$ in.?

San Diego

Del Mar
Chinese New Year Food and Cultural Faire

Borrego Springs
Cinco de Mayo Festival

How many quarters can you count in $\frac{3}{4}$ in.?

ACTIVITY 2 **Matching Mixes**

Would you rather have 4 quarters or 1 dollar? What about 10 dimes or 100 cents? Just as these amounts are equal, $1\frac{1}{2}$ and $\frac{3}{2}$ mean the same thing. You choose which to use in different situations.

With Your Partner   Select five measurements from the map on page 219. Model them as mixed numbers. Trade numbers with your partner and turn each other's numbers into fractions greater than one.

1 Record the process you use to get your results.

2 What patterns do you find in the numbers? How could you use multiplication and addition to change the mixed numbers? Write a rule.

3 Test your rule with these mixed numbers: $1\frac{1}{3}$, $2\frac{2}{3}$, $4\frac{1}{6}$, $6\frac{2}{5}$. Have your partner check your work by drawing a picture.

How many halves are there in $1\frac{1}{2}$? How can that help you change any mixed number to a fraction greater than one?

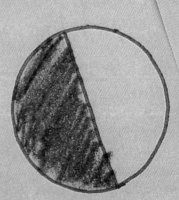

$$\frac{4}{3} =$$

How many wholes are there in $\frac{4}{3}$?

ACTIVITY OPTION

Where do you find mixed numbers in your life? Make up five problems to exchange with your partner. Use mixed numbers and fractions greater than one.

With Your Partner Write five different measurements as fractions greater than one. Trade fractions with your partner and turn each other's fractions into mixed numbers.

1 Record the process you use to get your results.

2 What patterns do you find in the fractions? How could you use division to change the fractions? Write a rule.

3 Test your rule with these fractions: $\frac{8}{3}$, $\frac{13}{2}$, $\frac{7}{5}$, $\frac{12}{6}$. Have your partner check your work by drawing a picture.

What You'll Need
- *Fraction Tool or ruler*
- *10 blank cards*

Mixing It Up

With Your Group Select two of the following games to play in any order you choose.

1 **Estimation Game** Each person chooses an object. Then everyone in the group guesses the length of each object. Record the estimates and measure the object.

The person whose estimate comes closest receives four points, the second closest gets three, the third closest two, and the fourth closest one. At the end of the game, the player with the most points wins!

To earn double points, show your estimates as mixed numbers and as fractions greater than one.

Key length

Estimate = 1 in.

Actual: $\frac{7}{8}$ in.

2 **Scavenger Hunt** Translate each of these fractions greater than one into mixed numbers. Have each person find objects whose estimated lengths, in inches or feet, match each number. Measure all the objects. Whoever has the closest estimates wins!

$$\frac{7}{2}, \frac{5}{4}, \frac{13}{4}, \frac{43}{8}$$

③ Concentrate Both players make five pairs of cards. Each pair includes one card with a mixed number on it and one card with the same number written as a fraction greater than one. Place the cards face down. Take turns trying to turn over a pair of cards with matching numbers. Keep the cards when you make a match. Play until all the cards are gone.

Try It!

Change the following fractions greater than one into mixed numbers. Order them from least to greatest.

1. $\frac{7}{4}$ 2. $\frac{17}{3}$ 3. $\frac{4}{2}$

4. $\frac{21}{5}$ 5. $\frac{35}{10}$ 6. $\frac{8}{7}$

Copy the square onto dot paper. In the square draw a shape that has the given perimeter. Name the part of the whole square you have drawn.

7. 6 units   8. 12 units

9. 14 units   10. 4 units

11. 8 units   12. 16 units

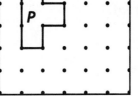

Perimeter P = 10 units
$P = \frac{1}{9}$ of square

Think About It

13. Describe how you ordered the fractions in Exercises 1–6.

Investigation

A Fraction of Time

Mutale, a fifth grader in Zambia, goes to school from noon to 5:00 P.M. each day. A group of her friends attends the same school from 7:00 A.M. to noon. Here's how Mutale spends her day.

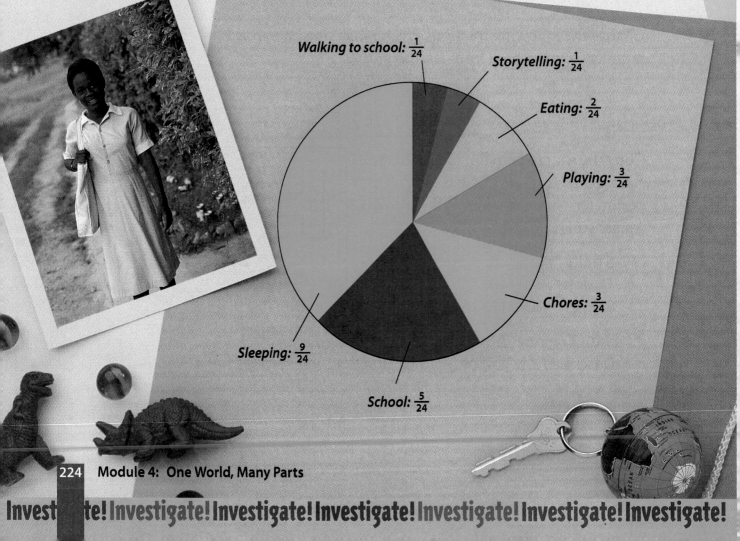

Walking to school: $\frac{1}{24}$
Storytelling: $\frac{1}{24}$
Eating: $\frac{2}{24}$
Playing: $\frac{3}{24}$
Chores: $\frac{3}{24}$
School: $\frac{5}{24}$
Sleeping: $\frac{9}{24}$

In this investigation you will collect data on how you spend the hours of your day. Then you will compare your day with Mutale's. If you prefer, you can compare your day with another person's.

How will you record each activity? You may round each time to the nearest half hour or hour. How might rounding make your total greater or less than 24 hours?

Tuesday

7:30 – 8:00   Get ready and eat breakfast

8:00 – 8:30   Walk to school

8:30 – 12:00   School

12:00 – 12:30   Lunch

12:30 – 3:30   School

3:30 – 5:30   Play with friends

5:30 –

1 Pick a typical day. Throughout the day make notes in your journal.

What to Include in My Report

- journal entries of the time I spent on each activity
- a graph or chart showing how my day is divided into fractions
- a comparison of my day with the typical day of a fifth grader from a different country.

2 Change the hours you spend on each activity into a fraction of your typical day. Use your Fraction Tool to make a circle graph like Mutale's.

3 Make a report to your class. Why should the fractions of your day total exactly $\frac{24}{24}$?

Ask Yourself

☐ What kinds of things do you do each day?
☐ How much time do you spend on each activity?
☐ How many hours are there in a day?
☐ Do your fractions add up to a whole day? Why or why not?
☐ How can you show the information you have found?

Adding and Subtracting Fractions

Fraction Addition

Look around you and you'll discover a world of fractions. Choose a country you would like to learn more about. Then build a boxed scene, or diorama, to display what you have learned. You might include flags, recipes, maps, charts, and a list of languages.

How does Mexico's flag show the fraction $\frac{1}{3}$?

What languages would you hear in your country?

What will you display about the country you choose?

BRAZIL

Languages Spoken
English
German
Italian
Portuguese
official language
Spanish
Tupian

What fraction of all the languages spoken in Brazil is Tupian?

ᴬᶜᵀᶦᵛᴵᵀʸ 1 Summing Sames

With Your Group   Discuss how you can use the blueprint below to figure out the dimensions of the paper you will need to make the diorama.

What You'll Need
• *Fraction Tool or inch ruler*
• *construction paper*

1 Write equations to show your paper's length and width. Then use fraction models to help you find the sums and check your answers.

2 Look at the equation for the width of the paper:

$2\frac{1}{8} + 6\frac{1}{4} + 2\frac{1}{8} = n$

How could you use the Commutative and Associative properties of addition to rewrite this problem to make it easier to solve?

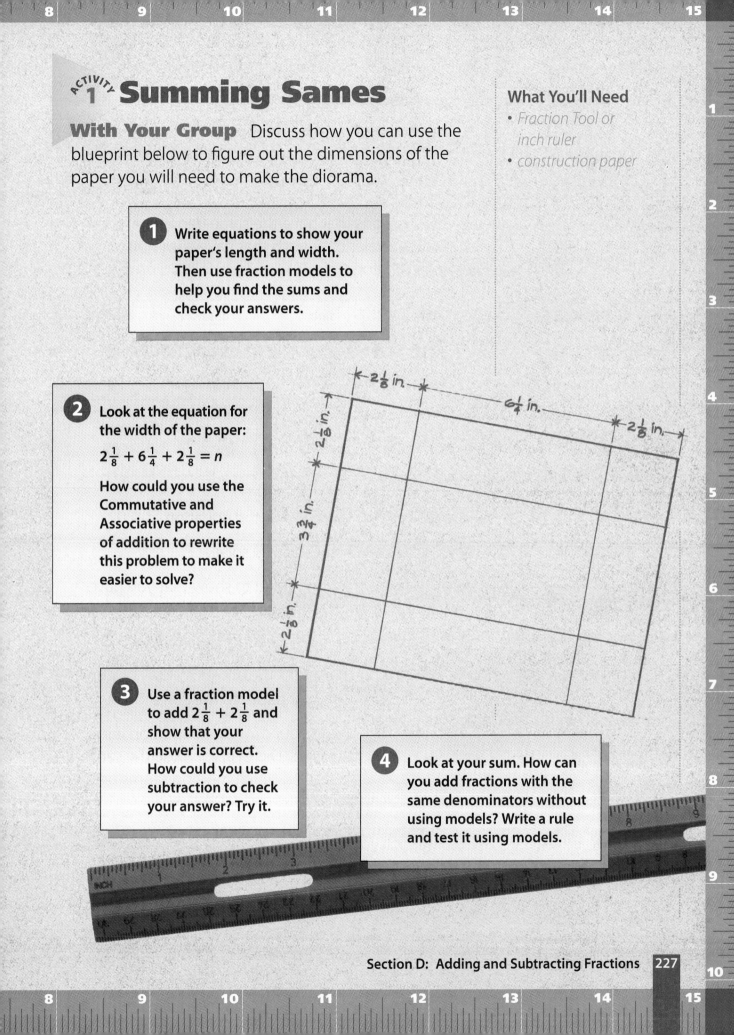

$2\frac{1}{8}$ in. $6\frac{1}{4}$ in. $2\frac{1}{8}$ in.

$2\frac{1}{8}$ in.

$3\frac{3}{4}$ in.

$2\frac{1}{8}$ in.

3 Use a fraction model to add $2\frac{1}{8} + 2\frac{1}{8}$ and show that your answer is correct. How could you use subtraction to check your answer? Try it.

4 Look at your sum. How can you add fractions with the same denominators without using models? Write a rule and test it using models.

Section D: Adding and Subtracting Fractions   **227**

DRAWING TO LEARN

Tracing Tool *Use your Tracing Tool to model the equation on this page. Explain how drawing a picture of the equation helped you find equivalent fractions and common denominators.*

ACTIVITY 2 Adding Unlikes

With Your Partner   You have solved part of the problem, but how can you find the width of the paper you'll need to make the base of your box? You know how to do the following:

- Add fractions that have the same denominators.
- Find equivalent fractions that have common denominators.

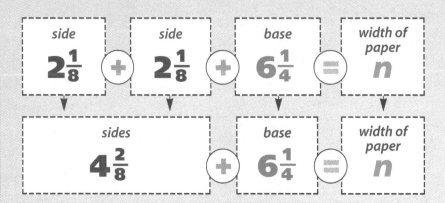

side $2\frac{1}{8}$ **+** side $2\frac{1}{8}$ **+** base $6\frac{1}{4}$ **=** width of paper n

sides $4\frac{2}{8}$ **+** base $6\frac{1}{4}$ **=** width of paper n

Use what you know to solve the equation.

1 Record your steps as you solve.

2 Choose a fraction model to show that you have found the right answer.

3 Use the same process to find the length of the paper. Use the blueprint.

4 Cut your paper to the correct size.

5 Share your process of addition with the class. Did everyone use the same method? Which method seems best? Why?

On Your Own Now make your box.

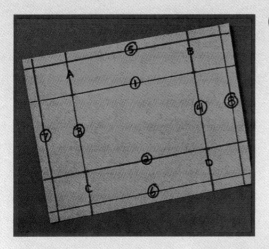

6 Follow the drawing to make lines 1, 2, 3, and 4, and half-inch borders labeled 5, 6, 7, and 8. These borders will become the tabs that attach to the top of the box. Label segments *A, B, C,* and *D* as shown.

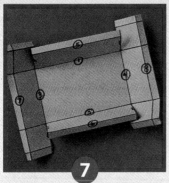

7

Fold lines 1–4 inward. Unfold so the paper is flat. Next fold lines 5–8 outward and unfold. Cut line segments *A, B, C,* and *D*.

8

Create your diorama. Decorate the inside of your box with the objects and pictures you have chosen. Keep in mind which way is up and which panels are top and bottom.

9

Fold the creased sides up to create a box, keeping the flaps on the outside of the box. Glue the sides together.

10

Cut the corners down to the $\frac{1}{2}$-in. folds you made and bend the flaps away from the box. You will use the opened flaps later to attach the top.

CONNECT AND COMMUNICATE

Try writing your answers in simplest terms.

ACTIVITY 3 Boxed In

On Your Own Figure out what size paper you would need to build the two boxes below. Compare your answers with a friend's. Then write a rule for adding mixed numbers with different denominators.

1

←— $3\frac{1}{8}$ in. —→ ←— $4\frac{3}{16}$ in. —→ ←— $3\frac{1}{8}$ in. —→

$3\frac{1}{8}$ in.

$2\frac{3}{16}$ in.

$3\frac{1}{8}$ in.

2

←— $4\frac{1}{4}$ in. —→ ←— $5\frac{3}{16}$ in. —→ ←— $4\frac{1}{4}$ in. —→

$4\frac{1}{4}$ in.

$3\frac{1}{2}$ in.

$4\frac{1}{4}$ in.

Do You Remember?

Try It!

Find the sums. Change any fraction greater than one into a mixed number, and write your answers in simplest terms.

1. $\frac{1}{2} + \frac{1}{3}$ 2. $\frac{7}{8} + \frac{2}{3}$ 3. $\frac{3}{10} + \frac{1}{2}$

4. $4\frac{1}{2} + 9\frac{7}{10}$ 5. $1\frac{4}{5} + 2\frac{5}{6}$ 6. $12\frac{7}{10} + 3\frac{1}{5}$

For each amount write the fewest pennies, nickels, dimes, quarters, and dollars you would get in change from a $5 bill.

7. $.28   8. $1.92   9. $2.06   10. $3.55   11. $4.73

Think About It

12. Write a sentence telling why you need to find a common denominator before you can add fractions that have different denominators.

Fraction Subtraction

ACTIVITY 1 Framing the Box

With Your Class Make a frame for your box. First cut your paper to the length and width shown on the blueprint. Then find the length and width of the window. Use what you know to write two equations to find the window's dimensions.

What You'll Need
- *Fraction Tool or inch ruler*
- *construction paper*
- *scissors*

How wide is each border? What numbers do you need to subtract to find the length and width of the window?

$2\frac{3}{16}$ in.

$2\frac{7}{16}$ in.

$2\frac{7}{16}$ in.

$9\frac{1}{4}$ in.

$2\frac{3}{16}$ in.

9 in.

What is the width of the paper? What is the length?

REASONING AND PROBLEM SOLVING

Think about equivalent fractions for one:
$1 = \frac{1}{1}, \frac{2}{2}, \frac{3}{3}, \frac{4}{4}$
Explain why writing 9 as $8\frac{16}{16}$ will help you subtract.

Section D: Adding and Subtracting Fractions 231

ACTIVITY 2 **Opening the Window**

With Your Group Find your own way to figure out how large the window on your box should be.

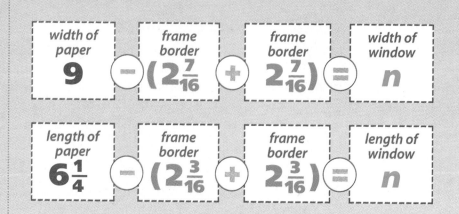

width of paper		frame border		frame border		width of window
9	$-$	$(2\frac{7}{16}$	$+$	$2\frac{7}{16})$	$=$	n

length of paper		frame border		frame border		length of window
$6\frac{1}{4}$	$-$	$(2\frac{3}{16}$	$+$	$2\frac{3}{16})$	$=$	n

Think about what makes these subtractions different from others you have done. How can you use what you know to figure out the length and width of your window? You can take the following steps:

• Rename a whole number as a mixed number.
• Write equivalent fractions with the same denominators.
• Add and subtract fractions with the same denominators.

1 Use what you know to find the window's length and width.

2 Check your answers with your Fraction Tool, ruler, or another model.

3 Compare your group's method with other groups'.

REASONING AND PROBLEM SOLVING

Why can you subtract $4\frac{14}{16}$ from 9 to find the width of the window? Why might you simplify $4\frac{14}{16}$ before subtracting?

4

Using the blueprint and your calculations, draw the window in the center of the frame and cut it out.

5

Decorate the frame. Visually center your box on the back of the frame. Glue the $\frac{1}{2}$-in. flaps to the frame to attach it.

ACTIVITY 3

Making a Difference

With Your Partner   Maria took these steps to subtract fractions that have different denominators. Explain what Maria did in each step. How does her method compare with yours?

$$4\tfrac{1}{3} - 2\tfrac{5}{8} = n$$ — *Why can't she subtract yet?*

$$4\tfrac{8}{24} - 2\tfrac{15}{24} = n$$ — *What does she have to do before she can subtract?*

$$3\tfrac{32}{24} - 2\tfrac{15}{24} = n$$ — *Can she subtract now?*

ACTIVITY OPTION

Describe the rule and complete.

Input	$\frac{3}{4}$	$\frac{5}{8}$	$\frac{1}{2}$	$\frac{7}{10}$
Output	$\frac{1}{4}$	$\frac{1}{8}$	0	n

Then make up a chart for your partner to fill in.

Section D: Adding and Subtracting Fractions   **233**

Inching Along

What You'll Need
- *gameboard*
- *scissors*
- *crayons or markers*
- *spinner*

ACTIVITY 4 Measure for Measure

With Your Group Knowing how to add and subtract fractions and mixed numbers will make you a winner at this game. Use the ruled board to check your work. Here's how to play.

1 Make 25-30 fraction cards. Use 2, 4, or 8 as denominators. Make a few bonus cards, too. Then make an addition/subtraction spinner.

add
+
$6\frac{1}{2}$
⊕

subtract
$\frac{3}{8}$
⊕

2 For the first turn, each player takes a card from the addition pile and moves to the number on the card. Be sure to record the number in your notebook.

3 For the second turn, each player spins to decide whether to take a card from the addition or subtraction pile. Add or subtract the number you picked from the one in your notebook. The result tells you how far to move on the board. Now it's the next player's turn.

4 If you pick a bonus card (marked with a star), keep it and select another addition or subtraction card. Bonus cards allow you to change the sign on this turn or a different turn. Use your bonus card when it will help you get to a starred space on the board and advance more quickly.

5 The first player to the finish line wins!

Do You Remember?

Try It!

Add only the mixed numbers whose sums are greater than ten.

1. $9\frac{4}{10} + \frac{7}{8}$　　**2.** $4\frac{2}{5} + 5\frac{5}{6}$　　**3.** $\frac{7}{8} + 9\frac{1}{16}$　　**4.** $1\frac{5}{8} + 8\frac{2}{3}$

Find only the differences that are less than four.

5. $6 - 2\frac{5}{8}$　　**6.** $13\frac{2}{3} - 9\frac{4}{5}$　　**7.** $5 - 1\frac{3}{8}$　　**8.** $16\frac{1}{4} - 11\frac{2}{3}$

9. Place each answer from Exercises 1–8 on a number line.

Estimate quotients to the nearest 100 for these division exercises.

10. $45\overline{)9{,}300}$　　**11.** $14\overline{)6{,}200}$　　**12.** $20\overline{)56{,}902}$

13. $5\overline{)98{,}765}$　　**14.** $33\overline{)99{,}999{,}999}$　　**15.** $5\overline{)2{,}012}$

Think About It

16. How can you estimate a sum or difference, as in Exercises 1–8, without changing to a common denominator?

Looking Back

Choose the right answer. Write *a, b, c,* or *d* for each question.

Use the flag to answer Exercises 1–3.

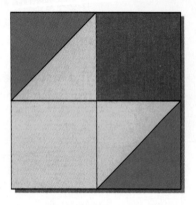

1. Find the fraction colored blue.

   a. $\frac{1}{2} - \frac{1}{2}$ b. $\frac{1}{2} \times \frac{1}{2}$

   c. $\frac{3}{4} \times 1$ d. $\frac{1}{8} + \frac{1}{4}$

2. Find the fraction colored yellow.

   a. $\frac{1}{8} \times 3$ b. $1 - \frac{2}{3}$

   c. $\frac{1}{8} \times 4$ d. $\frac{1}{2} + \frac{1}{4}$

3. Measure and compare to find the largest perimeter.

   a. yellow portion
   b. blue portion
   c. whole flag
   d. all perimeters are equal

4. On the number line below, *P* is closest to this number.

   a. $\frac{15}{16}$ b. $\frac{7}{8}$

   c. $\frac{3}{4}$ d. $\frac{9}{10}$

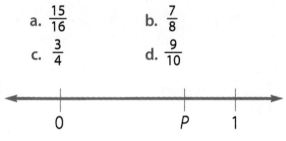

5. Choose the set of fractions that is ordered from least to greatest.

   a. $\frac{3}{6}$ $\frac{3}{8}$ $\frac{3}{9}$ $\frac{3}{10}$

   b. $\frac{2}{3}$ $\frac{3}{4}$ $\frac{4}{5}$ $\frac{5}{6}$

   c. $\frac{1}{8}$ $\frac{2}{10}$ $\frac{3}{5}$ $\frac{4}{16}$

   d. $\frac{2}{5}$ $\frac{3}{8}$ $\frac{4}{10}$ $\frac{5}{8}$

6. Choose the set of numbers that is ordered from greatest to least.

   a. $\frac{11}{4}$ $2\frac{1}{3}$ $\frac{18}{8}$ $2\frac{1}{16}$

   b. $2\frac{2}{5}$ $1\frac{3}{4}$ $\frac{60}{20}$ $\frac{17}{10}$

   c. $\frac{5}{4}$ $\frac{3}{2}$ $1\frac{2}{3}$ $1\frac{1}{6}$

   d. $3\frac{5}{16}$ $\frac{25}{8}$ $\frac{20}{4}$ $2\frac{1}{2}$

7. Find two numbers whose greatest common factor is 16.

   a. 32 and 60
   b. 64 and 116
   c. 24 and 72
   d. 48 and 80

8. Which results in a product of 24?

   a. $\frac{2}{3} \times 36$　　　b. $\frac{1}{2} \times 48$

   c. $\frac{3}{4} \times 32$　　　d. a, b, and c

9. The estimated quotient 60 makes sense for which one of these division exercises?

   a. $12\overline{)932}$　　　b. $6\overline{)3,600}$
   c. $4\overline{)349}$　　　d. $39\overline{)2,463}$

10. Choose the set of equivalent fractions.

    a. $\frac{1}{4}$　$\frac{25}{100}$　$\frac{5}{20}$　$\frac{7}{30}$

    b. $\frac{8}{10}$　$\frac{16}{20}$　$\frac{4}{5}$　$\frac{12}{15}$

    c. $\frac{2}{3}$　$\frac{6}{12}$　$\frac{4}{9}$　$\frac{12}{18}$

    d. $\frac{3}{8}$　$\frac{16}{40}$　$\frac{6}{16}$　$\frac{9}{24}$

Use these equations to answer Exercises 11–12.

a. $\frac{2}{3} \times \frac{3}{8} = n$　　　b. $\frac{4}{5} \times \frac{5}{8} = n$

c. $\frac{5}{6} \times \frac{3}{9} = n$　　　d. $\frac{5}{6} \times \frac{9}{10} = n$

11. Which product is greatest?

12. Which product is least?

13. Find the number that does not equal $1\frac{2}{8}$.

    a. $\frac{5}{4}$　　　b. $\frac{10}{8}$

    c. $\frac{28}{24}$　　　d. $\frac{20}{16}$

14. Find the number that equals $\frac{20}{16}$.

    a. $1\frac{1}{3}$　　　b. $1\frac{1}{4}$

    c. $1\frac{1}{2}$　　　d. $1\frac{1}{6}$

Find _n_ for the following.

15. $1\frac{1}{2} + n = 1\frac{2}{3}$

    a. $\frac{3}{6}$　b. $\frac{1}{4}$　c. $\frac{1}{3}$　d. $\frac{1}{6}$

16. $n - \frac{3}{8} = 1\frac{5}{8}$

    a. $1\frac{2}{8}$　b. 2　c. $1\frac{1}{4}$　d. $2\frac{1}{4}$

17. Find the possible dimensions of a rectangle whose area is $\frac{3}{4}$ square inch.

    a. $\frac{1}{2}$ in. $\times \frac{3}{8}$ in.

    b. $\frac{2}{3}$ in. $\times \frac{9}{16}$ in.

    c. $\frac{1}{4}$ in. $\times 3$ in.

    d. $\frac{1}{2}$ in. $\times 2$ in.

Check Your Math Power

18. There are many mixed numbers between $4\frac{1}{2}$ and $4\frac{3}{4}$. List at least ten of them. Then write an explanation or draw a chart to show how you arrived at your answer.

Investigations

MODULE 4

Sizing Up the World

There are many different ways the world can be broken into parts. Fractions can help you compare and better understand the different parts of your world.

Investigation
A

A Nation of Nations

In this investigation you will explore South America and use fractions to relate its parts.

238

1 **Compare** the countries in South America using the data on the chart. Find the fraction of South America's total population and area that is represented by each country. Use rounding to help you work with these large numbers.

2 **Research** other information about countries in South America. Include any fractions you find in your report.

3 **Write** a report comparing the population of South American countries with their area. Use circle graphs of your fractions to analyze the data and draw conclusions about what this data tells you.

4 **Share** your graphs and data with your class. Be prepared to defend your data and conclusions.

South America

Country	Area in square meters	Population
Argentina	1,065,189	32,663,000
Bolivia	424,165	7,156,000
Brazil	3,286,470	148,000,000
Chile	292,257	13,286,000
Colombia	439,735	33,777,000
Ecuador	109,483	10,751,000
French Guiana	43,740	101,000
Guyana	83,000	748,000
Paraguay	157,047	4,798,000
Peru	496,222	22,361,000
Suriname	63,037	402,000
Uruguay	68,037	3,121,000
Venezuela	352,143	20,189,000

Source: *The World Almanac and Book of Facts*

Keep in Mind

Your report will be judged by how well you do the following things.

- ☐ Describe each country as a fractional part of a whole.
- ☐ Use appropriate mathematical terms to describe how you worked with the data to make the fractions.
- ☐ Show your discoveries using charts and graphs.
- ☐ Analyze your data and draw conclusions about how sets of data relate.

Investigation B — A World of Fractions

Choose any country in the world. Describe your country, using five different fractions. Then make a poster for your country. Include a chart or graph of your data. Point out where and how you used estimation with your data. Share your poster with your class.

Ongoing Investigation — Fractions of "Who We Are"

Use fractions to describe the population you are investigating. For example, you might find the fractions of the total population by different age groups, ethnic groups, or regions. Display your data in a circle graph or chart. What conclusions can you draw from your data?

Faster, Higher, Stronger

The three words above are the Olympic motto. Every two years, athletes from around the world join in a colorful opening ceremony. Then they compete in all types of sporting events. In this module you will learn how Olympic races are measured in metric units. You will use multiplication and division with decimals to score diving, gymnastics, and other events.

SECTION A

By a Split Second

SECTION B

Sizing It Up

SECTION C

You Be the Judge

SECTION D

Olympic Legends

Let the Games Begin!

People have been racing each other for thousands of years. The ancient Greeks held athletic contests at Olympia every four years to honor their god Zeus. Legend says the hero Hercules founded the games. In this excerpt, what kind of race is being run?

D o you remember
    How you won
That last race . . . ?
How you flung your body
At the start . . .
How your spikes
Ripped the cinders
In the stretch . . .
How you catapulted [hurled]
Through the tape . . .
Do you remember . . . ?

From "To James" by Frank Horne

1 Be an Olympian

Ancient Olympians competed to see who could throw a spear, called a javelin, the farthest. With your group see who can throw a long, slender balloon the farthest.

Balloon Javelin Scores

Gina   1 m 40cm

Miguel

Gary

Rhonda

2 Keep Track and Record

Measure and record the throws. Who is the class champion? The Greeks crowned champions with olive wreaths. How do people honor athletes today?

Investigations Preview

Learning to measure length, mass, and capacity with the metric system can help you develop "metric sense."

Paper Towel Olympics (pages 262–263)

Which paper towel is the strongest and holds the most water? Knowing how to measure in milliliters, millimeters, and grams will help you find out which towel wins the gold medal.

Who's Fastest? (pages 286–288)

Knowing how to use multiplication to convert units of measure will help you compare your speed with that of Olympic athletes, animals, or vehicles.

LESSON 1 Splitting Seconds

In Your Journal List three situations in which a difference of less than one second was important.

What You'll Need
• *centimeter ruler*

Olympic races are often decided by a fraction of a second. In sprint events, for example, several runners may finish within one half second of the winner. Quick reactions are important in these races. Here is a test of your reaction time.

ACTIVITY 1 Who's the Quickest?

With Your Partner How quickly can you catch a falling centimeter ruler? To help you measure, you can use **decimals**—numbers that show tenths, hundredths, and so on.

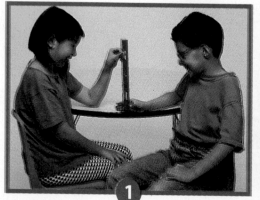

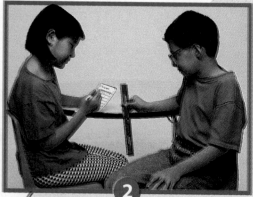

Drop and Catch

One student sits with an arm over the edge of a desk. The other holds the centimeter ruler, zero end down.

Judge the Catch

Your partner drops the ruler. Grab it as fast as you can. Record the centimeter mark at the top of your thumb. Try three catches.

Record Your Data

Copy the chart below. In the first column, record the distance the ruler traveled to the nearest centimeter. Then convert the centimeters into fractions of a **meter.** One meter is 100 centimeters long. In the third column write the fractions as decimals.

> **What fraction of a meter does each of the centimeters on the ruler represent?**

> **Why is it important to always measure to the same part of the thumb?**

Ruler Catch

cm	fraction	decimal
18	18/100	0.18

Tina

4 Compare Your Data

Order the decimals from least to greatest. Use >, <, and = to compare catches. Who had the fastest single catch? Who was fastest on average?

In the 1952 Olympics, four runners in the men's 100-m dash were timed at 10.4 seconds. How would you figure out how far each man ran in one tenth of a second?

ACTIVITY 2 Racing Against Time

On Your Own Study the table below. What changed in 1972?

1 Between 1928 and 1968, times are recorded in tenths. Order these times.

2 Between 1972 and 1992, times are recorded in hundredths. Order these times.

3 Order all the times. Who has the fastest time?

Women's 100-m Dash Gold Medal Winners

(Times shown in seconds)

Year	Winner	Time	Year	Winner	Time
1928	B. Robinson, United States	12.2	1972	R. Stecher, East Germany *	11.07
1932	S. Walsh, Poland	11.9	1976	A. Richter, West Germany *	11.08
1936	H. Stephens, United States	11.5	1980	L. Kondratyeva, Soviet Union	11.06
1948	F. Blankers-Koen, Holland	11.9	1984	E. Ashford, United States	10.97
1952	M. Jackson, Australia	11.5	1988	F. Griffith Joyner, United States	10.54
1956	B. Cuthbert, Australia	11.5	1992	G. Devers, United States	10.82
1960	W. Rudolph, United States	11.0			
1964	W. Tyus, United States	11.5			
1968	W. Tyus, United States	11.0			

* Between 1949 and 1990, Germany was divided into two countries.

Source: *The 1993 Information Please Sports Almanac*

ACTIVITY 3 Down to . . . ?

With Your Group In the decimal system, numbers can get greater and greater. Can they also get smaller?

1 What Comes Next?

The bar below shows the place-value system. Start at the left. What happens each time you move one place to the right? What should be the name of the column on the far right? Discuss with your group.

Thousands	Hundreds	Tens	Ones	.	Tenths	Hundredths	?

When reading numbers, say *and* for the decimal point. For 6.1, say *six and one tenth.*

Men's Singles Luge Top 3 Finishers

(Times shown in seconds)

Georg Hackl, Germany

45.190

45.351

46.026

45.796

Markus Prock, Austria

45.356

45.330

46.075

45.908

Markus Schmidt, Austria

45.243

45.416

46.254

46.029

Source: *New York Times,* February 11, 1992

2 Scoring the Luge

Use the place value chart to help you understand the times in the luge race. The luge (*loozh*) is a sled. The rider lies on his or her back. For each athlete, order the times from fastest to slowest. Estimate to the nearest tenth a sum for each athlete's times. Now add the times together. Based on the sums, who wins the gold medal?

③ Adding Thousandths

The number 0.001 shows one **thousandth**. Add 0.001 and 0.001 on your calculator. How many times would you add 0.001 to reach 0.01? 0.1? 1.0? In your journal describe the pattern you notice. Then explain why your calculator shows this sequence: 0.019, 0.02, 0.021. Why doesn't it show 0.020?

Decimal Pattern:

1. $0.001 + 0.001 =$

Do You Remember?

Try It!

Write each fraction as a decimal. Write a division statement that you can do on your calculator to check your answer.

1. $\frac{63}{100}$ 2. $\frac{19}{100}$ 3. $\frac{1}{100}$ 4. $\frac{217}{100}$

For each pair below, choose the greater and write it in words.

5. 36.2, 36.21   6. 8.9, 8.801   7. 1.482, 1.842   8. 4.01, 4.1

Find the fraction not in simplest terms. Write it in simplest terms.

9. $\frac{7}{16}$, $\frac{5}{30}$, $\frac{16}{25}$ 10. $2\frac{7}{10}$, $3\frac{7}{15}$, $4\frac{7}{35}$ 11. $\frac{6}{9}$, $\frac{6}{7}$, $\frac{6}{11}$

12. $5\frac{3}{16}$, $7\frac{5}{32}$, $8\frac{10}{16}$ 13. $\frac{7}{12}$, $\frac{12}{12}$, $\frac{11}{12}$

Think About It

14. In Exercises 5–8, how did you determine which number was greater?

Fill In the Blanks

Are all sevens equal? Which is more: seven pennies or seven dollars? Is place value important?

ACTIVITY 1 Building Numbers

With Your Class In this game you will try to build different types of numbers. You will use a spinner to generate digits. After each round, everyone should discuss the strategies used.

What You'll Need
- *spinner*

6 5 8 1

1 Draw four blanks. Spin for a number. Decide which blank to place your number in. Try to build the greatest number. Continue spinning until all blanks are filled. Then play again to make the smallest number.

Grocery stores usually round up. If three items sell for $.50, then one item sells for $.17.

2 Draw two rows of four blanks. Build two numbers that have the greatest sum possible. Then try to build the greatest difference possible.

3 Draw four blanks with a decimal point after the first blank. Build decimals that you will round. Write your own rule for rounding. Start by building the largest number possible after rounding to the ones' place.

4 Build numbers that will be the greatest after rounding to
- the tenths' place
- the hundredths' place

Now try creating the smallest number possible after rounding. Discuss how this will change your strategy for building decimals.

5 Compare rules for rounding. A common rule is to look at the digit to the right of the place you are rounding to. If it's 5 or greater, round up. If it's less than 5, round down.

Draw a chart or picture showing the numbers from 0.0 to 0.9. Then show the range of hundredths that rounds to that number of tenths. What rounding rule did you use?

Replay the game. Add a rule that you cannot use a digit twice while building a number.

Sports Technology

Technology has helped improve athletic performance. Improvements have helped athletes run faster, throw farther, and jump higher. To find out more, answer ten of the questions below.

1 **1956** Egil Danielsen of Norway threw a new style of javelin 85.71 m. He beat the old Olympic record by 11.93 meters. What was the previous record?

2 **1956** Rounded to the nearest whole number, how far did Danielsen throw the javelin?

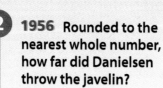

1950	1960	1970

Winning Pole Vault Heights	
1952	4.55 m
1956	4.56 m
1960	4.70 m
1964	5.10 m
1968	5.40 m
1972	5.50 m

Source: *The New Encyclopædia Britannica*, Volume 25, 1992

3 **1964** Fred Hansen of the United States became the first pole vaulter to win a gold medal using a fiber-glass pole. Round the results in the chart to the nearest tenth.

4 **1964 – 1980** Note the trend in pole vault heights from 1964 to 1972. Predict the winning height for 1976. Explain your prediction.

5 **1964** How much higher was the winning vault in 1964 than in 1960? Do you think the fiber-glass pole caused this difference? Explain.

6 **1985** Rule changes required a new javelin. It was designed to make throws 9 to 12 m shorter. Imagine that Egil Danielsen had used this javelin in 1956. What would have been the range of his throw?

7 **1986** The highest speed recorded on a normal racing bicycle is 71.323 kilometers per hour. One specially designed bike went 105.429 kilometers per hour. How much faster was this bike than a normal racing bike?

8 **1990s** Racing cyclists use about $\frac{9}{10}$ of their energy against friction from the air. If a cyclist uses 410.88 calories during a one-hour ride, estimate how many calories are used against air friction.

1980

1990

9 **1976** Nadia Comaneci of Romania scored a perfect 10.00 on the uneven bars. How does place value help explain why the scoreboard showed her score as 1.00?

10 **1988** Bicycles used by the U.S. Olympic team cost about $2,200 each. How much would 17 of these bicycles have cost?

11 **1988** The chart shows the medal winners in the men's 1,500-m wheelchair race. What was the time difference between the first- and third-place finishers?

1988 Men's 1,500-m Wheelchair Race

Mustapha Badid: 3 minutes, 33.51 seconds
Paul Van Winkel: 3 minutes, 33.61 seconds
Craig Blanchette: 3 minutes, 34.37 seconds

Source: *Sports Illustrated*, July 17, 1989

LESSON
3

How Big?
How Much?

CONNECT AND COMMUNICATE

In Your Journal Look for metric measurements on labels at the grocery store. Select different items with a combined mass of more than 2 kg. Describe your choices in your journal.

lympic races are measured in metric units. For example, sprinters compete in the 100-m dash. The table below shows some common metric units. Look under Measurement in the Tool Kit to find the names of other metric units. What is the relationship between each metric unit and the next larger unit?

Metric Units		
Length	**Mass**	**Capacity**
millimeter (mm) 0.001 meter	milligram (mg) 0.001 gram	milliliter (mL) 0.001 liter
centimeter (cm) 0.01 meter	centigram (cg) 0.01 gram	centiliter (cL) 0.01 liter
decimeter (dm) 0.1 meter	decigram (dg) 0.1 gram	deciliter (dL) 0.1 liter
meter (m)	gram (g)	liter (L)
kilometer (km) 1,000 meters	kilogram (kg) 1,000 grams	kiloliter (kL) 1,000 liters

^{ACTIVITY} 1 Tri-Beanathon

With Your Group Try these three experiments in any order. When you're done, order your group members' scores for each event. Make a chart or picture that shows the scores.

What You'll Need
- *beans*
- *cup marked in millimeters*
- *meter stick*
- *scale*
- *straws*

Bean Lift Hold a sheet of paper at one end. Place one dried bean at a time on the other end. How many beans can the paper hold up? How can you measure their mass? Will you measure in grams or kilograms?

Bean Blow Lay a meter stick flat. In one breath, blow a dried bean along the stick. Record your score. What unit did you use?

Bean Hold Fill one hand with dried beans. Pour your handful into a cup marked in milliliters. Record your score. How can you write your answer in liters?

TOOLS AND TECHNIQUES

In the bean hold activity, you measure your hand's capacity with beans. List three other items you could use instead of beans. What are the advantages and disadvantages of each?

Estimation Race

How will knowing the lengths of some items help you estimate the lengths of others?

What You'll Need
- *gameboard*
- *game pieces*
- *metric ruler*

ACTIVITY 2 ## How Close Are You?

With Your Group Use metric measurements to play the estimation race with three other players. Place game pieces at Start on the gameboard.

1 **Estimate** the length of an object. Record your estimate on a chart.

2 **Measure** the object. Find the difference between your estimate and the measurement. Record the measurement and the difference.

3 **Order** your estimate with the others in your group. Record your rank in your group.

4 **Move** ahead on the playing board. The player with the closest estimate moves four spaces. The next closest moves three, and so on.

ACTIVITY OPTION

Design your own game that uses estimates of metric measures. How will you reward players for making accurate estimates?

Ranking Estimates

Item	Estimate	Actual	Difference	Rank
Milk Carton	15 cm			

Do You Remember?

Try It!

For each group, order the measurements from least to greatest.

1. 2 km, 62 cm, 4 m

2. 14 km, 18 cm, 22 m

3. 2 kg, 68 g, 3,200 g

4. 71 L, 25 kL, 1,286 mL

Tell whether each number is greater when rounded to hundredths or tenths.

5. 4.057   **6.** 17.692   **7.** 10.045   **8.** 1.929

Order the fractions from least to greatest. Then round each mixed number to the nearest whole number.

9. $\frac{4}{5}$, $\frac{3}{10}$, $\frac{7}{20}$ **10.** $\frac{7}{8}$, $1\frac{1}{4}$, $\frac{13}{16}$ **11.** $2\frac{5}{6}$, $2\frac{2}{3}$, $2\frac{1}{12}$

12. $\frac{5}{7}$, $\frac{5}{6}$, $\frac{5}{11}$ **13.** $3\frac{7}{14}$, $3\frac{21}{28}$, $3\frac{5}{20}$

Think About It

14. If you measure the same object with a small and a large unit, which will give the larger number? Explain.

Connecting Metric Measures

How well can you use metric measures? Complete Activities 1 and 2. Then do either Activity 3 or Activity 4.

What You'll Need
- *balance scale*
- *classroom items*

ACTIVITY 1 Estimating Mass

With Your Group Mass is the amount of matter in an object. How accurately can you estimate the mass of items? For example, the mass of a nickel is 5 g. A juicy red apple has a mass of about 100 g.

1 Estimate the mass of five items in your classroom. Write down your estimates in order from least to greatest.

2 Find the mass of one item on a balance scale. Record your results.

DRAWING TO LEARN

To help you learn metric units, sketch each item you measure. Below it, write its mass.

Raisins ①
Yo-yo
Coins
Crayons ②
Sunglasses

How could you find the mass of a single raisin?

3 Review your other estimates. Do you want to revise any of them?

4 Find the mass of the other items. Continue to revise your other estimates.

How could you find the mass of six boxes of raisins?

ACTIVITY 2 Estimating Capacity

With Your Group Estimate the capacities of five containers. Then fill each with water. Pour the water into a metric measuring cup. How close were your estimates? One mL of water has a mass of 1 g. Bottled water is often sold in 1-L bottles. What's the mass of 1 L of water?

What You'll Need
• *metric measuring cup*
• *containers*

✔ **Self-Check** *Look at the measurements you made in Activity 2. Can you express each one in liters? in milliliters?*

Section B: Sizing It Up 259

Adjust your estimates based on the situation. Would you rather have too much or too little water at the track?

 Can You Move It?

ACTIVITY 3

On Your Own Imagine that you are the assistant coach of a track team. Assume that the team has 27 members. You need to carry 0.8 L of water to the track for each. The distance is 750 m. How will you do it?

1 How many liters of water do you need to move? How did you get your answer?

2 What mass of water do you need to take to the track? Explain.

3 How will you move the water? Will you need help carrying it?

How will you find the mass of the water you need to carry?

What size, shape, and number of containers will you use?

Estimate the length of each side of a cube that holds 1 L. How did you make your estimate?

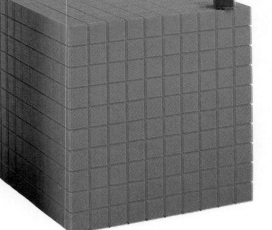

260

ACTIVITY 4 · What Can It Hold?

On Your Own

How can you use centimeter cubes to help you estimate how much a lunch box holds? Each centimeter cube takes the same space as 1mL. Now try to estimate how much three other containers hold.

Do You Remember?

Try It!

Which metric unit would you use to measure each item?

1. Length of a skateboard
2. Mass of a pencil
3. Mass of a person
4. Capacity of a drinking glass
5. Capacity of an aquarium
6. Width of a paper clip
7. Height of a building
8. Distance across a state

Match each fraction in simplest terms to its equivalent.

9. $\frac{3}{12}, \frac{4}{6}, \frac{6}{9}, \frac{1}{4}$

10. $\frac{3}{18}, \frac{1}{9}, \frac{2}{18}, \frac{2}{12}$

11. $\frac{12}{16}, \frac{16}{20}, \frac{3}{4}, \frac{20}{25}$

12. $\frac{9}{27}, \frac{6}{21}, \frac{4}{12}, \frac{2}{7}$

13. $\frac{12}{24}, \frac{7}{12}, \frac{14}{24}, \frac{5}{10}$

Think About It

14. How did you decide which units to use in Exercises 1–8?

Paper Towel Olympics

Which brand of paper towels is best? How much water do paper towels hold? Do some brands hold more than others? Choose three different brands to investigate. Find out which deserves the gold medal.

1 How much water does each towel hold? Pour a thin layer of water into a pan. How many milliliters of water are in the pan? Place a towel in the pan. Soak it, and remove it. How much water is left in the pan? How much did the towel hold? Repeat this with each brand.

2 How strong is each towel? Wet a towel. Place weights on it one at a time. How much will it hold before it breaks? Try this with the other brands. How much did the strongest brand hold?

3 How fast does each towel pick up water? Hold the edge of a towel on a water surface for one minute. In millimeters, measure how far the water climbs up the towel. How far does the water climb with the other brands?

Determine the overall winner of the Paper Towel Olympics. For each of the three events, give the first place brand 10 points. Give 5 points for second place and 2 points for third place. Which brand won the most total points?

Ask Yourself

☐ What makes a paper towel good?
☐ Which towel is the best?
☐ Why are milliliters a better unit than liters for this investigation?
☐ How can you record the results?
☐ Did all students get similar results? Explain.

Diet of Champions

Good nutrition is important to everyone, including athletes. The charts show the fractions of the minimum daily requirements (MDR) of vitamin C, calcium, and iron that you would get from one serving of 12 common foods. Use this information to answer the questions.

Milk Products
2–3 servings per day

	Cheese	Skim Milk
Vitamin C	0	$\frac{1}{30}$
Calcium	$\frac{1}{5}$	$\frac{3}{10}$
Iron	$\frac{1}{90}$	$\frac{1}{180}$

1 An athlete drinks 800 mL of milk each day. How many liters of milk does the athlete drink in a week?

2 Each day a runner runs 3,000 m twice, 100 m nine times, and 200 m seven times. How many kilometers does the runner run in a week?

Vegetables
3–5 servings per day

	Carrots	Peas
Vitamin C	$\frac{1}{10}$	$\frac{1}{3}$
Calcium	$\frac{3}{100}$	$\frac{3}{100}$
Iron	$\frac{1}{36}$	$\frac{1}{6}$

3 What fraction of the 12 foods have no vitamin C?

4 Which gives a greater fraction of the MDR of calcium, cheese or skim milk? How much greater?

5 How much more than the MDR of vitamin C will a person get from four servings of peas?

6 What fraction of the MDR of calcium is in one serving of skim milk and one serving of bread?

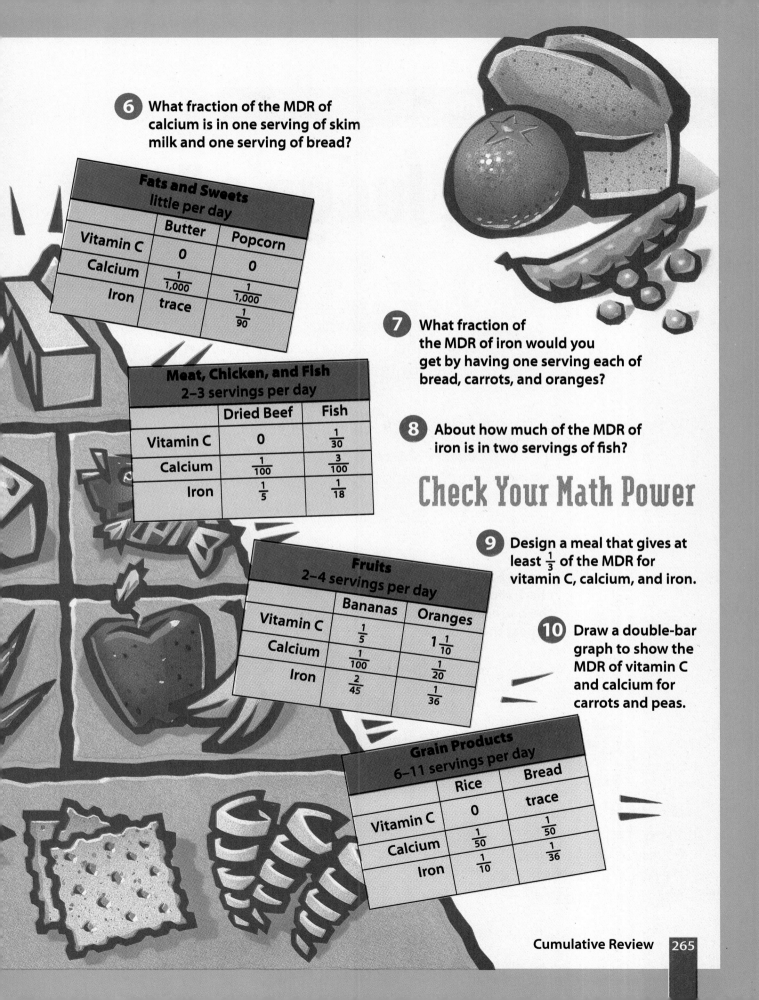

Fats and Sweets
little per day

	Butter	Popcorn
Vitamin C	0	0
Calcium	$\frac{1}{1,000}$	$\frac{1}{1,000}$
Iron	trace	$\frac{1}{90}$

Meat, Chicken, and Fish
2–3 servings per day

	Dried Beef	Fish
Vitamin C	0	$\frac{1}{30}$
Calcium	$\frac{1}{100}$	$\frac{3}{100}$
Iron	$\frac{1}{5}$	$\frac{1}{18}$

7 What fraction of the MDR of iron would you get by having one serving each of bread, carrots, and oranges?

8 About how much of the MDR of iron is in two servings of fish?

Check Your Math Power

9 Design a meal that gives at least $\frac{1}{3}$ of the MDR for vitamin C, calcium, and iron.

10 Draw a double-bar graph to show the MDR of vitamin C and calcium for carrots and peas.

Fruits
2–4 servings per day

	Bananas	Oranges
Vitamin C	$\frac{1}{5}$	$1\frac{1}{10}$
Calcium	$\frac{1}{100}$	$\frac{1}{20}$
Iron	$\frac{2}{45}$	$\frac{1}{36}$

Grain Products
6–11 servings per day

	Rice	Bread
Vitamin C	0	trace
Calcium	$\frac{1}{50}$	$\frac{1}{50}$
Iron	$\frac{1}{10}$	$\frac{1}{36}$

LESSON 5 The Judge's Eye

Judges use various tools to determine the winners at the Olympics. Which events are judged with clocks? What other tools are used? Which Olympic games are judged by the eye?

What You'll Need
- *meter stick*
- *ball*

ACTIVITY 1 Judge with Your Eye

With Your Group You can predict with multiplication. Try this activity to find out how.

1. **Drop a ball from 1 m. On a chart, record the height of the bounce in meters. Repeat three times.**

DRAWING TO LEARN

In a picture, show each student's estimate of the bounce height. How does the picture show which estimate is most typical?

Ball Bounce Results

Bounce	Judges' Estimates			Best Estimate
1	0.65	0.76	0.69	0.7
2				
3				

2 Did everyone record the same bounce for the dropped ball? Talk about any differences. Agree on the best estimate of the height.

3 List three ways you could change the height of the ball's bounce.

4 How can you predict the bounce of the ball when dropped from twice as high? How can you use multiplication to help you?

TOOLS AND TECHNIQUES

Calculator Using your calculator, how can you show the height of a typical bounce? How would you find an average? Would adding the measurements help?

ACTIVITY 2 From Twice as High

With Your Partner Assume a ball dropped from 1 m has a 0.7-m bounce. Look at the sketch below. How can you predict the bounce of the ball when dropped from 2 m?

1 How can you use multiplication to help you predict the height of the bounce? Think about the products below.

$$\begin{array}{r} 70 \\ \times 2 \\ \hline 140 \end{array} \qquad \begin{array}{r} 7 \\ \times 2 \\ \hline 14 \end{array} \qquad \begin{array}{r} 0.7 \\ \times 2 \\ \hline 1.4 \end{array}$$

How is $\frac{7}{10} \times \frac{2}{1}$ related to 0.7×2?

Drop=2m
Bounce=2x?

Drop=1m
Bounce=0.7m

2m

1m

2 Discuss which product above will help you predict the height of the bounce. Which product do you choose? Defend your choice.

CONNECT AND COMMUNICATE

In Your Journal Sketch a diagram that shows that 0.7 × 2 will be less than 2.

3 Look at your data for the ball your group dropped from 1 m. Use a sketch and multiplication to predict the bounce of the ball when it is dropped from 2 m. Drop the ball. How close was your prediction?

ACTIVITY 3 · From Half?

With Your Partner Assume that a ball bounced 0.7 m when dropped from 1 m. Look at the sketch below. Predict how high the ball will bounce when dropped from 0.5 m.

What You'll Need
• meter stick
• ball

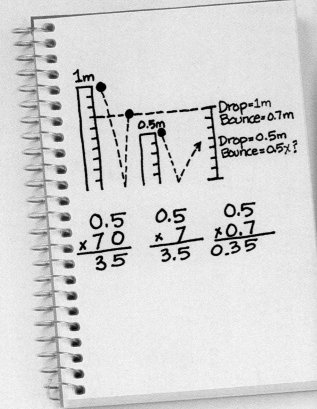

1 **Choose the product from above that best represents the bounce of the ball dropped from 0.5 m.**

2 **Use your data from Activity 1 to predict the bounce of your ball when it is dropped from 0.5 m. Check and discuss your prediction.**

Chart the results for dropping a ball from 0.5 m, 1 m, and 2 m. Use the chart to predict the height of the bounce when you drop the ball from 1.5 m and from 4 m.

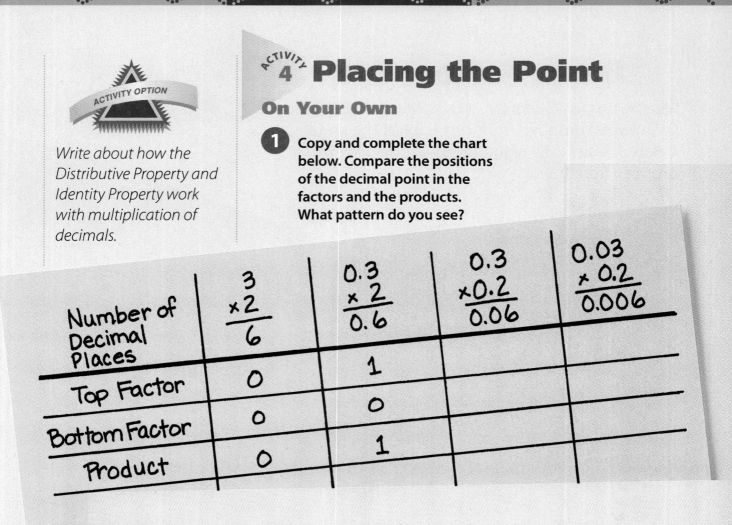

ACTIVITY OPTION

Write about how the Distributive Property and Identity Property work with multiplication of decimals.

ACTIVITY 4 Placing the Point

On Your Own

1 Copy and complete the chart below. Compare the positions of the decimal point in the factors and the products. What pattern do you see?

	3 ×2 ___ 6	0.3 × 2 ___ 0.6	0.3 ×0.2 ___ 0.06	0.03 × 0.2 ___ 0.006
Number of Decimal Places Top Factor	0	1		
Bottom Factor	0	0		
Product	0	1		

2 Copy the products on the right. Use the pattern you found in step 1 to help you place each decimal point. Use a calculator to check your placement.

1.3
× 2
___
26

2.3
×4.5
___
115
92
___
1035

0.94
× 8.6
___
564
752
___
8084

0.123
0.546
___
738
492
615
___
67158

3 Find each product. Check your answers with a calculator.

2.3
×5.4
___

7.6
×7.6
___

0.34
× 5.6
___

2.46
×8.56
___

4 Write a rule for multiplying decimals.

ACTIVITY 5 By 10 or by 100

On Your Own Use your calculator to explore some patterns in decimal multiplication.

✔ **Self-Check** *What happens to a decimal when you multiply it by 10 or 100?*

1 Write down ten decimals. Use your calculator to multiply each by 10. Do you see a pattern? How can you get a correct answer without using your calculator?

2 Use your calculator to multiply ten decimals by 100. Is there a pattern? Can you multiply a decimal by 100 without your calculator?

3 Write a rule for multiplying decimal numbers by 10 or by 100. Share your rule with the class.

Do You Remember?

Try It!

Work only exercises that have products less than 3.1.

1. $5 \times 0.6 = $ ■
2. $0.5 \times 0.6 = $ ■
3. $0.05 \times 0.6 = $ ■
4. $0.04 \times 3 = $ ■
5. $0.14 \times 13.45 = $ ■
6. $12.62 \times 1.61 = $ ■

Order the fractions from least to greatest. Round the least and greatest to the nearest whole numbers.

7. $\frac{2}{3}, \frac{1}{6}, \frac{5}{9}, \frac{5}{6}$

8. $1\frac{1}{2}, 1\frac{1}{10}, 1\frac{1}{5}$

9. $\frac{3}{4}, \frac{3}{8}, \frac{3}{12}, \frac{3}{3}$

10. $2\frac{3}{8}, 1\frac{7}{8}, 2\frac{1}{8}, 1\frac{5}{8}$

11. $\frac{1}{10}, \frac{99}{100}, \frac{9}{1,000}, \frac{9}{100}$

Think About It

12. Review your answers to 1, 2, and 3. Describe the pattern.

LESSON 6 Who Wins?

REASONING AND PROBLEM SOLVING

How could making an ordered list help you with this activity?

Greg Louganis won two gold medals in diving for the United States at the 1988 Olympics. Judges use multiplication to figure diving scores.

ACTIVITY 1 How Do They Judge?

With Your Group   One dive by Louganis was a reverse $3\frac{1}{2}$ somersault. Here is how judges figured his score for that dive.

> ### Drop and Add
>
> **1** Seven judges give individual marks to a dive. A mark can be 0 through 10. They drop the highest mark and the lowest mark. Imagine that Louganis got four 9.0's and three 8.5's on this dive. Which scores will you drop?
>
> **2** Add the remaining marks together. What is the sum for this dive?

How does dropping the highest and lowest marks make the scoring more fair?

Multiply

3 Multiply the sum by a number that measures how hard a dive is. This number is called the degree of difficulty. A reverse $3\frac{1}{2}$ somersault has a high degree of difficulty—3.5. Find the product for Louganis's dive.

4 Finally, multiply the product from Step 3 by 0.6. What score did Louganis get for this dive?

Discuss

5 Discuss how dives are scored.
   a. Would it make a difference to reverse Steps 3 and 4?
   b. Write a number sentence that shows Steps 2, 3, and 4.

Diving In

Each of the following questions is about the 1988 Olympics. Answer eight of your choice.

1 Tan Liangde, a Chinese diver, did a reverse somersault $2\frac{1}{2}$ pike. The judges gave him marks of 6.5, two 8.0's, an 8.5, and three 7.5's. What marks should you drop?

2 Greg Louganis did a $2\frac{1}{2}$ reverse somersault pike. The judges gave him an 8.0, five 8.5's, and a 9.0. After dropping the highest and lowest marks, what was the total of the remaining scores?

Layout or straight position

Pike position

3 Here are scores for five of Louganis's dives: 49.59, 73.92, 84.63, 76.50, and 80.85. Round each to the nearest whole number.

4 Tan Liangde did a reverse somersault $2\frac{1}{2}$ pike with a 3.0 difficulty. The judges gave him a 6.5, two 8.0's, an 8.5, and three 7.5's. What was his final score?

The inward pike dive is one of the simplest dives performed in Olympic meets. It has a degree of difficulty of 1.4.

5 What would Tan's score be if the 6.5 had been an 8.0?

The reverse $3\frac{1}{2}$ somersault is such a dangerous and difficult dive that few divers even attempt it. It has a very high degree of difficulty—3.5.

Forward

Back

Reverse

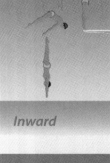
Inward

Twist

6 Louganis did a back $2\frac{1}{2}$ somersault. The marks were two 9.0's, four 8.5's, and an 8.0. His score was 77.40. Explain how you would find the degree of difficulty.

7 Louganis's second to last dive was a reverse $1\frac{1}{2}$ somersault with $3\frac{1}{2}$ twists. The degree of difficulty was 3.3. The judges gave him 7.5, 8.5, four 9.0's, and a 9.5. What was his final score?

8 Louganis's last dive was the "dive of death." The degree of difficulty was 3.5. The judges' marks were two 7.5's, two 7.0's, one 8.0, and two 8.5's. What was his final score?

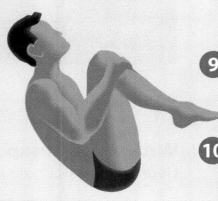
Tuck position

9 Compare Louganis's last two dives. Which score was higher?

10 If Louganis's last dive had a degree of difficulty of only 2.5, what marks could he have received to get the same score as he got for the "dive of death"?

LESSON 7

Best on Average

As in diving, judges score gymnastics. However, the judges don't just add gymnastics marks together. They average them. One of the stars on the 1992 U.S. Olympic team was Betty Okino.

In Your Journal Many sports statistics are averages. Make a list of all the sports averages you hear or see in one week.

ACTIVITY 1 Balance the Score

With Your Group How is gymnastics scored? Here are some sample marks from judges.

Judges' Marks					
9.60	9.65	9.80	9.70	9.75	9.75

1 Write the judges' marks in order, from highest to lowest. Cross out the highest and the lowest.

2 The score is the average of the four remaining marks. The average is the score a gymnast would get if all judges gave the same mark. Here are some ways to estimate an average.

TOOLS AND TECHNIQUES

You can use a computer graphing program to create bar graphs.

Try marking the scores end to end on a long strip of paper. One centimeter could equal one point from a judge. Fold to show the average.

The average will be between the highest and lowest marks. How could a number line show the range of possible averages?

Create a bar graph showing the judge's marks. Can you borrow from long bars and add to short ones to show how to average?

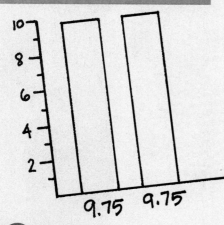

3 Use one of these methods or one of your own to find the average score. Share your method and your answer with the class.

What else can you judge? With a group of friends, rate several books, movies, or foods. Find the average score for each.

ACTIVITY 2 Rate the Worst Joke

With Your Group Now you get to be a judge in a bad-joke contest. Who can tell the worst joke?

1 Look through joke books and agree on a bad joke. Select one student to tell it to the class.

2 Students rate each joke told. Scores can range from a low of 0 to a high of 3.0. Give ratings in tenths of a point.

3 Find the average score in your group for each joke. Order the averages. Which joke got the highest average score? Did anyone get an unusual number as the average? Why would you call it unusual?

4 Compare scores with those of other groups. Discuss ways to calculate averages.

ACTIVITY 3 By the Numbers

With Your Partner How did you find an average score? Here are two ways.

1 Imagine that one student got a total of 2.6 points from three judges. How do you know the average is less than 1? more than 0.1? Copy the squares below on a piece of paper. Cut the squares to find the average. How will trading whole squares for tenths help?

✓ **Self-Check** *Why does a decimal in tenths divided by a whole number sometimes give an answer in hundredths? For example, why does 6.3 ÷ 2 = 3.15?*

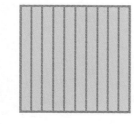
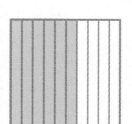

2 Look at this example. Answer each question.

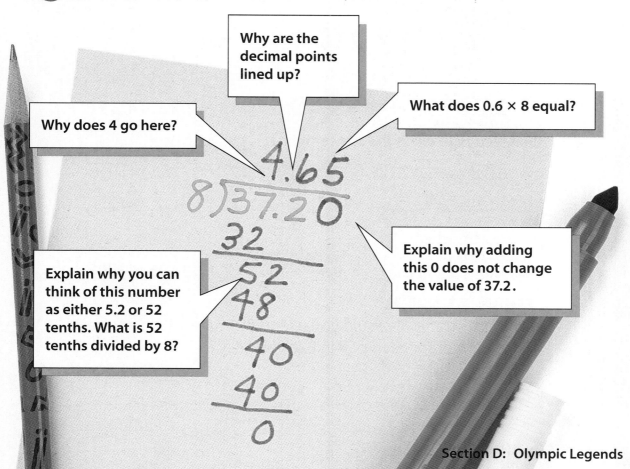

Why are the decimal points lined up?

What does 0.6 × 8 equal?

Why does 4 go here?

Explain why adding this 0 does not change the value of 37.2.

Explain why you can think of this number as either 5.2 or 52 tenths. What is 52 tenths divided by 8?

$$
\begin{array}{r}
4.65 \\
8\overline{)37.20} \\
32 \\
\hline
52 \\
48 \\
\hline
40 \\
40 \\
\hline
0
\end{array}
$$

REASONING AND PROBLEM SOLVING

Estimate the answer to each exercise before solving it.

ACTIVITY 4 **Roll for It**

With Your Partner Roll number cubes to create five exercises for your partner to answer.

1 Roll one number cube five times to fill the blanks:

$$\underline{}\,\overline{)\underline{}.\underline{}\,\underline{}\,\underline{}}$$

2 Solve your partner's exercises. Check your partner's answers by multiplying.

$3\overline{)6.14}$

Do You Remember?

Try It!

What is the average of each set of numbers?

1. 2.6, 3.4 **2.** 4.8, 6.3, 7.2 **3.** 1.1, 2.2, 3.3, 4.4, 5.5

For each pair, write the answer which is greater.

4. $6\overline{)28.2}$ $6\overline{)15.48}$ **5.** $7\overline{)16.8}$ $4\overline{)16.8}$

6. 14.2 ÷ 2 20.44 ÷ 4 **7.** 42.1 ÷ 8 54.2 ÷ 11

Find the product.

8. 1.679 × 100 **9.** 0.98 × 10 **10.** 14.26 × 100

Think About It

11. What strategies could you use to estimate which answer is greater for each pair in Exercises 4–7?

Who Shoots Best?

What was the greatest basketball team ever? The 1992 U.S. Olympic team included so many great players that people called it the Dream Team. Who was the best shooter on the team?

Top Scorers on the Dream Team			
Player	Field Goal Shots Made	Field Goal Shots Taken	Total Points
Charles Barkley	59	83	144
Michael Jordan	51	113	119
Karl Malone	40	62	104
Chris Mullin	39	63	103
Clyde Drexler	37	64	84

Source: *The 1993 Information Please Sports Almanac*

Dream Data

With Your Class Analyze the data in the chart above.

1 **Discuss** what *best* means. How many different ways can you measure shooting skill?

2 **Estimate** how many one-, two-, and three-point shots each player made. Field goals are worth two or three points. Free throws are worth one point. Explain how you made your estimate.

In Your Journal *Sketch a bar graph showing how many field goal shots each player took. On each bar, shade in the number of shots made. Which bar is filled the most?*

ACTIVITY 2 How's Your Aim?

With Your Group Find out how well you can shoot. Stand 2 m from a wastebasket. Shoot balls of wastepaper into it. Is the best shooter one who makes 5 out of 6 shots or 8 out of 10?

1 Each student shoots eight times. Record the fraction of shots made and the fraction missed.

2 Use your calculator to change each fraction to a decimal. What decimal represents the fraction of the shots you made?

3 How would you change fractions to decimals, using pencil and paper? Recall that a fraction is a way to show division. In your journal describe how to change a fraction to a decimal.

3 Rate the Pros

With Your Group Use the chart from page 281. Calculate a decimal to represent the fraction of shots each Dream Team player made. Round to the nearest thousandth. Who was the most accurate shooter?

Chris Mullin
Shots taken 63

Do You Remember?

Try It!

Change these fractions to decimals. Round to the nearest thousandth.

1. $\frac{1}{2} =$ 2. $\frac{3}{11} =$ 3. $\frac{3}{8} =$

4. $\frac{7}{20} =$ 5. $\frac{7}{9} =$ 6. $\frac{8}{12} =$

Change each decimal to a fraction in lowest terms.

7. $0.875 =$ 8. $0.75 =$ 9. $0.625 =$

Round to the nearest tenth.

10. 4.62   11. 8.92   12. 14.25

13. 20.149   14. 84.453

Think About It

15. In Exercises 7–9 above, how many fractions could you write for each decimal? Explain your answer.

Looking Back

Choose the right answer. Write *a, b, c,* or *d* for each question.

1. Which number sentence is incorrect?

   a. 4.8 cm + 0.2 cm = 5 cm
   b. 0.71 kg − 0.22 kg = 0.49 kg
   c. 2,700 mL − 200 mL = 250 mL
   d. 14.2 km + 2 km = 16.2 km

2. Rounded to the hundredths' place, which number doesn't match the others?

   a. 4.349   b. 4.344
   c. 4.354   d. 4.353

3. The volume of each small cube is 1 cubic centimeter. How many cubic centimeters are in the large cube?

   a. 125   b. 25
   c. 1,000   d. 100

4. Between which two numbers is $\frac{3}{4} \times \frac{1}{8}$?

   a. 0 and $\frac{1}{2}$ b. 1 and $1\frac{1}{2}$
   c. $\frac{1}{2}$ and 1   d. $1\frac{1}{2}$ and 2

5. Look at this pattern:
   1.0, 0.875, 0.75, 0.625, 0.5.
   What number continues the pattern?

   a. 0.4   b. 0.35
   c. 0.375   d. 0.425

6. Which ticket package offers the best price per ticket?

   a. 7 tickets for $90.00
   b. 4 tickets for $52.00
   c. 5 tickets for $63.00
   d. 3 tickets for $37.50

7. Which of these numbers is greatest when rounded to the tenths' place?

   a. 347.459
   b. 347.447
   c. 347.382
   d. 347.441

Medals Won in the 1992 Summer Olympics				
Country	Gold	Silver	Bronze	Total
Unified Team*	45	38	29	112
United States	37	34	37	108
Germany	33	21	28	82
China	16	22	16	54

*Athletes from countries once part of the Soviet Union

Source: *The 1993 Information Please Sports Almanac*

8. Which country won the most bronze medals?

   a. Unified Team   **b.** United States
   c. Germany   **d.** China

9. As a fraction of its total medals, which country won the most silver medals?

   a. Unified Team   **b.** United States
   c. Germany   **d.** China

10. Which has the largest product?

   a. 4.65×9.78
   b. 46.5×97.8
   c. 46.5×9.78
   d. 4.65×97.8

Check Your Math Power

Answer each item with a drawing or a short answer.

11. Look at the chart above. Draw a pictograph to show the number of gold medals each country won.

12. Imagine you purchased a pen for $1.19, a notebook for $3.49, and a ruler for $0.89 with a $10 bill. Describe two sets of change that would give you at least five quarters.

13. Imagine you want to use a balance scale to find the mass of some objects to the nearest 5 g. Each object has a mass between 5 g and 100 g. For example, an object may have a mass of 10 g, 45 g, or 83 g. The store sells balance "weights" of any multiple of 5 g from 5 g to 50 g. You want to buy the fewest "weights" necessary to find the mass of any of your objects. Which "weights" would you buy? Explain your reasoning.

14. Explain how to measure 1 L of water using only the two containers shown.

Investigations

Who's Fastest?

What is your fastest self-powered speed? Is your rate of speed faster than an Olympic champion swimmer? a sprinter? How many times faster is your fastest speed than is your favorite walking speed?

Investigation A

Compare Your Own Fastest Times

1 Measure a 50-m distance on the playground or in a park.

2 How fast can you walk 50 m? How much faster can you run that distance?

3

Experiment with other self-powered ways that you use to move around. You might use a bicycle, roller skates, skateboard, or wheelchair. Record how fast you travel 50 m.

Individual Champions in the 1992 Olympics

Champion	Event	Distance	Time
Patrick Ortlieb	Downhill skiing	2,905 m	1 min 50.37 s
Yevgeny Sadovyi	Swimming	400 m	3 min 45.00 s
Linford Christie	Dash	100 m	9.96 s
Georg Hackl	Luge	1,250 m	45.190 s

Source: *The 1993 Information Please Sports Almanac*

4 Look at the chart above. Convert the rates of speed to make them easier to compare. What is each athlete's average time in seconds for traveling 1 m? How do you compare with the athletes?

Time to Travel 1 Meter

1. Luge

$$1{,}250 \overline{)45.190}$$ 0.03

37 50

Keep In Mind

Your report will be judged by how well you do the following things.

☐ How well do you show what you know about multiplication to help you solve the problem?

☐ How well do you describe your results?

☐ How clearly do you show and explain your thinking?

Investigation B — Add an Engine

Research to find speeds for vehicles with motors. How fast do cars, ships, trucks, spacecraft, and snowmobiles travel? Will you compare top speeds or average speeds? Write a report that compares motorized speeds with the speeds of Olympic athletes.

Computer Option Use a computer spreadsheet or a database program to organize, analyze, and present your vehicle data. Select information to include in your report.

Investigation C — Compare Animals' Speeds

Find information about the speeds at which wild animals run, swim, or fly. How do these animals' speeds compare with the speeds of Olympic athletes? Prepare a visual presentation comparing the speeds of animals and Olympic athletes.

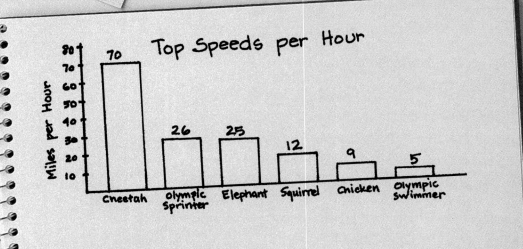

Top Speeds per Hour

Animal/Athlete	Miles per Hour
Cheetah	70
Olympic Sprinter	26
Elephant	25
Squirrel	12
Chicken	9
Olympic Swimmer	5

MODULE 6

Visual Math

Try designing a kite, making a mural, or graphing data about your class. In each of these activities, you'll use the geometry concepts and the tools and techniques of visual math explored in this module.

SECTION A

Mapping

SECTION B

Angles and Scale

SECTION C

Scale Drawing

SECTION D

The Shape of Data

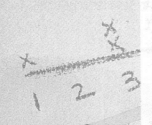

Shape a Trip

A map is a helpful tool when you are planning a trip. Use the map on page 291 to plan some voyages.

1 Point to Point

Where would you like to travel? Pick three points. Estimate their latitude and longitude to the nearest five degrees.

2 Triangle Trip

Use your Tracing Tool or tracing paper to mark your round-trip route. Label the latitude and longitude of two of the points. Plan another triangle trip and mark the latitude and longitude for two stops.

③ Where Have You Been?

Exchange map tracings. Put each labeled point at the right place on the map. Fill in missing latitude and longitude numbers. List the places on your partner's trip. See if you got the places right!

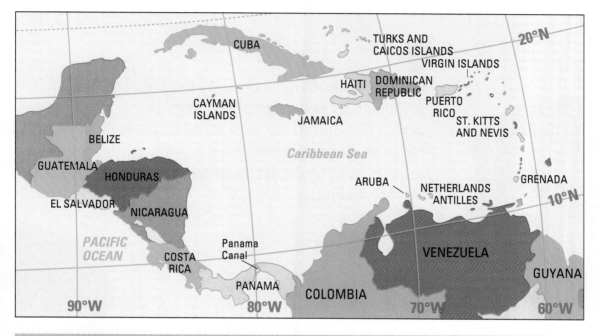

Investigations Preview

Learn about grids, scale, and geometric shapes. They can help you design kites, plan trips, or make a book of your own.

Kite Making (pages 320–321)
How would you build an original kite?
Understanding scale drawing will help you.

Lights! Shapes! Action! (pages 350–352)
What do you need to know to make a picture seem to move?
Use what you learn about scale and grids to help you design a flip book.

Word Bank
- angle
- coordinate grid
- data
- degree
- line plot
- line segment
- median
- mode
- ratio
- vertex

LESSON
1

Around the World

In 1992 Captain Bill Pinkney became the first African American to sail around the world alone. Students all across the United States tracked Captain Pinkney and his boat, *Commitment*. The students plotted points on a world map to show the latitude and longitude of the boat on each day.

"How do you know where you live? When you have latitude and longitude you have an address in the ocean or anywhere in the world."

Captain Bill Pinkney

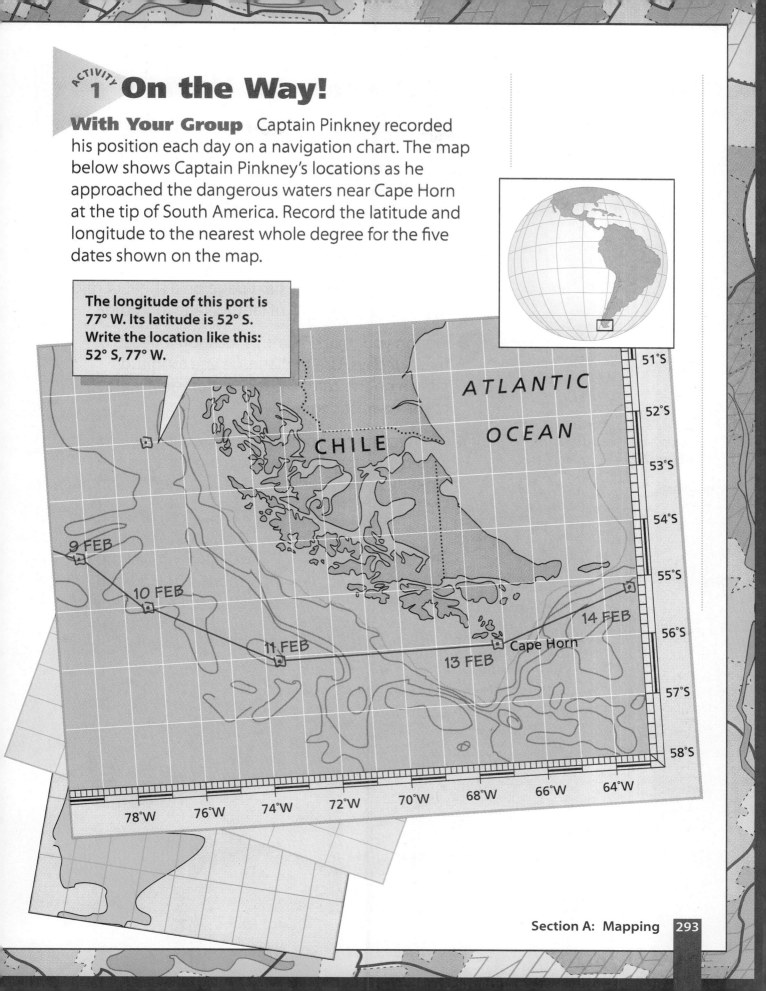

ACTIVITY 1 On the Way!

With Your Group Captain Pinkney recorded his position each day on a navigation chart. The map below shows Captain Pinkney's locations as he approached the dangerous waters near Cape Horn at the tip of South America. Record the latitude and longitude to the nearest whole degree for the five dates shown on the map.

> **The longitude of this port is 77° W. Its latitude is 52° S. Write the location like this: 52° S, 77° W.**

9 FEB

10 FEB

11 FEB

13 FEB

14 FEB

Cape Horn

CHILE

ATLANTIC OCEAN

51°S
52°S
53°S
54°S
55°S
56°S
57°S
58°S

78°W 76°W 74°W 72°W 70°W 68°W 66°W 64°W

What You'll Need

- *grid paper*

How would you round minutes to the nearest degree?

Each day Captain Pinkney recorded his location and observations in his log.

ᴬᶜᵀᴵⱽᴵᵀʸ 2 Around the Horn

On Your Own About two months after rounding Cape Horn, Captain Pinkney wrote the entries in the log below. His entries show that degrees of latitude and longitude can be divided into minutes. There are 60 minutes in a degree. Use the the log entries and the information on the next page to make your own map of this part of Captain Pinkney's voyage.

1 Copy the map on the next page on a sheet of grid paper. Label the lines of latitude and longitude.

2 Plot on your map Pinkney's location for each of the four days. Use the latitude and longitude shown on the card. These numbers are rounded to the nearest degree.

3 Connect the four points you have plotted. How would you describe the general direction of Pinkney's travel during these four days?

4 On which of the four days did Captain Pinkney travel the farthest? How can you tell?

April 1992

22°53′S 39°29′W
Week 15 100-266 Thursday 9

KWS·578
SOUTHBOUND II (Hurricane)

20°52′S 38°26′W
Week 15 101-265 Friday 10

KWS 578

19°37′S 38°14′W
Week 15 102-264 Saturday 11

KWS·578
MKWN 3 (creighton)

17°57′S 38°02′W
Week 15 103-263 Sunday 12

KWS 578 KIZ 837
WOM (IN3)

2°E

3°E

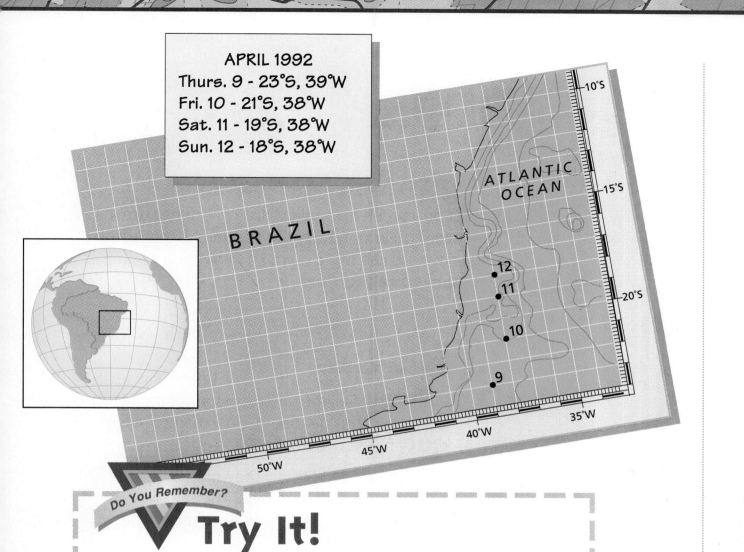

APRIL 1992
Thurs. 9 - 23°S, 39°W
Fri. 10 - 21°S, 38°W
Sat. 11 - 19°S, 38°W
Sun. 12 - 18°S, 38°W

Do You Remember?

Try It!

Tell whether you are traveling north, south, east, or west as you move from 18° S, 38° W to the point given.

1. 18° S, 40° W   **2.** 16° S, 38° W   **3.** 18° S, 36° W

4. 20° S, 38° W   **5.** 14° S, 38° W   **6.** 18° S, 32° W

Round the decimals to the nearest thousandth. Write the decimals in order from least to greatest.

7. 0.1103   **8.** 0.3127   **9.** 3.02166

10. 1.2344   **11.** 0.2739   **12.** 3.1118

Think About It

13. Write a brief explanation of how you found the answers to Exercises 1–6.

Geoboard Maps

You've seen how sailors like Bill Pinkney use maps to record their routes. Try the activities in this lesson to see how you can make maps of something as simple as figures on a geoboard.

ACTIVITY 1 Mapping Shapes

With Your Group

1. Make a list of all the different kinds of figures you can find on this geoboard. How many of each kind of figure can you find?

2. Draw each of the figures shown on the geoboard on your own geoboard map. The sample geoboard map on the next page shows the trapezoid done for you.

3. Notice that a single letter is used to label each point on the geoboard map. How is this system simpler than latitude and longitude?

Use the definitions in the box to help you answer Exercises 4–7.

4 You can name a figure with the letters of its vertexes. For example, the trapezoid on the map is *PTYZ*. Use the letters to name all the other figures on your map.

5 Each side of a figure is a line segment. For example, segment $\overline{PZ}$ forms one side of the trapezoid. Name the other three sides.

6 Each line segment is part of a line. To name the line, add arrows like this: $\overleftrightarrow{PZ}$. Choose three other segments on your geoboard map. Name the line that each segment is part of.

7 Name two segments that are part of parallel lines.

ACTIVITY OPTION

Use a geoboard or geoboard map. Make as many congruent triangles as you can without overlapping. How many squares can you show at one time using nine pegs?

- A **line** is a set of points that extends on and on in both directions.
- A **line segment** is part of a line and has two endpoints.
- A **ray** is a set of points that extends in one direction from an endpoint.
- **Parallel lines** are lines in a plane that never intersect.
- **Perpendicular lines** form right angles.
- A **vertex** is a point where two sides of a figure intersect.

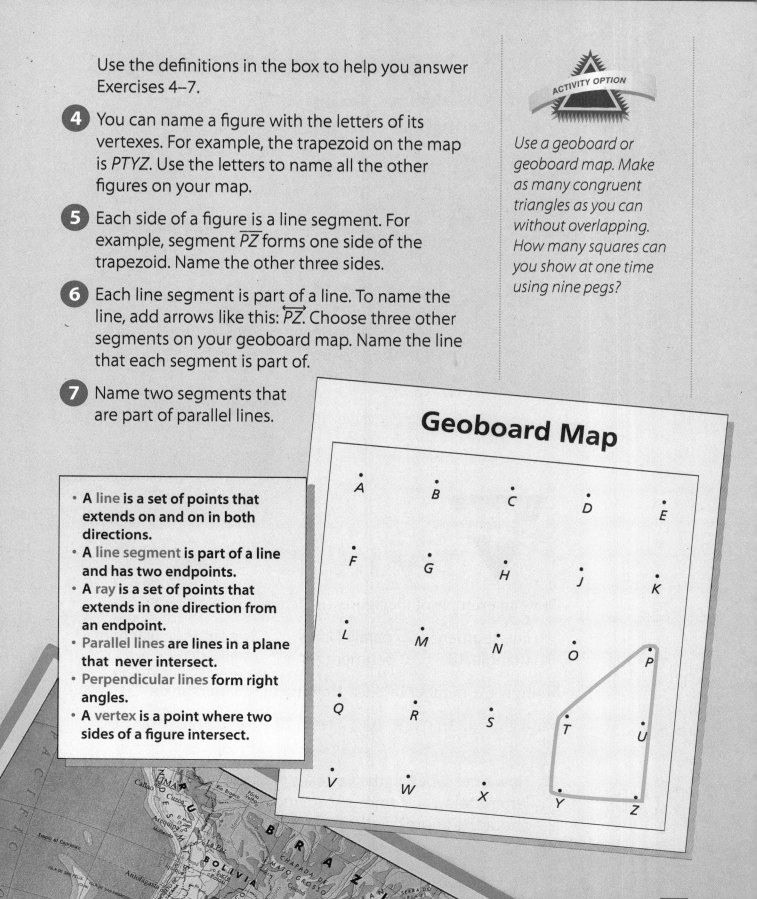

Geoboard Map

What You'll Need
- *geoboard*
- *rubber bands*

Use terms you've learned, such as parallel *and* vertex, *when you ask questions for the mystery game.*

ACTIVITY 2 Geoboard Mystery

With Your Group Use your geoboard for a mystery game.

1 One player uses one rubber band to make a mystery shape. Keep it secret!

2 The other players take turns asking yes-or-no questions about the mystery figure. Use the answers to help you draw the mystery figure on your map.

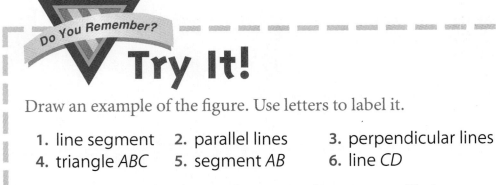

Do You Remember?

Try It!

Draw an example of the figure. Use letters to label it.

1. line segment   2. parallel lines   3. perpendicular lines
4. triangle *ABC*   5. segment *AB*   6. line *CD*

Multiply the number by 0.54. How are the answers alike?

7. 4.2   8. 3.1   9. 0.1   10. 0.20   11. 8.65

Think About It

12. How does labeling the vertexes of a figure with letters help you communicate more clearly about the figure?

Finding the Way

ACTIVITY 1 You Are Here

With Your Group The diagram below shows another way to map the trapezoid from the geoboard in Lesson 2. This kind of map is called a **coordinate grid.** Each point on the grid is named by an **ordered pair** of numbers. These numbers, or coordinates, tell where the point is located.

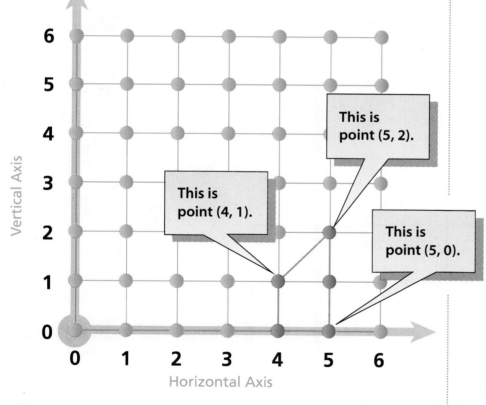

This is point (5, 2).

This is point (4, 1).

This is point (5, 0).

Vertical Axis

Horizontal Axis

1 Name the other vertex of the trapezoid. How did you decide in which order to write the numbers?

2 Find point (4, 3). Which number shows the horizontal distance? the vertical distance?

✔ **Self-Check** *How would you explain to a friend how to use ordered pairs to locate points on a coordinate grid?*

▶ ACTIVITY 2 Connecting Points

What You'll Need
• *grid paper*

With Your Group Use grid paper to make your own coordinate grid. Plot each set of points below.

1 Connect the points to make three triangles.
  a. (5, 5), (4, 4), (5, 3)
  b. (3, 2), (2, 1), (3, 0)
  c. (6, 0), (6, 6), (0, 6)

2 What are the vertexes of a square 2 units by 2 units if one vertex is (0, 0)?

3 Draw across the grid a line that contains (3, 4) and (4, 3). Name two more points on this line.

▶ ACTIVITY 3 Coordinate Games

What You'll Need
• *grid paper*

With Your Partner Choose two games to play with a partner. Make your own coordinate grids.

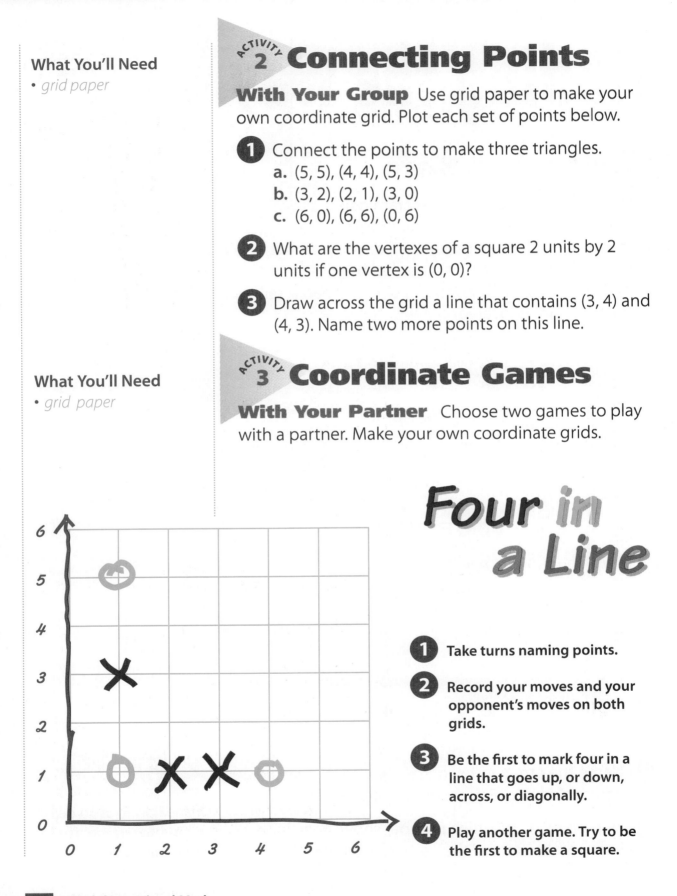

Four in a Line

1 Take turns naming points.

2 Record your moves and your opponent's moves on both grids.

3 Be the first to mark four in a line that goes up, or down, across, or diagonally.

4 Play another game. Try to be the first to make a square.

Hidden TREASURE

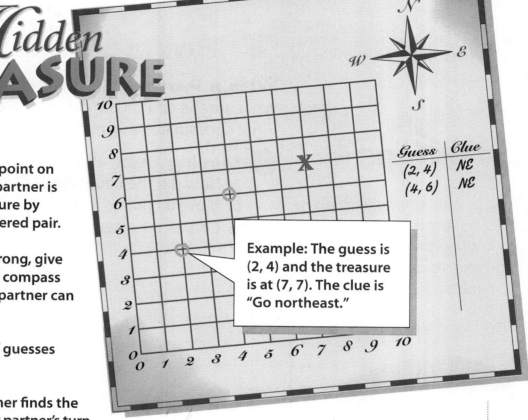

1. Secretly mark a point on your grid. Your partner is to find the treasure by guessing an ordered pair.

2. If the guess is wrong, give a clue, using the compass rose. Then your partner can guess again.

3. Keep a record of guesses and clues.

4. When your partner finds the treasure, it's your partner's turn to hide a treasure for you to find.

Example: The guess is (2, 4) and the treasure is at (7, 7). The clue is "Go northeast."

Guess	Clue
(2, 4)	NE
(4, 6)	NE

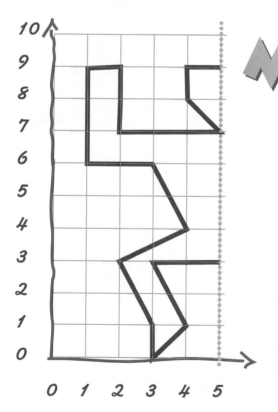

Mirror image

1. Draw a symmetrical figure by connecting points. Divide the figure on a line of symmetry.

2. Write the points of half the figure as a list of ordered pairs. List the points in the order in which they should be connected.

3. Exchange lists. Plot the points and complete your partner's drawing.

4. List the ordered pairs that make the other half of the figure. How does the second list compare with the first?

4 Moving on a Grid

What You'll Need
• grid paper

In Your Journal Sketch a figure to move on a grid. Write some directions and share them with a partner.

With a Partner Make a grid and move a boat! What are the coordinates of point *C* on the first boat? Write coordinates as you map the boat's movement.

1 **Moving Over** Place point *C* at (13, 7).
   a. How did the coordinates of point *C* change?
   b. Move all points the same number of units.
   c. Connect the new coordinates to draw the boat.

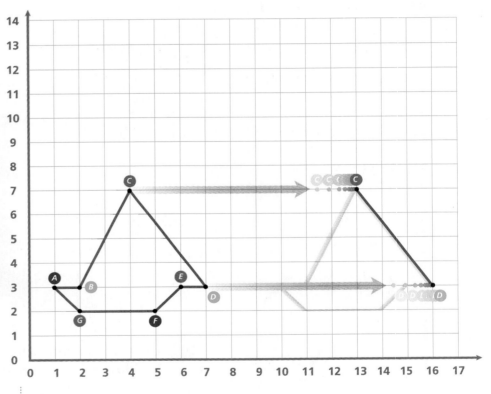

2 **Moving Up** Move the boat again.
   a. Place point *C* at (4, 14) and redraw the boat.
   b. Which coordinates changed? by how much?

3 **Moving Again**
   a. Move the boat so point *D* is at (16, 9).
   b. How did the coordinates change?

ACTIVITY 5 Growing on a Grid

What You'll Need
• *grid paper*

On Your Own By plotting points, you can show objects in different sizes.

1. **Draw one of these pictures on a grid.**

2. **Choose one of these ways to change the coordinates:**
   a. **Multiply all the coordinates by 2.**
   b. **Multiply only the first coordinate in each pair by 2.**
   c. **Multiply only the last coordinate in each pair by 2.**

3. **Plot the new coordinates to draw a new picture. How does it compare with your first drawing?**

4. **Add your picture to a class display.**

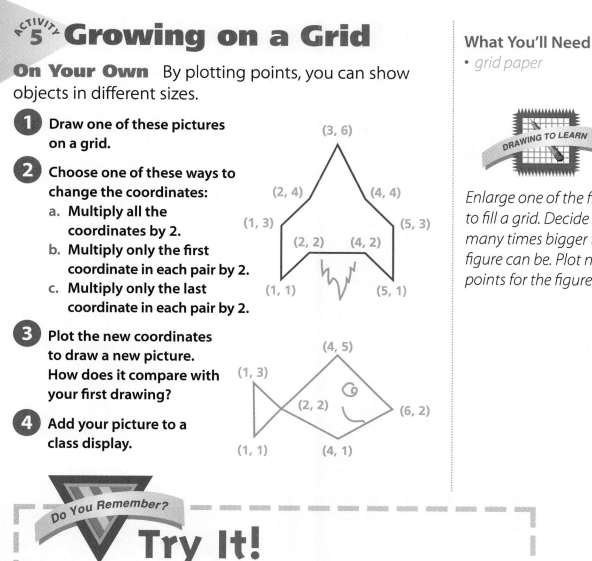

DRAWING TO LEARN

Enlarge one of the figures to fill a grid. Decide how many times bigger the figure can be. Plot new points for the figure.

Do You Remember?

Try It!

Draw an arrow to show the direction an object is moving if it begins at point (0, 0) and ends at each point.

1. (0, 3)   **2.** (2, 3)   **3.** (2, 2)   **4.** (4, 2)   **5.** (4, 0)

Write the measure in meters or grams.

6. 132 km   **7.** 5,000 cm   **8.** 12 kg   **9.** 1,600 mg   **10.** 0.5 km

Think About It

11. How do coordinates on a grid change when you move a figure to the left? up? down? to the right?

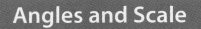

LESSON 4 Scaling a Kite

A map is a scale drawing of real places. If you know the scale of a map, you can find the actual distances between the places shown on the map. Large objects like buildings are also drawn to scale. American sculptor Tal Streeter made a scale drawing, much like the one on the left, of a large Japanese-style kite.

290 cm

180 cm

ACTIVITY 1 How Big Is It?

With Your Group You can figure out the scale of the kite drawing by comparing measurements.

1 Measure the length and width of the drawing. Measure the diagonal "bones." Record these numbers and the measurements of the real kite in your notebook.

2 How can you use division to figure out how many centimeters on the real kite equals 1 cm in the drawing? Use your answer to complete a scale for the drawing: 1 cm = ___ cm.

What is the relationship?

	Drawing	Real kite
Length	? cm	290 cm
Width	? cm	180 cm
Diagonals	? cm	? cm

3 Use your scale to find the length of the diagonals in the real kite.

What You'll Need
• *centimeter ruler*

TOOLS AND TECHNIQUES

You have used a map scale on maps in social studies. You will need a ruler to measure the distance between points on the kite drawing.

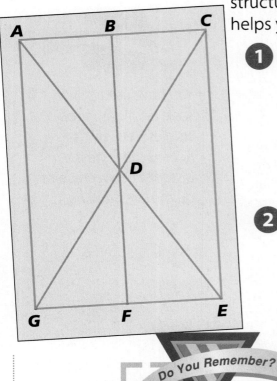

ACTIVITY 2 Angles and Kites

With Your Group This scale drawing shows the structure of a kite. Using letters to mark the key points helps you name the parts.

1 Two rays that share an endpoint form an **angle.** The endpoint they share is the vertex. The symbol ∠ means "angle." Use letters to name points of an angle. The middle letter always stands for the vertex.

　a. Find ∠ADC. Name the rays.

　b. What letter names the vertex?

2 Two angles are congruent if they are the same size.

　a. Trace ∠CDE on your Tracing Tool.

　b. Find an angle that is congruent to ∠CDE.

　c. Find an angle congruent to ∠ADF.

Do You Remember?

Try It!

For each angle, find a congruent angle in the figure above.

1. ∠ADC   2. ∠ADB   3. ∠GFD
4. ∠BCD   5. ∠ADG   6. ∠ACE

Plot each set of ordered pairs on a coordinate grid. Connect the points to form an angle with its vertex at the second point listed.

7. (1, 5), (1, 2), (4, 2)   8. (7, 4), (6, 1), (8, 1)
9. (12, 5), (10, 2), (12, 2)

Think About It

10. Are any of the angles you drew in Exercises 7–9 congruent? How can you tell?

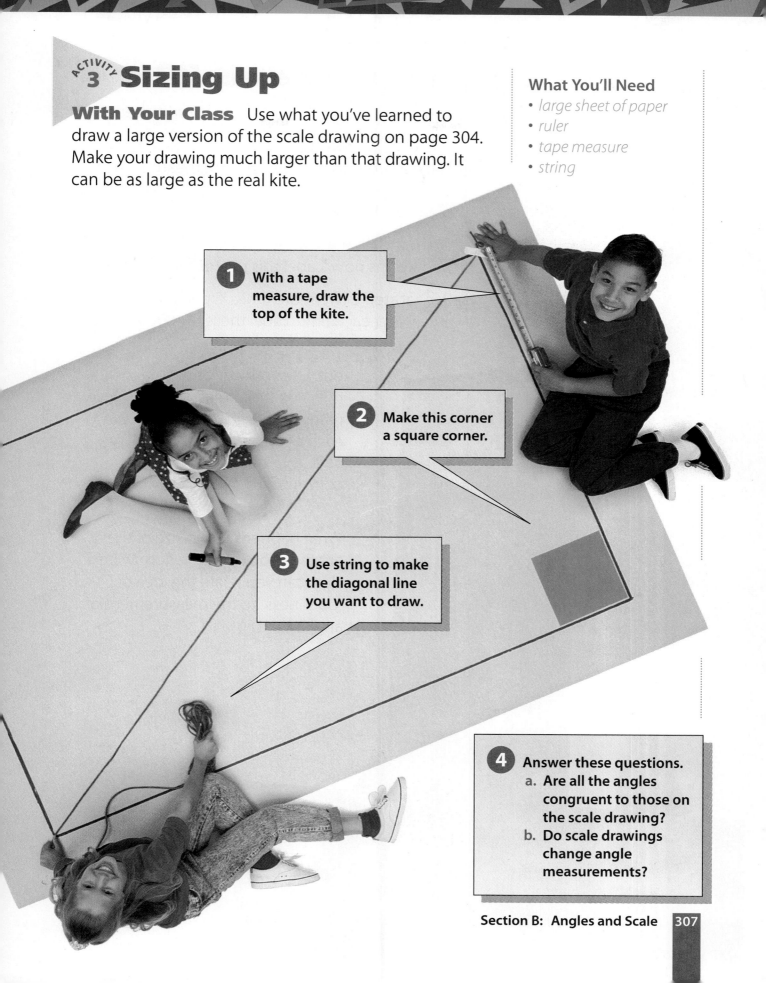

ACTIVITY 3 Sizing Up

With Your Class Use what you've learned to draw a large version of the scale drawing on page 304. Make your drawing much larger than that drawing. It can be as large as the real kite.

What You'll Need
- *large sheet of paper*
- *ruler*
- *tape measure*
- *string*

1 With a tape measure, draw the top of the kite.

2 Make this corner a square corner.

3 Use string to make the diagonal line you want to draw.

4 Answer these questions.
   a. Are all the angles congruent to those on the scale drawing?
   b. Do scale drawings change angle measurements?

⁴ How Open Is It?

With Your Group Try this activity with a door to explore comparing and measuring angles.

 1 Place a large sheet of paper underneath a door. Draw the ray made by the closed door. Use the hinge as the vertex. Label this ray *HA*.

2 Open the door a few inches. Draw the ray that the door forms now. Label this ray *HB*.

3 Repeat step 2 two more times. Open the door a little wider each time. Label these rays *HC* and *HD*.

4 Trace the angle below and cut it out. Use your cut-out angle to measure the angles you drew. How many of these angle units are in each of these angles?
   a. ∠ *AHB*
   b. ∠ *AHC*
   c. ∠ *AHD*

5 What happens to the size of the angle as you open the door wider? How can you relate the idea of "openness" to the measurement of angles?

 ACTIVITY 5 Standard Unit

On Your Own You worked out a way to measure the angles made by opening a door. The usual way to measure angles is with a small unit called a **degree.**

1 Make a Right Angle A **right angle** has 90°, but you can make one without measuring.

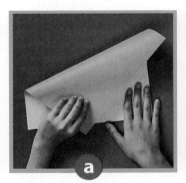 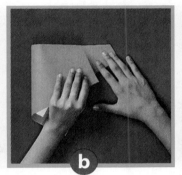 

a **Fold any piece of paper once.**

b **Fold it again with the edges of the first fold together.**

c **Use the square corner to draw and measure right angles.**

2 Draw Other Angles With your square corner, estimate and draw these angles.

45° 30° 60° 15° 150° 180°

3 Naming Angles Angles greater than a right angle are **obtuse angles.** Angles less than a right angle are **acute angles.** A straight line, 180°, is a **straight angle.**

a. Which of the angles you drew are obtuse angles? acute? straight?

b. Draw two acute angles and two obtuse angles. Label each angle.

REASONING AND PROBLEM SOLVING

What strategy did you use to draw acute and obtuse angles?

What You'll Need

- *Geometry Tool or protractor*
- *ruler*
- *grid paper*

☑ **Self-Check** *How close are your angle measurements to those made by other members of your group? Measure again until your measurements agree.*

ᴬᶜᵀᴵᵛᴵᵀʸ 6 A Friendly Protractor

With Your Group A protractor is a useful math tool. You can use it to measure angles.

1 On the Protractor Read the numbers, find the vertex, and follow these steps.

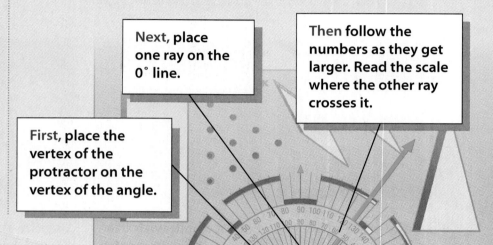

Next, place one ray on the 0° line.

Then follow the numbers as they get larger. Read the scale where the other ray crosses it.

First, place the vertex of the protractor on the vertex of the angle.

2 Measuring Angles Use a protractor to measure the door angles you made in Activity 4. Record your measurements.

3 Draw and Check Draw two acute angles. Write the number of degrees in each. Draw and label two obtuse angles.

4 Measure Again Use a protractor to measure the angles you drew in Activity 5. How accurate were your estimates?

5 Draw and Measure Draw an angle on paper. Exchange papers and measure angles. Draw an angle congruent to the one you measured.

6 **Angles Around** Draw a 30° angle. Draw another 30° angle so that the angles share one ray. Do it again and again until you get back to where you started.

    a. How many 30° angles did it take?

    b. What's the total number of degrees in a circle?

Draw a triangle. Measure all the angles. Are the bigger angles opposite the longer sides?

ACTIVITY 7 A Mathematical Star

On Your Own The figure below is a pentagram—a five-pointed star drawn inside a regular pentagon. It is sometimes called the Pythagorean pentagram because it was the symbol of a group of ancient Greek mathematicians led by Pythagoras. However, pentagram designs appeared even earlier in the art of the ancient Babylonians.

What You'll Need
- *Geometry Tool or protractor*
- *Tracing Tool*
- *ruler*

1 Are the triangles that form the five points of the star all congruent? Use your Tracing Tool to help you check.

2 Name two other pairs of congruent triangles in the pentagram.

3 How many degrees are in each point of the star? What is the total number of degrees in all five points?

4 Would your answers to Exercise 3 change if you enlarged the pentagram to twice the size shown? Write a few sentences to explain how you know.

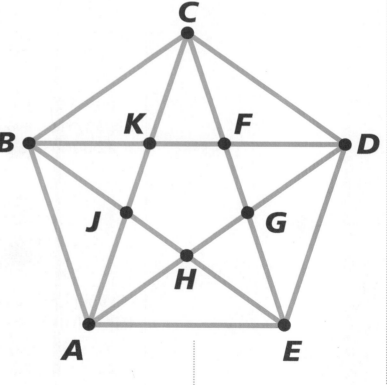

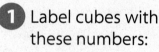

ESCAPE the WHEEL

An Angle Game

With Your Group You can play Escape the Wheel in groups of two, three, or four. The first player to get a game piece outside the wheel is the winner.

What You'll Need
- *Geometry tool or protractor*
- *gameboard*
- *2 cubes with degree labels*
- *game pieces*

Getting Ready

1 Label cubes with these numbers:

$$5°, \ 15°, \ 25°$$
$$35°, \ 45°, \ 55°$$

2 Choose your game piece. Use anything available, such as a button or a paper clip.

Play a different game. Take turns rolling one cube. On paper, draw an angle to match the number on the cube. The first person to have angles that total exactly 360° is the winner.

3 Put your game piece on a star. Roll the cubes. The player with the greatest roll starts the game.

Playing the Game

4 Measure the equal angles formed by the rays that intersect in the center of the wheel.

5 Roll both cubes. Add or subtract to find the number of degrees you can move your game piece. You can move in either direction.

6 If you land on an arrow, move in the direction of the arrow. Take turns until a player escapes the wheel.

Angles Around You

Look for angles in these objects. Answer the questions on a sheet of paper. Estimate when you can. Then check with a protractor.

Angle o' Clock

1 How many degrees is the acute angle formed by the clock hands?

2 At 2:45 will the hands form an acute angle or an obtuse angle?

Compass Points

3 How many degrees from north is east?

4 What direction is the arrow pointing when it points 45˚ west of south?

Cheese Wedge

5 Measure the angle in the wedge of cheese.

6 How many pieces of this size can you get from two circles of cheese?

Alphabet Angles

7 Which of these letters have acute angles? Which have obtuse angles? right angles?

8 Which letters have more than one kind of angle?

9 Name some letters that have no angles.

Crossed Sticks

10 Extend the rays to find the vertex of the angle formed by the chopsticks. How long is each chopstick from its tip to the vertex?

11 Measure the angle formed by the chopsticks.

Degree of Chance

12 How many degrees does each equal section of the spinner show?

13 Design and describe a spinner that has ten equal sections.

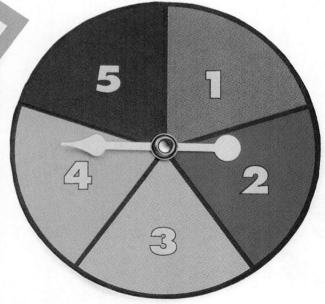

Think It Over

14 Find three ways to draw a right angle without using a protractor.

Flying Triangles

You can make a kite of almost any shape, but many kites are triangles. Look at the kites in the picture. How are they alike? How are they different?

A

B

C

D

F

E

Similar Triangles

With a Partner Triangles that are different sizes can be the same shape. If two triangles are the same shape, they are **similar triangles.**

  Which of the kites on the opposite page are similar? What can you say about the angles in similar triangles?

  Draw a kite to add to one of the sets of similar kites. Explain why your kite fits with the others in the set.

3 Draw or make your own set of three similar kites. Explain how your kites are similar.

Adding Up the Angles

With Your Group You know how to measure angles in triangles. Try the method below to find the measure of the three angles in one triangle. Repeat with at least two more triangles. Then make a generalization about the total number of degrees in a triangle.

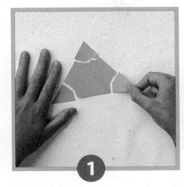

Tear the corners of the triangles.

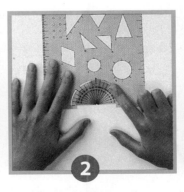

Put two corners together. Measure the angle.

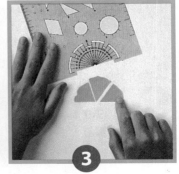

Add the third corner and find the total.

Make a list of properties that make triangles different. Try to list at least three. Use your list to help sort the triangles.

ACTIVITY 3 Sort by Your Rules

With a Partner   Investigate some ways you can sort triangles. To begin, think of ways these triangles are alike. Then find some differences. Sort them as many ways as you can think of.

1

2

3

4

5

6

ACTIVITY 4 Using Clues

With a Partner   Sort the triangles above by the length of their sides. Start by learning definitions that tell you what to look for. Then play a sorting game. The rules for the game are on the next page.

What You'll Need
- *Geometry Tool or protractor*
- *clue cards*
- *ruler*

CONNECT AND COMMUNICATE

In Your Journal Record what you have discovered about angles and sides in each kind of triangle.

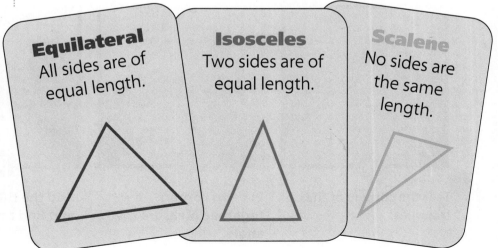

Equilateral
All sides are of equal length.

Isosceles
Two sides are of equal length.

Scalene
No sides are the same length.

triangle sort

To prepare the cards for this game, you will need an instruction sheet provided by your teacher.

1 Mix the cards and give five to each player. Stack the others face down. Turn one card from the pile face up and place it next to the pile.

2 Take turns drawing a card from either pile. Discard one in the face-up pile.

3 When a player gets five cards that describe one kind of triangle, that player names the triangle category.

Try It!

Measure the following angles:

1. ∠ABC   **2.** ∠CAB   **3.** ∠BCA   **4.** ∠DEF   **5.** ∠EFD

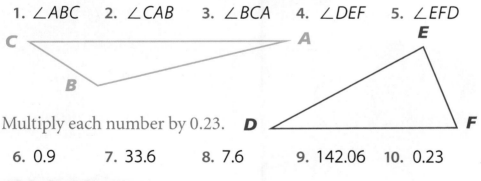

Multiply each number by 0.23.

6. 0.9   **7.** 33.6   **8.** 7.6   **9.** 142.06   **10.** 0.23

Think About It

11. How could you use your answers to Exercises 1 and 2 above to find the answer to Exercise 3 without measuring.

Investigation

Kite Making

Kites often fly high in the skies of Japan. They are a part of many celebrations. You might see thank-you kites and congratulations kites and kites that carry messages or pictures of heroes. There are giant kites and stamp-sized kites. The largest kite in the world was built in Japan. It was made of bamboo and paper and measured 63 ft in diameter. It is said that 150 to 200 people were needed to fly it.

Kites and Scale

You too can make a kite. Fly it or display it on the wall. Begin by making a scale drawing. Choose one of these activities.

Option 1

Choose a Japanese kite pictured on the opposite page or in a book or magazine.

1 Measure the sides of the kite. Measure the parts of the frame. Record all the measurements.

2 Figure out a scale for making the kite larger. Make a scale drawing of the kite.

3 Then, if you want to, make the large kite.

Option 2

Design a kite of your own. Build it if you would like to. Then make a scale drawing to show someone else how to build a kite just like yours. Show the scale you used and give the actual measurements of the kite.

Ask Yourself

☐ What scale will you choose to make your kite?
☐ In what unit of measurement will you make your scale drawing?
☐ How many times larger than the scale drawing will your real kite be?
☐ How could you explain your scale drawing to a friend?

The Captain's Sailboat

What must you do to plan a trip around the world in a sailboat? How would you build a boat? Look at this drawing of a boat like Captain Pinkney's *Commitment*.

1 Find the measures of angles *A, C, D, E, H,* and *J*. Measure one angle in each triangle, and use what you know about triangles to find the other angle. Write a sentence to show how you found each angle.

2 Make a $\frac{1}{2}$-size scale drawing for each of the triangular sails. Use your Geometry Tool or a protractor and a ruler. Label all the angles.

3 Describe the three triangles in the sails. Compare them, using the words *similar, congruent, right, scalene, equilateral,* and *isosceles*.

4 The *Commitment* is 47 ft long. Draw a scale to show how the picture compares to the actual boat. Use the scale to find the approximate height of the mast. Is 47 a prime or composite number? How do you know?

5 Is the mast a line of symmetry? Why or why not? Does the *Commitment* have another line of symmetry? If so, draw it.

SAIL 1

?

A

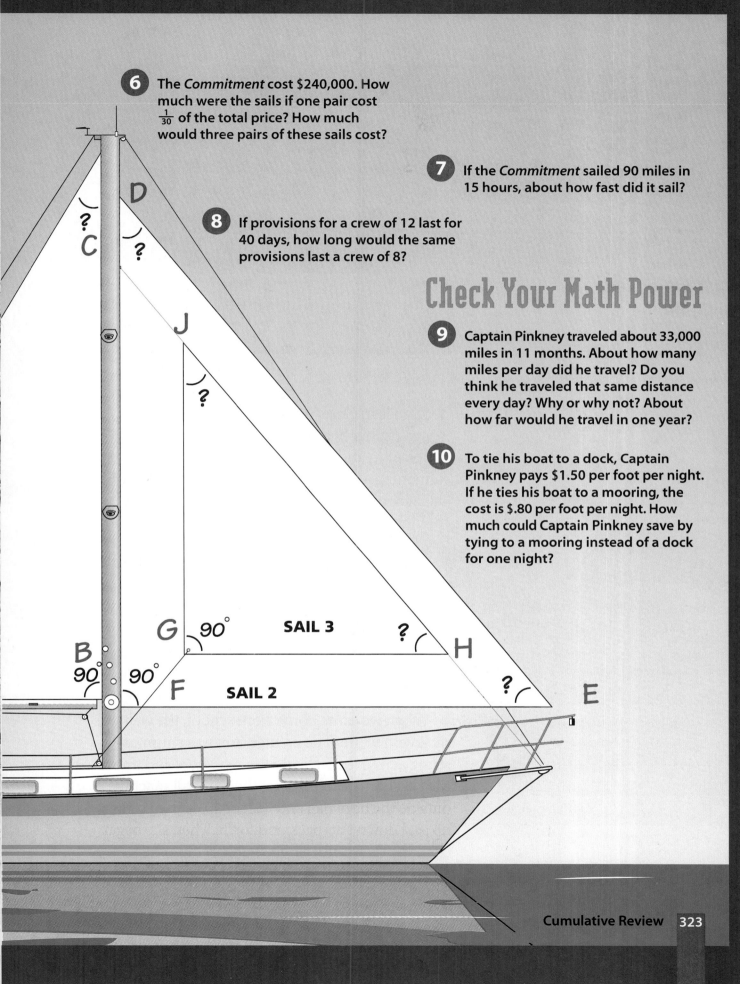

6 The *Commitment* cost $240,000. How much were the sails if one pair cost $\frac{1}{30}$ of the total price? How much would three pairs of these sails cost?

7 If the *Commitment* sailed 90 miles in 15 hours, about how fast did it sail?

8 If provisions for a crew of 12 last for 40 days, how long would the same provisions last a crew of 8?

Check Your Math Power

9 Captain Pinkney traveled about 33,000 miles in 11 months. About how many miles per day did he travel? Do you think he traveled that same distance every day? Why or why not? About how far would he travel in one year?

10 To tie his boat to a dock, Captain Pinkney pays $1.50 per foot per night. If he ties his boat to a mooring, the cost is $.80 per foot per night. How much could Captain Pinkney save by tying to a mooring instead of a dock for one night?

LESSON
6

The Big Picture

LITERATURE

In "The War of the Wall" by Toni Cade Bambara, an artist creates a huge wall painting to honor a young neighborhood man who died in a war. As you read, see if you can figure out the shortcut she uses.

I f you lean close," Lou said, leaning hipshot against her beat-up car, "you'll get a whiff of bubblegum and kids' sweat. And that'll tell you something—that this wall belongs to the kids of Talliaferro Street." I thought Lou sounded very convincing. But the painter lady paid us no mind.

She just snapped the brim of her straw hat down and hauled her bucket up the ladder.

"You're not even from around here," I hollered up after her. The license plates on her old piece of car said "New York." Lou dragged me away because I was about to grab hold of that ladder and shake it. And then we'd really be late for school.

When we came home from school, the wall was slick with white. The painter lady was running string across the wall and taping it here and there. Me and Lou leaned against the gumball machine outside the pool hall and watched. She had strings up and down and back and forth. Then she began chalking them with a huge hunk of blue chalk.

How Much Bigger?

What You'll Need
- *Geometry Tool or protractor*
- *centimeter ruler*

With Your Group You'll use the painter's short cut to make your own scale drawings in Activity 2. First, you need to know how to compare measurements.

1 Compare the Triangles What can you say about these two triangles? Use your ruler and protractor. Write down everything you discover. These questions will help.

> a. **What can you say about the angle measurements? Name all the pairs of equal angles.**
>
> b. **What can you say about the lengths of the sides?**
>
> c. **Which side is twice as long as side *AC*?**

2 Use a Ratio You can compare the lengths of two sides using a **ratio**. For example, side *EF* is twice as long as side *BC*. The ratio of *EF* to *BC* is 2 to 1. You can write this ratio as 2 : 1 or $\frac{2}{1}$.

> a. How would you write the ratio of side *BC* to side *EF*? Explain.
>
> b. What is the ratio of side *AC* to side *DF*?
>
> c. What is the ratio of side *CB* to side *FE*?

CONNECT AND COMMUNICATE

In Your Journal Draw a triangle similar to triangle DEF, with sides two times as long. Use what you know about angle measure and similar figures to help you.

What You'll Need

- *drawing paper*
- *crayons or markers*
- *ruler*
- *scissors*
- *tape*

TOOLS AND TECHNIQUES

What other methods can you use to blow up a picture? You can project the picture with an overhead projector onto a large piece of paper. Then you can draw the enlarged image.

ACTIVITY 2 Blow Up a Picture

With Your Group   The artist in "The War of the Wall" used ratio and a grid to blow up a picture. The directions at the bottom of this page show how. Choose an activity below or think up your own.

Draw a Big Friend!   Draw a life-sized picture of a friend. Trace a head-to-toe photo. Find out your friend's height—for example, 60 in. Then measure the height in the picture—for example, 6 in. Figure out the ratio. Use the grid system shown below.

Draw a Zoo!   Draw an animal life-size. Find a picture of an animal. Find out its actual size. Decide on a ratio. Use a grid to blow up the animal picture. Display your group's animals.

Blow It Up!   Make a bulletin-board mural. Choose a picture from a magazine. Measure the picture and the bulletin board. Find the ratio. Use the grid system.

1

Draw a grid over the small drawing.

2

Choose a ratio. Draw a large grid the correct size on your wall or paper.

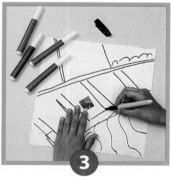

3

Redraw your picture, one grid square at a time, at the larger size.

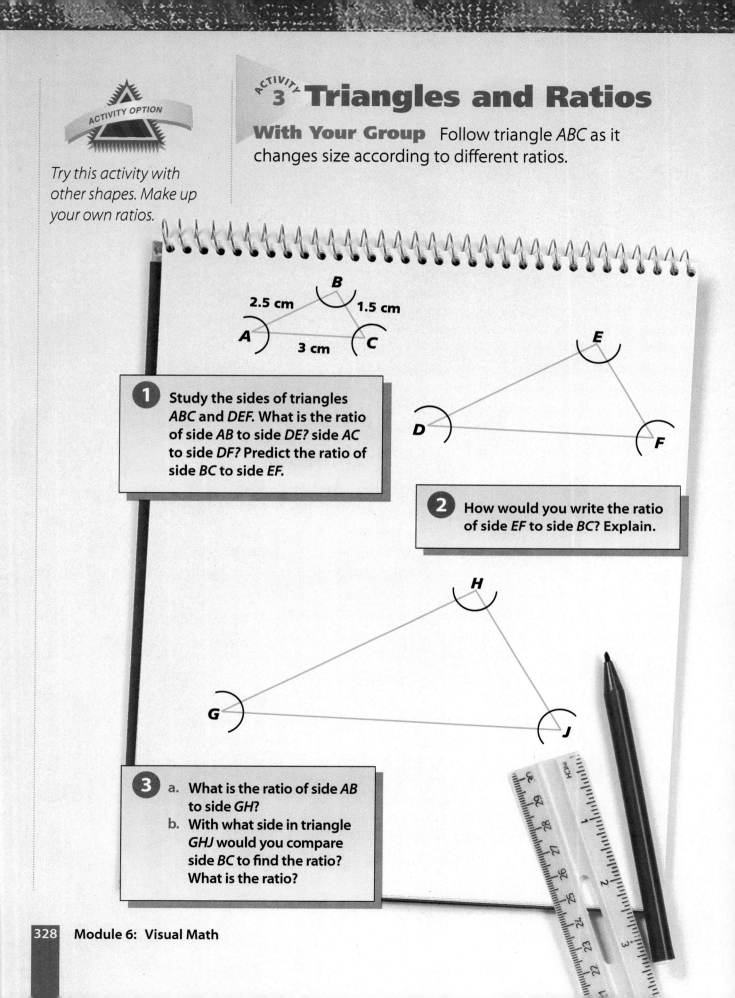

Triangles and Ratios

With Your Group Follow triangle *ABC* as it changes size according to different ratios.

ACTIVITY OPTION

Try this activity with other shapes. Make up your own ratios.

2.5 cm **B** **1.5 cm**
A **3 cm** **C**

E
D **F**

1 Study the sides of triangles *ABC* and *DEF*. What is the ratio of side *AB* to side *DE*? side *AC* to side *DF*? Predict the ratio of side *BC* to side *EF*.

2 How would you write the ratio of side *EF* to side *BC*? Explain.

H
G **J**

3 a. What is the ratio of side *AB* to side *GH*?
b. With what side in triangle *GHJ* would you compare side *BC* to find the ratio? What is the ratio?

4 Draw a new triangle with a ratio of 4 : 1 to triangle *ABC*.

a

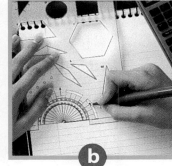
b

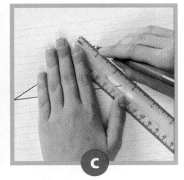
c

Multiply the length of each side of triangle *ABC* by four.

Draw the longest line. Measure the angle for the next line. Draw that line to the correct length.

Connect the two lines. Check to be sure the third line is in the correct ratio.

5 What ratio will make the longest side of triangle *ABC* as long as your desk? as your classroom? How long would the other two sides be for each new triangle?

Do You Remember?

Try It!

Write the ratio of the two sides given.

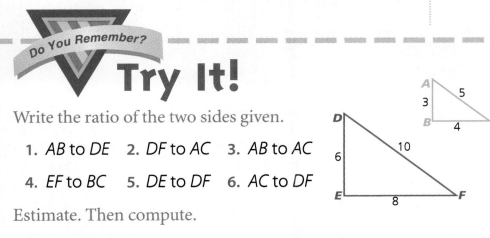

1. *AB* to *DE*   2. *DF* to *AC*   3. *AB* to *AC*

4. *EF* to *BC*   5. *DE* to *DF*   6. *AC* to *DF*

Estimate. Then compute.

7. $3.27 - 0.253$ 8. $0.96 + 2.954$ 9. $7.332 - 0.25$

10. $8.44 + 0.63$ 11. $10.366 - 0.412$ 12. $6.548 - 1.67$

Think About It

13. Are triangles *ABC* and *DEF* similar triangles? Explain your answer in writing.

Building Polygons

Now use triangles to build **polygons**—closed figures made entirely of line segments.

What You'll Need
• *drawing paper*
• *scissors*

ACTIVITY
1 **Cut and Combine**

With Your Group   Combine triangles to make **quadrilaterals,** or four-sided polygons. The six shapes at the bottom of this page are quadrilaterals.

1

Fold a sheet of paper in half. Cut out a triangle along the folded edge. Then unfold the triangle.

2

What kind of quadrilateral do you have? What can you say about the two triangles that make it up?

3

Cut across the fold line. Arrange the triangles into other quadrilaterals. Record your results.

4

Repeat steps 1–3 with another triangle. What generalizations can you make about the triangles that make up quadrilaterals? Describe your quadrilaterals.

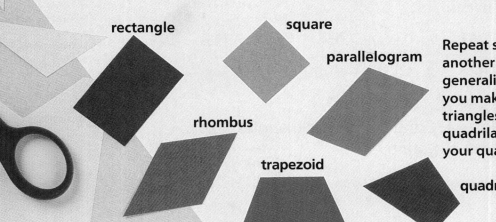

rectangle

square

parallelogram

rhombus

trapezoid

quadrilateral

ACTIVITY 2 More Than Four

With Your Group Measure the angles in a quadrilateral. Add them up. Record the number. Do the same with a pentagon and a hexagon. What pattern do you see?

Total Number of Degrees in Regular Polygons

Shape	sides	total degrees
Triangle	3	180
Quadri	4	?
Pentagon	5	?
Hexagon	6	?

ACTIVITY 3 Venning Shapes

With Your Group Look at the Venn diagram below. The outside shape stands for all quadrilaterals. What do the inside shapes stand for?

Draw a quadrilateral that is not a parallelogram.

Draw a parallelogram that is not a rectangle.

Why are trapezoids and parallelograms separate?

Which part of the diagram stands for figures that do not have two sets of parallel sides?

Why are squares shown inside rectangles and parallelograms?

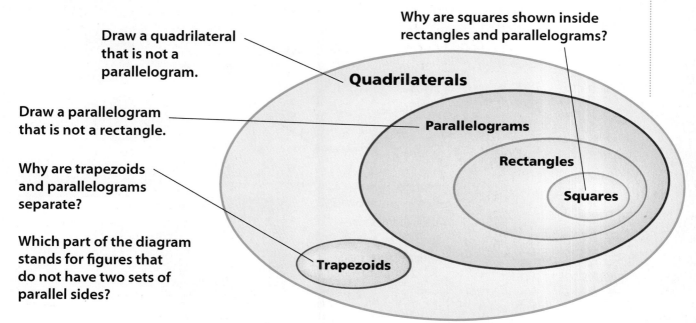

What You'll Need
- *Geometry Tool or protractor*
- *ruler*

What do you know about expressions that can help you find the pattern? First describe the pattern in words. Then use numbers and a variable. For instance, start with n × 180.

What You'll Need
- *Geometry Tool or protractor*
- *ruler*

Scale and Sketch

With Your Group Now try using polygons to help you blow up a picture. How big a lizard can you make on an $8\frac{1}{2}$-by-11-in. piece of paper? Compare your estimate with the lizard here to find the ratio you need. Follow these steps to make your lizard.

What You'll Need
- *Geometry Tool or protractor*
- *Tracing Tool or grid paper*
- *drawing paper*
- *ruler*

1 Measure the lizard. Estimate its final size. Find the ratio to compare the two sizes.

2 Start to break the lizard down into polygon shapes.

☑ **Self-Check** *Check your similar figures carefully. Are the angles the same? Are the sides all to the correct ratio? If so, your scaled-up animal should work out well.*

Draw a Cow!

If the lizard is too hard, try an animal with a simpler shape.

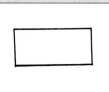

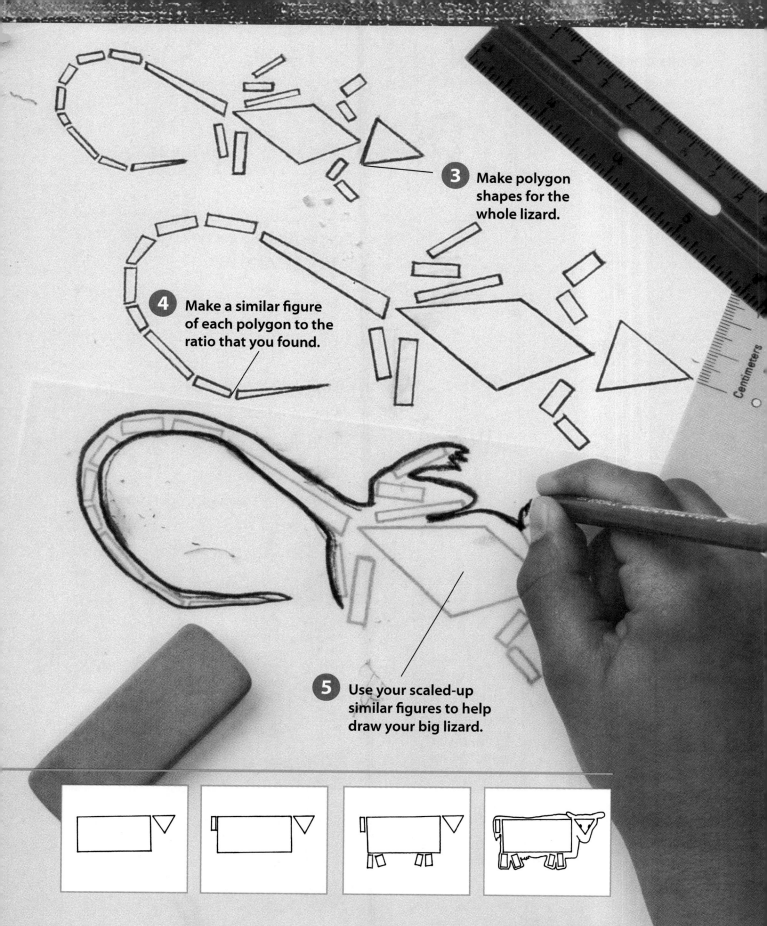

3 Make polygon shapes for the whole lizard.

4 Make a similar figure of each polygon to the ratio that you found.

5 Use your scaled-up similar figures to help draw your big lizard.

Polygon Games

Look for polygons in these patterns. Do the exercises on a separate sheet of paper. To help you keep track of the shapes, try labeling each polygon with a letter.

A

Find 'em

1 How many triangles can you find in Figure A? in Figure B?

2 How many quadrilaterals can you find in figure B?

3 How many pentagons can you find in figure A?

4 What other polygons can you find?

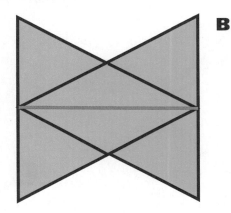

B

Keep Score!

5 In this polygon game you get 3 points for each triangle you find. You get 4 points for each quadrilateral. How many points can you make with the shapes you find in Figure C? Compare totals with a partner. Show each shape you found.

6 How many more points could you get if each pentagon were worth 5 points?

C

Sides and Angles

7 Score points by finding quadrilaterals in the flat figure below. Name them with the letters shown. Use the Score Card.

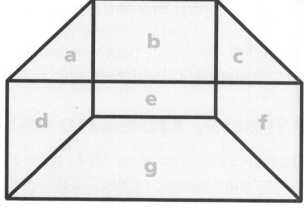

8 For one extra point each, tell what kind of quadrilateral you've found. Check your score against a partner's.

9 What other polygons besides quadrilaterals can you find?

Polygon Dinosaur

10 Now think about redrawing this dinosaur at different ratios. Measure the bottom side of each polygon. Tell the length of the dinosaur drawn at each ratio. (The top number in each ratio refers to the drawing shown.)

a. $\frac{1}{3}$ b. $\frac{1}{100}$

c. $\frac{1}{50}$ d. $\frac{20}{1}$

LESSON 8

Get the Facts!

Earlier in this module you used your math skills to make maps and scale drawings. In a similar way, you can also make visual displays of **data,** or numeric information. But first you'll need some data to work with. Try these activities to gather data about your own class.

ACTIVITY 1 Questions, Questions!

With Your Class One way to collect data is to take a survey. You can use a questionnaire like the one shown here.

1. Prepare your own questionnaire. Use any questions you like from the list shown. Add other questions that your class would like to gather data about.

2. Have each student answer all the questions. Collect all the questionnaires.

3. Agree on a plan for compiling the results of your survey.

Fifth Grade Question Sheet
Please answer the following questions.
1. How many hours of sleep do you get each night?
2. How many blocks away from school do you live?
3. How long is your hair (in inches)?
4. How many minutes of homework do you do each night ?

Tear It Up!

With Your Class Now collect some more data. See how many pieces you can tear a sheet of paper into in 15 seconds. Tear only one sheet at a time.

1 Start when your teacher says start. Tear until your teacher says stop. Count the pieces. Write your total.

2 List the class results on the board. Talk about what you see. Draw conclusions.

    a. What is the most frequent result? How do you know?

    b. What reasons can you think of for the differences in results?

    c. How do your class totals compare with the totals on the notebook?

Paper Tearing Scores

24 30 36 15 37
46 42 37 31 30
15 15 25 34 27
20 34 34 45 33
28 24 32 39 27

ACTIVITY OPTION

How high can you count in 30 seconds? What's your heartbeat after five pushups? Try these activities or make up your own.

Line 'em Up!

With Your Group Here is one way to organize data.

1 This **line plot** shows the tearing totals from the notebook on page 337. Answer the questions.

This *x* stands for a student. How many pieces did this student tear? Explain.

How would you describe this cluster of scores?

To find the range, subtract the smallest number (15) from the largest number. What is the range for this set of data?

What does each number across the bottom represent?

Organize some class data for a fact book. Use your class paper-tearing data or choose data from another question. Talk about the data. Describe it. Draw conclusions. Take notes. Write one or two paragraphs from the notes.

2 How many students tore fewer than 30 pieces? 30 or more pieces? Write your answers as:
   a. fractions
   b. percents (Remember, a percent has a denominator of 100.)
   c. decimals

3 Make a line plot of the tearing totals for your own class. Use the line plot to answer these questions.
   a. What is the range of the data?
   b. Are there any clusters? Describe them.

Middles and Mosts

With Your Group Often it's helpful to have one number you can use to summarize your data. You can use this number to compare different sets of data.

1 **A Mean Fifth Grader?** To find the **mean** for a set of scores, first add up all the scores. Then divide the total by the number of scores. Often people call the mean the average.

   a. Find the mean for the scores on the line plot shown in Activity 3.

   b. Find the mean for the results of your class's paper tearing.

   c. How do the two means compare?

2 **In the Middle** The **median** is the middle number in a set of data. If you have five numbers in order, the third number is the median. The median is also called the counting average.

   a. Find the median on the line plot on page 338.

   b. Find the median for your class's tearing data.

   c. How do the two medians compare?

3 **The Most Frequent** The number that occurs most often in a set of data is called the **mode.**

   a. Find the mode for the data on the sign below.

   b. What do you think the mode is for the data shown on the line plot on page 338? Explain.

4 **Write About It** Write a paragraph comparing the paper-tearing data for your class and for the class shown on the line plot. Which is best for comparing these sets of data—the mean, median, or mode?

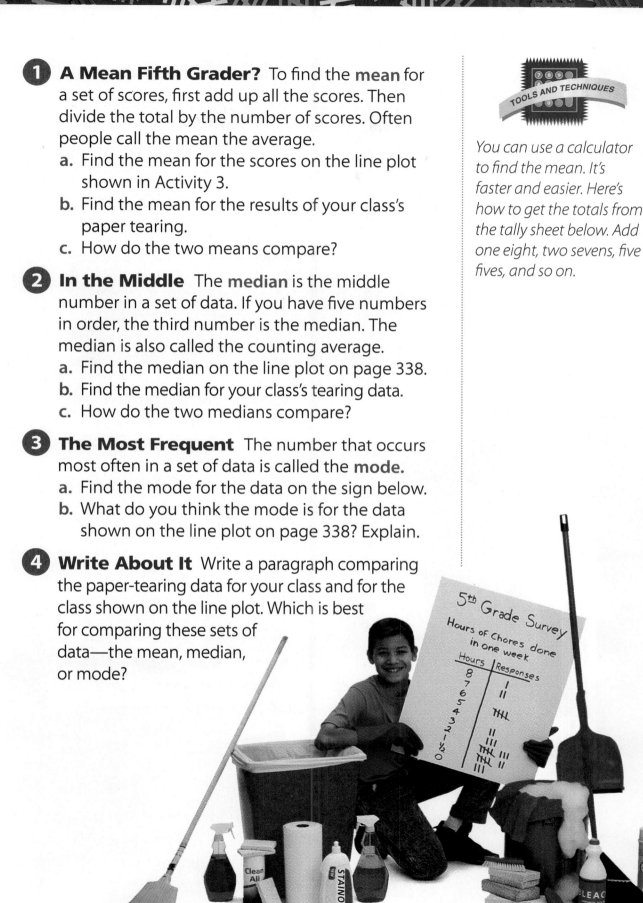

TOOLS AND TECHNIQUES

You can use a calculator to find the mean. It's faster and easier. Here's how to get the totals from the tally sheet below. Add one eight, two sevens, five fives, and so on.

5th Grade Survey
Hours of Chores done in one week

Hours	Responses
8	I
7	II
6	
5	↯↯↯
4	
3	II
2	III
1	↯↯↯ III
½	↯↯↯ II
0	III

ᴬᶜᵀᴵᵛᴵᵀʸ 5 Fruit and Books

With Your Group How many pieces of fruit do you eat in a week? How many books do you read in a month? Tally your class responses. Find the mean, median, and mode.

1 **Have a Banana!** Here's how many pieces of fruit two classes of fifth graders eat in a week.

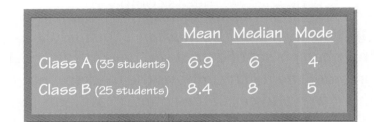

	Mean	Median	Mode
Class A (35 students)	6.9	6	4
Class B (25 students)	8.4	8	5

a. How do these classes compare with each other? with your class ?

b. One student in Class B eats 30 pieces of fruit a week. How does that affect the mean? the median? the mode?

c. Write a paragraph or two telling all you can about the data for Classes A and B and your class.

How Many Books? Here's what two classes of fifth graders said about how many books they read per month. Compare with your own class.

	Mean	Median	Mode
Class C (30 students)	4.8	4	3
Class D (27 students)	3.4	2	1

a. Which class reads more books? How does your class compare? How do you know?

b. Which number tells you the most about these classes and your own? Explain.

c. Write a paragraph or two telling all you can about these results and the results of your own class.

As you write up your conclusions, think about what the mean, median, and mode do not tell you about this data. What else would you like to know? Why?

Do You Remember?

Try It!

How long is your hair in inches? Here's what 20 fifth graders said.

3, 3, 7, 7, 2, 1, 2, 2, 3, 8, 10, 16, 4, 4, 4, 6, 2, 2, 3, 1

Make or find the following for this data.

1. line plot   2. cluster   3. range
4. mean   5. median   6. mode

What percent said the following number of inches? Change each percent to a decimal and a fraction.

7. 1–3   8. 7–8   9. 2–10   10. 4–7   11. 7–16

Think About It

12. Write a brief comparison of the mean, median, and mode for this set of data.

Plot It Out

ACTIVITY 1 Lots of Homework?

With Your Class Forty-five fifth graders answered this question: How many minutes of homework do you do each night? This **stem-and-leaf plot** shows the results.

1 Totals range from 2 to 210. Split each into tens and ones. For example, 45 is 4 tens and 5 ones. List tens as the stem.

2 Make the ones the leaves. How would you read these totals?

0	2, 5
1	
2	
3	
4	5
5	
6	
7	
8	
9	
10	
11	
12	
13	
14	
15	
16	
17	
18	
19	
20	
21	

0	2, 5
1	0, 0, 5
2	0
3	
4	0, 0, 0, 0, 0, 0, 0, 0, 0, 5
5	5, 5, 5, 5
6	0, 0
7	0, 0, 0, 0, 0, 0, 0, 0, 0, 0, 0, 0
8	0, 0
9	
10	
11	
12	
13	0, 0, 0, 0, 5
14	
15	
16	
17	
18	
19	
20	0
21	0

3 Keep plotting. The finished plot has an explanation for the reader.

4 Find the mean, median, and mode of the data on the stem-and-leaf plot.

5 Does anything surprise you? Explain.

6 What would you say about the students who said 2 minutes and 5 minutes?

 **How Do You Compare?**

With Your Group Put your class data about minutes of homework on a stem-and-leaf plot. Write a paragraph describing what your stem-and-leaf plot shows. How does your data compare with that shown on page 342?

Do You Remember?

Try It!

Look at the stem-and-leaf plot on page 342. How many totals are greater than the following?

1. 70   **2.** 45   **3.** 100
4. 35   **5.** 50   **6.** 120

Find each sum or difference. Order the answers from least to greatest.

7. $58.27 + 0.13$ **8.** $60.033 - 0.766$ **9.** $55.1 - 0.003$
10. $66.112 + 0.987$ **11.** $63.227 - 0.701$

Think About It

12. Which of the numbers in Exercises 1–6 are less than the median? How do you know?

Publish Your Facts!

Now write what you have learned from your data. You will put it all together in your fact book.

ACTIVITY 1 Write It Up!

With Your Group

Pick one of the questions your classmates answered.

1 Plot the data. Find the mean, median, and mode.

2 Discuss the data. Have one member take notes.
   a. What's the range? Do you see clusters?
   b. What does the middle tell you?
   c. What do you learn about fifth graders?

we sleep from $6\frac{1}{2}$ to 11 hours each night. Most of us sleep between 8 and 10 hours. Nine of 27 sleep 9 hours. That's the mode. The median is 9 and the mean is about 9. You can say our class average is 9 hours.

3 Write a few paragraphs about your data.
Use your notes. Write in everyday language.
Here's how one student did it.

Movies and Videos

0	0, 1, 2, 3, 3, 3, 3, 4, 4, 4, 5, 5, 6, 7, 8, 9
1	0, 0, 0, 1, 1, 1, 2, 4, 8
2	0, 0, 1, 1, 2
3	0

1/2 means 12 movies per month

How many movies or videos do you see in a month? Here's what we said!

We watch from 0 to 30 movies or videos a month. One person sees 30. No one else sees more than 22. The mean is about 10. The median is 9. These probably work better than the mode. It's 3. Most of us see fewer than 10 videos and movies a month. The next biggest group is in the tens.

The answers don't surprise me. Most of us see just enough. I think more than 15 is too many. You don't have time for homework. The person who sees 30 should probably watch less.

Does this student express the question clearly enough? Explain.

Does she talk about the data in everyday language? Does she choose the best middle? Explain.

Do you agree with her ideas about the data? Explain. What else might you say about this data? Write it down!

2 Put It Together!

With Your Group Now put together your part of the fact book. These steps might help.

1 **Exchange Papers** Trade papers with a group who worked with a different question.

2 **Check the Math** Look over the other group's data. Make sure their plots are correct. Did they make any mistakes in calculating the mean, mode, and median? Show any corrections they need to make.

3 **Edit the Writing** Read the paragraphs
carefully. Mark any corrections needed in spelling,
punctuation, or sentence structure. Suggest any
ways the group can make their writing clearer
and easier to understand. Then return the paper
to the group.

4 **Discuss and Finalize** Talk over the editing
and suggestions you received from the other
group. Prepare the final copy of your report.
Design and make a cover sheet for it.

✔ **Self-Check** *Ask
yourself about your
writing. Did you do the
following?*
· *Explain the question.*
· *Use a middle.*
· *Describe the data.*
· *Tell what's unexpected.*
· *Draw conclusions.*

Try It!

How many minutes do you think you can make a mint last in
your mouth? Here's a stem-and-leaf plot showing what some fifth
graders said. Write a sentence or two about each numbered item.

0	2, 2, 2, 5, 5, 5, 5, 6, 7, 7
1	0, 0, 0, 5, 5, 5, 8
2	0, 0, 0, 0, 0, 0
3	1
4	0, 5
5	
6	0

1. the mean, median, and mode
2. the biggest cluster
3. the range
4. where your own answer fits
5. a conclusion you draw from
   this data

Estimate the following in metric units. Measure to check.

6. length of your foot
7. mass of your protractor
8. capacity of a cup or mug
9. height of your classroom door
10. mass of a CD

Think About It
11. What kind of plot might make it easier to find clusters
    in the data above? Explain.

Looking Back

Choose the best answer. Write *a, b, c,* or *d* for each question.

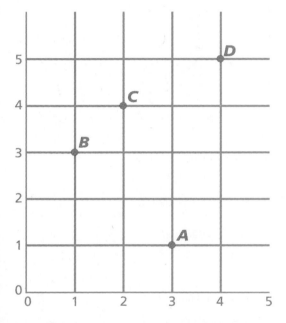

1. Which ordered pair is matched with the wrong point?

  a. *A*: (3, 1)   **b.** *B*: (1, 3)

  c. *C*: (4, 2)   **d.** *D*: (5, 4)

2. You want one number to tell the average amount of time fifth graders think they can keep a mint in their mouth. Which of these would not be useful?

  a. range   **b.** median

  c. mean   **d.** mode

3. A set of data shows ages when people learn to drive. The mode is 16. What does this tell you?

  a. Sixteen is the average age when people learn to drive.

  b. All people learn to drive at 16.

  c. More people learn to drive at 16 than any other age.

  d. Some people learn to drive before age 16 and some after age 16.

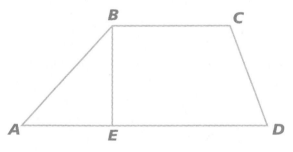

4. Which angle above is obtuse?

  a. ∠*BED*   **b.** ∠*ABC*

  c. ∠*ABE*   **d.** ∠*CDE*

5. The sum of 658 and 349 is closest to what number?

  a. 10   **b.** 10×10

  c. $10 \times 10 \times 10$ **d.** 100×100

6. Imagine a pentagon with all congruent angles. How many degrees would be in each angle?

    a. 180° **b.** 108° **c.** 60° **d.** 36°

7. A number doubles every step in a growth pattern (for example, 2, 4, 8, 16, 32). What is the ratio between the first and fourth numbers?

    a. $\frac{1}{4}$ **b.** $\frac{1}{8}$ **c.** $\frac{1}{2}$ **d.** $\frac{1}{32}$

8. Which is the best estimate of the total cost of this lunch:

    a. $7   **b.** $5   **c.** $6   **d.** $8

9. Which of the following defines an isosceles triangle?

    a. All sides are equal in length.
    b. No sides are the same length.
    c. Two sides are equal in length.
    d. One side is half the length of the other sides.

10. Which is true for the least common multiple of 14 and 21?

    a. It is a composite number.
    b. It is the product of 14 and 21.
    c. It is the difference between 14 and 21.
    d. It is the sum of 14 and 21.

Check Your Math Power

11. Using angles of 30°, 60°, and 90°, and a side of 5 cm, make a triangle with the largest perimeter possible.

12. Draw two block letters on a grid. Write directions for making the letters, using ordered pairs.

13. How many times can you snap your fingers in ten seconds? Sketch a stem-and-leaf plot that predicts what data for ten tries would look like. Then, look at the data your class collected for the class fact book. Make a stem-and-leaf plot to check your prediction.

14. Measure the quadrilateral. Make a scale drawing using a ratio of 4:1.

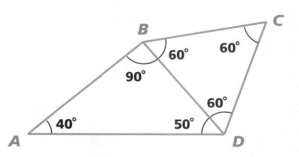

MODULE 6

Investigations

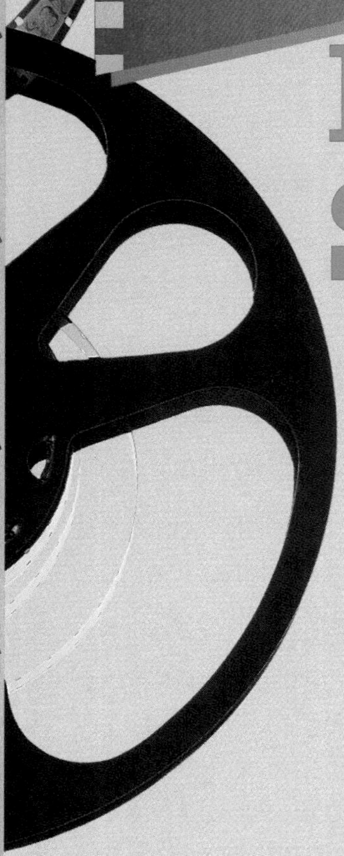

Lights! Shapes! Action!

Do you know how a movie works? Pictures flash by so quickly that they seem to move. A flip book works the same way. You flip the pages and see a slow-motion movie. Use the shapes and drawing skills you've learned to make a flip-book movie.

Investigation A

Polygon Flip

1 **Talk** with group members about how to show polygons moving in a flip book. Try these movements: growing, shrinking, sliding, turning, flipping. How can a coordinate grid help? Decide on three polygons to use.

2 **Fold** and cut your own sheet of grid paper into four equal pieces. Draw a horizontal and a vertical axis on each piece. Do this until you have 16 pieces.

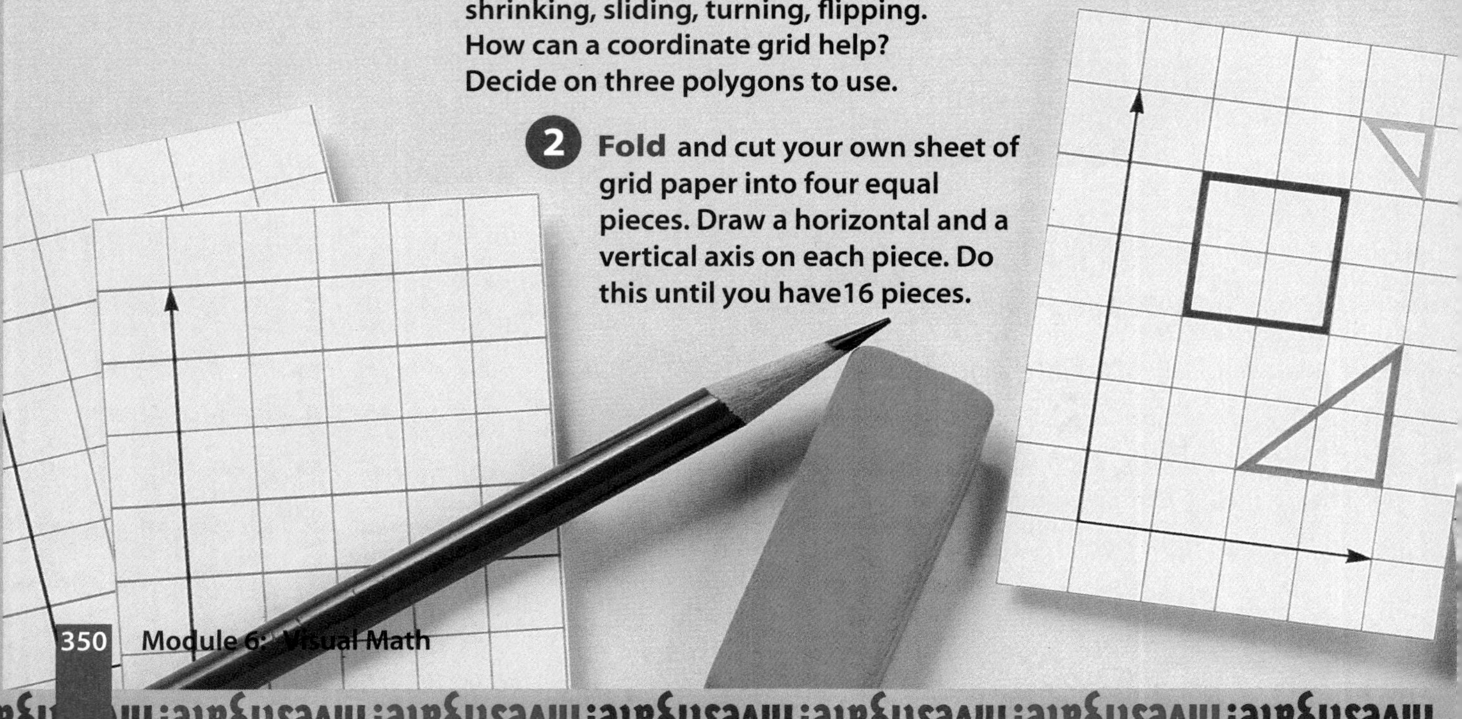

Draw your first shape. Redraw the shape on each following page. But make one small change each time. Use coordinates to help you draw each new scene.

Label the points. Write a description of the changes you made from page to page. Describe what happened to the angles and shapes.

Combine the sections your group created. Revise or add drawings if necessary. Use staples to connect them at the top. Then start the show!

Keep In Mind

Your work will be judged on these points:

☐ How did you use a grid, angle measure, similar polygons, and scale drawing to make your flip book?

☐ Do your written descriptions communicate your knowledge of these concepts?

☐ Did you label and draw your figures accurately and carefully?

Investigation B

Pentagram Pictures

Take another look at the pentagram on page 311. You've already found some pairs of congruent triangles in the pentagram. Now try these investigations.

1 How many triangles are there in the pentagram altogether? Use the letters to name each triangle, and make a list of all you find. How will you know when you have found them all?

2 Sort your list of triangles into sets of congruent triangles.

3 How many other polygons can you find in the pentagram?

4 How many sets of polygons can you find that are similar but not congruent? Is the pentagon in the center similar to the large pentagon? How can you tell?

5 Write a summary of what you found. Be sure to use your knowledge of angles, ratios, and polygons to describe your findings. Also include any other interesting discoveries you made about the pentagram.

Ongoing Investigation

Graphing "Who Are You"

Explore different techniques for plotting your population data. For example, try making a line plot of state populations from the 1990 census. Instead of x's, use the state abbreviations in your line plot. Then try making a stem-and-leaf plot of the same data. What are the advantages of each way of graphing your data?

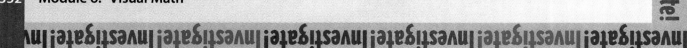

The circles at the top are labeled with the words **radius** (repeated around the first circle), **diameter diameter diameter diameter** (across the second circle), and **circumference** (written repeatedly around the third circle). The third circle shows its **Center**.

ACTIVITY 2 Measure and Chart

With Your Partner Look at the circles you made and the circles above. Where is the radius of each? Explain in your own words what **diameter** is. What is **circumference**?

What You'll Need
- *ruler*
- *at least 4 circular objects*
- *string*

1 In a chart like the one below, record the radius and diameter of the large circle you made. Fill in the chart with the radius and diameter of some of the other circles you drew. Explain how the radius and diameter are related.

2 Estimate the circumference of the circles above. How can you check your estimate? Think of more than one way to measure the circumference.

Object	Radius	Diameter	Circumference
cup	4.25 cm	8.5 cm	26 cm

CONNECT AND COMMUNICATE

3 Record the diameter and circumference of at least four circular objects. What do you notice about the relationship between the diameter and the circumference of a circle? Explain.

Write a definition for a circle. Your definition should allow someone who does not know what a circle is to draw one.

Section A: Going in Circles 357

Self-Check *Do you remember how to find a ratio? Look at the measurements for the cup in the sample chart. Write a division equation that shows how to get the ratio 3.06. Check by dividing.*

On Your Own The ratio of the circumference to the diameter of any circle is called **pi (π).** Mathematicians have figured the value of π to more than 2 billion decimal places.

Object	Diameter	Circumference	Ratio
cup	8.5 cm	26 cm	3.06
drum	25 cm	75.5 cm	3.02

4 Add a ratio column to the chart. Use your calculator to find the ratio. For each object, divide the circumference by the diameter. Round your answer to the nearest hundredth.

a. **What relationship do you see between the circumference and the diameter of each circle? Write this relationship as a ratio.**

b. **Does the size of the circle make any difference in the relationship? Explain.**

5 Measure the diameter of any two circles on these pages. Estimate the circumference of each circle. How can you check your results?

6 Since you usually don't need to find the exact circumference of a circle, you can use 3 or 3.14 as an estimated value of π. Showing π ≈ 3.14 means "π is approximately equal to 3.14."

You know the ratio π ≈ circumference ÷ diameter. The formula for the circumference of a circle is usually written this way:

Circumference ≈ π × diameter

Explain why writing the formula this way works. Give some examples.

Do You Remember?

Try It!

Estimate the circumference for the given diameter.

1. 2 in.   **2.** 3.25 cm   **3.** 8 yd   **4.** 76 ft

Estimate the diameter for the given circumference.

5. 3 ft   **6.** 63 cm   **7.** $37\frac{1}{2}$ in.   **8.** 86 in.

Which figures have the same perimeter? Explain.

9. 3 cm 4 cm 6 cm 2 cm 7 cm   **10.** 9 cm 5 cm 5 cm 9 cm   **11.** 7 cm 7 cm 7 cm 7 cm

Think About It

12. How did you find the circumference for Exercises 1–4 and the diameter for Exercises 5–8?

ACTIVITY OPTION

Make a copy of your chart, leaving some spaces blank. Exchange charts with a classmate. Find the missing numbers in each other's charts.

Spinner Land

What You'll Need
- *Geometry Tool or protractor*
- *compass*
- *ruler*

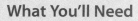
REASONING AND PROBLEM SOLVING

You know there are 360° in a circle. How can you use this to help you draw a spinner with any number of equal sections?

ACTIVITY 1 Dividing a Circle

With Your Group Here's how to use a compass to make some circles and divide them into equal sections. Use a protractor to measure the angles.

1

Open the compass to 2 in. Put the compass point at the center. Move the pencil to draw the circle. What is the circle's diameter?

2

Put the compass point on the circumference. Use the 2-in. opening of the compass to mark six equally spaced points on the circumference. Use the points to draw three diameters. Label this circle *spinner A*.

3 How could you divide a circle into three equal sections? Try it. Label this *spinner B*. Make a circle with five equal sections and label it *spinner C*.

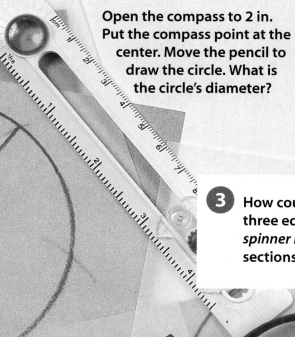

2 Taking Some Spins

With Your Group Number the sections of each of your spinners as shown below.

1

Straighten the outer part of a paper clip. Put your pencil point inside the loop of the paper clip.

2

Place the pencil point at the center of the circle. Spin the paper clip on each spinner to test your answers.

a. Spin on spinner A. Is the paper clip as likely to stop on 1 as on 2? Is 2 as likely as 3? Are all the numbers 1 through 6 equally likely? Explain your answer.

b. Look at spinners A and B. Comparing the two spinners, is it equally likely that you'll spin a 1 on each? Why or why not?

c. What is the probability of spinning a 4 on spinner B? on spinner C? Explain.

What You'll Need
- *4 spinners*

ACTIVITY 3 # What's in a Spin?

With Your Partner The possible results of spinning a spinner are called **outcomes.** You can write the outcomes in a **sample space.**

(1,2,3,4,5,6)

This is the sample space for spinner A. There are six possible outcomes.

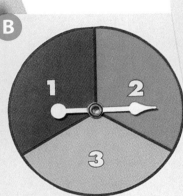

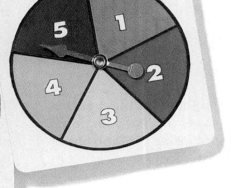

Probability Chart

	1	2	3
Spinner A	1 out of 6	1 out of 6	1 out of 6
Spinner B	1 out of 3	1 out of 3	1 out of 3

1 Write the sample space for spinner B. What is the sample space for spinner C?

2 Make a chart showing the probability, or chance, of getting each number from 1 to 6 on spinners A, B, and C. Why is the chance of spinning a 2 different for each spinner?

3 Choose one of the spinners to test probability. Predict the number of times each number will come up if you spin 50 times.

4 Test your predictions by spinning 50 times. Record and share your results.

5 For spinner B what is the probability of landing on 2? Why? Why is that probability not true for spinner D?

6 Predict the outcomes if you spin spinners B and D 30 times each. Make a spinner like D. Test your predictions. Share your results with the class.

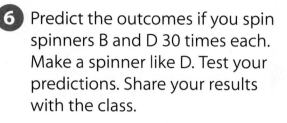

Try It!

Use the spinner at the right to complete Exercises 1–9.

1. Write the sample space.

2. Is the probability of spinning each number equally likely? Why or why not?

Name the probability of spinning each number.

3. 5 **4.** 1 **5.** 3 **6.** 0

7. an even number **8.** an odd number

9. a number less than 4

10. Group these polygons in three different ways. Explain your groupings.

square   triangle   quadrilateral
rectangle   hexagon   pentagon

Think About It

11. Explain this statement: The probability of spinning any number is always from 0 to 1.

Using a compass to draw circles and a protractor to measure angles is one way of making spinners. You can also use the Tracing Tool to trace spinners.

What's the Chance?

You may have heard someone say "It's like finding a needle in a haystack" or "When pigs fly!" These sayings refer to very unlikely events. In this section you will experiment to find out how likely an event is.

What You'll Need
• *2 coins*

ACTIVITY 1 **Flip a Coin**

With Your Partner
How many possible outcomes are there when you flip a coin? Consider the sample space (H,T). What percent of the time would you expect to flip a head? How many heads would you expect if you were to flip a coin 100 times?

$$\text{Probability} = \frac{\text{Number of ways an event can occur}}{\text{Total number of events}}$$

Probability of heads $= \frac{1}{2} = 0.50 = 50\%$

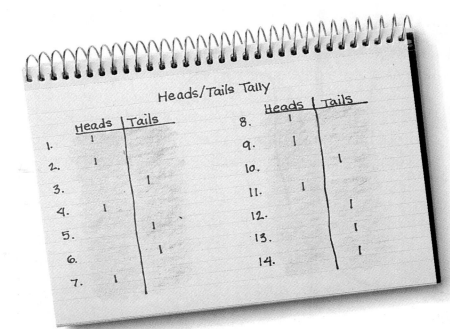

Heads/Tails Tally

	Heads	Tails
1.	I	
2.	I	
3.		I
4.	I	
5.		I
6.		I
7.	I	

	Heads	Tails
8.	I	
9.	I	
10.		I
11.	I	
12.		I
13.		I
14.		I

REASONING AND PROBLEM SOLVING

If someone flips a coin and says "Heads I win, tails you lose," what is the probability that you will win? What if the person says "Heads I win, tails I lose"?

1 **Flip** Flip a coin 25 times and record the results. Write your results, or **experimental probability,** as a ratio. Write the ratio as a fraction and as a percent. Flip the coin 25 more times and write the ratio for the 50 trials.

2 **Revise** Combine your data with data from another group. You will then have the results from 100 flips. Write the experimental probability and the predicted probability. Look at the experimental probability and the predicted probability. How did the probabilities compare as the number of flips increased? Predict the ratio for 1,000 coin flips.

365

What You'll Need
- *compass*
- *Geometry Tool or protractor*
- *ruler*
- *2 paper clips*

ACTIVITY 2 # Circle Graph Spinners

With Your Partner   Create a spinner with ten equal parts. Use a different color or letter in each part.

1 Predict   Make a list of your predicted probability for each outcome. Write each prediction as a ratio in fraction form.

Out of 100 spins, 6 landed on red. Draw this result as a circle graph. Explain what the product tells you. Can multiplying $\frac{6}{100} \times 360$ help?

2 Experiment   Carry out 100 **trials,** or spins, and record the experimental probability. Use your data to create a circle graph.

3 Compare   Compare the predicted probability with the experimental probability. What do you notice about the circle graph and the spinner?

With Your Class   What is the favorite vegetable of your schoolmates? Conduct a survey of 100 fellow students. Then create a circle graph to show the survey results. If you were to turn this graph into a spinner, how do you think the results would compare?

✓ **Self-Check**   *How do you know whether you have created an accurate circle graph? Find the number of degrees in each section. Add the numbers. If the sum is 360, your graph is correct.*

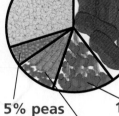

30% corn   **40% potatoes**

5% peas   **15% broccoli**

10% carrots

4 **Predict**   In 100 spins, how many ones do you think you will spin? twos? Make predictions for each outcome.

5 **Experiment**   Spin 100 times and record the results.

6 **Compare**   Write a paragraph comparing the results of your experiment with the data shown on the circle graph. How do the data on the circle graph and the results of the experiment differ? How are they alike? Why?

Tally of Results

Corn ⊮⊮ ⊮⊮ ⊮⊮ ⊮⊮⊮

Peas ⊮⊮ ⊮

Picture Prediction

Take a trip to the rain forest. Use what you know about probability to create a spinner and a gameboard about some rain forest creatures.

1 Explain how you know that the probability of each outcome on the spinner is $\frac{1}{6}$.

2 On your spinner what is the probability of spinning a bird?

3 Name an event on your spinner that has a probability of $\frac{1}{2}$.

4 Suppose you could change your spinner. How might you make the probability of spinning a snake $\frac{2}{3}$?

You are going to create a gameboard that has 25 spaces. Answer Exercises 5–10 about the gameboard.

5 The ratio of toucans to macaws on the spaces should be 2:1. What are all the possible equal ratios you could have on the gameboard?

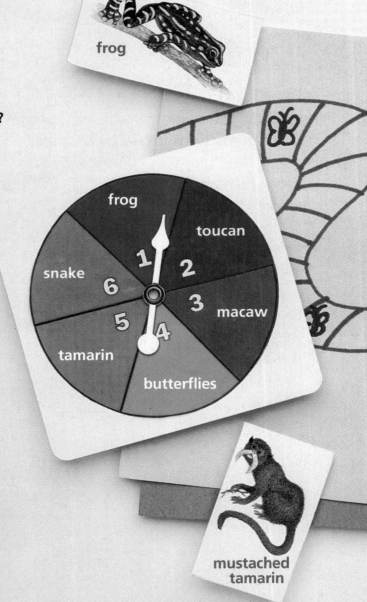

6 Nine spaces on the gameboard should have butterflies. The ratio of butterflies to frogs is 3:1. The ratio of frogs to snakes is also 3:1. How many of each of these animals should you show on the board?

7 The probability of landing on a space with a tamarin is 24%. Use equal ratios to find the number of tamarins on the 25-space gameboard.

8 Use the information you gained in Exercises 5–7 to design your gameboard. Place the animals in the 25 spaces in any order you wish.

9 What is the probability that you will land on a butterfly on your first spin? How do you know?

10 Read the rules and play the game with a partner. Then describe any changes you would make to the game.

Rules of the Game

1. Spin the spinner. Move the number of spaces shown.

2. What animal did you land on? Your score is the number of points for that animal shown on the spinner.

3. The player with the most points at the end of the rain forest is the winner.

toucan

butterflies

macaw

snake

What's Next?

You've worked with probability experiments in which the possible outcomes are known. Now try some experiments in which the outcomes are not known.

ACTIVITY 1 It's in the Bag

With Your Partner Conduct your own marbles-in-a-bag experiment.

What You'll Need
- *5 marbles*
- *1 bag*

1 You have five marbles in your bag. Each is red, blue, or green. You don't know how many of each color there are.
- Have one person draw ten times without looking in the bag. Replace the marble after each draw.
- Have the other person record the results.
- Based on your data, predict how many marbles of each color are in the bag.

2 Draw ten more times and record the results. Change your prediction if necessary. Draw ten more times and make a final prediction. Look into the bag to see if your prediction is correct.

Look at these marbles. Then write the probability for each outcome.

ACTIVITY 2 What's in the Bag?

With Your Partner Last time, you knew there were red, blue, and green marbles in the bag. This time you won't know the colors of the marbles. How will not knowing the colors change how you read your data?

1 Have each person take a bag and place five colored marbles in it. Do not let your partner know which colors you chose. Write the sample space and the probability of drawing each color. Estimate the number of each color you would expect to pick in 100 draws. Exchange bags with your partner.

2 Without looking in the bag, draw 100 times. Replace the marble after each draw. Record the results.

3 Use your data to write the experimental probability as a fraction, a decimal, and a percent. Predict the colors of the marbles in the bag. Look into the bag to check your prediction.

TOOLS AND TECHNIQUES

Try using a computer bar graph to show the outcomes of your probability experiments.

From looking at the data in this chart, what might you predict about the colors of the five marbles in the bag?

|||| |||| ||||| ||||| |||| ||||

371

January
||||

February
||

March
卌 |||

June
卌 |

July
||||

August
卌 |||

ACTIVITY 3 **Birthday Survey**

With Your Class How many students in your class were born in July? December? What would you predict? In this activity you will collect data and make predictions.

1 What is the probability of a person's birthday being in a particular month? Construct a sample space with all possible outcomes. What is the probability for each outcome?

2 Make a prediction of the number of birthdays per month based on the number of students in your class. Survey your class. Compare experimental probability with predicted probability.

January   April   July   August   September

3 Use your data to answer the following questions.

    a. If a new student were to come into your class, what is the probability that the student would have been born in January? Explain.

    b. Use your ratios to predict how many students in the fifth grade were born in each month.

    c. Suppose the fifth grade is representative of your school. Estimate the number of students in your school born in each month.

Conduct a survey of fifth graders' birthdays. Decide the number of students you will survey. Use your data to predict how many fifth graders were born on each day.

Do You Remember?

Try It!

There are 1 green, 2 blue, and 2 red marbles in a bag. Express the probability ratio for drawing each color in each of the following forms.

    1. as a fraction   **2.** as a decimal

    3. as a percent   **4.** in words

For the numbers 3, 4, 5, 8, 12, find the following:

    5. the mean   **6.** the median

    7. the mode   **8.** the range

    9. If 25 is added to the list, what is the mean?

    10. If 2 is added to the list, what is the median?

Think About It

11. Explain how you can change the way a probability is written from a fraction to a percent or decimal.

Investigation

Who Plays What?

Your town or neighborhood is going to build a recreation center. The center will include a gym, a swimming pool, and a recreation room. The planners need to know what equipment to buy.

To help plan the center's budget, you have been asked to conduct a survey of fifth graders and recommend activities. Your survey needs to identify fifth graders' six favorite activities.

1 Work with groups to survey fifth graders in your school. Use this data to predict the responses of all fifth graders in your area.

SOUTH PACKERS

374

2 Make a group presentation about the survey. Include a poster that clearly shows the survey results.

3 Each group member should also write a report. The report should give the results of the survey and make activity recommendations based on the results.

Basketball
IIII II

Volleyball
III

Video Games
IIII III

Arts and Crafts
IIII I

Water Polo
I

Table Tennis
II

Ask Yourself

☐ How can you use your knowledge of probability to make activity suggestions?

☐ What questions will you ask?

☐ Who will you ask? Why do you think it's important that you don't just survey your friends?

☐ How can you make sure that your questions are clear and that you can count the results?

☐ As you prepare your presentation, what is the clearest way to get your ideas across?

A History of Pi

Throughout the ages, mathematicians have been calculating the value of π. Solve these problems to find out more about pi. Use the time line.

1 1800 B.C. Babylonians find the area of a circle. They use a value of 3 for the ratio of the circumference to the diameter. Use this value to find the diameter of a circle with a circumference of 9 cm.

3 220 B.C. Archimedes of Greece estimates pi to be between $3\frac{10}{71}$ and $3\frac{1}{7}$. Use one of these values to find the circumference of a circle with a radius of 2 m.

B.C. A.D.

| 1800 B.C. | 1600 B.C. | | 200 B.C. | 0 | A.D. 200 | A.D. 400 | |

2 1650 B.C. In Egypt, Ahmes the scribe records the value of pi as $\left(\frac{4}{3}\right)^4$. An exponent tells you the number of times a number is used as a factor. $\left(\frac{4}{3}\right)^4 = \frac{4}{3} \times \frac{4}{3} \times \frac{4}{3} \times \frac{4}{3}$. Find the Egyptian value of pi as a fraction.

4 A.D. 470 Tsu Ch'ung-chih of China finds the value of pi to be between 3.1415926 and 3.1415927. Use these values to find the least and greatest circumference of a circle with a diameter of 4 cm.

5 A.D. 1579 François Viete of France uses regular polygons having 393,216 sides to find pi correct to nine decimal places. Draw and name some polygons with 3, 4, 5, 6, and 8 sides.

6 Draw polygons with greater and greater numbers of sides. What shape would Viete's polygon with 393,216 sides look like? Explain.

Check Your Math Power

9 A.D. 1949 In the United States, ENIAC, the first computer used for this purpose, finds pi to 2,037 decimal places. Suppose each digit on the printout is 2 mm wide and is printed on a 20-cm wide line. Describe how you would find the number of lines in the printout.

| A.D. 1000 | A.D. 1200 | A.D. 1400 | A.D. 1600 | A.D. 1800 | A.D. 2000 |

7 A.D. 1706 The single symbol π is used for the first time by mathematicians in England. About how many years ago was this?

8 A century is 100 years. For about how many centuries have people been studying pi?

10 A.D. 1991 David and Gregory Chudnovsky of the United States use supercomputers to find π to 2.16 billion decimal places. About how many times greater is the number of decimal places the Chudnovsky brothers used for pi in 1991 than ENIAC used in 1949? Explain how you got your answer.

LESSON 5

Probabilities

Do you play games? If so, you may do better if you know the probabilities involved. You can use your math skills to figure out the probabilites in many games.

What You'll Need
- compass
- Geometry Tool or protractor
- ruler
- 2 paper clips

ACTIVITY 1 Spin to Win

With Your Partner

1 Make two spinners like those shown on page 379. Then read the Spin and Guess rules.

Spin and Guess

1. Player 1 spins a number and records it.

2. Player 2 predicts whether the next spin will be greater than, less than, or equal to player 1's number.

3. Player 2 records the prediction and spins.

4. Players continue taking turns predicting and spinning. First player to get 21 points wins.

Scoring: A correct prediction earns one point for the player who made the prediction. An incorrect prediction earns one point for the other player.

2 Use spinner A to play the game. Look at your results. Describe the following probabilities:
- spinning any number
- spinning a number greater than your partner's
- spinning a number less than your partner's

In Your Journal Tell how you can use what you know about probability to improve your chances of winning a game.

If your partner spins a 4, which has the greater probability, a number less than 4 or greater than 4?

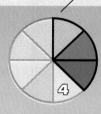

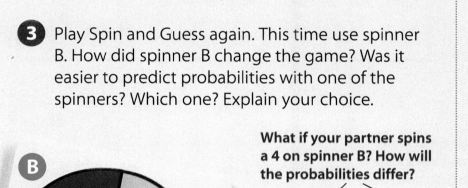

Less than 4   Greater than 4

3 Play Spin and Guess again. This time use spinner B. How did spinner B change the game? Was it easier to predict probabilities with one of the spinners? Which one? Explain your choice.

What if your partner spins a 4 on spinner B? How will the probabilities differ?

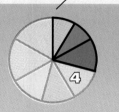

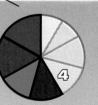

Less than 4   Greater than 4

379

What You'll Need
• *cube labeled 1–6*

A 1–6 number cube has the same probabilities as a spinner with six equal parts.

 The Odds on Odds

On Your Own   You need to roll a 1, 3, or 5 to win a game. What you learned about probability with spinners will help you find the probability of rolling the number you need.

1 Make a sample space showing all the possible outcomes of rolling a 1–6 number cube. Write the probability of each outcome.

2 Look at the sample space. Write the probability of rolling any odd number (1, 3, or 5). Roll the cube 24 times. Record the results. Do the results agree with your predicted probability?

You know the probability of each single event. How can addition help you find the probability of rolling 1, 3, or 5? How does this mathematical probability compare with your trials?

$$\frac{1}{6} \quad \frac{1}{6} \quad \frac{1}{6}$$

$$\frac{3}{6} \quad or \quad \frac{1}{2}$$

3 How do you find the probability of rolling a 4 or a 6? of rolling an odd number or a 2? a 4 or a number less than 4?

³ᴬᶜᵀᴵⱽᴵᵀʸ **Drop It**

With Your Group Sometimes you can't easily figure out a probability. The only way to find out could be to try something again and again—to experiment. Think about dropping a paper cup. It can land on its side, its top, or its bottom. What's the probability of each outcome? Follow Steps 1–5 to find out.

What You'll Need
- *paper cup*
- *3 unbreakable cylinders*

1 Drop a paper cup 20 times from a height of 3 ft. Record the results. Use your results to state a probability for each type of landing.

2 Compare your results with those of other groups. Would probabilities change if you added all the class trials together? Try it.

3 Look at three different cylinders. Write your prediction for each type of landing for each cylinder. Explain your predictions.

④ Drop each cylinder 20 times from a height of 5 ft. Record the results. If other groups used similar cylinders, add their results to yours.

⑤ Use your results to state the experimental probability of each kind of landing. State the probabilities as ratios and compare them with your predictions.

Do You Remember?

Try It!

Refer to the spinners below for Exercises 1–5.

1. Where are even and odd equally probable?
2. On which one is an even number least likely?
3. On which one is a 1 the most likely outcome?
4. On which is an odd number most likely?
5. Which numbers have a probability of 0.25?

A. **B.** **C.**

Write the probability.

6. Roll 3 on a 1–10 number cube.
7. Roll 2 or 4 on a 1–6 number cube.
8. In 2 flips of a coin get heads and tails.
9. Spin a 5 on spinner C above.
10. Spin an odd number on spinner B above.

Think About It

11. Write an explanation of how you decided where even and odd were equally likely in Exercise 1.

How Many Ways?

LITERATURE

Mike and his four friends have started a club. They decide to vote to elect a club president.

I passed the pencil to Rob and watched him out of the corner of my eye as he wrote down a name. He seemed pretty confident. When everyone had finished, he collected all the slips of paper. Then he began to read off the names written on them:

"Rob. Bubba. Mike. Andy. Kenny."

It took a minute to sink into all our heads that everyone had gotten one vote. We all must have voted for ourselves! Then everyone tried to laugh, but I guess we were all a little embarrassed. The problem was how to make the vote come out right the next time.

Bubba said, "We'll just make it a rule that nobody's allowed to vote for himself."

"How are you going to do that," I asked, "if you don't know who they voted for?"

From Some Friend!
by Carol Carrick

383

What You'll Need

- *counters in 4 different colors*

Making Arrangements

With Your Group   In the next election each boy could vote for two different people. Discuss how this solution might work out.

1 Find at least ten ways this election could come out. Making an organized list is a problem solving strategy you might try.

2 People sometimes don't know who is running in an election. They may vote for the first name on the ballot. Pick four students to run for office. Estimate how many ballots you will need in order to list their names in as many different arrangements as possible.

> Vote for one
> ☐ Christina
> ☐ Keith
> ☐ Brenda
> ☐ Donna

ACTIVITY OPTION

Play disc jockey. Pick four songs you like. Make a sample space to show all the possible orders in which you can play them.

3 Use different-colored counters to stand for the students' names. See how many different ways you can arrange them. Was your prediction correct?

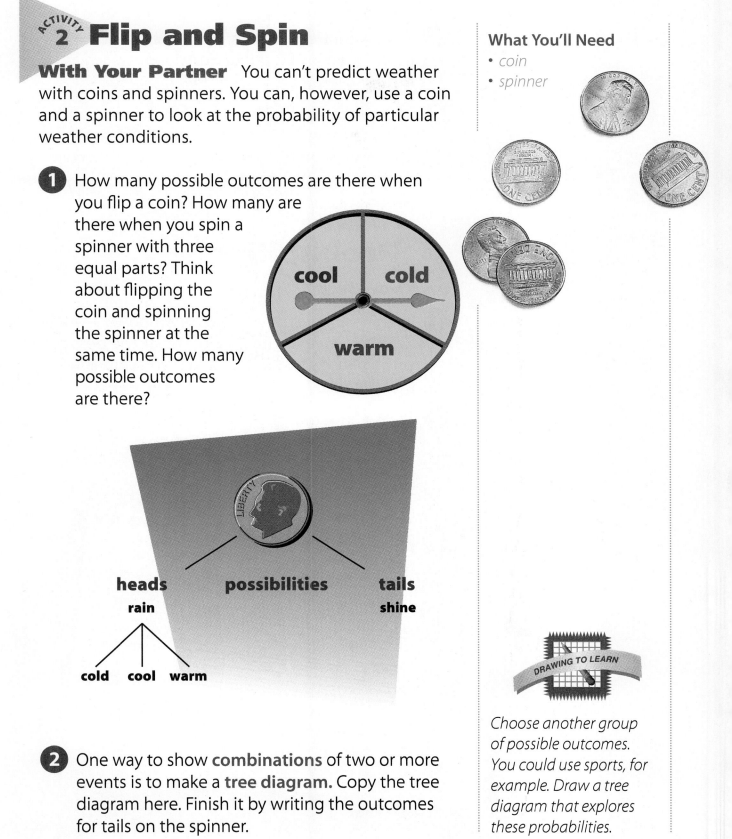

ACTIVITY 2   Flip and Spin

With Your Partner You can't predict weather with coins and spinners. You can, however, use a coin and a spinner to look at the probability of particular weather conditions.

What You'll Need
- *coin*
- *spinner*

1 How many possible outcomes are there when you flip a coin? How many are there when you spin a spinner with three equal parts? Think about flipping the coin and spinning the spinner at the same time. How many possible outcomes are there?

cool   cold

warm

heads   possibilities   tails

rain   shine

cold   cool   warm

2 One way to show **combinations** of two or more events is to make a **tree diagram.** Copy the tree diagram here. Finish it by writing the outcomes for tails on the spinner.

DRAWING TO LEARN

Choose another group of possible outcomes. You could use sports, for example. Draw a tree diagram that explores these probabilities.

How can you find the probability of events happening at the same time? Think about the relationship between the number of outcomes for each event and the total number of outcomes.

3 Using your tree diagram, list all the possible combinations of weather descriptions, such as *rainy and cold.*

4 What is the probability of getting the rainy-and-cold outcome? Write the probability of each outcome. Then test your predictions with a coin and a spinner. Write a paragraph to describe your results.

ACTIVITY 3 Probability

On Your Own

1 Imagine equal-space spinners numbered 1–4 and 1–5. Draw tree diagrams showing all the possible combinations for flipping a coin and spinning the spinners.

2 Think about the tree diagrams you have made. Copy and complete the chart showing the possible number of combinations.

Coin Flip Outcomes	Spinner Outcomes	Combinations
2	2	4
2	3	6
2	4	
2	5	

3 Look at your completed chart. How could you find the total number of combinations for two events without drawing a tree diagram? Justify your answer.

4 Tell how many outcomes are possible from flipping a coin, spinning a 1–3 spinner, and rolling a 1–6 number cube. Tell the outcomes without drawing a tree diagram.

☑ **Self-Check** *After drawing a tree diagram, how can you find and read all the combinations you made?*

Do You Remember?

Try It!

Make a tree diagram to show all the possible outcomes of a spinner with equal yellow, blue, and red parts and a 1–6 number cube. Use the diagram to state each probability.

1. blue and any odd number
2. yellow and 3
3. red and an even number *or* 1
4. red *or* blue and 3 *or* 6
5. yellow *or* blue and any even number

Tell whether the answer will be greater or less than 2. If less than 2, find the exact answer.

6. 0.947×2.1
7. 5.01×0.45
8. 0.04804×4.3
9. 2.418×1.5
10. 10.55×0.25
11. 4.01×0.5

Think About It

12. How can you use multiplication to find the outcomes for two events, such as using a coin *and* a number cube? Give examples.

LESSON 7 Play the Game

At the end of this module you will create a game of your own. This lesson and the next one will start you thinking about what goes into making a game.

ACTIVITY 1 Chance or Strategy?

Some games depend on chance. Other games use strategy. If you've played checkers, you've probably used a strategy—a plan for winning.

With Your Partner Play and discuss *shisima* and *nim*. Decide which game to play first. Talk about dreidel as well. Which games involve chance? How about strategy? Which is the most important in each game?

Nim probably originated in China. Players line up an odd number of sticks in a row. Each player in turn picks up 1, 2, or 3 sticks. The player who picks up the last stick loses. Play a few times with 11 sticks. Then try it with 15 sticks. Then try 21.

What You'll Need
- *21 sticks or crayons*
- *6 game pieces*

REASONING AND PROBLEM SOLVING

When you figure out a strategy for winning nim, explain it to your partner. Then play a game or two to see what happens when both players know the strategy.

Shisima is a game played by the Tiriki people in Kenya. The name *shisima* means "sources of water." The playing pieces are *imbalavi,* or "water insects." Players take turns moving their pieces one at a time along the straight or curved lines. The first player to get three pieces in a straight line wins.

Dreidel is traditionally played at Chanukah. Players put a number of counters into a pile. They take turns spinning the dreidel like a top. The Hebrew letter that lands face up tells the player to take a number of counters from the pile or to put more in. Play ends when one player gets all the counters.

With Your Class Think of games you like to play. Write the headings *Chance* and *Strategy* on the board. Take turns writing the names of games under the headings. The class should agree on which heading is better for each game. If anyone doesn't know a game, the person naming it can describe how it is played.

Choose a game someone in your group can bring to class. Play it for 10–15 minutes. Then discuss how chance and strategy are involved in the game. Present your conclusions to the class.

What You'll Need

- *2 cubes labeled 1–6*

2 # Fair or Foul?

With Your Partner   Use what you know about probability as you play the following game.

1 Play Math Roll. Is it fair? Why or why not?

Math Roll

1. One player is "even"; the other is "odd."

2. Take turns rolling two number cubes. Subtract the smaller number from the greater number.

3. If the difference is an even number, the even player wins a point. (Zero counts as even.)

4. If the difference is an odd number, the odd player scores.

5. The first player to get ten points wins.

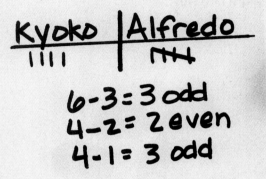

Kyoko | Alfredo
|||| | ~~||||~~

6 − 3 = 3 odd
4 − 2 = 2 even
4 − 1 = 3 odd

Kyoko | Alfredo
~~||||~~ || | |||

6 × 3 = 18 even
4 × 2 = 8 even
4 × 1 = 4 even

TOOLS AND TECHNIQUES

How can you best find out which game is more fair? Would a diagram help? Would a sample space help? Explain.

2 Play a second game of Math Roll. Follow the same rules, but instead of subtracting, multiply the two numbers. Use the product to tell whether the even player or the odd player wins a point. Is this version fair? Explain.

ACTIVITY 3 Find the Fair One

With Your Group

What You'll Need
• *spinner*

1. Discuss the games you listed on the chalkboard in Activity 1. Are all of them fair? Explain.

2. Make up rules for a game that uses the spinner shown here. Your game can also use number cubes or coins.

3. Play the game to test the rules. Is it a fair game? Revise it if you need to. Then trade with another group and try each other's game.

Do You Remember?

Try It!

Tell which is most important in each game—chance or strategy.

1. checkers
2. chess
3. dreidel

4. tick-tack-toe
5. scissors, paper, stone

Write fractions $\frac{1}{2}$ or greater as a percent. Write others as decimals.

6. $\frac{3}{4}$
7. $\frac{1}{5}$
8. $\frac{6}{10}$

9. $\frac{1}{20}$
10. $\frac{3}{25}$
11. $\frac{35}{50}$

Think About It

12. What games are more fun to play—games of chance, games of strategy, or games that involve both chance and strategy? Explain your choice and give examples.

LESSON 8

GALAXY

What You'll Need
- *gameboard*
- *2 paper clips*
- *game pieces*

ACTIVITY 1 ▶ Play and Revise

With Your Group Play a game or two of Galaxy in a group of three players. Assign one player to keep a record of each spin.

1 Players take turns. Use the two spinners on the board to move toward the finish. Spin a paper clip on each spinner. The sum of the two numbers spun tells how many planets a player moves toward the finish.
- Player 1 can move only after spinning an odd number.
- Player 2 moves only after spinning an even number (but not doubles, which are the same number on both sides).
- Player 3 moves only by spinning doubles.

✔ **Self-Check** *To make sure you understand the rules of the game, try explaining them to a classmate.*

2 A player may land on a planet occupied by another player's marker. If that happens the one there first moves back one planet.

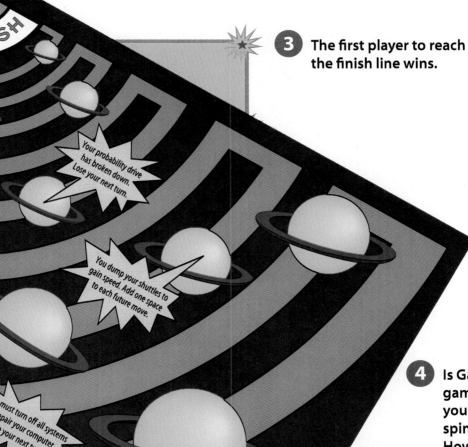

3 The first player to reach the finish line wins.

4 Is Galaxy a fair game? What does your record of spins tell you? How would a tree diagram help you decide whether the game is fair?

5 Revise the game. You can change any rules, but keep the gameboard and two spinners. Share your changes with the class. As other groups explain their changes, decide whether they have made a fair game.

Section D: What Makes a Game a Game?   393

In Your Journal *Explain how knowing about probability can improve your chances of winning at tick-tack-toe.*

ACTIVITY 2 **Winning**

On Your Own Do you have a usual first move when you play tick-tack-toe? Are some spaces better choices than others as a first move? Draw a series of diagrams showing all possible ways of winning after various first moves. Which is the best? Which is the worst? Why? Explain your strategy to your group.

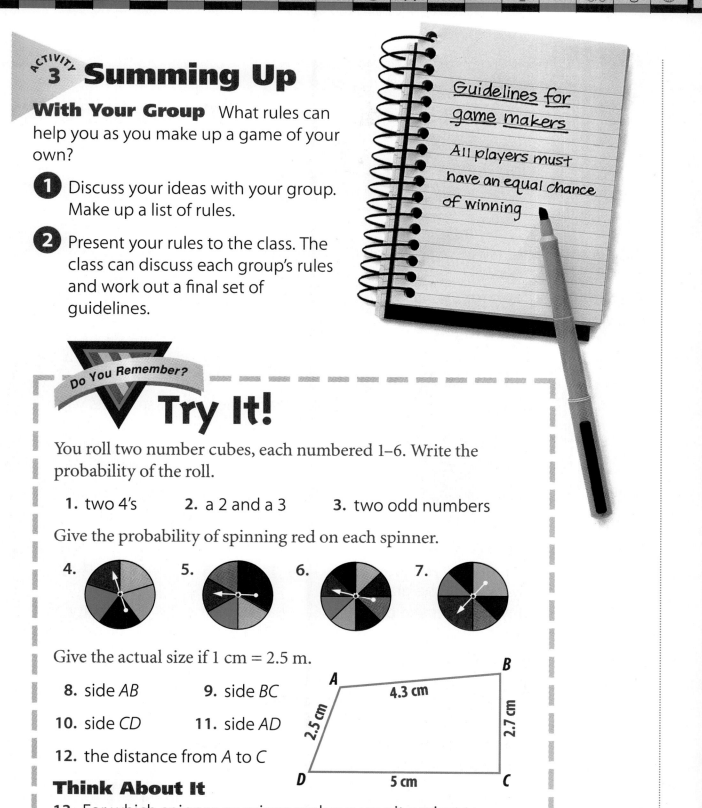

ACTIVITY 3 Summing Up

With Your Group What rules can help you as you make up a game of your own?

1 Discuss your ideas with your group. Make up a list of rules.

2 Present your rules to the class. The class can discuss each group's rules and work out a final set of guidelines.

Guidelines for game makers

All players must have an equal chance of winning

Do You Remember?

Try It!

You roll two number cubes, each numbered 1–6. Write the probability of the roll.

1. two 4's   **2.** a 2 and a 3   **3.** two odd numbers

Give the probability of spinning red on each spinner.

4.   **5.**   **6.**   **7.**

Give the actual size if 1 cm = 2.5 m.

8. side *AB*   **9.** side *BC*

10. side *CD*   **11.** side *AD*

12. the distance from *A* to *C*

A — 4.3 cm — B
2.5 cm ... 2.7 cm
D — 5 cm — C

Think About It

13. For which spinner or spinners above was it easiest to figure the probability of spinning red? Explain why.

Looking Back

Choose the best answer or answers.

Use the circle graph for Exercises 1–6. Write *a, b, c,* or *d.*

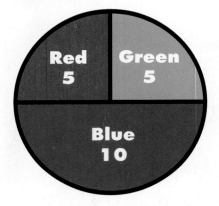

Favorite Colors of 20 Students

1. What can you tell from the graph?
   a. Half as many students like blue as like green.
   b. Students like red and green equally.
   c. Twice as many students like green as like blue.
   d. Twice as many students like red and green as like blue.

2. What part of the group of students surveyed liked green?

   a. 25%   b. $\frac{1}{4}$ c. 0.33   d. 12

3. If 8 more students were surveyed, how many would probably like green?
   a. 1   b. 2   c. 3   d. 4

4. What is the ratio of students who like red to those who like blue?
   a. $2:1$ b. $4:1$ c. $1:3$ d. $1:2$

5. If this graph were a spinner, what would be the probability of landing on green?

   a. $\frac{1}{2}$ b. $\frac{1}{3}$ c. $\frac{1}{4}$ d. $\frac{2}{3}$

6. What would be the probability of landing on yellow?
   a. 0.5   b. 0.33   c. 0.25   d. 0

Use the circle below for Exercises 7–8.

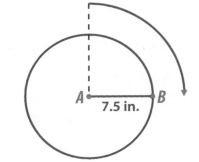

7. What is the circle's diameter?
 a. 7.5 in. **b.** 23.5 in.
 c. 15 in.   **d.** 22.5 in.

8. Imagine the circle as a piece of cardboard that is rolled the distance shown by the arrow. What distance along its circumference has it rolled?
 a. ≈ 11.78 in. **b.** ≈ 44.16 in.
 c. ≈ 5.88 in. **d.** ≈ 15.32 in.

Base your answers to Exercises 9–12 on the tree diagram.

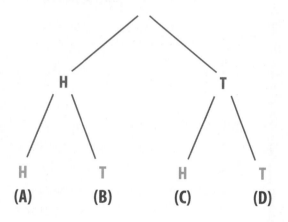

 (A) (B) (C) (D)

9. What should the outcome labeled (A) be?
 a. T, H **b.** H, T **c.** H, H **d.** T, T

10. What should outcome (C) be?
 a. T, H **b.** H, T **c.** H, H **d.** T, T

11. What is the probability of flipping two coins at the same time and getting heads and tails?
 a. $\frac{1}{4}$ **b.** 3 : 4
 c. 0.50   **d.** 100%

12. What is the probability of flipping two heads?
 a. 25 : 50   **b.** 25%
 c. $\frac{3}{4}$ **d.** 5%

Use the line segments and a Geometry Tool for Exercises 13–15. Write *a, b, c,* or *d*.

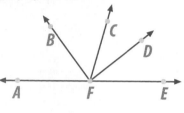

13. What is the measure of ∠*DFE*?
 a. 40° **b.** 45° **c.** 50° **d.** 55°

14. Which angle is 75°?
 a. *BFE* **b.** *AFC* **c.** *BFC* **d.** *CFE*

15. Which angle is 105°?
 a. *AFB* **b.** *AFC* **c.** *BFD* **d.** *CFD*

Check Your Math Power

16. Draw a spinner for which the chance of spinning a 1, 2, or 3 is not equally likely. Describe the angles in your spinner segments.

17. Make up rules for a fair game using the spinner made for Exercise 16.

18. Draw a tree diagram for which one possible outcome is heads, tails, and 3. What is the probability of that outcome?

Play and Probability

Evidence of board games has been found in Egyptian tombs and in ancient ruins. *Go,* an ancient game from China, has been traced as far back as 2356 B.C. Variations of games like checkers and tick-tack-toe have been played all over the world for hundreds of years.

Some games use unusual gameboards. This two-player game, called *puluc,* uses ten ears of corn and ten counters. *Puluc* is played by the Quiché Indians who live in the highlands of Guatemala. Many Quiché Indians are farmers. They use the materials available to them to play *puluc.*

Investigation
A

A Game of Your Own

What materials around you would you use to create a game of your own? You can make any kind of game you like. Remember to use what you know about chance and strategy to make your game fair.

1 Write a list of rules and an explanation of your game.

2 Play your game with classmates or friends. Use players' comments to revise your game and to make it more fun.

3 Present your game to the class.

Keep in Mind

Your game will be judged on the following.

☐ How did you use what you know about fair games and probability to write your rules?

☐ How clearly did you express the object of the game and how players can win?

☐ How did you use other players' comments to revise your game?

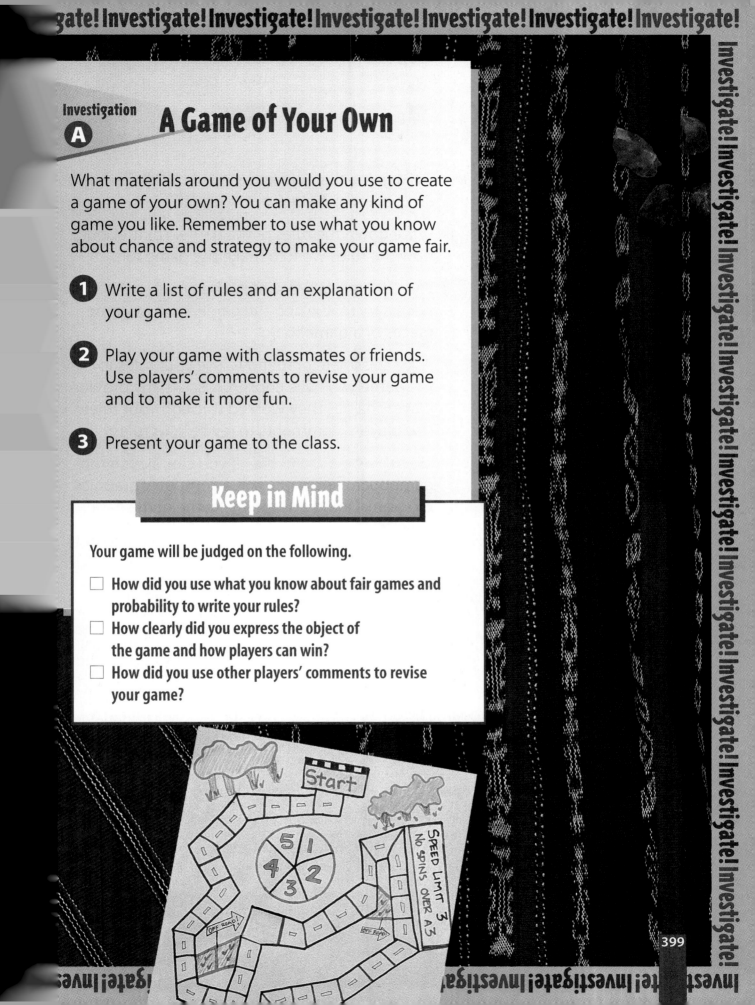

399

One Student's Process

Investigation
B

Rules of the Game

Think of a game that you know how to play. Could you explain to someone else how to play it?

1 Write down the rules of the game. Think about how the rules work to make the game fun.

2 If you'd like, make a sketch of any objects necessary for playing the game, such as game pieces or a gameboard.

3 Ask a classmate or friend to use your rules to play the game you have chosen. Discuss any problems players had as they worked through your rules. Use players' comments to revise your rules.

Computer Option If you can, sketch the gameboard and pieces on a computer graphics program. Doing this will make the game easier to revise.

Investigation
C

Vice Versa

You made a list of chance and strategy games in Section D. Pick one game listed under *Chance* and one game listed under *Strategy*. Write the rules for each.

How do the rules make one a game of chance and the other a strategy game? How can you change the rules to make the game of chance into a game of strategy? the game of strategy into a game of chance?

Rewrite the rules and ask friends or classmates to play the games. Discuss the results of play and use players' comments to revise the rules.

The Shape of Things to Come

Did you know that a 15-year-old boy invented earmuffs to keep his ears warm when he skated? Recently a kindergarten student dreamed up elastic shoelaces to ease taking off shoes! People make inventions to do jobs better or faster. Sometimes they invent things simply to have fun. You may not know it yet, but your good ideas can make you an inventor too!

Space: The Third Dimension

Volume: Going Cubic

Rate, Ratio, and Function

Formula for an Invention

The Art of Invention

In this Japanese folktale, a young farmer has saved his village twice by following his mother's advice. Now, to save their village one last time, they must invent "... a drum that sounds without being beaten."

The young farmer hurried home breathlessly. "Mother, Mother, we must solve another terrible problem or Lord Higa will conquer our village!" And he quickly told his mother about the impossible drum.

His mother, however, smiled and answered, "Why, this is the easiest of them all. Make a drum with sides of paper and put a bumblebee inside. As it tries to escape, it will buzz and beat itself against the paper and you will have a drum that sounds without being beaten."

From "The Wise Old Woman"
by Yoshiko Ushida

Word Bank

- cubic unit
- face
- net
- space figure
- three-dimensional object
- volume

① Dream Big

How would you have solved the problem of inventing the magic drum? Use your imagination on a problem you face.

② Use Mathematics

Mathematics helps inventors see shapes in space, draw scale models, figure rates of work, and test inventions. What math do you think the inventor of the paper drum may have used?

③ Make a List

What job could an invention do for you? Begin to write notes and sketch your invention in your journal. Describe or draw a picture of something you want to build.

Investigate! Investigate! Investigate! Investigate! Investigate! Investigate! Investigate! Investigate! Investigate! Investigate! Investigate! Investigate! Investigate! Investigate!

Investigations Preview

Imagining, brainstorming, planning, drawing, measuring, building, and sharing your work with others—with these skills you can invent anything.

Making an Aquarium (pages 424–425)
How would you design a happy home for fish? Knowing about volume will help you carry out your plan.

A World of Toys (pages 446–448)
What kind of toy can you build? Making a scale drawing will get your design off the ground.

Investigate! Investigate! Investigate! Investigate! Investigate! Investigate! Investigate! Investigate! Investigate! Investigate! Investigate! Investigate!

LESSON 1 Shapes in Space

Making your invention will involve building shapes in space. Use the polygons you know to make shapes in space, or **space figures.**

base

What You'll Need
- *toothpicks*
- *gumdrops or softened beans*

ACTIVITY 1 Going Up!

With Your Class You can measure polygons in two dimensions: length and width. Space figures, or **three-dimensional objects,** have the added dimension of height.

- Polygons make up the **faces** of space figures.
- A cube is a space figure in which all the faces are squares.

Look around your classroom. Make a list of polygons and space figures you see.

With Your Partner

1 Try making some space figures. Make a square with toothpicks and gumdrops.

2 Use more toothpicks and gumdrops to turn your square into a cube. Make a copy of the chart at the right, and record how many faces, edges, and vertexes your cube has.

3 Use a triangle as the base for another space figure. Make a rectangle the base for a third space figure. Record what you find on your chart. Use the same bases and build at least five other space figures.

Base Shape	Number of Faces	Number of Vertexes	Number of Edges
■			
▲			
▮			

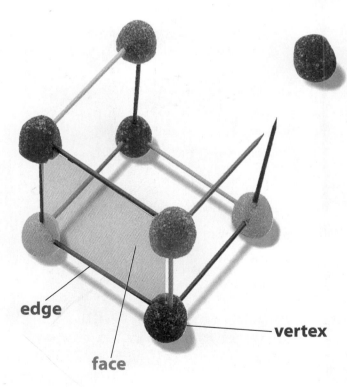

edge

face

vertex

CONNECT AND COMMUNICATE

Copy the chart on this page. Include the glossary definitions for base, face, vertex, and edge. Then fill in the numbers on the chart.

- *a variety of common objects having flat faces or curved surfaces*

DRAWING TO LEARN

In Your Journal Sketch a common object, like a lamp or a television. Then describe the object in terms of the two- and three-dimensional figures that it contains.

ACTIVITY 2 **What's My Shape?**

With Your Partner Do the next three activities in whatever order you choose. Afterward, discuss with another pair of students what you learned about three-dimensional shapes.

1 Look at the shapes on these pages. Figure out which number should go in each gray box. Then make and fill out a chart like the one on page 405.

2 Gather 20 objects, some with curved faces and some with flat faces. Take turns sorting your shapes into at least two piles. Base your sorting on something shared, such as the number of faces. Your partner must figure out how you grouped your piles.

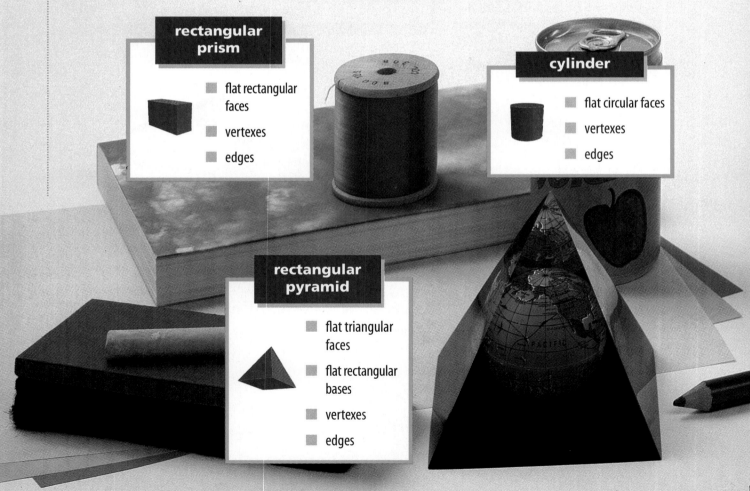

rectangular prism
- ■ flat rectangular faces
- ■ vertexes
- ■ edges

cylinder
- ■ flat circular faces
- ■ vertexes
- ■ edges

rectangular pyramid
- ■ flat triangular faces
- ■ flat rectangular bases
- ■ vertexes
- ■ edges

3 Put a shape behind your back. Your partner must guess its name in ten questions or less. Here are just a few possible questions:

- Does your shape have curved faces?
- How many vertexes does your shape have?
- Are all the faces congruent?
- Are all the edges congruent?
- Is one or more of the faces a triangle?

Take turns with your partner. After you have played this game for a while, tell what helped you get better at guessing the shapes.

How can knowing the number of congruent faces help you identify a space figure? What else do you need to know?

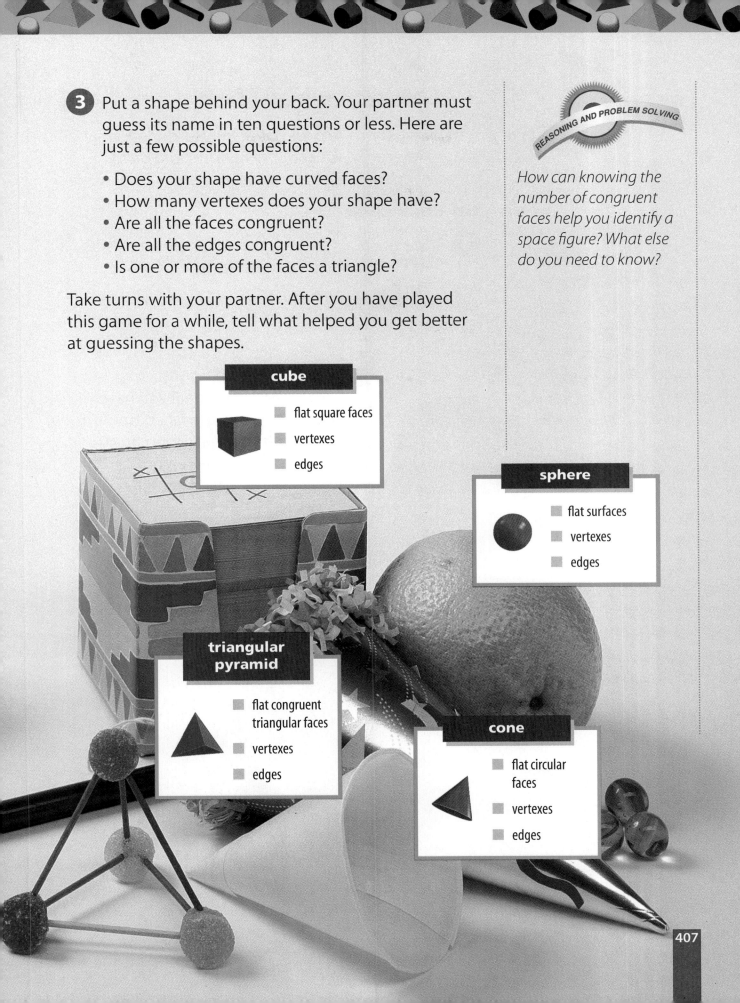

cube
- flat square faces
- vertexes
- edges

sphere
- flat surfaces
- vertexes
- edges

triangular pyramid
- flat congruent triangular faces
- vertexes
- edges

cone
- flat circular faces
- vertexes
- edges

3 Making a Net

A **net** is a pattern that folds into a three-dimensional shape. You can make and fold nets to build many different space figures.

What You'll Need

- *small cardboard boxes*
- *scissors*
- *grid paper*
- *tape*

TOOLS AND TECHNIQUES

How could slitting your box down the sides help you draw its net?

On Your Own

1 Trace the box you brought from home to see its net. First outline the largest face.

2 Carefully tip the box along one edge. Now trace the face that lies next to the first one.

3 Keep tipping your box at each edge until you have traced all the faces. Now cut out your net. How can you fold it to make a box?

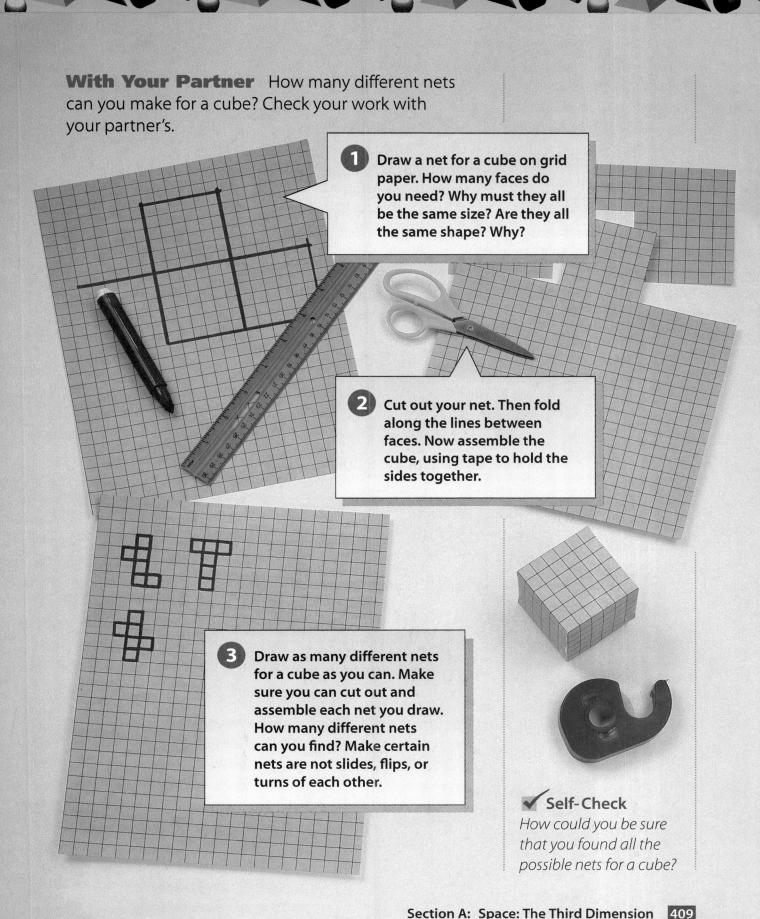

With Your Partner How many different nets can you make for a cube? Check your work with your partner's.

1 Draw a net for a cube on grid paper. How many faces do you need? Why must they all be the same size? Are they all the same shape? Why?

2 Cut out your net. Then fold along the lines between faces. Now assemble the cube, using tape to hold the sides together.

3 Draw as many different nets for a cube as you can. Make sure you can cut out and assemble each net you draw. How many different nets can you find? Make certain nets are not slides, flips, or turns of each other.

✔ **Self-Check**
How could you be sure that you found all the possible nets for a cube?

Make a net for another space figure and give it to a friend to build.

On Your Own Make a net for a pyramid with a rectangular base, like the one shown in this picture. How many different nets can you find for this shape? If the pyramid had a triangular base, could you make more or fewer nets? How do you know?

Do You Remember?

Try It!

Make a net for each of the following figures.

1. **2.** **3.**

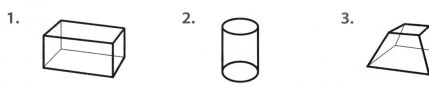

Name two objects for each three-dimensional shape.

4. cylinder   **5.** cone   **6.** sphere

7. cube   **8.** rectangular prism   **9.** pyramid

Use $\frac{4}{25}$, $\frac{2}{5}$, $\frac{7}{20}$, $\frac{9}{10}$, and $\frac{1}{2}$. Write the number that fits each description as both a fraction and as a percent.

10. greatest fraction   **11.** least percent   **12.** odd percent

13. between 35% and 50%   **14.** $\frac{2}{5} < n < \frac{9}{10}$

Think About It

15. How did you figure out a way to make the net for Exercise 3? Write a brief description of your process.

Taking Up Space

You can use your visual skills to help you understand shapes in space.

ACTIVITY 1 Building Blocks

With Your Partner

1 Build as many different space figures as you can using four centimeter cubes. The cubes must touch along one whole side.

2 Make a chart like the one below. How can you tell that each of your figures is not just a slide, flip, or turn of another figure?

3 Repeat this activity with five cubes and six cubes. Which figures had the greatest number of faces showing? the least number? How do you know?

What You'll Need
• *centimeter cubes*

Write a formula to predict the greatest number of faces that will show in a space figure made of n cubes.

Figure	Number of Cubic Units	Number of Faces
	4	18
	4	

411

Shape Up!

Imagine these space figures from different points of view. Then choose any seven exercises plus Exercise 10.

1 Sketch a figure with a triangular base. Record the number of sides, vertexes, and edges.

2 Sketch two figures that fit exactly through the triangular hole and explain how you know. Then repeat for the circular and square holes.

3 What is the least number of colors you could paint Figure F so that no two sides that share an edge are the same color?

4 Which space figure on these pages has the greatest number of flat faces?

5 Which space figure on these pages has the greatest number of edges?

A

B

C

6 If you painted the outside of Figure *F*, how many faces of each corner cube would you color? Make a chart showing the number of faces each of the smaller cubes would have painted.

7 Make the same chart as you did in Exercise 6 for a cube made up of eight smaller cubes.

D

8 Compare the figures made up of small cubes. Find the object that has the most small cubes. How many cubes does it have?

9 Choose one figure made up of small cubes and write down its letter. How many cubes might be hidden from your view? Defend your answer.

E

10 Suppose that a triangular prism and a cube had the same size base and height, and were made of the same material. Which do you think would weigh more? Explain.

F

LESSON 3

Fill It Up!

DRAWING TO LEARN

What containers do you use each day? Sketch or describe some unusual containers, or invent one of your own.

Containers that look very different may still have the same **volume.** Volume, the amount of space contained in a space figure, is usually measured in **cubic units.**

A cubic centimeter (cm³) is the volume of a cube with every edge measuring 1 cm. How long is each edge of a cubic inch (in.³)?

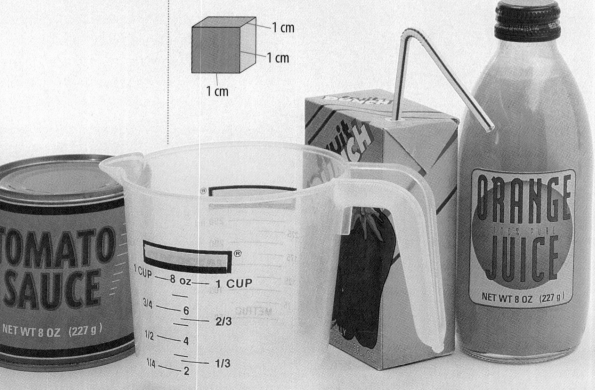

1 cm
1 cm
1 cm

1 CUP — 8 oz — 1 CUP
3/4 — 6
— 2/3
1/2 — 4
1/4 — 2 — 1/3

Each of these containers can hold 8 fl oz. Do you think they all have the same volume? Explain.

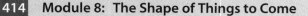

ACTIVITY 1 Blocking It In

With Your Group Sometimes you can estimate that one shape holds more than another simply by looking. Sometimes, however, you need to know exactly how much a container holds. How can filling it help? Make your own boxes to see!

What You'll Need

- *centimeter grid paper*
- *scissors*
- *tape*
- *centimeter cubes*

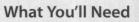

How do standard units, such as cubic centimeters and cubic inches, make it easier to measure and communicate volume?

1

Each student gets a quarter sheet of grid paper. Cut out a congruent square from each of the four corners.

2

Fold up the sides and tape the edges.

3

Select one box from your group. Estimate how many centimeter cubes will fit in the box. Make a chart to record your group's estimates of each box's volume.

4

Fill the box to the top with your cubes. Count and record. Repeat with the other boxes. How can you improve your estimates each time?

What You'll Need
- *centimeter cubes*
- *boxes from Activity 1*

REASONING AND PROBLEM SOLVING

How can a layer of cubes help you find area?

ACTIVITY 2 Layer by Layer

With Your Group How might filling boxes in layers help you think of volume? Trade boxes with another group and use layering to help you find the volume of the boxes. Discuss with your group any patterns you find. Discuss how you found the volume.

How many cubes does the first layer of this block have? How can you tell without counting each cube?

1 Choose a box. Use centimeter cubes to cover its base. Record how many cubes you used in one layer.

2 Put another layer of cubes in your box. Did you use the same number of cubes as in the first layer? Why?

3 Layer cubes until your box is full.
- How many layers high is your box?
- How many cubes fit altogether?

Record the volume on your chart. Repeat with the rest of the boxes.

Box	Area of Base	Number of Layers	Volume
1	60 cm²	2	120 cm³
2			

3 Beyond Blocks

With Your Group How could you find the volume if you do not have enough cubes to fill even one layer? Find another box to measure—a cereal box, shoe box, or jewelry box. Think about how you could use standard units of measurement instead.

What You'll Need
- cardboard box
- centimeter cubes
- ruler

TOOLS AND TECHNIQUES

What operation can you use to help you find volume? How can a calculator help?

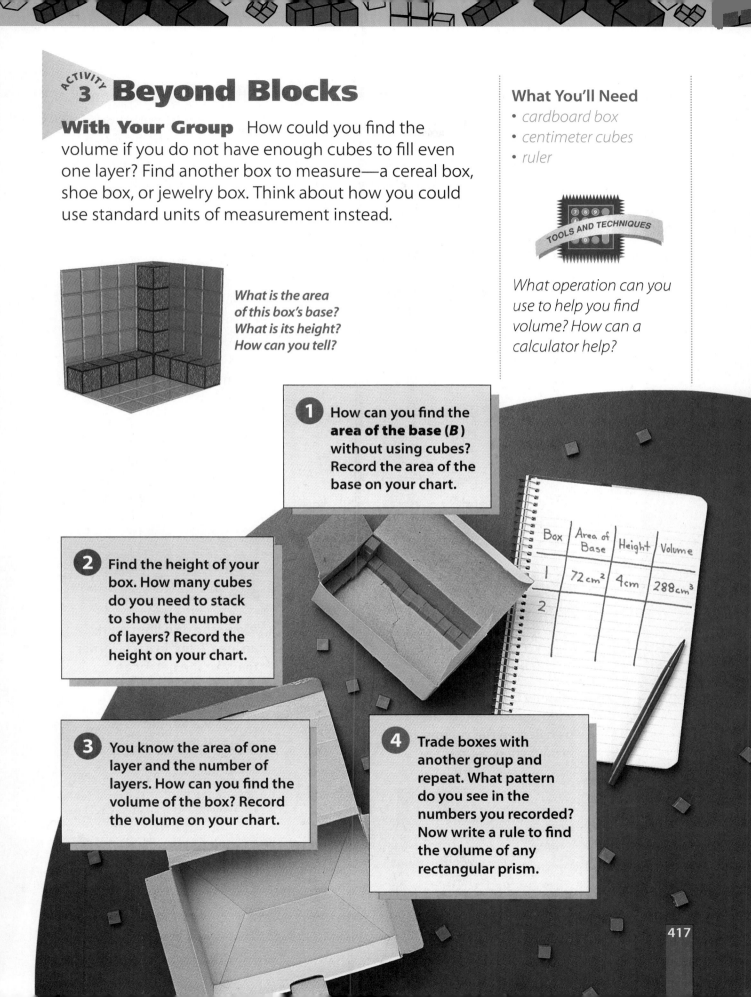

What is the area of this box's base? What is its height? How can you tell?

1 How can you find the **area of the base (B)** without using cubes? Record the area of the base on your chart.

2 Find the height of your box. How many cubes do you need to stack to show the number of layers? Record the height on your chart.

Box	Area of Base	Height	Volume
1	72 cm²	4 cm	288 cm³
2			

3 You know the area of one layer and the number of layers. How can you find the volume of the box? Record the volume on your chart.

4 Trade boxes with another group and repeat. What pattern do you see in the numbers you recorded? Now write a rule to find the volume of any rectangular prism.

417

What You'll Need
- *grid paper*
- *ruler*

On Your Own Now test the rule you discovered for finding volume. Go back to the boxes you made in Activity 2. Use your rule and your ruler to find the volume of each box. Do you get the same answers as you did when you counted cubes? Why or why not?

ACTIVITY 4 Baffling Boxes

With Your Group If you make different open boxes from the same size paper, which box will have the greatest volume? Will it be the box with the smallest square cut out? the box with the largest square cut out? Try this activity and see.

1 Mark out a 15-cm-by-15-cm area on grid paper.

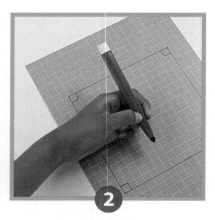

2 Along the grid lines mark an area 1 cm² in each corner to make the net for an open box.

3 Identify the length, width, and height of the box. Record the volume in your chart.

length	width	height	volume
13cm	13cm	1cm	169cm³
11 cm	11 cm	2cm	

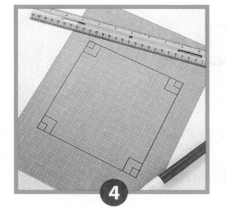

4 Mark out the next larger square you could cut out of each corner to make a box. Repeat, recording the new volume.

5 Continue marking and recording all the boxes you could make. Which box had the greatest volume? Did the answer surprise you?

ACTIVITY OPTION

Find the dimensions of a box with a volume of 48 in.^{3} and a base larger than 1 in.^{2} that will take up the least room on your desk.

Do You Remember?

Try It!

Give dimensions for two boxes with volumes of 100 cm^3.

1. length __?__   width __?__   height __?__

2. length __?__   width __?__   height __?__

Estimate the volume in cubic centimeters for rectangular prisms with these dimensions. If the volume is greater than 1,000 cm^3, find the exact volume. Use a calculator.

3. 6 cm by 23 cm by 9 cm   **4.** 12 cm by 25 cm by 2 cm

5. 16 cm by 48 cm by 8 cm   **6.** 26 cm by 11 cm by 9 cm

State the probability for rolling green if the given number of faces of a game cube are painted green.

7. 1   **8.** 2   **9.** 3   **10.** 4   **11.** n

Think About It

12. How can you find the dimensions of a box with a volume of 100 cm^3?

Shapes That Contain

Meet the Liter

What You'll Need
- *thousands' cube*
- *centimeter cubes*

CONNECT AND COMMUNICATE

In Your Journal
A decimeter (dm) is 10 cm long. Make a list of other words you know with the Latin root decem, meaning "ten."

With Your Class Learning about liters will help you invent different containers with the same volume. A thousands' cube holds exactly 1 L of water.

1 This cube is 1 dm long by 1 dm wide by 1 dm high. What is its volume? Explain how 1 L, 1 dm^3, and 1,000 cm^3 are related.

2 A ones' cube is 1 cm^3. How many ones' cubes does the thousands' cube contain?

3 In the metric system, *milli-* means "one-thousandth." What fraction of a liter is a milliliter? How are 1 mL and 1 cm^3 related? Explain how you know.

4 How many milliliters of water would this container hold if it were full? About how many milliliters of water does it contain now?

5 If this container were 3 dm long, 2 dm wide, and 4 dm high, how many liters of water could it hold? How do you know?

6 One cubic centimeter (cm^3), or 1 mL, of water has a mass of 1 g. Since 1 kg equals 1,000 g, what is the mass of 1 L of water? Explain your answer.

ACTIVITY 2 Liters Short and Tall

With Your Partner What shapes of liter containers have you seen? Think of a rectangular prism that holds a liter. If its base measures 10 cm by 10 cm, how high does it need to be? Choose one of these two activities.

ACTIVITY OPTION

Tape sheets of centimeter grid paper together to make a net for one of your liter containers. Explain why your container would or would not be practical to hold milk or juice.

1 Make a chart to show the length, width, and height of at least ten different 1-L containers. Use your calculator to check that your containers will each hold exactly 1 L (1,000 cm³ or 1,000 mL).

Box	Length	Width	Height
A	10 cm	10 cm	
B	5 cm		
C			

A
10 cm × 10 cm

B
10 cm
5 cm

C
5 cm
5 cm

2 Sketch ten different 1-L containers. Make sure to label their dimensions. Use your calculator to check that your containers will hold exactly 1 L.

Sketch four differently shaped containers. Describe a use for each container. Explain how each container's shape matches its use. Record each container's volume and its dimensions.

What You'll Need

- *grid paper*
- *ruler*
- *a variety of space figures*

ACTIVITY 3 **A Different Shape**

With Your Partner From soup cans to jelly jars, containers are all shapes and sizes. How could you estimate the volume of a container that is a cylinder or a triangular prism?

 Use what you know to explain how you would estimate the volumes of the shapes on this page.

 Choose three space figures you find in your classroom. Estimate their volumes in cubic centimeters or cubic inches and explain your thinking.

What measurements will you need?

How could tracing the base on a sheet of grid paper help you estimate the area of the base?

By what number should you multiply the base to estimate the volume?

Do you think your estimate will be high? low? about right? Explain.

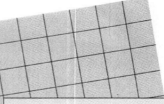

ACTIVITY 4 **Build a Bottle**

On Your Own Now make a container of any shape to hold 300 mL of fluid, an average serving for one. How many cubic centimeters is that?

What You'll Need
- *grid paper*
- *scissors*
- *tape*

1 Sketch your container. What dimensions do you need to determine?

2 What dimensions will give you a volume of 300 mL?

3 Draw a net and cut it out to build your container.

4 Show your container to your class. Explain how you designed it and determined its volume.

Do You Remember? **Try It!**

List the area of the base and the height of three different triangular prisms that have the given volumes.

  1. 250 mL   **2.** 20 L

Sketch a cylinder 8 cubes high. Estimate its volume if its base holds the given number of cubes.

  3. 16   **4.** 49   **5.** 25   **6.** 4   **7.** 64

Write the number of red marbles in a bag of 100 marbles if the following is true.

  8. $\frac{2}{5}$ are red.   **9.** 33% are *not* red.   **10.** 1 of 10 is red.

Think About It

11. Explain in writing how you found the area of the base and the height of the triangular prisms in Exercise 1.

Investigation

Making an Aquarium

Create a home for a rainbow of tropical fish from Brazil, the Philippines, or your local pet shop. Design an aquarium to display your treasures. Use the information on this page to determine all the dimensions of your tank, including its volume. Then show your aquarium design to your classmates.

Tetra
2 in.
Brazil

Guppy
1 in.
Venezuela

To give your fish breathing room, allow 1 in. of fish per gallon of water. A 10-gal tank can hold fish that have no more than 10 in. of combined length. Which combinations of fish would fit in a 10-gal tank?

4 in.

5 in.

11.5 in.

Did you know that 1 gal of water takes up about 230 in.³? How could you use this information and your calculator to figure out some possible dimensions for a 2-gal tank? a 10-gal tank?

Blue Tang
4 in.
Philippines

Neon
1 in.
Peru

Angel
3 in.
Brazil

Will an angelfish swim peacefully with a neon in your aquarium? You can find the answer in a book about tropical fish or on a visit to a pet store.

Ask Yourself

- ☐ How will you choose which fish to put in your aquarium?
- ☐ What volume does your aquarium need to be to fit the fish you chose?
- ☐ What different shapes could you use for your design?
- ☐ How can you tell that the design you selected gives your fish enough breathing room?
- ☐ How could you explain your aquarium design to a friend?

Zebra
2 in.
India

Make sure your aquarium report includes

- a sketch with all the dimensions marked
- the math you used to determine volume
- a list of the fish you chose and your reasons for choosing them
- any outside research you did on the fish

Clownfish
1 in.
Philippines

AQUARIUM MATH

FISH Tetra = 2 in.
      Angel = 3 in.
      Neon = + 1 in.
      total   6 in.

WATER 6 in. fish
       6 gal water

$6 \times 230 \text{ in.}^3 = 1380 \text{ in.}^3$

AQUARIUM

parts	dimensions	Volume
cube	10 in. × 10 in. × 10 in.	1000 in.³
cylinder	8 in.² × 5 in.	40 in.³
triangular prism	20 in.² × 17 in.	340 in.³

★ Total Volume = 1380 in.^3

Area of Base = 100 in.²

cylinder

triangular prism

Base = 20 in.²

Base = 8 in.²

Top view (Area of Bases)

cube

Side view (heights)

scale ½ in. = 1 in.

425

Gumming Up the Works

The Maya people of Central America enjoyed chewing the chicle, or sap, of the sapodilla plant more than 1,000 years ago. In the 1800s North Americans added flavors to the chicle and began to sell chewing gum. The gumball machine was invented in the 1880s.

1 Name two space figures you can see on this page.

2 You have a bag with 6 gumballs: 2 red, 3 yellow, and 1 green. If you pull one gumball from the bag, what event would have a probability of $\frac{1}{6}$? $\frac{0}{6}$? $\frac{6}{6}$? $\frac{1}{2}$?

3 What percent of the gumballs below is red? white? pink?

4 Name a fraction that shows what part of these gumballs are blue, red, or pink. Write three different ways to show this number.

5 For every 20 gumballs in this machine, 4 are red, 3 are green, 2 are yellow, 1 is white, and 10 are other colors. What is the probability your nickel will get you a green gumball? a red? a yellow?

6 If this gumball machine were 9 gumballs long, 8 wide, and 13 high, about how many gumballs could fit in it altogether? Round your answer to the nearest hundred.

7 Draw a net for the canister, or base, of one of the gumball machines you see on these pages.

Check Your Math Power

8 Draw two circles on your paper. Measure and label them to show circumference, diameter, radius, and center.

9 Draw and label the dimensions for a gumball machine that has a volume of 8,000 cm^3.

10 Choose the number of gumballs of each color your machine will hold. Draw a circle graph to show the probability of getting each color.

LESSON **5** Scaling New **Heights**

What do you need to know to understand how an invention works? In this section you will explore a common invention, the stapler. What information do you get from the scale drawing below?

What You'll Need
• *grid paper*
• *ruler*

ACTIVITY **1** **Sizing Up Your Class**

With Your Partner Choose a simple object, like a book. Measure each surface. Now make a full-scale drawing of your object on a sheet of grid paper. Show all the measurements in three different views.

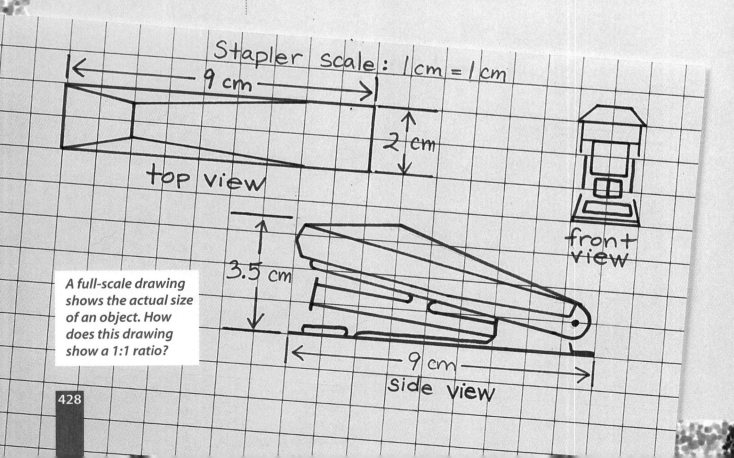

Stapler scale: 1 cm = 1 cm

9 cm

2 cm

top view

front view

3.5 cm

9 cm

side view

A full-scale drawing shows the actual size of an object. How does this drawing show a 1:1 ratio?

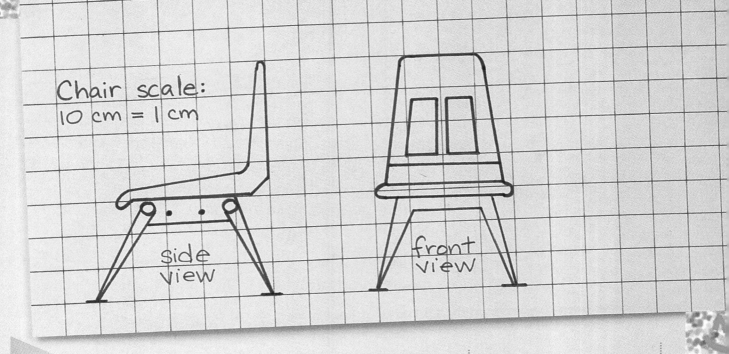

Chair scale:
10 cm = 1 cm

side view

front view

2 Bring It Down to Size

With Your Partner Choose a large, simple object, such as a chair, to draw. Why can't you make a full-scale drawing of this object on your grid paper?

What You'll Need
- *grid paper*
- *ruler*

 1 Measure and record your object's dimensions.

2 Use what you know about scale drawing to select a ratio that lets you to fit the object onto grid paper.

What is the actual height of the chair drawn above?

3 Draw your object on the grid paper, using the scale you chose. Show at least two different views. Record the scale you used and label your views.

TOOLS AND TECHNIQUES

Explain how finding equivalent ratios can help you decide how big to make an object in a scale drawing.

What You'll Need
- *grid paper*
- *ruler*

Computer designers never draw full-scale pictures of circuits because these circuits are so tiny. What scale would you use to draw an average-sized circuit of $\frac{1}{4}$ in. by $\frac{1}{4}$ in.? Explain.

ACTIVITY 3 The Big Picture

With Your Partner Scale drawing can also show a small object in greater detail. Select a small object or part of an object in the classroom. Measure and record the object's dimensions. Pick a scale that will let you draw a larger version of the object. Draw your picture on grid paper and label the scale.

enlargement of staple
scale is 1 cm = 5 cm

side view   front view

Do You Remember?

Try It!

Name an object you might draw using each scale.

1. 10 ft : 1 in.
2. 1 ft : 6 in.
3. 1 ft : 1 in.
4. 1 ft : $\frac{1}{4}$ in.
5. 1 in. : 5 in.
6. $\frac{1}{4}$ in. : 5 in.

Find the circumferences of circles that have the radii below. Describe any patterns you find.

7. 8 in.
8. 4 in.
9. 2 in.
10. 1 in.

Think About It

11. Explain how you decided on an object you might draw using the scale 10 ft : 1 in.

Go with the **Flow**

Scale drawings can show you how a stapler looks, but how does it work? A **flowchart** maps all the steps in a job such as stapling.

DRAWING TO LEARN

Have you started thinking about the contraption you are going to build? As you plan, draw a flowchart to show how your invention will work.

To use a stapler.

Push down on top of stapler.

Blade pushes staple out and through paper.

▸ACTIVITY 1 **Charting a Course**

With Your Partner Make a diagram showing all the steps involved in using a stapler. What will make the diagram a good flowchart? Agree on a diagram that shows each step.

With Your Class Discuss how you could use a flowchart to show activities like brushing your teeth or multiplying three numbers on a calculator.

What You'll Need
- *stapler*
- *grid paper*
- *markers or crayons*

Section C: Rate, Ratio, and Function   **431**

What You'll Need
- *scissors*
- *paste*
- *markers or crayons*

Following Each Step

On Your Own Make a flowchart or decision tree to show an activity such as selecting an after-school snack. A decision tree is a flowchart that shows all the steps in making a decision. Swap charts with a classmate and see whether you can follow all the steps on each other's chart.

ACTIVITY OPTION

Draw a simple flowchart to show how to play your favorite video or board game. Try to explain your game in ten steps or less.

HUNGRY? NO YES

Set fork down.

Put fork in spaghetti.

Twirl fork.

Lift fork.

Swallow.

Are the ends of the spaghetti dangling? YES NO

YUM (chew it up)

Open mouth and insert fork. JUST RIGHT TOO HOT

Blow on spaghetti.

Take fork out of mouth.

Explain how making a flowchart could help you solve a math problem.

With Your Partner   Look at the steps above for baking bread. Cut out all the items on your activity worksheet. Add the missing steps and correct their order to make a flowchart that works.

Do You Remember?

Try It!

Make flowcharts for the following activities:

   1. making a sandwich   **2.** solving $5 + (3 \times 6) + (10 \div 2)$

Draw a triangle with the angles 90° 45° 45°. Then make a similar triangle using the given ratio for the length of the sides.

   3. 4 : 1   **4.** 2 : 5   **5.** 7 : 3

Write how you know the answer will be greater than or less than one. If less than one, find the exact answer.

   6. 2×3 **7.** $\frac{3}{4} \times \frac{1}{8}$ **8.** $\frac{1}{3} \times 2$ **9.** $\frac{1}{3} \times \frac{2}{3}$ **10.** $\frac{2}{3} \times 2$

Think About It

11. Write an explanation of how you determined all the steps you needed to make your flowcharts in Exercise 1.

Function at the Junction

CONNECT AND COMMUNICATE

In Your Journal *Describe some places you think functions are used every day. Include what you think are the inputs and the outputs.*

What You'll Need
- *index cards*
- *markers or crayons*
- *game pieces*
- *gameboard*
- *number cube*

Each time you push the stapler, only one staple comes out. One push = one staple is a function. It pairs an input, a push, with an output, a staple. Find the outputs below when the inputs are 1, 2, and 3.

1. $n \times 2$
2. $n + 3$
3. $(2 \times n) - 1$
4. $15 - (n \times 5)$

ACTIVITY 1 Input/Output

On Your Own Make four cards for four different function machines.
- On the front of each card show at least three inputs and three outputs.
- Write the rule on the back.

Input	Output
8	5
9	6
10	7

rule ─── n × 3

1 Stack your function machine cards with the input/output side showing.

With Your Group See whether all the outputs and rules each of you made are correct. Then copy your cards. Each group should have one copy of each function card made by the other groups.

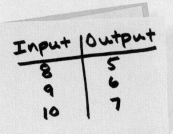

2 Draw a card and roll the cube.

Input	Output
2	0
4	0
5	0
8	0
11	0

Explain why this table could have at least two function rules.

Junction Bonus

If you land on one of these spaces, pick an extra function card and roll again. Answer correctly and advance your game piece down the short path. Answer incorrectly and advance your game piece down the long path.

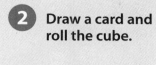

3 If you correctly state the rule on the card, move the number of spaces shown on the cube.

What You'll Need

- *rubber band*
- *thread spool*
- *thin straws*
- *tape*
- *ruler*
- *paper clip*
- *wax-paper cup*
- *1-hole punch*
- *cardboard*

The Great Spool Race

With Your Group Select a spool to race. Which do you think will go faster, a small or a large spool?

1 Mark the side of the spool. Record the distance the spool travels in one rotation and in two rotations.

2 Make a function table to show distance traveled per rotation. What is the function rule?

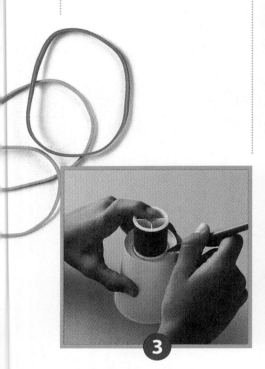

3 Trace the spool on the bottom of a wax-paper cup. Cut out the tracing. Make a second, smaller cardboard circle.

4 Use a hole punch to put a hole in the center of the circles. Use a short straw and tape to hold the rubber band on one end of the spool.

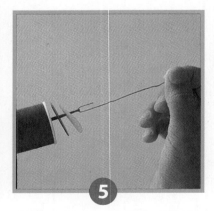

5 Use a bent paper clip to help you pull the rubber band through the hole in the spool and the cardboard and wax-paper circles.

straw for winding

wax-paper washer

Completed Racer

6 On the other end, use a straw longer than the diameter of the spool. Wind this straw ten times. Now your racer is ready to test. Put it down and see if it works. The straw will drag and keep the racer straight.

A rate is a ratio that compares two measures. What measures of distance and time did you compare to find your racer's rate of speed?

What You'll Need
- *masking tape*
- *ruler*
- *spool racer*
- *stopwatch or clock with second hand*

ACTIVITY 3 Let the Race Begin!

With Your Class In a corner of your classroom, use masking tape to mark a 2-ft track. Have two students keep time. Now test how fast your racers go. Record the time of each racer and graph your results. How did size affect your racer's speed? Predict how fast racers with larger wheel diameters would go.

Try It!

Make function machines for the following rules. Show at least five input and output numbers.

1. $n \div 5$
2. $(n \times 2) - 1$
3. $(n - 2) \div 2$
4. $n \times \frac{3}{4}$
5. $(2 \times n) + 15$
6. $30 - (n + 2)$

Draw 4 circles with the following measurements.

7. a diameter of 3 in.
8. a radius of 2 in.
9. a diameter of 6 cm
10. a circumference of about 22 in.

Think About It

11. What tips could you give to another fifth grader about how to figure out function rules?

LESSON
8

Planning for Success

TOOLS AND TECHNIQUES

How to Brainstorm
- *Write down every idea.*
- *Let everyone give ideas.*
- *Discuss ideas only after writing them all down.*

Have you ever heard of "the real McCoy"? Elijah McCoy, an African American inventor who lived from 1843 to 1929, made fine products for machinery. "The real McCoy" came to mean something of the highest quality. Brainstorming can give you ideas for a high-quality invention. Then you will bring it to life.

ACTIVITY 1 Storming Your Brain

With Your Class Make a list of problems you would like to solve. Then list inventions that could solve the problems.

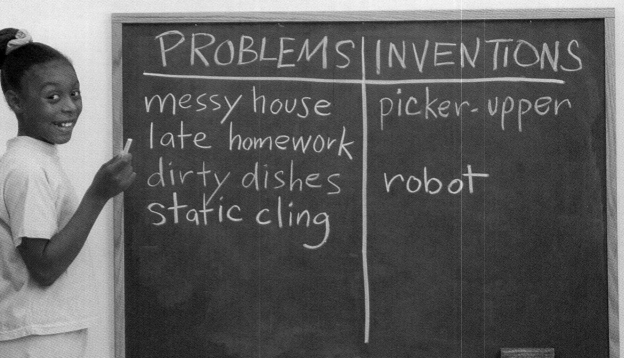

PROBLEMS	INVENTIONS
messy house	picker-upper
late homework	
dirty dishes	robot
static cling	

With Your Group Choose an invention your group would like to make. Be sure you can get the materials you will need to make it. One group decided to build a homework handler. They made a list of rules for their invention. What guidelines will your group use for your invention?

DRAWING TO LEARN

Sketch and describe an invention you would make if you could make anything in the world.

RULES FOR
HOMEWORK HANDLER

1. is easy to build

2. is made with supplies that are easy to find

3. can't hurt anyone

4. makes homework collection faster

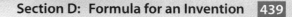

What You'll Need
- grid paper
- ruler
- materials for your invention
- scissors
- tape
- markers or crayons

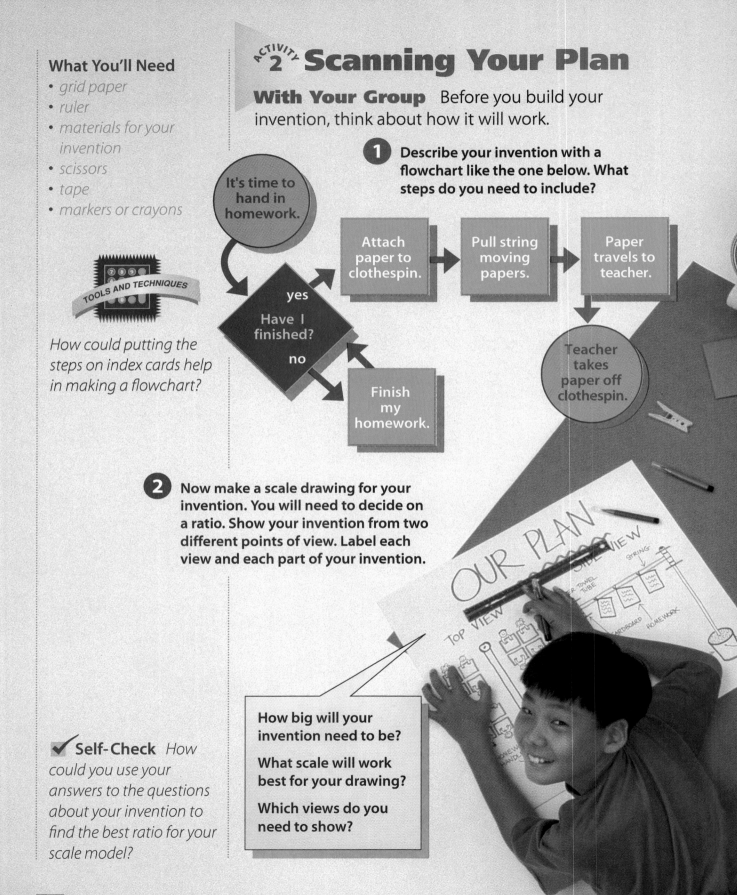

TOOLS AND TECHNIQUES

How could putting the steps on index cards help in making a flowchart?

Scanning Your Plan

With Your Group Before you build your invention, think about how it will work.

1 Describe your invention with a flowchart like the one below. What steps do you need to include?

It's time to hand in homework.

yes

Have I finished?

no

Attach paper to clothespin.

Pull string moving papers.

Paper travels to teacher.

Teacher takes paper off clothespin.

Finish my homework.

2 Now make a scale drawing for your invention. You will need to decide on a ratio. Show your invention from two different points of view. Label each view and each part of your invention.

How big will your invention need to be?

What scale will work best for your drawing?

Which views do you need to show?

✔ **Self-Check** *How could you use your answers to the questions about your invention to find the best ratio for your scale model?*

3 Now make a scale model of your invention. What materials can you use? Do you need to make a working model? Are you using three-dimensional figures and measures? How?

Did you make any changes in your original idea once you started developing your model? What changes did you make? Why?

Do You Remember?

Try It!

Use the ratio in Exercise 1 to draw a scale model of a window that is 24 in. by 36 in. Then choose two other ratios from Exercises 2–6 and sketch them. Explain one of your drawings.

1. 1 in. : 1 ft   **2.** 3 in. : 1 ft   **3.** $\frac{1}{2}$ in. : 1 ft
4. 4 in. : 1 ft   **5.** 2 in. : 1 ft   **6.** 1 in. : 2 ft

Find the ratio and write it in simplest form.

7. girls to all students in your class
8. boys to girls in your class
9. doors in your classroom to windows in your classroom
10. left-handed to right-handed students in your class

Think About It

11. Is the ratio you found for Exercise 10 greater than or less than the 1 : 10 ratio of left-handed to right-handed people in the general public? Write why you know.

Working It Out

Now it's time to put your plan into action! How will you know if your invention works?

ACTIVITY 1 Put It to the Test

With Your Group Before testing your invention, do what a scientist would do: predict what you think will happen. Record your prediction.

1 **Test** your invention to see if it works.

2 **Record** the results of your test, such as how fast your invention works and any problems you find.

3 **Analyze** your data. Did your invention work as you predicted? If not, explain what you think happened.

Before testing your invention, review your flowchart to be sure you have included all the steps needed to make it work.

5 Report the data you collected. Write a lab report, outline, or story. Add charts or graphs if you like. Include your prediction and an explanation of your test results. End with ideas for improving your invention.

4 Revise your invention to make it work better. Test it again. Be sure to collect and analyze your data.

Test Run	Number of Papers	Time
without machine	24	8 min
with machine 1	24	4 min
with machine 2	24	5 min

Do You Remember?

Try It!

Use the chart for Exercises 1–4.

Time (min)	Cubes released
1	5
2	8
3	11
4	14
5	17

1. Predict the number of cubes at 7 min.
2. Describe the function rule for this machine.
3. How long would it take to fill a box that holds 32 cubes?
4. Graph the data in at least one way.

Find the circumference of a circle with the given diameter. Use $\pi \approx 3.14$.

5. 1 in.   6. 3 in.   7. 12 cm   8. 11 ft   9. $20\frac{1}{2}$ in.   10. 33 in.

Think About It

11. How did you use the function rule to determine the length of time to fill the box in Exercise 3?

Looking Back

Choose the best answer. Write *a*, *b*, *c*, or *d* for Exercises 1–10.

Use these figures to answer Exercises 1–4.

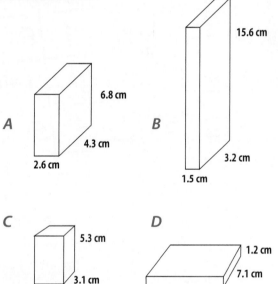

1. Use rounding to estimate. Find the space figure that has the smallest volume.

2. Which space figure's volume is closest to the volume of Figure *A*?

3. A cylinder with a base area of 10 cm² and a height of 7 cm has almost the same volume as which space figure?

4. If you added 2 cm to the longest dimension of Figure *C*, which space figure would it be closest to in volume?

Use this figure for Exercises 5–6.

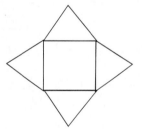

5. Which space figure could you build with this net?

   a. a cube
   b. a rectangular prism
   c. a rectangular pyramid
   d. a cylinder

6. The space figure you build with this net will have which of the following?

   a. as many edges as vertexes
   b. as many faces as edges
   c. as many faces as vertexes
   d. more vertexes than faces

7. Choose the space figure that has a curved surface and two flat faces.

   a. cylinder   **b.** sphere
   c. cone   **d.** cube

8. You have designed an unusual liter container with a base that measures $\frac{1}{2}$ cm by $\frac{1}{2}$ cm. How tall will it be?

   a. 4,000 cm   **b.** 250 cm
   c. 2,000 cm   **d.** 1,000 cm

9. Find the measurement that best describes angle *BAC*.

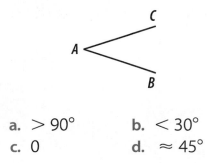

   a. $> 90°$ **b.** $< 30°$
   c. 0   **d.** $\approx 45°$

10. Complete this function table.

Input	Output
$\frac{2}{3}$	1
$\frac{1}{2}$	$\frac{5}{6}$
$\frac{1}{6}$	$\frac{1}{2}$
1	n

   a. $1\frac{1}{2}$ **b.** $1\frac{2}{3}$
   c. $1\frac{1}{3}$ **d.** $1\frac{1}{6}$

Check Your Math Power

Next to the name of each object, write a ratio that you could use to make a scale drawing of the object on $8\frac{1}{2}$-in.-by-11-in. paper. Explain your choices.

11. your desk

12. a safety pin

13. a telephone

14. the chalkboard

Copy the grid below.

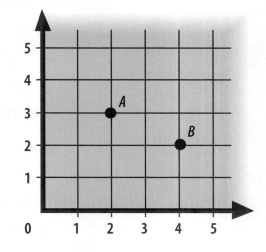

15. Use *A* and *B* as two vertexes of a polygon. Draw the polygon. Use ordered pairs to name each vertex.

16. How many different nets for open boxes can you fit on a 9-by-9 grid? Make each net from five squares. Draw the grid on your own paper and show how you got your answer.

MODULE 8 Investigations

A World of Toys

Children of all ages have always made their own toys, using simple materials they have found around them. What materials are these toys made of? What materials could you use to make a toy?

Investigation A — Playing Around

In this investigation you will make your own toy with found objects.

1 **Design** a toy using objects that would otherwise be thrown away. Brainstorm ways to make your toy. Decide which toy you will make and plan how to make it.

Oyoyotls
This noisemaker comes from Mexico. Shake the bamboo stick and hear the nutshells click and clack.

446

2 Construct your toy. Think about who will use the toy and how it will be used. Make sure your toy is sturdy and safe.

3 Display your toy and a poster showing a step-by-step plan of your invention process. Be prepared to answer questions about how your toy works and how to make it.

Keep in Mind

Your report will be judged by how well you do the following things.

☐ Explain how you made your toy. List materials so that someone else could make it.

☐ Use appropriate mathematical terms to describe any space figures your toy contains.

☐ Show a scale drawing of your toy with all the necessary measurements, including volume.

Cascarones
At a festival in Mexico you may see these decorated eggshells, filled with brightly colored confetti.

Scrap Bulldozer
A boy in Brazil made this bulldozer with wood, nails, string, and a tin can. It really works!

Investigations 447

Investigation B

Instant Festival

Make your own *cascarones*. The *cascarones* should hold 1 dm³ of confetti altogether. How many eggs will you need? Make a plan describing the *cascarones* you will make and how you will make them. Your plan should include your measurements and how you determined the volume for each *cascarón*. Share your *cascarones* and your plan with the class.

Ongoing Investigation

Wrapping Up "Who We Are"

It's time to prepare your final report on the "Who We Are" investigation. Review all the population data that you've gathered and prepare a presentation for your class. Be sure that your report includes

- graphs of your data
- Your conclusions about patterns of change in the data
- Your predictions about the population in 2020

Tool Kit
Contents

Problem Solving Strategies

Computation Tools

Technology

Data Collection

Drawing to Learn

Measurement

Ways to Solve Problems

On the next few pages, you'll find different strategies, or ways, for solving math problems. Learning these strategies will give you a powerful set of problem solving tools.

Problem

You have square tables for a party. Only one person can sit comfortably on each side. What is the greatest number of people you can seat at 1, 2, 3, 4, 5, and 6 tables if you want the tables to touch on at least one side?

Draw a Picture or a Diagram

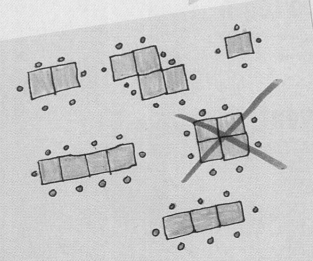

Drawing a picture or diagram can help you solve many problems. You will probably find it helpful to draw a picture when a problem asks you to arrange objects, work with shapes, or compare varying measurements in a space. (See Drawing to Learn on pages 470–471.)

Build a Model or Act It Out

Making a model with objects is another way to find solutions to a problem about arrangements. In this case, you could use blocks to show tables and counters to show chairs. You could move the blocks and counters all sorts of ways to find the best arrangements.

Use a Pattern

You may find a pattern when you are trying to solve some problems. If you do, use the pattern to predict numbers without doing extra calculations. Drawing a picture or making a table can also help you discover the pattern.

Steps

1. **Work through the first several steps of the problem. Drawing a picture often helps.**

2. **Write the numbers in a table and look for a pattern.**

3. **Use the pattern to complete the table.**

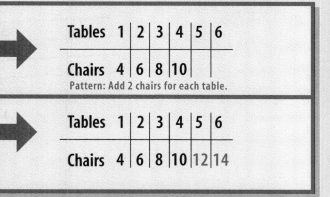

Tables	1	2	3	4	5	6
Chairs	4	6	8	10		

Pattern: Add 2 chairs for each table.

Tables	1	2	3	4	5	6
Chairs	4	6	8	10	12	14

Tool Kit

Problem Solving Strategies

What is the least number of coins you can use to make 35 cents? What is the greatest number of coins you can use? In how many different ways can you make 35 cents?

Organize Information

Some problems require you to make combinations or arrange data. In these cases, it helps to organize your information in a list, table, chart, or graph.

Write a List Making a list is one way to organize your information. Write down all the possibilities in a planned way.

Make a Table or Chart

If you find yourself writing the same words again and again, organize your information into a table. Making a table will save you time and space.

First you can list all the ways to make 35¢ using just one quarter.

Ways to Make 35¢

Quarters	Dimes	Nickels	Pennies
1	1		
1		2	
1			10
1		1	5
	3	1	
	3		5

Then you can write all the ways to make 35¢ using 3 dimes.

At the end of a day, you have $2.04 left. You can't remember exactly how much you took out of your home bank that morning. How can you figure it out?

▶ Work Backward

If you have ever lost something, you may have found it by tracing your steps backward. That's exactly how to use the strategy Work Backward. You'll want to use this strategy when you know the endpoint of a problem but not the information that leads to it.

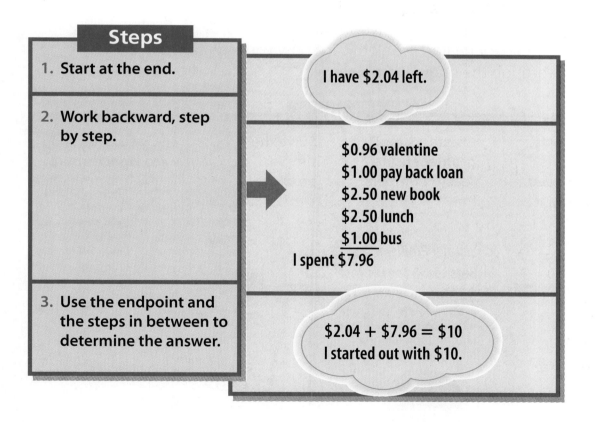

Steps

1. **Start at the end.**

   I have $2.04 left.

2. **Work backward, step by step.**

   $0.96 valentine
   $1.00 pay back loan
   $2.50 new book
   $2.50 lunch
   $1.00 bus
   I spent $7.96

3. **Use the endpoint and the steps in between to determine the answer.**

   $2.04 + $7.96 = $10
   I started out with $10.

Tool Kit

Problem Solving Strategies

Problem

A sporting goods store usually sells bats for $8.95. Now they're on sale for $6.98. If balls cost $4.95, how many bat-and-ball sets can you buy with $120?

Use a Simpler or Related Problem

Some problems seem hard because they involve lots of data or large numbers. Unnecessary data also makes problems difficult to solve. In such cases, working a simpler or related problem can show you how to work through the original problem.

Steps

1. Cut out words and numbers you don't need. (In this case, it doesn't matter that bats *used* to sell for $8.95.)

2. Create a simpler problem using "easy" numbers.

3. Solve the simpler problem.

4. Use that method to work through the first problem.

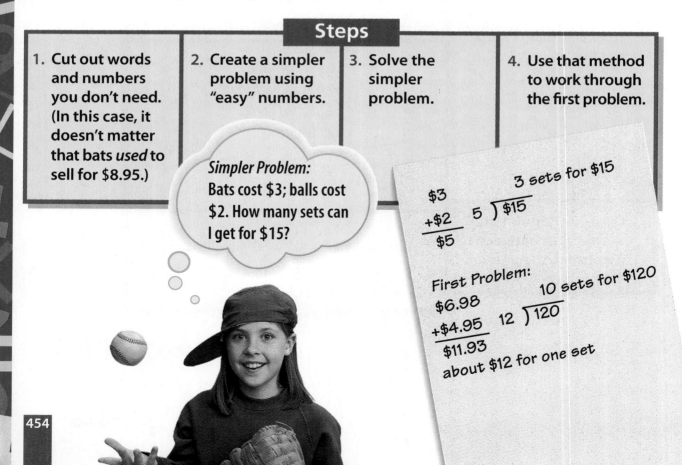

Simpler Problem:
Bats cost $3; balls cost $2. How many sets can I get for $15?

$$\begin{array}{r} \$3 \\ +\$2 \\ \hline \$5 \end{array}$$

5) $15   3 sets for $15

First Problem:
$$\begin{array}{r} \$6.98 \\ +\$4.95 \\ \hline \$11.93 \end{array}$$

12) 120   10 sets for $120

about $12 for one set

454

Find two numbers whose sum is 135 and whose difference is 21. What are they?

Guess and Check

Guess and Check is a strategy that helps you plunge right into a problem. First make a guess at an answer. Then check to see if it works. Use that information to decide if your next guess should be lower or higher.

Steps

1. **Make a guess.**

   How about 100 and 35?

2. **Check it out to see if it works.**

   $100 + 35 = 135$
   But $100 - 35 = 65$

3. **Use your guess to make a better guess.**

   The numbers must be closer to one another. Maybe it's 70 and 65:
   $70 + 65 = 135$. But $70 - 65 = 5$.

4. **Keep trying until you get the answer that works.**

   78 and 57?
   $78 + 57 = 135$
   $78 - 57 = 21!$

Computing by Steps

Use this part of the Tool Kit to review ways to add, subtract, multiply, and divide. You'll find methods for computing with paper and pencil as well as "in your head."

Paper and Pencil

These methods are helpful whenever you are using paper and a pencil to compute large numbers.

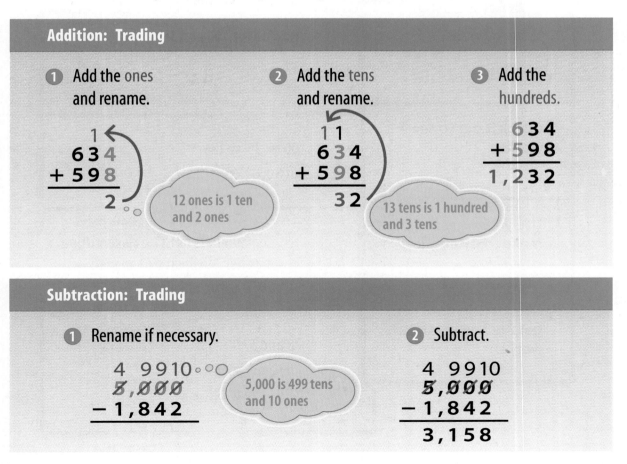

Addition: Trading

1 Add the ones and rename.

$$\begin{array}{r} 1 \\ 6\,3\,4 \\ +\,5\,9\,8 \\ \hline 2 \end{array}$$

12 ones is 1 ten and 2 ones

2 Add the tens and rename.

$$\begin{array}{r} 1\,1 \\ 6\,3\,4 \\ +\,5\,9\,8 \\ \hline 3\,2 \end{array}$$

13 tens is 1 hundred and 3 tens

3 Add the hundreds.

$$\begin{array}{r} 6\,3\,4 \\ +\,5\,9\,8 \\ \hline 1,2\,3\,2 \end{array}$$

Subtraction: Trading

1 Rename if necessary.

$$\begin{array}{r} 4\ \ 9\,9\,10 \\ 5,000 \\ -\,1,8\,4\,2 \end{array}$$

5,000 is 499 tens and 10 ones

2 Subtract.

$$\begin{array}{r} 4\ \ 9\,9\,10 \\ 5,000 \\ -\,1,8\,4\,2 \\ \hline 3,1\,5\,8 \end{array}$$

Addition: Decimals

① Line up the *decimal points* so you will be adding "like" quantities.

$$\begin{array}{r} 5.74 \\ 23.88 \\ +\,10.70 \\ \hline \end{array}$$

② Add the *hundredths* and rename.

$$\begin{array}{r} \overset{1}{} \\ 5.74 \\ 23.88 \\ +\,10.70 \\ \hline 2 \end{array}$$

③ Add the *tenths* and rename.

$$\begin{array}{r} \overset{2\ 1}{} \\ 5.74 \\ 23.88 \\ +\,10.70 \\ \hline 32 \end{array}$$

④ Add the *whole numbers*. Place a *decimal point* in the answer.

$$\begin{array}{r} \overset{1\ 2\ 1}{} \\ 5.74 \\ 23.88 \\ +\,10.70 \\ \hline 40.32 \end{array}$$

Subtraction: Decimals

① Change whole numbers to decimals. Line up the *decimal points*.

$$18.00\ -$$

(18 is 18.00)

② Rename if needed. Subtract the hundredths.

$$\begin{array}{r} {}^{9\ 10} \\ 18.\cancel{0}\cancel{0} \\ -\ 5.83 \\ \hline 7 \end{array}$$

③ Rename if needed. Subtract the tenths.

$$\begin{array}{r} {}^{7\ \ 9\ 10} \\ 18.\cancel{0}\cancel{0} \\ -\ 5.83 \\ \hline \end{array}$$

④ Subtract the *whole numbers*. Place the *decimal point*.

$$\begin{array}{r} {}^{7\ \ 9\ 10} \\ 1\cancel{8}.\cancel{0}\cancel{0} \\ -\ 5.83 \\ \hline \end{array}$$

Adding and Subtracting Fractions: Same Denominators

① See if the *denominators* are the same.

$$\frac{4}{5} - \frac{1}{5}$$

Same denominators

② Subtract the *numerators*. Write the *difference* over the common denominator.

$$\frac{4}{5} - \frac{1}{5} = \frac{3}{5}$$

Tool Kit

Computation Tools

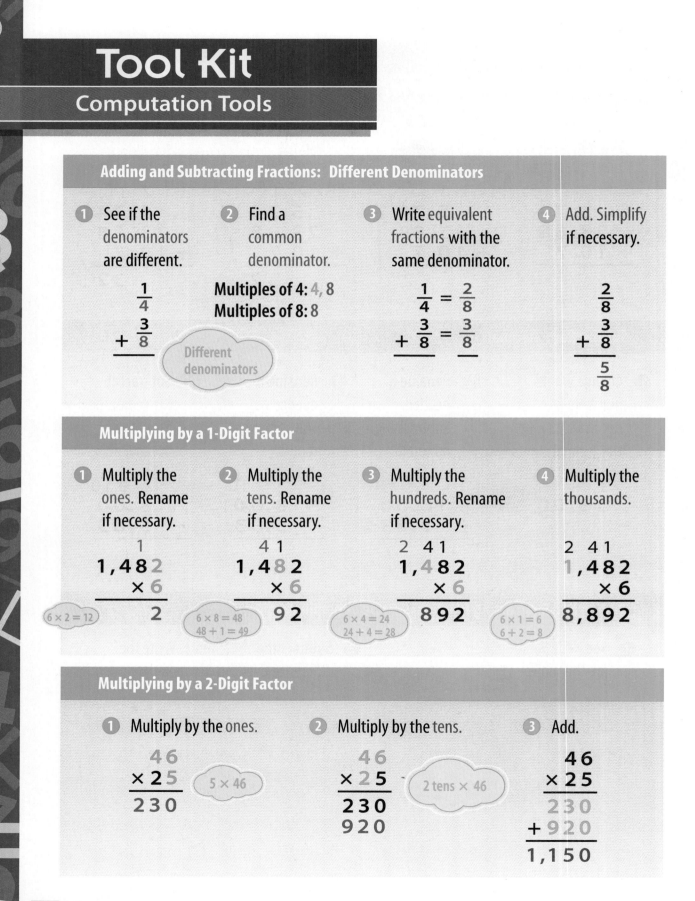

Adding and Subtracting Fractions: Different Denominators

1 See if the denominators are different.

$$\frac{1}{4}$$
$$+\frac{3}{8}$$

Different denominators

2 Find a common denominator.

Multiples of 4: 4, 8
Multiples of 8: 8

3 Write equivalent fractions with the same denominator.

$$\frac{1}{4} = \frac{2}{8}$$
$$+\frac{3}{8} = \frac{3}{8}$$

4 Add. Simplify if necessary.

$$\frac{2}{8}$$
$$+\frac{3}{8}$$
$$\frac{5}{8}$$

Multiplying by a 1-Digit Factor

1 Multiply the ones. Rename if necessary.

```
   1
1,482
×  6
    2
```
6 × 2 = 12

2 Multiply the tens. Rename if necessary.

```
  4 1
1,482
×   6
   92
```
6 × 8 = 48
48 + 1 = 49

3 Multiply the hundreds. Rename if necessary.

```
 2 41
1,482
×   6
  892
```
6 × 4 = 24
24 + 4 = 28

4 Multiply the thousands.

```
 2 41
1,482
×   6
8,892
```
6 × 1 = 6
6 + 2 = 8

Multiplying by a 2-Digit Factor

1 Multiply by the ones.

```
  46
×25
 230
```
5 × 46

2 Multiply by the tens.

```
  46
×25
 230
 920
```
2 tens × 46

3 Add.

```
  46
×25
 230
+920
1,150
```

Dividing by a 1-Digit Divisor

1 Decide how many digits are in the quotient.

$$7\overline{)534}$$

The first digit is in the tens' place.

2 Estimate the first digit.

$$7\overline{)534}$$ → 7

3 Multiply to find the number of tens shared. Subtract to find the tens left.

$$\begin{array}{r} 7 \\ 7\overline{)534} \\ -49 \\ \hline 4 \end{array}$$

4 tens

4 Trade the tens for ones. Share the ones.

$$\begin{array}{r} 76 \\ 7\overline{)534} \\ -49 \\ \hline 44 \\ -42 \\ \hline 2 \end{array}$$

7 × 6

Dividing by a 2-Digit Divisor

1 Decide how many digits are in the first quotient.

$$23\overline{)378}$$

The first digit is in the tens' place.

2 Estimate the first digit.

$$23\overline{)378}$$ → 1

3 Multiply to find the number of tens shared. Subtract to find the tens left.

$$\begin{array}{r} 1 \\ 23\overline{)378} \\ -23 \\ \hline 14 \end{array}$$

14 tens

4 Trade the tens for ones. Share the ones.

$$\begin{array}{r} 16 \\ 23\overline{)378} \\ -23 \\ \hline 148 \\ -138 \\ \hline 10 \end{array}$$

Multiplying Decimals

1 Multiply as with whole numbers.

$$\begin{array}{r} 32.6 \\ \times \ .05 \\ \hline 1630 \end{array}$$

2 Add the decimal places in the factors. Write that many decimal places in the product.

$$\begin{array}{r} 32.6 \\ \times \ .05 \\ \hline 1.630 \end{array}$$

← 1 decimal place
← 2 decimal places
← 3 decimal places

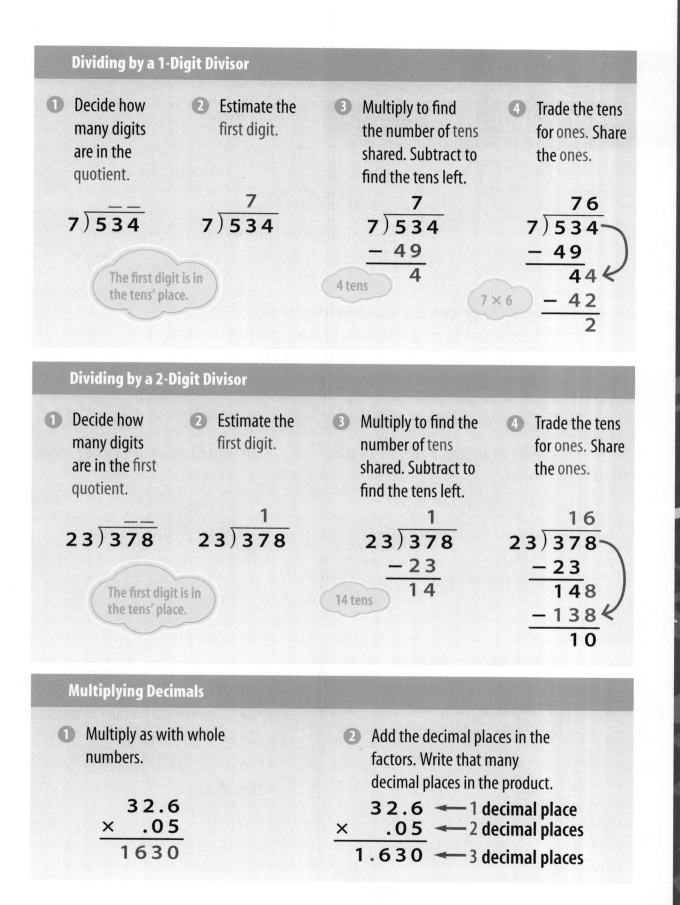

Tool Kit

Computation Tools

▶ **Mental Math**

Doing computation mentally can be faster than writing something down. Here are some strategies you can use for mental math.

Counting On or Counting Back

When you add or subtract numbers, you can count ahead or count back by multiples of ten. Then count ahead or back one number at a time.

Add: 28 + 43

Start with 28 and count ahead by 4 tens.

28 . . . 38, 48, 58, 68 . . .
Then count ahead by 3 ones.
68 . . . 69, 70, 71

Subtract: 88 − 32

Start with 88 and count back by 3 tens.

88 . . . 78, 68, 58 . . .
Then count back by 2 ones.
58 . . . 57, 56

Canceling Zeros

If both the divisor and dividend end in zeros, mentally cross out the same number of zeros in each. Then divide.

6,600 ÷ 200 = n

Cancel same number of zeros.

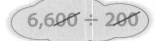

6,600 ÷ 200

Then divide.

66 ÷ 2 = 33

Multiplying Tens

When you multiply by multiples of 10, 100, or 1,000, multiply the nonzero digits. Then supply the zeros in the product.

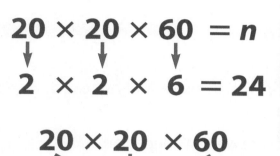

$$20 \times 20 \times 60 = n$$

$$2 \times 2 \times 6 = 24$$

First multiply the factors without the zeros.

$$20 \times 20 \times 60$$

$$24{,}000$$

Then count the number of zeros in the factors.

3 zeros

Supply the zeros in the product.

Compensation

When you add or subtract, changing one number to a round number can make solving easier. Then change your answer to compensate.

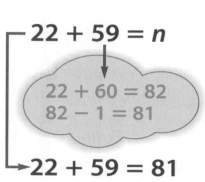

$$22 + 59 = n$$

$$22 + 60 = 82$$
$$82 - 1 = 81$$

$$22 + 59 = 81$$

Add 1 to 59 to get 60.
Subtract 1 from the answer to compensate.

Breaking Apart Numbers

You can break apart numbers to get numbers that are easier to use mentally. Breaking apart numbers in a multiplication problem is one way to use the Distributive Property.

Add

$$64 + 23$$

$$64 + (20 + 3) \quad \text{Break apart 23.}$$

$$(64 + 20) + 3$$

$$84 + 3 = 87$$

Think: 20 + 3

Multiply

$$9 \times 52$$

$$= (9 \times 50) + (9 \times 2) \quad \text{Break apart 52.}$$

$$= 450 + 18$$

$$= 468$$

Think: 50 + 2

Tool Kit

Computation Tools

▶ Estimation

Estimation is using mental math to get an answer that's close to the actual answer but not exact. When is it helpful to estimate?

- When an exact answer isn't necessary
- When you want to know if your answer is reasonable
- When there is no way of getting an exact number

Here are four estimation strategies.

Rounding
Rounding makes numbers easier to work with mentally.

Round Whole Numbers	*Round Decimals*	*Round Fractions*
To nearest 100	To nearest 1	To whole numbers
75 ⟶ 100	$6.59 → $7	$2\frac{2}{3}$ ⟶ 3
233 ⟶ 200	$136.98 → $137	$5\frac{1}{8}$ ⟶ 5

Rounding to Estimate Products
To get a quick multiplication estimate, round the factors.

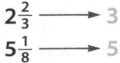

$$19 \times 665$$
$$\downarrow \qquad \downarrow$$
$$20 \times 700 = 14{,}000$$

Front-End Estimation

Use front-end estimation to quickly add money amounts.

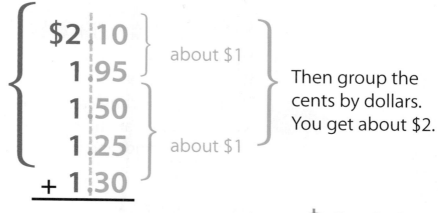

First group dollars. You get $6.

$2.10
1.95 } about $1

1.50
1.25 } about $1
+ 1.30

Then group the cents by dollars. You get about $2.

$6.00 + about $2.00 = about $8.00

Compatible Numbers

Compatible numbers are numbers that are easy to divide. You can use compatible numbers to help estimate quotients and the products of some fractions and whole numbers.

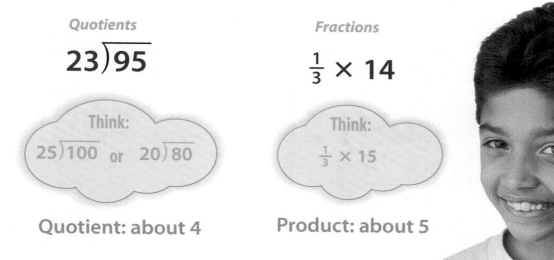

Quotients

$23\overline{)95}$

Think:
$25\overline{)100}$ or $20\overline{)80}$

Quotient: about 4

Fractions

$\frac{1}{3} \times 14$

Think:
$\frac{1}{3} \times 15$

Product: about 5

Electronic Tools

Computers and calculators can help you solve problems, calculate numbers, and present work. The trick is in knowing how and when to use them.

Computer

Computers can help you collect, organize, and analyze large amounts of data. With different kinds of software, you can create diagrams, charts, tables, graphs, and pictures.

Software Software programs are the instructions that tell a computer what to do. Drawing programs, spreadsheets, word processing packages, and computer games are all software.

Drawing Programs Pictures can help you solve a problem or explain an idea. Using drawing software is a fun and easy way to make all kinds of pictures. And on the computer you can always change your picture.

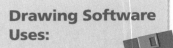

Drawing Software Uses:

- draw pictures
- make patterns
- illustrate stories
- create floor plans

Spreadsheets/Graphs

Spreadsheet programs are very useful when you are working with lots of numbers. Spreadsheets have columns and rows, like a table. You can enter your own numbers or have the computer calculate them for you. Then you can sort, rearrange, and even graph your information.

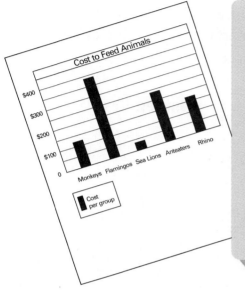

Cost to Feed Animals

The spreadsheet added the total cost.

	A	B	C	D	E	F	G
1	Cost of Feeding Animals Each Week in Wildlife Park						
2							
3	Animals	Number	Cost/One	Total Cost			
4							
5	Monkey	8	$17.00	$136.00			
6	Flamingo	12	$32.00	$384.00			
7	Sea Lion	4	$11.00	$44.00			
8	Anteater	2	$115.00	$230.00			
9	Rhino	1	$165.00	$165.00			
10							
11	SUM	27	$340.00	$959.00			

Databases

With database software you can organize large amounts of data, including words, dates, and numbers. A database is a great place to put survey results because it can sort through all the answers in the survey. For example, for this survey, the database can search for how many boys have pet hamsters or what kind of pet is owned by the most students.

	Name	Male/Female	Age	Pets	
1	Mark Ellis	M	11	dog	parrot
2	Sue Linn	F	12	fish	
3	Reggie Brown	M	10	dog	
4	Cassie Houston	F	12	dog	cat
5	Rosa Rodriguez	F	12	hamster	
6					
7					
8					
9					
10					
11					
12					
13					
14					
15					

Tool Kit
Technology

> ## Calculator
>
> Your calculator may be a little different from the one shown on these pages. Read the instructions that come with your calculator to learn how to use it.

Examples:

Division
This calculator will divide and show the remainder.

$173 \div 15$

173 [INT ÷] 15 [=] | Q 11 R 8 |

Fractions
This calculator will compute with fractions, change fractions to mixed numbers, and simplify fractions.

$\frac{26}{3} \times \frac{51}{4}$

26 [/] 3 [×] 51 [/] 4 [=] | 1326/12 |
[Ab/c] | 110⌣6/12 |
[Simp] [=] | 110⌣3/6 |
[Simp] [=] | 110⌣1/2 |

Mixed Numbers
This calculator will compute mixed numbers.

$4\frac{1}{5} + 6\frac{3}{8}$

4 [+] 1 [/] 5 [+] 6 [+] 3 [/] 8
[=] | 10 23/40 |

Percents
This calculator will find percents.

What is 40% of 75?

40 [%] [×] 75 [=] | 30 |

Parentheses
This calculator will perform multiple calculations in the order you want.

$2 \times (4 + 5)$

2 [×] [(] 4 [+] 5 [)] [=] | 18 |

1 Memory

M+ Stores the number on the display in memory, or adds the displayed number to any value already in memory

M− Subtracts the displayed number from memory

MR Displays the value stored in memory

x⌒\M Exchanges the number on the display with the number in memory

2 Clearing

ON/AC Clears the memory, display, and operation

Backspace Clears the last digit entered

CE/C Clears the last entry

CE/C **CE/C** Clears the display but not the memory

3 Display

Shows the digits of your work

4 Fractions and Decimals

F⌒D Changes decimals to fractions, fractions to decimals

5 Negative Numbers

+⌒− Changes positive numbers to negative numbers

6 Repeats

= Can be used to repeat an operation with the same number:

4 **+** 2 **=** 6
= 8
= 10

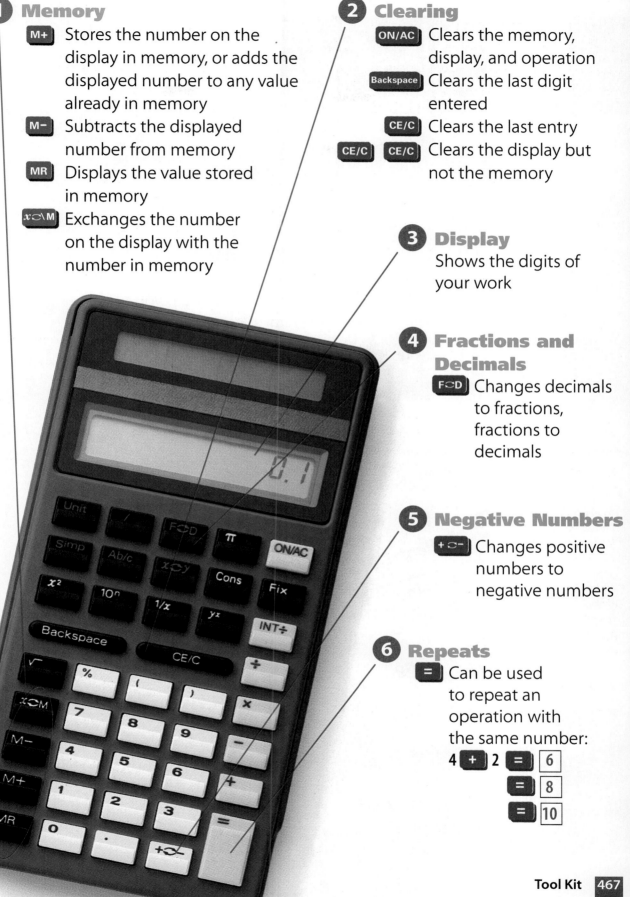

Working with Data

Data refers to facts of all kinds. Numbers, statistics, dates, and responses to interviews are all examples of data. Here are some steps to help you plan and organize data at several stages.

Eight Steps to Good Data Collection

Possible Questions
- How much has my state's population changed?
- How much did our class grow last year?
- What kinds of arrays are found in grocery stores?

Ways to Collect Data
- counting
- measuring
- observing
- researching
- interviewing
- experimenting

1 Begin with a Question
Choose a question that you can answer by collecting data from several people or sources.

2 Plan Your Strategy
Choose a way to collect data. Where will you go for information? What kind of data are you likely to collect? How can you share it?

3 Collect and Record the Data
This could be as simple as a few tally marks in response to a question or as complex as making several graphs.

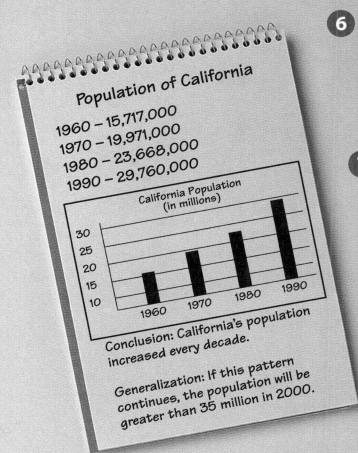

Population of California

1960 – 15,717,000
1970 – 19,971,000
1980 – 23,668,000
1990 – 29,760,000

California Population
(in millions)

30
25
20
15
10

1960   1970   1980   1990

Conclusion: California's population increased every decade.

Generalization: If this pattern continues, the population will be greater than 35 million in 2000.

6 Draw a Conclusion

What does the data tell you about your original question? Does it describe something? Does it allow you to make comparisons?

7 Use Your Conclusion

You may be able to use your conclusion as a basis for a prediction, generalization, or decision.

8 Look Back/Look Ahead

As you look over the results of your data collection, you may want to begin the process again with a related or refined question. Or you may wish to test the theory you developed.

4 Organize the Data

Review and arrange your data. What's the best way to categorize your data?

5 Represent Your Data

What's the best way to display your data? A table? A chart? A graph? Now you're ready to share your results.

How does California's growth compare to that of other states?

Drawing as a Math Tool

Drawing can help you discover, understand, and share key concepts in math. Use your Drawing to Learn tools to make a variety of precise shapes and measurements.

Drawing to Discover

Drawing can lead to discovery. For example, if you draw what you know about a problem, you often find the solution. If you draw a chart, you can see how groups of numbers relate. And drawing helps you discover your own creative ideas about math.

As you draw, patterns appear that you might not have noticed otherwise.

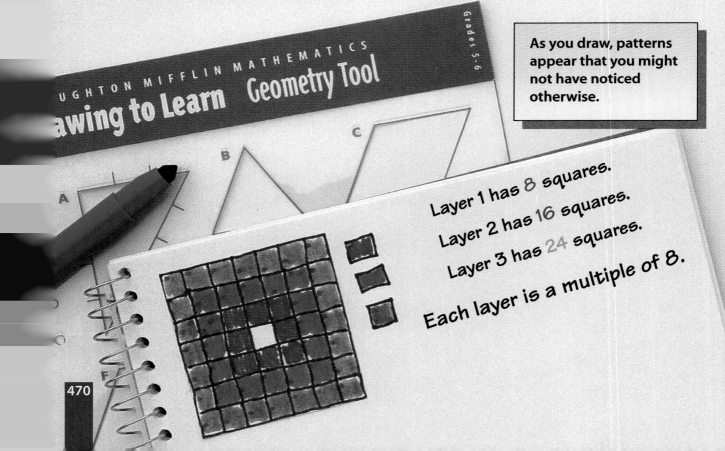

Layer 1 has 8 squares.
Layer 2 has 16 squares.
Layer 3 has 24 squares.

Each layer is a multiple of 8.

Drawing to Understand

To simplify the steps of a process, pick up a pencil and start to draw. Drawing can also help you understand key concepts in math, including the basic computations of adding, subtracting, multiplying, and dividing.

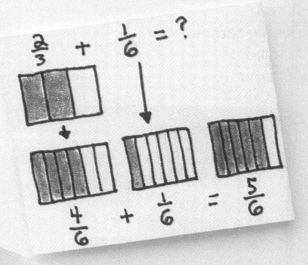

You can use drawing to create your own system for understanding a key math concept.

Drawing to Share

Pictures, diagrams, graphs—all these are visual ways to share information. You can pack a great deal of data into a drawing.

People can point to your graph and ask questions or give feedback.

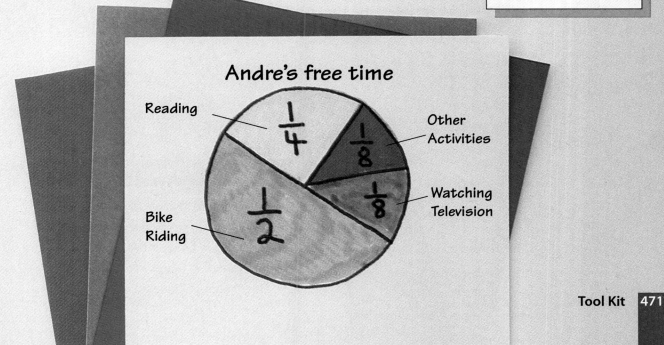

Measurement Tools

The charts on this page identify common measures. Check the glossary and index for more information on specific terms.

	Customary	Metric
Length	1 foot (ft) = 12 inches (in.) 1 yard (yd) = 3 feet (ft) or 36 inches (in.) 1 mile (mi) = 5,280 feet (ft)	1 centimeter (cm) = 10 millimeters (mm) 1 decimeter (dm) = 10 centimeters (cm) 1 meter (m) = 10 decimeters (dm) 1 kilometer (km) = 1,000 meters (m)
Capacity	1 cup (c) = 8 fluid ounces (fl oz) 1 pint (pt) = 2 cups (c) 1 quart (qt) = 2 pints (pt) 1 gallon (gal) = 4 quarts (qt)	1 liter (L) = 1,000 milliliters (mL) 1 kiloliter (kL) = 1,000 liters (L)
Mass/ Weight	1 pound (lb) = 16 ounces (oz) 1 ton (t) = 2,000 pounds (lb)	1 gram (g) = 1,000 milligrams (mg) 1 kilogram (kg) = 1,000 grams (g)
Temperature	*Fahrenheit* freezing point = 32° F boiling point = 212° F	*Celsius* freezing point = 0° C boiling point = 100° C

Time
1 minute (min) = 60 seconds (s) 1 hour (h) = 60 minutes (min) 1 day = 24 hours (h) 1 week = 7 days 1 year = 52 weeks

Module 5.1 Section A

a For use with Lesson 1 (pages 4–7)

Which pairs are congruent? For each congruent pair, write whether the second figure is a slide, flip, or turn.

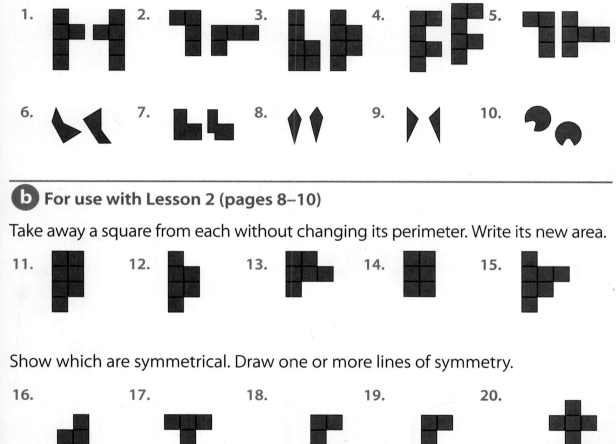

b For use with Lesson 2 (pages 8–10)

Take away a square from each without changing its perimeter. Write its new area.

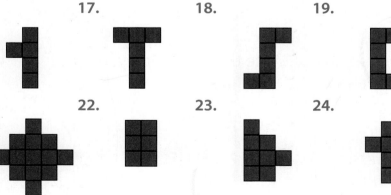

Show which are symmetrical. Draw one or more lines of symmetry.

16.   17.   18.   19.   20.

21.   22.   23.   24.   25.

Module 5.1 Section B

a For use with Lesson 3 (pages 14–17)

Show two possibilities for Step 3 in each pattern.

1. ○ ● ○ ● ●   2. ○ ● ● ○ ● ●

Step 1   Step 2   Step 1   Step 2

3. 1, 4   4. 6, 24   5. 1,000, 500   6. 2, 8

7. 600, 300   8. 2, 4   9. 3, 12   10. 5, 30

b For use with Lesson 4 (pages 18–21)

Find the total for these steps of the pattern. Use your calculator.

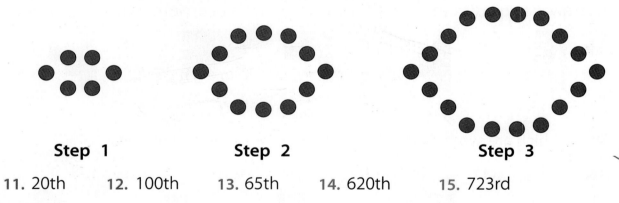

Step 1   **Step 2**   **Step 3**

11. 20th   12. 100th   13. 65th   14. 620th   15. 723rd

Find the 20th step in each sequence. Write the expression you used.
Use *n* for the number of the step.

16. 5, 10, 15   17. 4, 8, 12   18. 11, 12, 13   19. 6, 12, 18

For *n* = 8 solve each expression.
20. $n - 3$ 21. $n \times 6$ 22. $n \times n$ 23. $n + n$

For *n* = 12 solve each expression.
24. $n - 3$ 25. $n \times 6$ 26. $n \times n$ 27. $n + n$

Module 5.1 Section C

---

a **For use with Lesson 5 (pages 24–26)**

On which of the patterns you made do these numbers share the same color?

1. 13, 27, 41   2. 44, 20, 4   3. 32, 44, 8   4. 38, 48, 98

5. 30, 4, 42   6. 34, 58, 4   7. 19, 26, 40   8. 5, 33, 37

9. 14, 29, 34   10. 33, 24, 45   11. 55, 28, 64   12. 15, 50, 78

---

b **For use with Lesson 6 (pages 27–30)**

Use this pattern: orange, blue, green, purple, red. What color will
these squares be?

13. 13   14. 16   15. 48   16. 65   17. 71

18. 60   19. 82   20. 54   21. 27   22. 59

23. 51   24. 94   25. 100   26. 123   27. 252

---

c **For use with Lesson 7 (pages 31–33)**

Write an equation for three different paths between each pair of numbers.

28. 35 to 53   29. 22 to 54   30. 87 to 39   31. 5 to 31

32. 44 to 68   33. 30 to 14   34. 32 to 78   35. 73 to 60

36. 5 to 25   37. 18 to 13   38. 95 to 89   39. 19 to 1

What does z equal on a hundreds' board?

40. $z + 20 = 84$ 41. $28 - z = 23$ 42. $53 - z = 23$

Module 5.1 Section D

ⓐ For use with Lesson 8 (pages 34–37)

Find the first two common multiples of each of the following pairs of numbers.

1. 3 and 7	**2.** 2 and 3	**3.** 4 and 5	**4.** 5 and 8
5. 5 and 2	**6.** 3 and 6	**7.** 2 and 7	**8.** 3 and 8
9. 2 and 5	**10.** 4 and 7	**11.** 9 and 5	**12.** 5 and 25

ⓑ For use with Lesson 9 (pages 38–43)

Find all the factors of the following numbers.

13. 40	**14.** 99	**15.** 32	**16.** 72	**17.** 100
18. 45	**19.** 132	**20.** 54	**21.** 64	**22.** 36
23. 31	**24.** 18	**25.** 35	**26.** 80	**27.** 51

Tell whether each of the following is prime or composite.

28. 40	**29.** 32	**30.** 15	**31.** 13	**32.** 36
33. 23	**34.** 19	**35.** 4	**36.** 25	**37.** 73

Answer these questions about prime numbers.

38. What is the smallest prime number?

39. What is the only even prime number?

40. What are the only factors for every prime number?

41. How many prime numbers are less than 50?

42. How many prime numbers are squares?

Draw a design, using the squares on graph paper. Use your picture to answer the questions.

43. Write a multiplication sentence to show the number of smallest squares in your picture.

44. Locate a polyomino in your picture. Redraw the polyomino as if it had flipped.

Module 5.2 Section A

ⓐ For use with Lesson 1 (pages 52–57)

Write each number in two ways.

1. 4,305

2. twelve thousand, four hundred nineteen

3. 256 hundreds

4. 709,031

5. 3,486 tens

6. two million, four hundred fifty-six thousand

7. 3,926

8. 2,566,932

9. 345 hundreds

10. 2,482

11. 230,100

12. two hundred thousand, three

13. 60,480

14. thirty-three million, five thousand

ⓑ For use with Lesson 2 (pages 58–61)

Use the population chart on page 60 to answer the following.

15. What two states are closest in population?

16. What is the difference in population between those two states?

17. What state has about $\frac{1}{3}$ the population of Michigan?

18. What two states together have about 40 million people?

19. What two states together exceed California in population?

20. By how much do those states exceed California?

21. What states' populations exceed the combined population of Oregon and Ohio?

22. What state's population is closest to the difference between California and Texas?

Module 5.2 Section B

a For use with Lesson 3 (pages 62–67)

Round the following to the place value of the digit indicated.

1. 3,4$\underline{5}$6
2. 6$\underline{7}$,047
3. 2$\underline{0}$9,554
4. 3$\underline{4}$5
5. $\underline{3}$8
6. 99,$\underline{4}$72
7. $\underline{7}$,902
8. $\underline{1}$34,505
9. 5$\underline{3}$9
10. 1,$\underline{7}$16
11. $\underline{8}$09
12. $\underline{4}$53
13. $\underline{2}$,836
14. 2$\underline{0}$9,326
15. 9$\underline{7}$2

b For use with Lesson 4 (pages 68–71)

Find y.

16. $3 \times y = 33$
17. $4 \times 12 = y$
18. $9 \times y = 9$
19. $45 = 3 \times y$
20. $14 \times 13 = y$
21. $20 \times y = 100$
22. $21 \times y = 63$
23. $y = 30 \times 12$
24. $17 \times y = 34$
25. $14 \times 18 = y$
26. $29 \times y = 0$
27. $9 \times y = 0$
28. $26 \times y = 52$
29. $y \times 16 = 48$
30. $57 \times 3 = y$

c For use with Lesson 5 (pages 72–77)

Rewrite the number sentences, using the Associative or Commutative Property. Then find the product.

31. $20 \times 32 = n$
32. $16 \times 40 = n$
33. $100 \times 45 = n$
34. $200 \times 11 = n$
35. $50 \times 29 = n$
36. $19 \times 60 = n$
37. $100 \times 13 = n$
38. $25 \times 37 = n$
39. $71 \times 17 = n$
40. $93 \times 22 = n$
41. $70 \times 40 = n$
42. $12 \times 68 = n$
43. $98 \times 22 = n$
44. $103 \times 26 = n$
45. $59 \times 62 = n$

Module 5.2 Section C

(a) **For use with Lesson 6 (pages 80–85)**

Find the area and perimeter for rectangles with a length of 5 of the given unit and the following widths.

1. 12 ft	2. 11 in.	3. 16 ft
4. 17 in.	5. 42 ft	6. 35 cm
7. 100 m	8. 38 m	9. 13 ft
10. 27 ft	11. 91 ft	12. 60 in.

Find at least two possible dimensions if the area is the following.

13. 24 ft²	14. 30 ft²	15. 40 cm²
16. 25 in.²	17. 50 yd²	18. 60 m²

(b) **For use with Lesson 7 (pages 86–91)**

Rewrite the expressions, using the Distributive Property. Then find the products.

19. 34×22	20. 18×67	21. 31×55
22. 86×63	23. 29×51	24. 62×76
25. 105×43	26. 85×18	27. 53×78
28. 90×40	29. 250×75	30. 300×84

Use the Distributive Property to rewrite the expressions. Then find the products.

31. $(3 \times 20) + (20 \times 20)$	32. $(5 \times 16) + (80 \times 16)$	33. $(7 \times 10) + (8 \times 10)$
34. $(9 \times 10) + (12 \times 10)$	35. $(4 \times 40) + (5 \times 40)$	36. $(100 \times 2) + (100 \times 30)$

Module 5.2 Section D

a For use with Lesson 8 (pages 92–97)

Find the averages of the following lists.

1. 21, 23, 46, 45, 60

2. 1, 2, 3, 4, 5, 6, 7, 8, 9

3. 150, 200, 300, 350

4. 10, 100, 1,000, 10,000, 100,000

5. 13, 34, 47, 81, 128, 209, 335

6. 78, 86, 75, 90, 83, 97, 80, 91

7. 145, 200, 99, 107, 74

8. 0, 3, 3, 6, 11, 13, 24, 35, 50, 65

9. 0, 50, 100, 150, 200

10. 500, 625, 750, 900, 1,000

Find five possible numbers that would give the average shown.

11. 25

12. 50

13. 100

14. 200

b For use with Lesson 9 (pages 98–107)

Find the quotient and remainder.

15. $135 \div 7$

16. $151 \div 8$

17. $199 \div 9$

18. $178 \div 9$

19. $256 \div 5$

20. $256 \div 6$

21. $256 \div 7$

22. $1,000 \div 8$

23. $89 \div 8$

24. $101 \div 9$

25. $457 \div 3$

26. $296 \div 2$

Find the missing remainder or dividend.

27. $48 \div 5 = 9 \, \text{R}n$

28. $96 \div 6 = 16 \, \text{R}n$

29. $85 \div 3 = 28 \, \text{R}n$

30. $n \div 6 = 8 \, \text{R}4$

31. $37 \div 4 = 9 \, \text{R}n$

32. $n \div 6 = 9 \, \text{R}1$

33. $74 \div 5 = 14 \, \text{R}n$

34. $n \div 2 = 45 \, \text{R}1$

35. $68 \div 7 = 9 \, \text{R}n$

Module 5.3 Section A

a For use with Lesson 1 (pages 116–119)

Name the amount of change to be returned from the purchase.

1.
Amount Owed	Paid With
$6.45	$10 bill

3.
$17.02	$20 bill, 1 nickel

2.
Amount Owed	Paid With
$18.97	$20 bill

4.
$4.79	$5 bill, 4 pennies

Determine whether the correct amount of change was returned.
Describe any corrections that need to be made.

5.
Total Bill	Paid	Change
$5.97	$10	4 $1 bills, 3 pennies

7.
$1.49	$5	2 $1 bills, 2 quarters, 1 penny

6.
Total Bill	Paid	Change
$35.50	$50	1 $10 bill, 1 $5 bill, 2 quarters

8.
$18.65	$20	1 1$ bill, 1 quarter, 1 dime

b For use with Lesson 2 (pages 120–123)

Estimate the total amount of purchase by rounding to the nearest dollar.

9. $1.29, $1.95, $4.50, $.99, $3.26

10. $3.45, $1.87, $3.25, $2.19, $.65

Use front-end estimation to find the total amount of the purchase.

11. $1.52, $.98, $2.50, $1.79, $6.12

12. $1.15, $1.89, $5.55, $1.19, $.75

c For use with Lesson 3 (pages 124–127)

Divide by multiples of 10.

13. $10\overline{)60}$

14. $20\overline{)60}$

15. $30\overline{)60}$

16. $30\overline{)65}$

17. $50\overline{)350}$

18. $50\overline{)3,500}$

19. $50\overline{)360}$

20. $50\overline{)365}$

21. $30\overline{)270}$

22. $60\overline{)427}$

23. $50\overline{)408}$

24. $80\overline{)655}$

Module 5.3 Section B

a **For use with Lesson 4 (pages 128–131)**

Solve.

1. The container for your fruit punch holds 64 oz. You have to put 4 c water and 1 c mix in the container. Is the container large enough? How do you know?

2. A bottle of milk is marked $\frac{1}{2}$ gal. Another bottle is marked 2 qt. Do the containers hold the same amount? Explain how you know.

3. Draw a diagram that shows how cups, pints, and quarts are related.

4. A 1-lb loaf of bread is divided into 2 equal pieces. How many ounces does each piece weigh?

b **For use with Lesson 5 (pages 132–137)**

Estimate quotients that have two places. Use guess and check to find quotients with only one place.

5. $14\overline{)37}$
6. $48\overline{)567}$
7. $53\overline{)624}$
8. $33\overline{)125}$

9. $64\overline{)138}$
10. $57\overline{)430}$
11. $63\overline{)237}$
12. $624 \div 16$

Use the data. Find the price per sandwich. Use multiplication on your calculator, and guess and check to solve.

13. 1 oz chicken on Italian bread
14. 1 oz turkey on rye bread
15. 2 oz turkey on Italian bread
16. 1 oz chicken and 1 oz turkey on whole-wheat bread
17. 1 oz chicken on whole-wheat bread

> Whole-wheat bread: $1.92 for 24 slices
> Italian bread: $2.00 for 20 slices
> Rye bread: $2.40 for 16 slices
> Chicken: $5.60 per pound
> Turkey: $4.48 per pound

c **For use with Lesson 6 (pages 138–141)**

Decide which is the better buy.

18. Tomato sauce: 1 lb 8 oz for $3.36 or 18 oz for $2.70

19. Juice: frozen, which makes 64 oz for $3.20, or fresh, 1 gal for $5.12

Module 5.3 Section C

a For use with Lesson 7 (pages 144–147)

Solve for *n*.

1. $(624 - 32) \times 2 = n$
2. $37 \times 14 = n$
3. $260 \div 20 = n$
4. $(12 \times 8) + 15 = n$
5. $1,256 + 17 + 334 = n$
6. $(26 + 24) \div 10 = n$
7. $8 \times n = 728$
8. $100 \div n = 20$
9. $(24 \times 8) - 2 = n$

Match the equation to the situation.

10. Joe has \$2 more than Maria. Joe has \$18. How much money does Maria have?

   a. $n + \$2 = \$18$ b. $n = \$18 - \$2$ c. $n \times 2 = \$18$ d. $n = \$18 + \$2$

---

b For use with Lesson 8 (pages 148–154)

Estimate the first digit of the quotient. Name the place of the digit. Check your answer by multiplying.

11. $27 \overline{)62}$

12. $38 \overline{)902}$

13. $45 \overline{)1,680}$

14. $18 \overline{)4,756}$

Make a chart that shows how to share the money.

15. $\$816 \div 24$
16. $\$8,750 \div 35$
17. $\$1,872 \div 36$

---

c For use with Lesson 9 (pages 155–159)

Divide. Check your answer by multiplying.

18. $56 \overline{)75}$

19. $38 \overline{)97}$

20. $62 \overline{)254}$

21. $75 \overline{)1,000}$

22. $80 \overline{)2,006}$

23. $16 \overline{)6,407}$

24. $28 \overline{)8,740}$

25. $45 \overline{)5,128}$

Module 5.3 Section D

a For use with Lesson 10 (pages 160–163)

Use the graph to answer.

1. Which type of show is most popular?
2. How many people were surveyed?
3. How many fifth graders liked either comedy or music shows?
4. How many more fifth graders chose music shows than chose quiz shows?
5. Use the data below to make a graph.

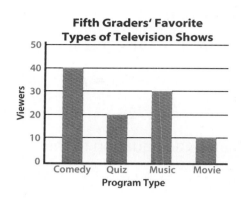

Fifth Graders' Favorite Types of Television Shows

Birthday Months of Mr. Chin's Class

Dec.	Jan.	Apr.	July	May	May	Jan.	Jan.	June	Sept.	Mar.	Mar.
June	Mar.	May	Aug.	Jan.	Apr.	Apr.	Oct.	Feb.	Sept.	Dec.	July
July	Apr.	Jan.	July	Dec.	Feb.	Sept.	Sept.	Mar.	Oct.	May	

b For use with Lesson 11 (pages 164–167)

Use the data in the chart to answer.

6. Round dollars to the nearest million.

7. On a pictograph each symbol stands for $2 million. If dollar amounts are rounded to the nearest million, how many symbols will each need?

8. Make a pictograph.

Dollars Spent in Advertising on WHMM	
Weekday **a.** 7 A.M.–9 A.M.	$970,000
b. 3 P.M.–5 P.M.	$3,664,000
c. 7 P.M.–9 P.M.	$12,520,000
Saturday **d.** 7 A.M.–9 A.M.	$5,944,000
e. 10 A.M.–noon	$6,278,000

c For use with Lesson 12 (pages 168–171)

Use the data to answer. Use a calculator.

9. Which show reaches the most people per dollar for advertising? How many people?

10. You have $1,000 for advertising. How can you reach the most people? Defend your choice.

Local Cable Television Data		
Show	Ad (30 seconds)	Viewers
Town News	$300	1,200
The Story Hour	$450	2,000
Talk! Talk! Talk!	$1,500	9,000
Local Sports	$500	2,200

Module 5.4 Section A

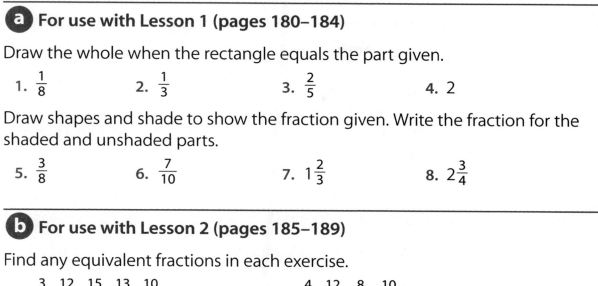

a For use with Lesson 1 (pages 180–184)

Draw the whole when the rectangle equals the part given.

1. $\frac{1}{8}$　　　2. $\frac{1}{3}$　　　3. $\frac{2}{5}$　　　4. 2

Draw shapes and shade to show the fraction given. Write the fraction for the shaded and unshaded parts.

5. $\frac{3}{8}$　　　6. $\frac{7}{10}$　　　7. $1\frac{2}{3}$　　　8. $2\frac{3}{4}$

---

b For use with Lesson 2 (pages 185–189)

Find any equivalent fractions in each exercise.

9. $\frac{3}{4}, \frac{12}{16}, \frac{15}{20}, \frac{13}{14}, \frac{10}{15}$　　　10. $\frac{4}{5}, \frac{12}{20}, \frac{8}{10}, \frac{10}{8}$

11. $\frac{2}{3}, \frac{4}{9}, \frac{10}{15}, \frac{12}{18}$　　　12. $\frac{1}{3}, \frac{5}{15}, \frac{6}{12}, \frac{7}{21}$

13. $\frac{2}{5}, \frac{4}{10}, \frac{6}{18}, \frac{8}{12}$　　　14. $\frac{9}{24}, \frac{1}{3}, \frac{1}{4}, \frac{3}{8}$

---

c For use with Lesson 3 (pages 190–193)

Write a fraction to describe the following:

15. the part of the week that is not a weekend

16. the part of 1 yd that is greater than 1 ft

17. of the days of the week, the ones that begin with T or S

18. of the last decade, the number of years you have lived

19. of the days in a week, the number of days when there is no school

20. of the months in a year, the months with one syllable

21. the part of the letters in this sentence that is vowels

22. of the number words for 1 through 10, those that have more than three letters

Module 5.4 Section B

a For use with Lesson 4 (pages 194–199)

Estimate. Then use a calculator to find the products.

1. $\frac{1}{2} \times \frac{1}{2}$ 2. $\frac{1}{2} \times \frac{1}{4}$ 3. $\frac{1}{4} \times \frac{1}{2}$

4. $\frac{1}{4} \times \frac{1}{4}$ 5. $\frac{1}{3} \times \frac{1}{2}$ 6. $\frac{1}{3} \times \frac{1}{3}$

7. $\frac{1}{3} \times \frac{1}{4}$ 8. $\frac{1}{2} \times \frac{2}{3}$ 9. $\frac{1}{3} \times \frac{3}{4}$

b For use with Lesson 5 (pages 200–203)

Find the products. Draw arrays for multiplication where the product is a fraction less than 1.

10. $\frac{1}{4} \times \frac{7}{8}$ 11. $\frac{4}{7} \times \frac{3}{5}$ 12. $\frac{1}{3} \times \frac{1}{4}$

13. $\frac{3}{4} \times \frac{1}{5}$ 14. $\frac{1}{5} \times 20$ 15. $\frac{3}{4} \times \frac{2}{3}$

16. $\frac{8}{9} \times 1$ 17. $\frac{1}{5} \times \frac{2}{3}$ 18. $\frac{3}{4} \times 100$

c For use with Lesson 6 (pages 204–207)

Write three equivalent fractions.

19. $\frac{1}{2}$ 20. $\frac{2}{3}$ 21. $\frac{3}{4}$

22. $\frac{3}{8}$ 23. $\frac{5}{6}$ 24. $\frac{3}{10}$

25. $\frac{4}{9}$ 26. $\frac{1}{5}$ 27. $\frac{3}{16}$

d For use with Lesson 7 (pages 208–209)

Change these fractions to simplest terms.

28. $\frac{6}{12}$ 29. $\frac{8}{12}$ 30. $\frac{6}{8}$ 31. $\frac{4}{6}$

32. $\frac{4}{12}$ 33. $\frac{4}{8}$ 34. $\frac{8}{16}$ 35. $\frac{5}{10}$

36. $\frac{12}{18}$ 37. $\frac{10}{15}$ 38. $\frac{8}{24}$ 39. $\frac{25}{30}$

Module 5.4 Section C

a **For use with Lesson 8 (pages 212–217)**

Compare the fractions. Write >, <, or =.

1. $\frac{1}{2}$ ● $\frac{7}{12}$

2. $\frac{2}{5}$ ● $\frac{1}{3}$

3. $\frac{7}{8}$ ● $\frac{13}{16}$

4. $\frac{4}{16}$ ● $\frac{16}{64}$

5. $\frac{4}{9}$ ● $\frac{5}{6}$

6. $\frac{9}{20}$ ● $\frac{3}{8}$

Write each pair as equivalent fractions with the least common denominator.

7. $\frac{2}{3}, \frac{3}{4}$

8. $\frac{1}{5}, \frac{1}{2}$

9. $\frac{5}{6}, \frac{4}{9}$

10. $\frac{7}{8}, \frac{1}{6}$

11. $\frac{3}{4}, \frac{7}{10}$

12. $\frac{9}{16}, \frac{1}{2}$

Write each percent as a fraction.

13. 27%

14. 33%

15. 1%

16. 83%

17. 75%

18. 40%

19. 55%

20. 90%

21. 99%

Write each fraction as a percent.

22. $\frac{37}{100}$

23. $\frac{47}{100}$

24. $\frac{50}{100}$

25. $\frac{80}{100}$

26. $\frac{7}{100}$

27. $\frac{86}{100}$

28. $\frac{75}{100}$

29. $\frac{21}{100}$

30. $\frac{25}{100}$

---

b **For use with Lesson 9 (pages 218–223)**

Write the fractions greater than one as mixed numbers.

31. $\frac{17}{6}$

32. $\frac{25}{7}$

33. $\frac{30}{4}$

34. $\frac{19}{5}$

35. $\frac{21}{2}$

36. $\frac{100}{8}$

Write as fractions greater than one.

37. $7\frac{2}{3}$

38. $3\frac{9}{10}$

39. $11\frac{1}{2}$

40. $20\frac{3}{4}$

41. $8\frac{7}{8}$

42. $1\frac{99}{100}$

43. $7\frac{1}{2}$

44. $5\frac{1}{5}$

45. $2\frac{7}{10}$

Module 5.4 Section D

a For use with Lesson 10 (pages 226–230)

Find the sum. Change any fraction greater than one into a mixed number. Write your answer in simplest terms.

1. $\frac{3}{4} + \frac{1}{3}$

2. $\frac{5}{8} + \frac{1}{4}$

3. $\frac{2}{3} + \frac{1}{6}$

4. $\frac{1}{4} + \frac{7}{8}$

5. $\frac{1}{5} + \frac{5}{6}$

6. $\frac{2}{9} + \frac{1}{3}$

7. $\frac{9}{16} + \frac{5}{8}$

8. $\frac{7}{8} + \frac{1}{2}$

9. $\frac{2}{3} + \frac{4}{5}$

Draw a rectangle with the given length and width in inches. Label the drawing.

	10.	11.	12.	13.	14.	15.	16.	17.
length	$2\frac{1}{2}$	4	$6\frac{1}{2}$	$2\frac{3}{16}$	$7\frac{5}{8}$	$3\frac{1}{8}$	5	$2\frac{1}{2}$
width	3	$\frac{1}{2}$	$4\frac{3}{4}$	$4\frac{1}{4}$	$2\frac{1}{4}$	$2\frac{7}{16}$	$5\frac{1}{16}$	$\frac{5}{8}$

b For use with Lesson 11 (pages 231–235)

Add and write the sums in lowest terms.

18. $\frac{2}{5} + \frac{3}{10}$

19. $4\frac{5}{12} + 6\frac{1}{3}$

20. $\frac{5}{16} + \frac{7}{8}$

21. $\frac{2}{3} + \frac{5}{8}$

22. $\frac{4}{9} + \frac{5}{6}$

23. $1\frac{7}{8} + 2\frac{7}{10}$

24. $\frac{4}{5} + 3\frac{1}{2}$

25. $9\frac{1}{4} + \frac{5}{6}$

26. $\frac{1}{100} + \frac{1}{10}$

Subtract.

27. $\frac{7}{12} - \frac{1}{2}$

28. $\frac{3}{4} - \frac{3}{10}$

29. $\frac{9}{16} - \frac{3}{8}$

30. $\frac{4}{5} - \frac{3}{4}$

31. $10 - 4\frac{2}{3}$

32. $8 - 7\frac{13}{16}$

33. $1\frac{1}{3} - \frac{5}{6}$

34. $4\frac{1}{6} - 1\frac{1}{4}$

35. $8\frac{2}{5} - 2\frac{3}{10}$

Module 5.5 Section A

a **For use with Lesson 1 (pages 244–248)**

Write each fraction as a decimal.

1. $\frac{23}{100}$ 2. $\frac{9}{100}$ 3. $\frac{71}{100}$ 4. $\frac{20}{100}$ 5. $\frac{89}{100}$

6. $\frac{30}{100}$ 7. $\frac{29}{100}$ 8. $\frac{6}{100}$ 9. $\frac{50}{100}$ 10. $\frac{100}{100}$

11. Arrange the answers in Exercises 1–5 from greatest to least.

12. Which answer of Exercises 1–5 is closest to 1?

13. Which answer in Exercises 6–10 is the largest number?

14. Which answer in Exercises 6–10 is the smallest number?

b **For use with Lesson 2 (pages 249–253)**

Add or subtract these decimals.

15. $0.24 + 0.24$ 16. $5.7 + 3.1$ 17. $0.94 - 0.85$

18. $3.25 - 1.2$ 19. $0.88 + 0.8$ 20. $2.27 - 1.3$

21. $4 + 4.13$ 22. $10 - 1.1$ 23. $23.8 + 0.25$

Round to the place of the indicated digit.

31. 4.27   32. 6.39   33. 9.66

34. 12.09   35. 0.367   36. 5.45

37. 20.94   38. 1.051   39. 17.6

40. 99.01   41. 3.2931

Module 5.5 Section B

ⓐ For use with Lesson 3 (pages 254–257)

For each group put the measurements in order from greatest to least.

1. 9 m, 19 cm, 190 km
2. 13 L, 345 mL, 2 kL
3. 48 g, 12 kg, 109 g
4. 2,345 mL, 3 L, 17 kL
5. 4 km, 580 m, 6,700 cm
6. 150 m, 12 km, 1,000 cm,
7. 20 L, 1,000 mL, 1 kL
8. 100 g, 1 kg, 1.5 kg
9. 105 m, 100 cm, 1 km

Tell whether each number is larger when rounded to the nearest hundredth or to the nearest tenth.

10. 0.874
11. 35.208
12. 7.945
13. 0.006
14. 10.152
15. 8.472

16. Rewrite 467 kilograms as grams.

17. Rewrite 23,000 mL as liters.

ⓑ For use with Lesson 4 (pages 258–261)

Which metric unit would you use to measure each of the following?

18. mass of a brick
19. capacity of a picnic jug
20. length of a parking lot
21. capacity of an eyedropper
22. mass of a penny
23. distance to the equator
24. length of a brick
25. distance around bicycle wheel
26. mass of an adult
27. mass of a calculator
28. length of a desk
29. capacity of a cooking pan

Round to the nearest tenth.

30. 5.67
31. 12.019
32. 71.48
33. 8.036
34. 4.53
35. 0.91
36. 2.52
37. 0.074
38. 13.55

Module 5.5 Section C

ⓐ For use with Lesson 5 (pages 266–271)

Find the products.

1. 8×0.9
2. 0.7×6
3. 0.04×3
4. 5×0.45
5. 6.8×12.2
6. 4.09×0.16
7. 0.01×82
8. 4×6.19
9. 34.34×0.34
10. 10×6.2
11. 5×2.3
12. 0.3×0.6

ⓑ For use with Lesson 6 (pages 272–275)

For the following questions, refer to pages 274 and 275.

13. What would have been Tan Liangde's score on the reverse somersault $2\frac{1}{2}$ pike in problem 1 if the difficulty factor were 2.5?

14. What would have been Tan Liangde's score on the reverse somersault $2\frac{1}{2}$ pike in problem 1 if the judge who gave him a 6.5 had given him a 6.0?

15. What would have been Louganis's score on the $2\frac{1}{2}$ reverse somersault pike with a 3.5 degree of difficulty if all the judges had given him a score of 8.2?

16. What would have been Tan Liangde's score on the reverse somersault $2\frac{1}{2}$ pike in problem 4 if all the judges had given him a score of 8.1?

17. What would have been Louganis's score for the "dive of death" had all the judges given him an 8.6?

18. Which diver will get a higher score: one who receives all 10's on an inward pike or one who receives all 7's on a "dive of death"?

Find the larger product for each pair.

19. 0.6×3 or 2×0.3
20. 0.8×0.3 or 0.8×1.5
21. 3.8×5 or 4.1×5
22. 0.31×3 or 3.1×3
23. 4.1×3.8 or 4.1×3.12
24. 0.07×100 or 0.6×50
25. 4.25×6.41 or 1.35×10.2
26. 0.3×2.8 or 1.2×15

Module 5.5 Section D

a For use with Lesson 7 (pages 276–280)

Find the average for each set of numbers.

1. 12.4, 15.6, 11, 14.2

2. 78, 89, 94, 66, 100

3. 1, 2, 3, 4, 5, 6, 7, 8, 9, 0

4. 3.6, 2.9, 4.0, 3.2

5. 0, 0, 3, 4.8, 0.7

6. 1, 10, 100, 1,000

7. 5, 5, 5, 5, 5,

8. 10, 11, 12, 13, 14

Estimate which of each two sets has the greater average.

9. $\{12, 5, 9, 2\}$ or $\{1, 8, 5, 12\}$

10. $\{0.4, 1.8, 3.6\}$ or $\{0.04, 0.18, 3.6, 3.9\}$

11. $\{19, 35.78, 21.1\}$ or $\{22.4, 46.9, 36.23, 50\}$

12. $\{3, 5, 7, 11\}$ or $\{2, 4, 6, 8, 10\}$

13. $\{6, 6, 7, 8, 8\}$ or $\{5, 6, 6, 6, 7\}$

14. $\{15, 12, 14, 13\}$ or $\{25, 5, 20, 6\}$

15. $\{0, 1, 2, 3, 4\}$ or $\{2, 1, 2, 3, 4\}$

b For use with Lesson 8 (pages 281–283)

Change these fractions to decimals. Round to the nearest hundredth.

16. $\frac{1}{4}$

17. $\frac{1}{8}$

18. $\frac{11}{25}$

19. $\frac{4}{15}$

20. $\frac{1}{11}$

21. $\frac{7}{32}$

22. $\frac{3}{4}$

23. $\frac{5}{6}$

Change each decimal to a fraction in lowest terms.

24. 0.50

25. 0.125

26. 0.33

27. 0.005

28. 0.95

29. 0.72

30. 0.375

31. 0.80

32. 0.166

33. 0.65

34. 0.30

35. 0.45

Module 5.6 Section A

ⓐ For use with Lesson 1 (pages 292–295)

Tell if you are traveling north, south, east, or west as you move from point *A* to point *B*.

1. *A* is 10° S, 40° W, and *B* is 8° S, 40° W.

2. *A* is 10° S, 40° W, and *B* is 10° S, 45° W.

3. *A* is 15° N, 40° W, and *B* is 10° N, 40° W.

4. *A* is 40° N, 110° W, and *B* is 45° N, 115° W.

ⓑ For use with Lesson 2 (pages 296–298)

Use the diagram to name the following.

5. perpendicular lines
6. line segment

7. parallel lines
8. a right angle

Draw an example of the following.

9. triangle *DEF*
10. a line parallel to *DF*
11. a line perpendicular to *DF*

12. an angle whose vertex is *R*
13. an angle whose vertex is *S*
14. a 180° angle

ⓒ For use with Lesson 3 (pages 299–303)

Locate the following points on a coordinate grid.
Draw an arrow from each point to (0, 0).

15. (3, 1)
16. (5, 2)
17. (4, 5)

18. (2, 0)
19. (1, 6)
20. (1, 3)

21. (0, 4)
22. (5, 5)
23. (6, 3)

24. (4, 7)
25. (5, 4)
26. (3, 2)

Write *left, right, up,* or *down* to indicate movement between the following points.

27. (0, 0) to (0, 8)
28. (5, 5) to (5, 1)
29. (9, 6) to (5, 6)
30. (0, 4) to (0, 2)

31. (1, 10) to (10, 10)
32. (7, 4) to (7, 7)
33. (2, 9) to (9, 9)
34. (6, 0) to (2, 0)

Module 5.6 Section B

Measure the following angles with your protractor.

1.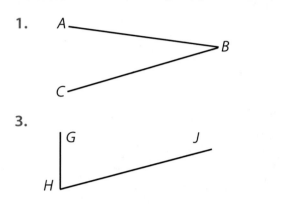

2.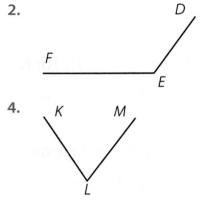

3.

4.

Draw the following angles.

5. 20°   6. 45°   7. 100°   8. 155°   9. 80°   10. 120°

ⓑ **For use with Lesson 5 (pages 316–323)**

Name each kind of triangle.

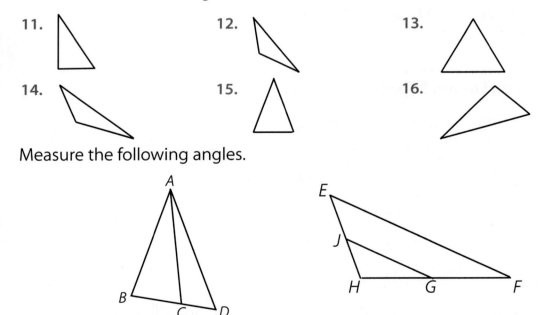

11.

12.

13.

14.

15.

16.

Measure the following angles.

17. *ABC* 18. *ACD* 19. *ADC*   20. *HJG*   21. *JEF*   22. *EFG*   23. *HGJ*   24. *GJE*

Module 5.6 Section C

a For use with Lesson 6 (pages 324–329)

Find the lengths of similar triangles, using the following ratios.

Ratio Sides	Ratio Sides	Ratio Sides
1. $\frac{2}{1}$ 3, 4, 5	2. $\frac{4}{1}$ 3, 8, 11	3. $\frac{3}{2}$ 4, 6, 8
4. $\frac{3}{1}$ 10, 13, 17	5. $\frac{1}{2}$ 8, 14, 18	6. $\frac{2}{3}$ 12, 18, 21
7. $\frac{1}{4}$ 12, 16, 24	8. $\frac{4}{5}$ 10, 25, 35	9. $\frac{1}{10}$ 100, 80, 40
10. $\frac{3}{8}$ 24, 40, 56	11. $\frac{9}{4}$ 8, 12, 16	12. $\frac{12}{1}$ 2, 7, 13

b For use with Lesson 7 (pages 330–335)

Use the drawing to answer the following questions.

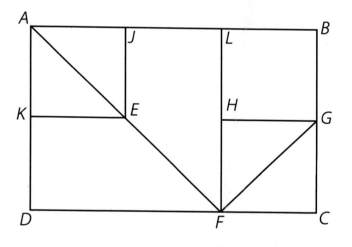

13. Name all the triangles you can find.
14. Name a pentagon.
15. Name all the quadrilaterals you can find.
16. Name two sets of parallel lines.
17. Name two sets of perpendicular lines.
18. Name a pair of congruent triangles.
19. Name two similar triangles.
20. Name a square.
21. Name an obtuse angle.
22. Name an acute angle.

Module 5.6 Section D

a For use with Lesson 8 (pages 336–341)

Use the data on the graph for Exercises 1–4.

1. range
2. mean
3. median
4. mode

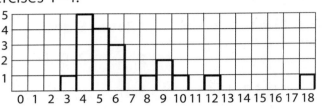

b For use with Lesson 9 (pages 342–343)

Age of U.S. Presidents at Inauguration	
4	9 8 6 9 7 2 3 6
5	7 7 7 8 7 4 1 0 2 6 4 0 5 4 1 6 5 1 4 1 5 6 2
6	1 1 8 4 5 0 2 1 9 4

Use the stem-and-leaf plot to answer the following.

5. Find the mode.   6. Find the range.   7. Find the median.
8. How many were inaugurated at age 61?
9. How many were older than 65?
10. How many were younger than 47?
11. At what ages between 50 and 59 were no presidents inaugurated?
12. At what ages between 60 and 69 were no presidents inaugurated?

c For use with Lesson 10 (pages 344–347)

Use the stem-and-leaf plot to answer
the following.

3					
2		4	3		
1	2	4	0	2	1
0	1	2	3	4	5

13. Find the mean.   14. Find the median.
15. Find the mode.   16. Find the range.
17. Find the biggest cluster.
18. How many values are greater than 24?
19. How many values are less than 12?
20. How many values are between 20 and 40?

Module 5.7 Section A

a **For use with Lesson 1 (pages 356–359)**

Estimate the circumference for circles with the following diameters.

1. 4 cm
2. 5 in.
3. 10 yd
4. 1 mi
5. 20 ft
6. 3 m

Estimate the diameter for a circle with the following circumference.

7. 3.1 m
8. 44 in.
9. 314 mi
10. 62 ft
11. 100 m
12. 13 yd
13. 9.4 yd
14. 75 ft
15. 28 cm

b **For use with Lesson 2 (pages 360–363)**

Use the spinner to answer Exercises 16–25.

16. Write the sample space.

17. Is the probability of spinning each number equally likely? Why or why not?

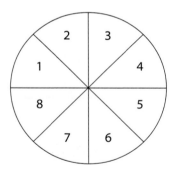

Find each probability.

18. 4
19. 0
20. 1
21. even number
22. odd number
23. number less than 4
24. 7 or 8
25. sum of two even numbers

Module 5.7 Section B

a For use with Lesson 3 (pages 364–369)

Use the spinner to answer Exercises 1–10.

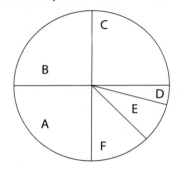

1. Write the sample space.

2. What outcome(s) is (are) most likely?

3. What outcome(s) is (are) least likely?

4. What outcomes have an equal probability?

5. About what percent of outcomes will be A?

6. About what percent of outcomes will be A, B, or C?

On 100 spins, about how many of the outcomes will be the following?

7. F

8. E

9. D

10. F, E, or D

---

b For use with Lesson 4 (pages 370–377)

A bag contains 2 white, 8 blue, 10 red, and 12 yellow marbles. Write the probability for randomly drawing each of the following.

11. white

12. blue

13. red

14. yellow

15. not red

16. white, red, or yellow

17. blue or white

18. green

19. white, blue, red, or yellow

20. not white or red

21. not red or yellow

22. not white, blue, red, or yellow

Module 5.7 Section C

a For use with Lesson 5 (pages 378–382)

Find the probability.

1. Even number on a 1–6 number cube

2. odd number on a 1–6 number cube

3. prime number on a 1–12 spinner

4. multiple of 3 on a 1–10 spinner

5. number greater than 4 on a 1–6 number cube

6. number less than 5 on a 1–10 spinner

7. 0 on a 1–6 number cube

8. 8 on a 0–8 spinner

9. prime number on a 1–6 number cube

10. number less than 6 on a 1–6 number cube

11. number greater than 2 on a 1–6 number cube

12. number greater than 6 on a 1–6 number cube

13. number less than 5 on a 1–4 spinner

14. composite number on a 1–8 spinner

15. factor of 8 on a 1–10 spinner

16. multiple of 4 on a 1–10 spinner

17. factor of 100 on a 1–100 spinner

18. multiple of 10 on a 1–100 spinner

b For use with Lesson 6 (pages 383–387)

Make a tree diagram to show all possible outcomes of a coin flip and a 1–4 spinner, then find each probability.

19. H, even

20. T, odd

21. H, 2

22. H, 2, 3, or 4

23. T, not 1

24. H, 4

Module 5.7 Section D

a For use with Lesson 7 (pages 388–391)

Tell whether chance or strategy is more important in each
of the following games.

1. bridge
2. spinning a spinner
3. throwing number cubes
4. dots
5. tic-tac-toe
6. darts
7. checkers
8. concentration

b For use with Lesson 8 (pages 392–395)

Rolling two number cubes labeled 1–6, find the probability
of the following outcomes.

9. 6 and 1
10. 1 and 6
11. two even numbers
12. odd sum
13. 6 and 5
14. sum of 3
15. sum of 7
16. sum of 9
17. sum of 6
18. What sum is most likely?

Use this spinner to determine the probability of these outcomes.

19. even number
20. odd number
21. zero
22. number greater than 3
23. outcome of 3
24. prime number
25. number less than 4
26. whole number

Module 5.8 Section A

a **For use with Lesson 1 (pages 404–410)**

Describe the objects from which the following nets were made.

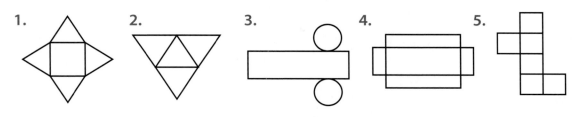

1. 2. 3. 4. 5.

Draw a net for each of the following shapes.

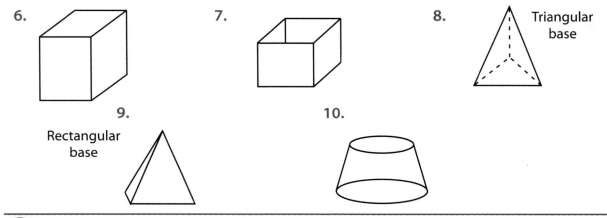

6. 7. 8. Triangular base

9. Rectangular base 10.

---

b **For use with Lesson 2 (pages 411–413)**

Find the number of cubes that would have 1, 2, 3, 4, 5, and 6 faces painted if each figure's entire surface were painted.

 11. 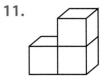 12.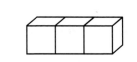

13. 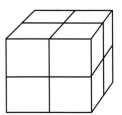 14.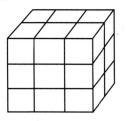

Module 5.8 Section B

a **For use with Lesson 3 (pages 414–419)**

How many cubes would it take to build each solid?

1.

2.

3.

4.

5.

6.

Give the dimensions of two different boxes with the given volume.

7. 200 cm³

8. 180 cm³

9. 360 cm³

10. 1,000 cm³

11. 1,000,000 cm³

12. 440 cm³

13. 8 cm³

14. 27 cm³

15. 81 cm³

Estimate the volume of the rectangular prism. Then find the volume.

16 length = 11 cm, width = 9 cm, height = 12 cm

17 length = 26 m, width = 33 m, height = 48 m

18 length = 1 mm, width = 1 cm, height = 1m

19 length = 98 cm, width = 203 cm, height = 495 cm

20 length = 10 cm, width = 20 cm, height = 12 cm

21 length = 15 cm, width = 15 cm, height = 15 cm

b **For use with Lesson 4 (pages 420–423)**

Find an area of the base and height for the volume of each prism.

22. volume = 1,800 cm³

23. volume = 2,800 cm³

24. volume = 900 m³

25. volume = 4,480 cm³

26. volume = 11,000 m³

27. volume = 1,000,000 cm³

Module 5.8 Section C

ⓐ For use with Lesson 5 (pages 428–430)

Find a scale that would be suitable for drawing each.
1. kitchen   2. pliers   3. school grounds   4. parking lot   5. model train

6. bicycle   7. airplane   8. desk chair   9. fountain pen   10. paper clip

---

ⓑ For use with Lesson 6 (pages 431–433)

Draw a triangle with angles of 30°, 60°, and 90°. Then make a similar triangle, using the following ratios.
11. 2 : 1   12. 3 : 2   13. 1 : 2   14. 2 : 3   15. 1 : 4

Draw an equilateral triangle. Then make a similar triangle, using the following ratios.
16. 4 : 1   17. 3 : 2   18. 2 : 1   19. 2 : 3   20. 1 : 2

Draw an acute triangle. Then make similar triangle, using the following ratios.
21. 1 : 2   22. 3 : 2   23. 1 : 2   24. 1 : 5   25. 5 : 1

ⓒ For use with Lesson 7 (pages 434–437)

Copy the function machines. Show five different input and output values.

26 $n + 10$

Input n	Output $n + 10$

27. $n \times n$

Input n	Output $n \times n$

28. $n \div 11$

Input n	Output $n \div 11$

29. $5 - n$

Input n	Output $5 - n$

30. $(n \times 3) - 17$

Input n	Output $(n \times 3) - 17$

31. $n \times n \times n$

Input n	Output $n \times n \times n$

32. $n - 100$

Input n	Output $n - 100$

33. $(4 - n) \times 4$

Input n	Output $(4 - n) \times 4$

Module 5.8 Section D

ⓐ For use with Lesson 8 (pages 438–441)

Find the ratio for each of the following scales.

1. 1 in. = 1 ft   2. 1 in. = 1 yd   3. 1 in. = 1 mi   4. 1 in. = 50 mi

5. 1 in. = 1,000 ft   6. 1 in. = 100 ft   7. 1 in. = 40 ft   8. 1 in. = $\frac{1}{4}$ mi

9. 1 in. = 100 yd   10. 1 in. = 5 mi   11. 1 in. = 10 yd   12. 1 in. = 100 yd

Use this data to write a ratio in simplest form:
Boys = 8, Girls = 10, Left handers = 3, Right handers = 15

13. ratio of boys to girls

14. ratio of girls to students

15. ratio of left handers to right handers

16. ratio of left handers to students

ⓑ For use with Lesson 9 (pages 442–443)

Use the table for the following exercises.

17. Predict the output for 20.

18. Predict the output for 100.

19. Describe the function rule.

20. Predict the input for an output of 11.

21. Predict the input for an output of 59.

22. Graph the data.

Input	Output
10	0
11	1
12	2
13	3
22	12

23. Complete this chart.

Input	3	4	5	6	7
Output	9	16	25		

24. Complete this chart.

Input	9	10	11	12	13
Output	20	22	24		

25. Describe the function rule.

26. Describe the function rule.

Glossary

A

acute angle (p. 309) An angle that measures less than 90°.

angle (p. 309) Two rays that share an endpoint. See *ray*.

area (p. 8) The number of square units in the surface of a shape.

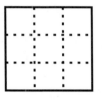

Area is 9 square units.

area of the base (*B*) (p. 417) Area of the bottom of a three-dimensional shape.

arrangement (p. 384) A special way of setting out or ordering a collection of things.

Associative Property of Addition (p. 227) Changing the grouping of the addends does not change the sum. Example:

$$(4 + 3) + 7 = 14$$
$$4 + (3 + 7) = 14$$
$$so \quad (4 + 3) + 7 = 4 + (3 + 7)$$

Associative Property of Multiplication (p. 72) Changing the grouping of the factors does not change the product. Example:

$$(2 \times 5) \times 4 = 40$$
$$2 \times (5 \times 4) = 40$$
$$so \quad (2 \times 5) \times 4 = 2 \times (5 \times 4)$$

average (p. 92) A number that stands for a set of numbers. See also *mean, median*.

axis (p. 162) A line that shows the horizontal or vertical scale of a graph.

B

bar graph (p. 164) A graph that uses bars to compare data.

billion (p. 54) The number equal to 1,000 × 1,000 × 1,000. In standard form, a billion is written as 1,000,000,000.

C

capacity (p.128) The amount a container can hold.

centigram (cg) (p. 254) A metric unit for measuring mass. 100 cg = 1 gram

centiliter (cL) (p. 254) A metric unit for measuring capacity. 100 cL = 1 liter

centimeter (cm) (p. 254) A metric unit for measuring length. 100 cm = 1 meter

circumference (p. 357) The distance around a circle.

combination (p. 385) An arrangement of things in which the order does not matter.

Glossary

common denominator (p. 214) A common multiple of the denominators of two or more given fractions. A common denominator of $\frac{2}{3}$ and $\frac{1}{4}$ is 12.

common factor (p. 42) A number that is a factor of two or more given numbers. The common factors of 8 and 12 are 1, 2, and 4.

common multiple (p. 36) A number that is a multiple of two or more numbers. 12 is a common multiple of 2, 3, 4, and 6.

Commutative Property of Addition (p. 227) Changing the order of the addends does not change the sum. Example:

$$7 + 4 = 11$$
$$4 + 7 = 11$$
$$\text{so} \quad 7 + 4 = 4 + 7$$

Commutative Property of Multiplication (p. 72) Changing the order of the factors does not change the product. Example:

$$5 \times 8 = 40$$
$$8 \times 5 = 40$$
$$\text{so} \quad 5 \times 8 = 8 \times 5$$

compatible numbers (p. 135) Numbers that divide easily for use in estimating. Sometimes called friendly numbers.

composite number (p. 41) Any whole number greater than 1 that is not a prime. 10 is a composite number.

cone (p. 407) A solid with one circular face and one vertex.

congruent (p. 6) Having the same size and shape.

coordinate grid (p. 299) A grid in which the points are named by ordered pairs called coordinates. See *ordered pair* for illustration.

cube (p. 407) A solid in which all six faces are congruent squares.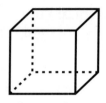

cubic unit (p. 414) A unit used to measure the volume of a solid. A cubic centimeter is the volume of a cube with every edge measuring 1 cm.

cup (c) (p. 131) A unit of capacity in the U. S. Customary System. 2 c = 1 pint

cylinder (p. 407) A solid with circular bases and no corners.

D

data (p. 336) Numbers that give information.

decigram (dg) (p. 254) A metric unit for measuring mass. 10 dg = 1 gram

deciliter (dL) (p. 254) A metric unit for measuring capacity. 10 dL = 1 liter

decimal (p. 244) A number that uses the place-value system and a decimal point. Another way to write fractions with denominators of 10, 100, 1,000, and so on. Examples: 0.2 and 1.75

decimal fraction See *decimal*.

decimal point (p. 247) The point that separates the whole number from the fractional part of a number.

decimeter (dm) (p. 254) A metric unit for measuring length. 10 dm = 1 meter

degree (°) (p. 309) A unit for measuring angles.

denominator (p. 180) The bottom number of a fraction. It shows the total number of equal parts. The denominator in the fraction $\frac{2}{3}$ is 3.

diagonal (p. 309) A line segment that joins two vertexes, yet is not a side.

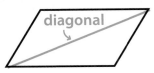

diameter (p. 357) A line segment through the center of a circle that has its two endpoints on the circle.

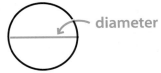

Distributive Property (p. 86) The product of a factor and a sum is equal to the sum of the products. Example:
$$5 \times (3 + 2) = (5 \times 3) + (5 \times 2)$$

dividend (p. 100) The number being divided in division. In the equation 36 ÷ 4 = 9, the dividend is 36.

divisible (p. 39) Capable of being divided without a remainder. Example: 24 is divisible by 3 because 24 ÷ 3 = 8.

divisor (p. 100) The number that divides the dividend in division. In the equation 30 ÷ 5 = 6, the divisor is 5.

double-bar graph (p. 164) A graph that uses two bars for each category to compare data.

E

edge (p. 405) The line segment formed when two faces of a solid meet.

equation (p. 32) A number sentence stating that two quantities are equal. Example: 9 × 6 = 54.

equilateral triangle (p. 318) A triangle with three sides of equal length.

equivalent fractions (p. 185) Fractions that name the same number. $\frac{1}{3}$ and $\frac{2}{6}$ are equivalent fractions.

estimate (p. 10) An answer that is not exact.

even number (p. 15) A number that is a multiple of 2. Examples: 2, 8, 22, 46

event (p. 354) A set of one or more outcomes.

experimental probability (p. 365) The probability that is found by doing an experiment.

expression (p. 19) Numbers and/or variables connected by operation signs. Examples: $n \times 5$, $4 + 37$, $k \div 5$

F

face (p. 404) A flat surface of a solid.

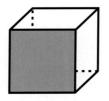

factor (p. 38) A number being multiplied to obtain a product. In the equation $4 \times 6 = 24$, the factors are 4 and 6.

flip (p. 6) Reflecting a figure about a line.

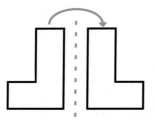

flow chart (p. 431) A chart that maps all the steps in a job or process.

fluid ounce (fl oz) (p. 129) A unit for measuring capacity in the U.S. Customary System. 8 fl oz = 1 cup

fraction (p. 178) A number that shows part of a whole unit. $\frac{1}{2}$, $\frac{4}{5}$, and $\frac{5}{7}$ are fractions.

front-end estimation (p. 122) An estimation strategy in which you use front-end digits first and then adjust if necessary.

G

gallon (gal) (p. 129) A unit for measuring capacity in the U.S. Customary System. 1 gal = 4 quarts

gram (g) (p. 254) A metric unit for measuring mass. 1,000 g = 1 kilogram

grid (p. 27) Parallel and perpendicular line segments that form a pattern of squares or rectangles.

gross (p. 145) A group of 12 dozen, or 144, items.

H

hexagon (p. 331) A polygon with 6 sides and 6 angles.

hundredth (p. 244) One of 100 equal parts. In the decimal 0.86, the number 6 is in the hundredths' place.

I

inch (in.) (p. 219) A unit of length in the U.S. Customary System. 12 in. = 1 foot

isosceles triangle (p. 318) A triangle with two sides having equal length.

K

kilogram (kg) (p. 254) A metric unit for measuring mass. 1 kg = 1,000 grams

kiloliter (kL) (p. 254) A metric unit for measuring capacity. 1 kL = 1,000 liters

kilometer (km) (p. 254) A metric unit for measuring length. 1 km = 1,000 meters

L

least common multiple (LCM) (p. 37) The least of the common multiples of two or more numbers. The LCM of 4 and 6 is 12.

line (p. 297) A set of points that extends on and on in both directions.

line graph (p. 65) A graph with a line that shows changes over time.

line of symmetry (p. 10) A line that separates a figure into two matching parts.

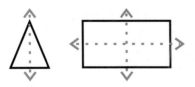

line plot (p. 338) A plot that uses *x*'s to order data along a line.

line segment (p. 297) A part of a line with two endpoints.

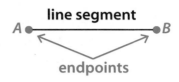

liter (L) (p. 254) A metric unit for measuring capacity. 1 L = 1,000 milliliters

lowest terms See *simplest terms*.

M

mass (p. 258) In an object, the actual amount of matter not subject to the force of gravity.

mean (p. 339) The quotient found by dividing the sum of a group of numbers by the number of addends.

median (p. 339) The middle number in a set of data after the data are arranged in order from least to greatest. If you have five numbers in order, the third is the median.

meter (m) (p. 245) A metric unit for measuring length. 1 m = 100 centimeters

mile (mi) (p. 12) A unit of length in the U.S. Customary System. 1 mi = 5,280 feet

milligram (mg) (p. 254) A metric unit for measuring mass. 1,000 mg = 1 gram

milliliter (mL) (p. 254) A metric unit for measuring capacity. 1,000 mL = 1 liter

Glossary

millimeter (mm) (p. 254) A metric unit for measuring length. 1,000 mm = 1 meter

million (p. 52) A number equal to 1,000 × 1,000. In standard form a million is written as 1,000,000.

mixed number (p. 220) A number that consists of a whole number and a fraction. $2\frac{1}{2}$ is a mixed number.

mode (p. 339) The number that appears most often in a set of data.

multiple (p. 35) The product of a given number and any whole number. A multiple of 3 is 15.

net (p. 408) A two-dimensional pattern that folds into a three-dimensional object. This net forms a pyramid.

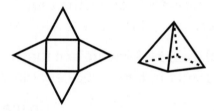

net weight (p. 140) The weight of a product without packaging.

numerator (p. 180) The top number of a fraction. It shows the number of parts chosen. The numerator in the fraction $\frac{2}{3}$ is 2.

obtuse angle (p. 309) An angle that measures more than 90°.

> 90°

octagon (p. 377) A polygon with eight sides.

odd number (p. 15) A number that is not a multiple of 2. Examples: 3, 7, 19, 21

ordered pair (p. 299) A pair of numbers that shows the location of a point on a grid. The ordered pair for the point on the coordinate grid below is (4, 2).

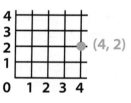

ounce (oz) (p. 129) A unit for measuring weight in the U.S. Customary System. 16 oz = 1 pound

outcome (p. 362) A possible result. Each number or color on a spinner is a possible outcome.

P

parallel lines (p. 297) Lines that are the same distance apart at all points.

parallelogram (p. 330) A quadrilateral with opposite sides parallel.

pentagon (p. 329) A polygon with five sides.

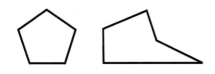

pentomino (p. 6) A polyomino made of five squares.

percent (p. 216) Hundredths written with a % sign. Example: $0.33 = \frac{33}{100} = 33\%$

perimeter (p. 8) The distance around any figure.

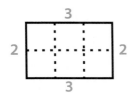

The perimeter is 10 units.

period (p. 54) A group of three digits within a whole number, named by starting at the right. The first three periods in a number are ones, thousands, and millions.

Millions	Thousands	Ones
987,	654,	321

perpendicular lines (p. 297) Two lines that intersect to form right angles.

pi (π) (p. 358) A number that is the ratio of the circumference to the diameter of any circle. Circumference = π × diameter. π ≈ 3.14

pictograph (p. 166) A graph that uses pictures to show data.

pint (pt) (p. 129) A unit of capacity in the U.S. Customary System. 1 pt = 2 cups

point (p. 290) An exact location. Points are usually labeled with capital letters.

polygon (p. 330) A closed figure made from line segments.

polyomino (p. 4) A pattern of squares in which adjoining squares share at least one side.

pound (lb) (p. 129) A U.S. Customary unit of weight. 1 lb = 16 ounces

prime number (p. 41) A number with only two factors—itself and 1. An example of a prime number is 7.

prism (p. 406) A solid with a top face that is congruent to its base, or bottom face. The top and bottom can be any polygon. The other faces are rectangles.

probability (p. 354) The chance that something will happen, usually expressed as a ratio between 0 and 1.

product (p. 38) The answer in multiplication. In the equation 8 × 6 = 48, the product is 48.

protractor (p. 310) A tool for measuring angles.

pyramid (p. 410) A solid with a polygon for a base and triangles for faces.

Q

quadrilateral (p. 330) A polygon with four sides.

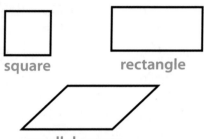

square   rectangle

parallelogram

quart (qt) (p. 129) A unit of capacity in the U.S. Customary System. 1 qt = 2 pints

quotient (p. 100) The answer in division. In the equation 56 ÷ 7 = 8, the quotient is 8.

R

radius (p. 356) A line segment from the center to a point on the circle.

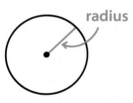

radius

range (p. 338) The difference between the greatest and the least numbers of given data.

ratio (p. 325) A pair of numbers used in a comparison or rate situation. Example: 2 bicycles to 3 cars = $\frac{2}{3}$ or 2:3 or "two to three."

ray (p. 297) A part of a line with one endpoint. A ray goes on and on in one direction.

ray *RS*

rectangle (p. 330) A parallelogram with all angles right angles.

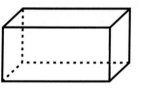

rectangular prism (p. 406) A prism in which all faces are rectangles.

rectangular pyramid (p. 406) A pyramid with a rectangular base.

remainder (p. 103) The number left over when division is complete.

repeating decimal A decimal in which a sequence of digits repeats endlessly. Examples: 33.33 . . . , 0.257257257 . . .

rhombus (p. 330) A parallelogram with all sides equal.

right angle (p. 309) An angle that measures 90°.

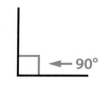

← 90°

rounding (p. 310) Replacing a number by the nearest ten, hundred, thousand, and so on, to make it easier to use. 67 rounded to the nearest ten is 70.

S

sample space (p. 362) A list of all the possible outcomes of an experiment.

scale (p. 305) The ratio of size in a drawing to actual size.

scale drawing (p. 305) A drawing made by using a scale.

scalene triangle (p. 318) A triangle with no two sides having the same length.

sequence (p. 17) A set of items whose order is determined by a rule or pattern.

sides (p. 318) The segments that make up a polygon.

similar triangles (p. 317) Triangles that have congruent angles and are the same shape.

simplest form (p. 208) See *simplest terms*.

simplest terms (p. 208) The form in which both terms of a fraction have no common factor greater than one. In simplest terms $\frac{3}{6}$ is $\frac{1}{2}$.

simplify (p. 208) To write a shorter or easier form of a fraction or expression.

space figure (p. 404) See *three-dimensional object*.

sphere (p. 407) A solid that is made up of all the points that are the same distance from one point called its center.

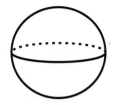

square (p. 330) A rectangle with all sides congruent.

standard form (p. 55) The simplest way to show a number using digits. The standard form of 3 tens and 6 ones is 36.

stem-and-leaf plot (p. 342) A way to show data. Usually, the tens' digits are "stems" and the ones' digits are "leaves." The plot below shows this data: 20, 29, 31, 42, 45, 48.

stem-and-leaf plot	
2	0, 9
3	1
4	2, 5, 8

straight angle (p. 309) An angle that measures 180°.

survey (p. 160) Information gathered by asking questions and recording answers.

symmetry (p. 9) What a flat shape has when a line, called a *line of symmetry*, can separate the shape into two matching parts.

T

terms of a fraction (p. 180) The numerator or denominator.

thousandth (p. 248) One of 1,000 equal parts. In the decimal 0.568, the number 8 is in the thousandths' place.

three-dimensional object (p. 404) An object that has the three dimensions: length, width, and height.

ton (t) (p. 129) A unit of weight in the U.S. Customary System. 1 t = 2,000 pounds

trapezoid (p. 330) A quadrilateral with exactly one pair of parallel sides.

tree diagram (p. 385) A picture used to count the way things can be combined.

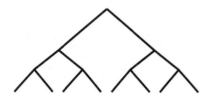

trial (p. 366) Each try in a probability experiment, such as spinning a spinner.

triangular pyramid (p. 407) A pyramid that has a triangle as its base.

U

unit price (p. 138) The cost of one unit. Example: If a 20-pound bag of dog food costs $10, the unit price is $10 ÷ 20, or 50¢ per pound.

V

variable (p. 19) A letter or symbol that holds a place for a number. n is the variable in this equation: $4 + n = 7$

vertex (p. 297) The common endpoint of two rays or two segments. The point where three or more edges of a solid meet.

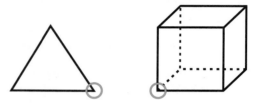

volume (p. 414) The amount of space inside a solid shape.

W

word form (p. 55) The name of a number spelled out in words. The word form for 5,823 is *five thousand, eight hundred twenty-three*.

Z

Zero Property of Multiplication (p. 38) The product of zero and any other number is zero. Example:
$$5 \times 0 = 0$$

Index

Index

Index

Dividend, 100

Divisibility, 39

Division
  calculator activities using, 56–57, 123
  checking, using multiplication, 97, 124–125, 133–134, 149, 280
  compatible numbers, 152, 463
  decimals and, 279–280
  dividend, 100
  divisor, 100
  equations, 145, 146–147
  estimating with, 78–79, 100–101, 102–103, 116, 125, 135, 148–149, 152–154, 459, 463
  explaining, 100–101, 148, 153, 155, 159, 279
  finding factors, 39, 40, 41
  games using, 105, 134–135
  interpreting remainders, 158–159
  measurement and, 128–129, 130, 131, 132–133
  mental math with, 125–128, 133, 135, 149, 152–154, 460, 461, 462, 463
  modeling, 93, 102–103, 150–151
  money and, 126–128, 134, 150–151
  by multiples of ten, 78–79, 124–125
  one-digit divisors, 100–101, 102–103, 104–105, 459
  patterns in, 124–125, 148–149
  problem solving and, 90–91, 92, 93, 94, 95, 96, 98, 99, 100–101, 102–103, 104–105, 110–112, 126–127, 132–133, 134, 135, 136–137, 138–139, 140–141, 142–143, 145, 146–147, 148–149, 150–151, 152–154, 155, 156–157, 158–159, 160, 161, 162–163, 164–167, 168–169, 170–171, 174–176, 208–209, 210–211
  quotient, 100
  recording, 156–157
  remainders and, 158–159
  by tens, 124–125
  two-digit divisors, 137, 148, 150–151, 152–154, 155, 156–157, 158–159, 459

  two- and three-digit quotients, 125, 148–156
  unit pricing and, 136–137, 139–139
  writing about, 97, 149, 153

Distributive Property of Multiplication, 86–87, 270, 461

Divisor, 100

Double bar graphs, 164–165

Drawing to Learn, 19, 33, 73, 85, 100, 150, 185, 201, 251, 266, 283, 303, 311, 414, 422

E

Edge, 405

Equation,
  defined, 32
  writing, 18–19, 20–21, 22–23, 28–29, 32, 33, 146–147, 273, 434–435

Equilateral triangle, 318

Equivalent fractions, 182, 185–189, 206–207, 214–215, 231–232, 426

Estimation
  of angle measures, 314
  of area, 68–69, 70–71, 73, 84, 86–87, 89
  compatible numbers and, 152, 463
  from data, 60–61, 94, 252–253, 281, 376–377
  of differences, 235
  division and, 78–79, 100–101, 102–103, 135, 152–154, 463
  front-end, 122, 463
  large numbers and, 50–51, 52–53, 54–55, 56–57, 58–59, 60–61, 65, 74–75, 76–77
  of latitude and longitude, 290–291
  of metric measurements, 256–257, 258, 259, 260, 261
  multiplication and, 74–75, 76–77, 195, 266–267, 268, 269, 463
  of perimeter, 10, 68–69, 180
  problem solving and, 63, 64, 65, 66–67, 415
  of proportion in shapes, 180–181, 182–183, 184
  reasonable, 67, 68–69, 74
  rounding divisors, 153

  rounding to tens or hundreds, 122, 462
  using smaller numbers, 170, 450
  of volume
    of million objects, 50–51, 78–79
    of space figures, 414, 415, 416, 417–419, 420, 421, 422, 423
  when to use, 63, 64, 462

Event, 364

Experimental probability, 356

Exponent, 82–83

Expression
  defined, 19
  writing, 20–21, 23, 28–29, 32, 33, 434

F

Face, 404

Factor
  defined, 38
  finding, 39, 40, 41

Flips, slides, and turns, 6–7, 47, 302, 303, 350–352

Flowchart, 431, 432–433, 440

Fluid ounce, 129, 133, 472

Foot, 218, 472

Formulas
  area of rectangle, 80–81, 416–417
  circumference of circle, 359
  perimeter of rectangle, 80

Fractions
  addition of, 226–227, 228–229, 230, 457
  arrays modeling multiplication of, 198–199, 200–201, 202–203, 206–207
  calculator activities using, 195, 208–209, 282–283, 466
  comparing and ordering, 214–215, 223, 231
  decimals and, 246–248, 282
  denominator, 180
  division and, 282
  equivalent, 185, 186–187, 188, 189, 206–207, 214–215, 231–232, 426, 458
  estimating, 180–181, 182–183, 195, 196–197
  least common denominator, 214–215
  least common multiple, 37, 214–215

Index

Index

Multiplication (cont.)
  predicting outcomes, 68, 266–267, 268, 269
  problem solving and, 34–35, 36–37, 38, 39, 40, 41, 42–43, 68–69, 70–71, 72, 73, 74–75, 80–81, 82–83, 84, 85, 86–87, 88, 89, 194–195, 196–197, 198–199, 200–201, 202–203, 204–205, 206–207, 266–267, 268, 269, 270, 271, 272–273, 274–275, 276–277, 278–279, 280, 281, 282, 283, 286–288
  product, defined, 38
  properties of, 71, 72, 86–87, 88, 90–91, 97, 200, 206, 270
  table, 34–35, 36–37, 38, 39
  two-digit factors, 74–75, 87–88, 89, 458
  whole numbers
    basic facts, 34–35, 36–37, 38, 39, 40, 41, 42–43
    patterns in , 34–35, 36–37, 56–57, 74–75

N

Net
  defined, 408
  drawing, 423, 427
  making, 408–410
Number line, 277
Numbers
  comparing and ordering, 58–59, 60–61, 65, 66–67
  modeling. *See* Modeling.
  rounding. *See* Rounding.
  standard form, 55
  word form, 55
Number sense. *See also* Data; Estimation; Logical reasoning, reasonable answers; Proportional reasoning.
  large numbers, 50–51, 52–53, 54–55, 56–57, 58–59, 60–61, 65, 74–75, 76–77, 78–79, 146–147, 247–248, 249–251
  number relationships, 153
  operation sense, 140–141, 145–147, 417
  place value and, 50–51, 52–53,

54–55, 56–57, 102–103, 247–248, 249–251, 270–271
  rounding for estimation, 63, 64, 65, 153, 462
  time lines and, 376–377
  units of measure and, 130
Numerator, 180

O

Obtuse angle, 309
Ongoing Investigation, xiv–xvi, 112, 240, 352, 448
Open-ended problems. *See* Logical reasoning, open-ended problems.
Ordered pair, 299, 300, 301, 302, 303
Ordering. *See also* Comparing.
  data, 58–59
  decimals, 246
  fractions, 214–215
  flowcharts and, 431, 432–433
Organized list, 85, 136, 384, 385–386, 452
Ounce, 129, 472
Outcome, 362–363

P

Parallel lines, defined, 297
Parallelogram, 183, 331
Patterns
  charts and, 52–53, 54–55, 124–125
  creating
    growth patterns, 14–15, 16
    L-numbers, 14
    repeating patterns, 24–25, 26
    square numbers, 15
  describing, 2–3, 14–15, 16, 17, 18, 19, 20–21, 22–23, 26, 41, 56–57, 103, 154, 331
  division and, 28–29, 56–57, 123, 148–149
  finding, 4, 18–19, 34–35, 36–37, 56–57, 123, 148, 209, 270
  growth, 14–15, 16
  on hundreds' board, 24–25, 26, 27, 28–29, 31, 32, 33
  in large numbers, 56
  multiples of ten and, 52–53,

56–57, 124–125
  multiplication tables and, 34–35, 36–37
  poetry and, 30
  predicting, 14–15, 16, 17, 18–19, 21, 24–25, 26, 27, 28–29, 195, 270–271
  prime numbers and, 40–41
  problem solving and, 4–5, 6–7, 8, 9, 10, 11–13, 14–15, 16, 17, 18–19, 20–21, 22–23, 24–25, 26, 27, 28–29, 30, 31–32, 33, 34–35, 36–37, 38, 39, 40, 41, 42–43, 46–48, 434–435
  writing expressions based on, 19, 20–21, 22–23, 28–29, 31, 32, 33, 39, 72
Pentagon, 331
Pentagram, 311, 352
Pentominoes, 6–7
Percent, 216–217, 371
Perimeter, 8, 80–81, 84
Period, 54
Perpendicular lines, 297
Pi, 358–359
Pictographs, 19, 60–61, 166
Pint, 129, 472
Place value. *See also* Decimals.
  in addition, 456, 457
  billions and, 54–55
  charts, 52–53, 54–55, 247
  comparing, 52–53, 247
  decimals and, 247, 248, 270, 271, 457, 459
  in division, 102–103, 134
  game using, 249–251
  hundreds and, 52–53, 54–55, 56, 102–103, 156–157, 456, 458
  hundred thousands and, 54–55
  large numbers and, 50–51, 52–53, 56–57, 65, 74–75, 78–79
  millions and, 50–51, 52–53, 56–57, 65, 74–75, 78–79
  modeling using base ten blocks, 52–53, 102–103
  ones and, 102–103, 459
  period, 54
  problem solving and, 52–53, 54–55, 56–57, 58–59, 60–61, 102–103, 246, 247, 248, 253, 270–271

Index

Acknowledgments

Text *(continued from page iv)*

Extensive efforts to locate the rights holder were unsuccessful. If the rights holder sees this notice, he or she should contact the School Division Rights and Permissions Department, Houghton Mifflin Company, 222 Berkeley Street, Boston, Massachusetts 02116. **62** From *Pride of Puerto Rico: The Life of Roberto Clemente,* by Paul Robert Walker. Orlando, Florida: Harcourt Brace Jovanovich Publishers, 1988. **144–45** From *The Toothpaste Millionaire,* written by Jean Merrill, illustrated by Jan Palmer. Copyright © 1972 by Houghton Mifflin Company. Reprinted by permission of Houghton Mifflin Company. **204** From "Down the Rabbit-Hole" in *Alice in Wonderland,* by Lewis Carroll. Originally published in 1865 by Macmillan, London, as *Alice's Adventures in Wonderland,* written by Lewis Carroll, illustrated by Sir John Tenniel. **242** From "To James," in *Notes Found Near a Suicide,* by Dr. Frank S. Horne, poet and housing administration official under Presidents Roosevelt and Truman. Uncle of Lena Horne and great uncle of Gail Lumet Buckley, author of *The Hornes: An American Family.* Originally published in *Crisis,* 1925, under the pseudonym Xavier I. Reprinted by permission of Gail Lumet Buckley. **324** From *The War of the Wall,* by Toni Cade Bambara. Reprinted by permission of the author. **386** From *Some Friend,* by Carol Carrick. New York: Clarion Books, Ticknor & Fields, a Houghton Mifflin Company, 1979. **402** From "The Wise Old Woman," in *The Sea of Gold and Other Tales from Japan,* by Yoshiko Uchida. New York: Charles Scribners, 1965.

Illustrations

54 Phil Scheuer. **67** Phil Scheuer (t). **78–79** Catherine Twomey. **264–65** Mike Kasun. **274–75** Dale Glasgow. **324–25** Ruben Ramos. **424–25** Andrea Tachiera. **432** Chris Reed.

Photography

Front cover Allan Landau. **Back cover** Sharon Hoogstraten. **i** Allan Landau. **ii–iii** Allan Landau. **vi** University Press of Florida (l); Aric Attas (tr); Sharon Hoogstraten (br). **vii** Sharon Hoogstraten. **viii** Sharon Hoogstraten. **ix** Sharon Hoogstraten (tl, bl); © David Cannon, Allsport (r). **x** Sharon Hoogstraten. **xi** Sharon Hoogstraten (tl, tr); Allan Landau (b). **xii–xiii** Allan Landau. **xiv** Allan Landau. **xv** Sharon Hoogstraten. **xvi** Allan Landau. **1** Courtesy University Press of Florida. **2** Sharon Hoogstraten; Allan Landau (l). **3** Allan Landau (l). **4** Courtesy University Press of Florida (b). **4–5** Sharon Hoogstraten (t). **6–7** Aric Attas. **8** Allan Landau. **9** Courtesy of Gordon Menzie Studio (b). **10** Tony Stone Worldwide (t); Allan Landau (b). **11** Independence National Historical Park Collection (t). **12** Courtesy of the Geography & Map Division, Library of Congress (tl). **14–15** Aric Attas. **16** Aric Attas. **17** Sharon Hoogstraten. **18** Allan Landau (t); Aric Attas (b). **19** Sharon Hoogstraten; Aric Attas (b). **20** Allan Landau. **22–23** Collection of Ivory Freidus, photo by Togashi. **24** Aric Attas. **25** Giorgio Ventola. **26** Sharon Hoogstraten. **27** Giorgio Ventola. **28** Giorgio Ventola; Aric Attas (t, b). **32** Sharon Hoogstraten. **33** Aric Attas. **34** Sharon Hoogstraten. **35** Sharon Hoogstraten (t); Giorgio Ventola (b). **36** Sharon Hoogstraten. **37** Sharon Hoogstraten. **40–41** Sharon Hoogstraten. **43** The Museum of Modern Art, New York. **45** Sharon Hoogstraten (b). **46–47** Sharon Hoogstraten. **48** Allan Landau. **49** Allan Landau (b). **50–51** Sharon Hoogstraten. **53** Allan Landau. **55** Ed Nagel. **56–57** Sharon Hoogstraten. **58** Sharon Hoogstraten. **59** Allan Landau. **62–63** Sharon Hoogstraten. **64** Allan Landau. **67** Sharon Hoogstraten. **68–69** Sharon Hoogstraten. **72–73** Allan Landau. **74** © Tom Tracy, Tony Stone Worldwide (c). **74–75** Sharon Hoogstraten. **76–77** Sharon Hoogstraten. **77** Allan Landau (t). **78** Allan Landau (c). **80–81** Sharon Hoogstraten. **83** Allan Landau. **84–85** Sharon Hoogstraten. **87** Sharon Hoogstraten. **88–89** Sharon Hoogstraten. **90** Allan Landau. **92** Sharon Hoogstraten. **93** Sharon Hoogstraten. **94** Sharon Hoogstraten. **95** Allan Landau. **96** Sharon Hoogstraten. **98–99** Allan Landau. **100** Allan Landau. **101** Sharon Hoogstraten. **102–3** Sharon Hoogstraten. **104–5** Sharon Hoogstraten. **106–7** Sharon Hoogstraten. **110** Allan Landau (t, b). **110–11** Sharon Hoogstraten. **111** Allan Landau (t). **112** Sharon Hoogstraten. **113** Sharon Hoogstraten. **114–15** Ed Nagel. **116–17** Sharon Hoogstraten. **117** Allan Landau (b). **118** Sharon Hoogstraten. **119** Sharon Hoogstraten. **120–21** Ed Nagel. **123** Sharon Hoogstraten (t); Allan Landau (b). **124–25** Sharon Hoogstraten. **126–27** Sharon Hoogstraten. **128** Allan Landau. **128–29** Sharon Hoogstraten. **130** Sharon Hoogstraten. **131** Sharon Hoogstraten. **132** Allan Landau. **132–33** Sharon Hoogstraten. **133** Sharon Hoogstraten. **134** Allan Landau (l). **134–35** Ed Nagel. **135** Susan Andrews (l, r). **136–37** Sharon Hoogstraten. **140–41** Sharon Hoogstraten. **142–43** Allan Landau. **146** Sharon Hoogstraten (l); Allan Landau (r). **147** Sharon Hoogstraten. **150–51** Allan Landau. **152–53** Sharon Hoogstraten. **154** Sharon Hoogstraten. **155** Allan Landau. **158–59** Sharon Hoogstraten. **160–61** Ed Nagel. **161** Allan Landau (r). **163** Sharon Hoogstraten. **165** Sharon Hoogstraten; Allan Landau (l, r). **166** Sharon Hoogstraten. **167** Allan Landau.

168–69 Sharon Hoogstraten. 170 Allan Landau. 171 Allan Landau; Allan Landau (l, r). 174 © Willi Dolder, Tony Stone Worldwide (tl); © Leonard Lee Rue III, Tony Stone Worldwide (bl); © Tom Ulrich, Tony Stone Worldwide (br). 174–75 Chris Harvey, Tony Stone Worldwide; Sharon Hoogstraten (l, b, r). 175 Tony Stone Worldwide (bl); © Thompson and Thompson, Tony Stone Worldwide (br). 177 Tony Stone Worldwide. 178 Allan Landau. 179 Aric Attas (l, b). 182 Allan Landau. 183 Aric Attas. 184 Allan Landau. 185 Aric Attas. 186 Allan Landau (tl); Sharon Hoogstraten (tc, tr, bl, br). 188 Allan Landau. 189 Aric Attas. 190–91 Sharon Hoogstraten. 194 Allan Landau. 195 Aric Attas. 196–97 Sharon Hoogstraten. 198 Allan Landau. 199 Aric Attas. 200–201 Aric Attas. 202–3 Aric Attas. 205 Aric Attas (t, c); Allan Landau (b). 206–7 Allan Landau. 210–11 Sharon Hoogstraten. 212 Allan Landau. 213 Allan Landau. 218–19 Aric Attas. 220 Allan Landau (c). 220–21 Aric Attas. 222 Aric Attas. 223 Allan Landau. 224 Pam Hasegawa (l). 224–25 Aric Attas. 226 Allan Landau (l). 226–27 Aric Attas. 228–29 Sharon Hoogstraten. 229 Allan Landau (t, cl, c, cr, bl). 231 Sharon Hoogstraten. 232–33 Sharon Hoogstraten. 233 Allan Landau (l, r). 234 Aric Attas (l). 234–35 Allan Landau. 238–39 Aric Attas. 240 Aric Attas. 241 © Rick Rickman, Duomo Photography (c). 241 Aric Attas. 242 Allsport/Vandystadt (l); © Al Tielemans, Duomo Photography (tr). 242–43 Aric Attas. 243 Allan Landau (l, r). 244 Allan Landau (l, r). 244–45 Allan Landau. 246 UPI/BETTMANN (t); Sharon Hoogstraten (c). 246–47 © Bob Martin, Allsport. 248–49 Sharon Hoogstraten. 250–51 Allan Landau. 252 UPI/BETTMANN (t); Rob Tringali, Jr., Sportschrome East/West (bl). 252–53 Focus on Sports (bc). 253 C. Michael Lewis (tl); © David Cannon, Allsport (tr); UPI/BETTMANN (br). 254–55 Sharon Hoogstraten. 255 Allan Landau (tl, tc, tr). 256 Allan Landau. 257 Sharon Hoogstraten. 258–59 Sharon Hoogstraten. 261 Sharon Hoogstraten. 262 Allan Landau (b). 262–63 Sharon Hoogstraten. 263 Allan Landau (t, b). 266–67 Allan Landau. 268–69 Sharon Hoogstraten. 270–71 Sharon Hoogstraten. 272 Allan Landau. 273 Focus On Sports. 276 Allsport/Vandystadt. 277 Allan Landau (tl); Sharon Hoogstraten (r). 278 Allan Landau. 279 Sharon Hoogstraten. 280 Sharon Hoogstraten. 281 © Rick Rickman, Doumo Photography. 282 Allan Landau. 283 Sharon Hoogstraten. 286 Allan Landau (bl, br). 286–87 Aric Attas. 287 Allan Landau (tl). 288 Aric Attas. 289 Sharon Hoogstraten. 290 Allan Landau. 292 Allan Landau. 294 Allan Landau. 296–97 Allan Landau. 302 Allan Landau. 304 Tal Streeter, The Art of the Japanese Kite, Weatherhill Inc. 305 Allan Landau. 306–7 Allan Landau. 308 Allan Landau. 309 Allan Landau (tl, tc, tr). 310 Sharon Hoogstraten. 312–13 Allan Landau. 314–15 Sharon Hoogstraten. 316 Allan Landau. 317 Allan Landau (bl ,bc, br). 319 Allan Landau. 320 Allan Landau (l). 320–21 Sharon Hoogstraten. 326 Allan Landau (bl, bc, br).

327 Susan Andrews. 328 Allan Landau. 329 Allan Landau (tl, tc, tr). 330 Allan Landau (tl, tc, tr); Sharon Hoogstraten (b). 331 Ralph Brunke. 332 Ralph Brunke (t, c); © John W. Banagan, Image Bank (b). 332–33 Allan Landau. 336 Allan Landau (l, r). 337 Sharon Hoogstraten (t); Allan Landau (b). 339 Allan Landau. 340 Allan Landau. 342 Sharon Hoogstraten. 343 Allan Landau. 344–45 Sharon Hoogstraten. 346 Allan Landau. 350–51 Sharon Hoogstraten. 351 Allan Landau (tl, tc, tr). 353 Sharon Hoogstraten. 354 Allan Landau. 355 Sharon Hoogstraten (t). 356 Allan Landau (cl, c, cr, b). 357 Allan Landau (b). 358–59 Aric Attas. 360 Allan Landau (l, r). 360–61 Sharon Hoogstraten. 361 Allan Landau (l, r). 362–63 Sharon Hoogstraten. 364 Allan Landau. 365 Aric Attas (t); Allan Landau (b). 366 Allan Landau. 367 Allan Landau. 368–69 Sharon Hoogstraten. 369 Colin Prior, Tony Stone Worldwide (t). 370 Aric Attas (l). 370–71 Allan Landau. 371 Aric Attas (r). 372–73 Aric Attas (t). 372 Allan Landau (b). 373 Allan Landau (b). 374–75 Sharon Hoogstraten. 376 Stock Montage (tr); British Museum (b). 377 UPI/BETTMANN (t); Stock Montage (c); © Joe Pineiro, Columbia University (b). 378–79 Sharon Hoogstraten. 380 Sharon Hoogstraten. 381 Allan Landau. 382 Aric Attas. 383 Sharon Hoogstraten. 384–85 Sharon Hoogstraten. 386–87 Sharon Hoogstraten. 388 Sharon Hoogstraten. 389 Aric Attas (tr, b). 390 Sharon Hoogstraten. 391 Aric Attas. 393 Allan Landau. 394 Sharon Hoogstraten (t); Allan Landau (b). 395 Aric Attas. 398–99 Aric Attas. 399 Sharon Hoogstraten (b). 400 Allan Landau (t ,c, b). 401 Allan Landau. 402–3 Sharon Hoogstraten. 403 Sharon Hoogstraten (b). 404 Allan Landau (l); Sharon Hoogstraten (r). 405 Sharon Hoogstraten (l); Allan Landau (r). 406–7 Sharon Hoogstraten. 408 Susan Andrews. 409 Sharon Hoogstraten. 410 Sharon Hoogstraten. 411 Sharon Hoogstraten. 415 Allan Landau (tl, tr, bl, br). 416 Allan Landau. 417 Allan Landau. 418 Sharon Hoogstraten (tl, tr). 418–19 Sharon Hoogstraten. 419 Sharon Hoogstraten (tl, tr). 421 Sharon Hoogstraten. 422 Sharon Hoogstraten. 423 Sharon Hoogstraten. 425 Allan Landau (br). 426 Sharon Hoogstraten (l, br). 427 Sharon Hoogstraten. 428–29 Sharon Hoogstraten. 429 Allan Landau (r). 430 Sharon Hoogstraten. 431 Sharon Hoogstraten. 433 Sharon Hoogstraten. 434–35 Sharon Hoogstraten. 436 Susan Andrews (t, tl, tr, cl, c, cr). 436–37 Sharon Hoogstraten. 438–39 Allan Landau. 440–41 Allan Landau. 442 Allan Landau (b). 442–43 Allan Landau. 443 Sharon Hoogstraten (r). 446 Allan Landau (c). 446–47 Sharon Hoogstraten. 447 The Caplan Collection at The Children's Museum of Indianapolis (b). 448 Sharon Hoogstraten; Allan Landau (t, c, b). 449 Aric Attas (tl, tr); Allan Landau (b). 450 Sharon Hoogstraten. 451 Sharon Hoogstraten. 452 Sharon Hoogstraten. 454 Allan Landau. 460 Allan Landau. 463 Allan Landau. 467 Aric Attas. 468–69 Sharon Hoogstraten. 469 Allan Landau (b). 470–71 Aric Attas.